D1553370

Cooperative Threat Reduction,
Missile Defense, and the Nuclear Future

Cooperative Threat Reduction, Missile Defense, and the Nuclear Future

Michael Krepon

A HENRY L. STIMSON CENTER BOOK

COOPERATIVE THREAT REDUCTION
© Michael Krepon, 2003

First published 2003 by
PALGRAVE MACMILLAN™
175 Fifth Avenue, New York, N.Y. 10010 and
Houndmills, Basingstoke, Hampshire, England RG21 6XS.
Companies and representatives throughout the world.

PALGRAVE MACMILLAN is the global academic imprint of the Palgrave Macmillan division of St. Martin's Press, LLC and of Palgrave Macmillan Ltd. Macmillan® is a registered trademark in the United States, United Kingdom and other countries. Palgrave is a registered trademark in the European Union and other countries.

ISBN 0-312-29556-1

Library of Congress Cataloging-in-Publication Data
Krepon, Michael, 1946–
Cooperative threat reduction, missile defense, and the nuclear future/by Michael Krepon.
    p. cm.
ISBN 0–312–29556–1
        1. Nuclear weapons—United States. 2. United States—Military policy.
3. Nuclear disarmament. 4. Nuclear arms control—Verification.
5. Deterrence (Strategy) 6. Ballistic missile defenses—United States.
7. World politics—21st century. I. Title.

UA23 .K77696 2002
355.02'17—dc21   2002029244

A catalogue record for this book is available from the British Library.

Design by Newgen Imaging Systems (P) Ltd., Chennai, India.

First edition: January, 2003
10 9 8 7 6 5 4 3 2 1

Printed in the United States of America.

Dedicated to Alessandra, Joshua, and Misha
The happy conjunction of Altoona, Pennsylvania
and Sharon, Massachusetts

Contents

Preface and Acknowledgments

T his book was mostly written at odd hours in what used to be a tool shed behind the house. For the transformation of the tool shed into a windowed office where I can gaze out onto woods and cow pasture, I owe much to Len Wishart's carpentry skills.

Many people helped me to write this book by pointing me in the direction of research material, answering questions, commenting on various chapters, and pointing out analytical shortcomings and factual errors. My appreciation goes to Gary Ackerman, Ken Allen, Dana Allin, Khalid Banuri, Rajesh Basrur, Barry Blechman, Doug Englund, David Goldfischer, Thomas Graham, Jr., Rose Gottemoeller, Dennis Gormley, Siegfried Hecker, Steven Hildreth, William Hoehn, Kim Holmes, Rebecca Johnson, Ken Keating, David Koplow, Kenneth Luongo, Michael McDevitt, Scott McMahon, James Mulvenon, Robert S. Norris, John C. Reppert, Alan Romberg, Karen M. Rohan, Gideon Rose, Phillip Saunders, Leonard Spector, Benjamin Self, Amy Smithson, Jonathan Tucker, Elizabeth Turpen, and Brian Woo. Their comments, guidance, and suggestions should not imply endorsement of the views presented here.

Chris Clary provided heavy lifting in every aspect of the preparation of this book. His help with research, fact checking, editing, and matters of style was invaluable. Research assistance was also provided by Sameer Ahmed, Chris Gagné, Sandhya Gupta, Pradeep Ramamurthy, and Jessica Trojak.

Some of these chapters appeared previously in somewhat or significantly different form in *Foreign Affairs, Survival, The Nonproliferation Review,* and *Great Decisions.* I thank these journal editors, who are listed above, for their helpful comments.

My association with St. Martin's Press/Macmillan, now Palgrave, goes back to my first book, *Strategic Stalemate,* published in 1984. Toward the end of this book, I realized I was writing a belated sequel. My sincere thanks go to my editor at Palgrave, Anthony Wahl, and the Vice President and Editorial Director at Palgrave (and my previous editor), Michael Flamini. My appreciation also goes out to Keith Povey and his colleagues for their keen editorial eyes.

I am grateful to the Henry L. Stimson Center's Board of Directors for their encouragement and support for my programming and writing projects. Special thanks go to George Perkovich who has the combined gifts of being able to think conceptually, analytically, and politically. In addition to participating in brainstorming sessions and commenting on chapters, he provided funding support for my work on nuclear issues while working at the W. Alton Jones Foundation. I also owe a great deal to David Speedie at the Carnegie Corporation of New York. Amidst the vagaries of the funding scene, David and Carnegie, led by Vartan Gregarian, have demonstrated an unwavering commitment to tackling the toughest issues of international security. The Stimson Center has no better supporters. In addition, my sincerest thanks go to Melanie Greenberg of the William and Flora Hewlett Foundation, and to Joan Rohlfing, Charles Curtis, and Sam Nunn of the Nuclear Threat Initiative for supporting my work on nuclear escalation control and conflict resolution issues in South Asia. Jonathan Fanton, Mitchel Wallerstein, and Kennette Benedict at The MacArthur Foundation, have generously supported my work analyzing the weaponization of space.

I have learned much from devoted practitioners of cooperative threat reduction at Sandia National Laboratories, where I serve as a consultant. They have my deepest respect and appreciation for the important work they do in the field under trying circumstances. Special thanks go to Dori Ellis.

My thanks also go to my students at the University of Virginia, with whom I re-read and discussed the classic texts of arms control. My own introduction to these topics came through the many courtesies of gifted mentors, especially Alton Frye, who has guided me in his gentle manner for two decades, first as the guiding force behind the International Affairs Fellowship program of the Council on Foreign Relations, and later as a Director of the Stimson Center.

I learned much from three practitioner/teachers who have left a lasting imprint and who will be greatly missed: McGeorge Bundy, who helped launch the Stimson Center and who had the knack of turning conversations into graduate seminars; Howard Stoertz, who was gifted with a keen analytical mind and who guided by asking the right questions; and Paul C. Warnke, who bore the slings and arrows of pursuing arms control with dignity, grace, and good humor.

Most important of all, I wish to thank my family for their support and unconditional love, despite my prolonged periods of mental preoccupation. They know well that far-off look on my face that comes when I'm editing an argument in my head.

MICHAEL KREPON
North Garden, Virginia
March 2002

Introduction

The Cold War has been replaced by asymmetric warfare, where weak states or terrorist groups strike at America's vulnerabilities while skirting U.S. military strength. Cold War security dilemmas, such as a massive "bolt out of the blue" missile attack and the rumble of Soviet tank armies across the German plain, have given way to very different surprise attack scenarios. Americans now dread highjackers who fly planes into buildings, trucks carrying "fertilizer bombs," and letters without return addresses that could be carrying strange, powdery substances. The leakage of deadly materials or weapons from aging Soviet stockpiles to bad actors is as much, if not more, of a threat to international security than the old Red Army and Strategic Rocket Forces. The Soviet Union was deterrable; suicide bombers are not.

During the Cold War, the United States succeeded in containing the Soviet Union through strong alliances, preventive diplomacy, nuclear deterrence, and conventional military capabilities. In asymmetric warfare, power projection capabilities, cohesive alliances, and preventive diplomacy remain essential, but nuclear weapons and tank armies are not very helpful. In fighting against unconventional foes, the most meaningful assets are likely to be the cooperation of nearby states, timely intelligence, air power, smart weapons, and agile ground forces.

The symbolic end of the Cold War occurred many times over, with the tearing down of the Berlin Wall and the statue of Felix Dzerzhinsky outside KGB headquarters in Moscow, or with the last lowering of the Soviet flag atop the Kremlin. Similarly, many events dramatized the advent of asymmetric warfare, including the demolition of the U.S. Marine barracks in Beirut, the bombing of the U.S. embassies in Kenya and Tanzania, or the attack on the *USS Cole* in Aden harbor by an explosives-laden pontoon boat. All of these incidents left their mark, but none of them resulted in vastly different conceptions of national security. After each of these shocks, the Pentagon continued to request and spend money in familiar ways. And after each wake-up call, members of Congress and the executive branch continued to wrangle over nuclear weapons, missile defenses, and strategic arms control in utterly familiar terms.

In this sense, the transition from Cold War to asymmetric warfare occurred rather precisely on September 11, 2001. When two hijacked planes slammed into the twin towers of the World Trade Center and another into the Pentagon, the immediacy of the terrorist threat and the inadequateness of U.S. readiness and response were watched by a stunned nation in real time. The scale, symbolism, and audacity of these suicidal attacks—and the thought of a fourth hijacked plane heading for Washington that never reached its target because passengers stormed the cockpit—will remain a permanent scar in the collective consciousness of an entire citizenry. After September 11, Americans knew without a shadow of a doubt that their Cold War conceptions of threat and response—downsized but not discarded in the decade after the collapse of the Soviet Union—were antiquated beyond repair. The paradigm shift from Cold War to asymmetric warfare was hardwired and fused on that day of national mourning and transformation.

The central organizing principle for U.S. national security during the Cold War was the containment of Soviet power and influence. The global contest between two great powers armed with many thousands of nuclear weapons required concepts and practices to prevent the strategic competition from crossing the nuclear threshold. Strategic stability was based, in part, on mutual acceptance of each other's power to wreak unimaginable damage. Assured destruction (soon labeled Mutual Assured Destruction, or MAD) was more than a fact of Cold War life; it was codified by treaties permitting huge offensive nuclear arsenals while expressly prohibiting national missile defenses.

Most of the creative thinking about nuclear weapons and arms control took place in the late 1950s and early 1960s. During this period, it was clear that the prevailing nostrums of massive retaliation and nuclear disarmament needed to be re-thought. Important books such as Henry A. Kissinger's *The Necessity for Choice*, Bernard Brodie's *Strategy in the Missile Age*, Thomas C. Schelling's and Morton H. Halperin's *Strategy and Arms Control*, Hedley Bull's *The Control of the Arms Race*, and a collective effort edited by Donald G. Brennan, *Arms Control, Disarmament, and National Security*, mapped new terrain. This body of work rejected the nuclear doctrine of massive retaliation, replacing it with notions of graduated nuclear deterrence. These authors also set aside the notional national objective of general and complete nuclear disarmament, creating in its place a new field of strategic arms control.

One of the most provocative authors during this time was Herman Kahn, who published a collection of essays under the title *Thinking About the Unthinkable*. Kahn went enthusiastically where few nuclear "theologians" dared to tread, applying the anodyne nuclear deterrence constructs of fellow theorists to war-fighting scenarios. While others dealt with the abstractions of deterrence and arms control theory, Kahn focused on how to "come to grips with the problems that modern technology and current international relations present to us."[1] The resulting work produced complex escalation ladders of nuclear weapons' use along with staggering estimates of death tolls. The enthusiasm with which Kahn approached this grim task was easily caricatured—Hollywood produced two memorable Kahn-like characters, Dr. Strangelove, played by Peter Sellers, and the woefully miscast Walter Matthau in *Fail Safe*—but he was a very real figure of the Cold War, attempting to apply cold logic and analysis to a numbingly terrifying nuclear stand-off.

After the events of September 11, 2001 we again need to come to grips with current international relations. During the Cold War, the unthinkable never happened. The unthinkable of asymmetric warfare has already happened, and could happen again and again. The time is ripe for a new wave of creative thinking about missile defenses, nuclear deterrence, and strategic arms control. We need to re-conceptualize containment, prevention, and response for a new era of asymmetric threats. Herman Kahn and others asked then what might happen if deterrence failed. Now we must ask similar questions in an entirely different context.

What value do missile defenses and nuclear weapons have against much weaker states or terrorist cells? How should the United States respond to new kinds of vulnerability as the world's sole superpower with no strategic competitor in sight for at least a decade? Should Washington continue to accept vulnerability to Moscow's strategic deterrent, and extend this construct to Beijing, the only "near peer competitor" (to use the Pentagon's term) on the horizon? How should the United States size its nuclear weapons and configure its target lists as the lone superpower? Where do missile defenses fit into a world of U.S. military predominance? After President George W. Bush's decision to withdraw from the Anti-Ballistic Missile (ABM) Treaty, what should replace MAD as a central organizing principle for nuclear arsenals and strategic arms control?

The Bush administration's decision to withdraw from the ABM Treaty leaves a significant void in U.S. national security policy—one that cannot be filled simply by deploying ballistic missile defenses. This void extends beyond the ABM Treaty, as the Bush administration has also walked away from the second Strategic Arms Reduction Treaty and a long-considered protocol to improve monitoring of the Biological Weapons Convention. Prior to this, Republican senators rejected the Comprehensive Test Ban Treaty. Some Republican officials and members of Congress are eager to resume nuclear testing and to proceed with the weaponization of space.

There is a strong working consensus in the United States on many essential elements of American security, such as the need for better intelligence capabilities and preventive diplomacy, more agile crisis management, superior conventional military capabilities, and an invulnerable nuclear deterrent. On the matter of arms control and the role of treaties, however, there is a great deal of debate. A new approach must be fashioned to fill the void created by partisan division over arms control, one that is geared to the shift from the Cold War to asymmetric warfare, and one that can generate sustained, bipartisan support in Washington and in other capitals.

The responsibility for the weakness of treaty instruments is, after all, widely shared. Treaty outliers, especially India, Pakistan, and Israel, have injured nuclear non-proliferation efforts. Countries that have bored away from within, such as North Korea, Iran, and Iraq, have done great damage, as have states that have placed commercial interests above the strengthening of treaty obligations, including France, Japan, and Germany. The globe's sole superpower, the United States, which has taken to using or discarding treaties at its convenience, has contributed disproportionately to this mess. The combined effects on treaty norms from wounds inflicted from the top down, from the mercantile powers, covert proliferators, and outliers are, of course, mutually reinforcing. The weaker the norms embedded in treaties, the more inclined U.S. skeptics will be to dispense with these compacts and resort to the role of global sheriff.

The growing void that was once filled by arms control and non-proliferation treaties comes at a time when nuclear, chemical, and biological weapons or materials are the top-most threats to national, regional, and international security. These dangers no longer emanate from Soviet strength, but from lax Russian security practices, insufficient export controls, tempting foreign offers, and criminal enterprises linked to governmental authorities. These dangers are also home grown in troubled regions where leaders seek domination or protection against their neighbors. The weapons America fears most provide the best insurance policy against Washington's military predominance. The most likely delivery vehicles for these deadly weapons are trucks, container ships, civilian airliners, and subway cars—not ocean-spanning missiles. The precepts of MAD have little applicability for these security dilemmas. Nor is a "one size fits all" concept of nuclear deterrence very useful in dealing with small states or terrorist groups that cannot match

America's strengths, so instead seek to exploit U.S. weaknesses. "Limited nuclear options" against terrorist cells are as obsolete as massive retaliation was in the 1950s against a nuclear-armed Soviet Union.

During the Cold War, Hawks and Doves fought fierce contests over nuclear weapons and arms control treaties. But as nuclear arsenals grew, both camps begrudgingly accepted (apart from one significant interlude) the constructs of MAD. That interlude—President Ronald Reagan's embrace of the Strategic Defense Initiative and nuclear abolition—led to surprising outcomes. At the end of the Reagan administration, MAD remained very much in place while advanced missile defenses remained on the shelf. But Reagan's twin challenges to nuclear orthodoxy, combined with Mikhail Gorbachev's bold initiatives, generated very deep cuts in nuclear arsenals. Their joint efforts also grievously damaged the theology of graduated nuclear deterrence by removing most of the European rungs on Herman Kahn's escalation ladder.

The strategic concept of MAD remained in place during the first decade after the demise of the Soviet Union, more from force of habit than from official endorsement. The Clinton administration shied away from an alternative conceptualization, and had this effort been made, it would have faced strenuous opposition from combative Republicans on Capitol Hill. Bipartisan constructs in the 1990s were rare phenomena and, in any event, large questions relating to the role of nuclear weapons and missile defenses were in such flux that the timing was not right for consensus building.

Instead, the Clinton administration devoted itself to implementing the extraordinary strategic arms reduction accords achieved during the last years of the Cold War. There was much unfinished business resulting from the breakthroughs generated by the serendipitous conjunction of Ronald Reagan and Mikhail Gorbachev. After an initial hesitancy, the administration of George H.W. Bush seized the opportunity to finalize accords reducing strategic forces. The Clinton administration sought to formalize these treaties through tortuous ratification processes and to proceed dutifully in step-by-step fashion to secure further reductions. These efforts met with only limited success because the demise of the Soviet Union undermined the rationale and the bipartisan support for treaties predicated on equality.

The Clinton administration was confident and adept in domestic policy but tentative abroad and weak in defending its foreign labors on Capitol Hill. After heroic efforts in helping to denuclearize states in the former Soviet Union, the Clinton team managed to secure the entry into force of the first Strategic Arms Reduction Treaty, concluded in 1991. But this was the only arms treaty ratified during President Clinton's watch without crippling reservations. The Chemical Weapons Convention squeaked through the Senate, heavily weighted with such conditions. Subsequent accords adapting the ABM Treaty to expressly permit advanced theater missile defenses were kept off the Senate's calendar for fear of their rejection by Senate Republicans. The Cold War's end not only widened the domestic political divide over the ABM Treaty, but also over the utility of nuclear weapons, symbolized by the Clinton administration's fixed pursuit of the Comprehensive Test Ban Treaty, and its uncompromising rejection by Senate Republicans.

By the end of the 1990s, the unraveling of the domestic U.S. consensus behind the twin pillars of MAD—huge offensive nuclear arsenals and a treaty-bound prohibition against national missile defense—was virtually complete. Treaty making lost bipartisan support when the Soviet Union collapsed and when the Comprehensive Test Ban Treaty appeared to constitute a threat to the U.S. nuclear stockpile. When Senate Republicans voted against ratification of the Test Ban Treaty, mostly in deference to future stockpile needs, they badly damaged the structural foundation for international control over nuclear weapons. Another support structure for strategic arms control, the ABM Treaty, was barely standing at the end of the Clinton administration.

The incoming administration of George W. Bush was eager to tear down this tottering structure, while treaty protectors feared the worst—the utter collapse of strategic arms control and the unraveling of nonproliferation regimes, with incalculable effects. Domestic paralysis on strategic arms control compounded these difficulties. Then came the tragic events of September 11, providing President Bush and his advisors far more freedom of action than their Hawkish predecessors. The demise of the Soviet Union, U.S. military dominance, and a wartime siege mentality made it relatively easy to walk away from treaties.

During the Cold War, Hawks and Doves agreed over ends while disagreeing over means.[2] With the end of the Cold War, partisans disagreed over ends as well as means. Conceptualists at one end of the political spectrum envisioned cooperative security; the other end championed the hard-edged, unapologetic maintenance of U.S. strategic superiority. The familiar contest between Hawks and Doves had now morphed into a divide between Dominators and Conciliators. Conciliators found themselves in the untenable position of defending MAD, as Dominators bashed MAD, while plotting the resumption of nuclear testing and the seizure of the high ground of space. Neither posture held much appeal to an American public that, when not uninterested, wanted favorable outcomes without negative consequences.

Public confusion deepened amid the contradictory conditions of American strategic superiority. The dichotomies of the Cold War were fairly clear. In the decade after the demise of the Soviet Union, contradictory tendencies became transposed. Globalization produced alienation, and power generated vulnerability. The old bromides of nuclear weapons, missile defenses, and strategic arms control did not cure these ills. Firmly held belief systems were challenged by asymmetric threats, but the objects of prior belief were too central to be discarded.

These mixed impulses could be reconciled—but not under the umbrella of MAD. Many elements of a new strategic concept began to take shape during the first decade after the Cold War, but did not cohere because political conditions were not ripe for synthesis. Republicans and Democrats alike on Capitol Hill readily acknowledged that the strategic arms reduction accords did not go far enough in reducing force levels. Support was also evident across the political spectrum to rely increasingly on informal and more flexible arrangements. Many called for reducing the alert status of nuclear forces, and no senior government official or military officer could convincingly explain why, a decade after the Soviet Union dissolved, thousands of nuclear weapons were ready to be launched within minutes of a command to do so. The post-Cold War U.S. nuclear war plan also remained incomprehensible and ripe for revision. Targeting lists were downsized, but not fundamentally rethought and explained to the American public.

Most important of all, a new practice, born of necessity, began to safeguard the dangerous weapons and materials residing in the former Soviet Union. These cooperative threat reduction efforts, initially championed on Capitol Hill by Senators Sam Nunn and Richard Lugar, were soon affixed with an acronym—CTR—which begat additional acronyms as new initiatives were spun off to address the multiple problems attendant on the Soviet Union's demise. CTR programs retained consensual support because they proved their worth in readily understood ways. At the century's end, CTR programs in the former Soviet Union secured the deactivation of over 5,000 nuclear warheads and many hundreds of launchers for an inter-continental nuclear attack. Further assistance was provided for the storage and transportation of nuclear weapons. Construction proceeded on a large, secure fissile material storage facility. The United States helped to improve the safety and security at Russian chemical weapons storage sites. Security upgrades were implemented for hundreds of metric tons of highly enriched uranium and plutonium. Radiation detection equipment was installed at Russian border crossings to help detect and interdict nuclear smuggling. Plutonium-laden fuel rods from nuclear power reactors were secured.

Cooperative threat reduction was potentially an open-ended pursuit, bounded by the political contours of U.S.–Russian relations, bureaucratic mindsets, and financial constraints. Taking the lead in this effort was the Pentagon, which helped to dismantle aging Soviet-era nuclear forces, and the U.S. nuclear weapon labs, which devised collaborative programs with their counterparts in Russia to protect fissionable material once used in bomb programs. The leadership roles in cooperative threat reduction played by the Departments of Defense and Energy were absolutely essential. Had these efforts been led by the Department of State and the now-defunct Arms Control and Disarmament Agency, they would have been politicized and hopelessly underfunded during the 1990s. Successful efforts required the backing of more powerful and better-funded sponsors. To be sure, the pursuit of CTR initiatives by agencies with institutional interests in the perpetuation of U.S. nuclear weapons and force levels led to awkward juxtapositions, but these mattered less than the new practices undertaken between former adversaries.

Cooperative threat reduction initiatives grew as the intellectual and political capital behind strategic arms control was shrinking. The Clinton administration added dramatically to this shift in capital flows by building considerably on Nunn–Lugar initiatives while proceeding quite tentatively on strategic arms control accords inherited from the administration of George H.W. Bush. Quietly, without much fanfare and below the horizon of partisan debate, the daily practice of cooperative threat reduction became the primary means of reducing the dangers associated with weapons of mass destruction. While bilateral treaties were tied up in the politics of ratification, legislative conditions, and domestic division, cooperative threat reduction initiatives expanded.

The inauguration of President George W. Bush sealed the rejection of MAD as a central organizing principle for strategic arms control. But what would replace it? On May 1, 2001, President Bush delivered a speech at the National Defense University calling for a "clear and clean break" with the past and challenging Americans and foreign nationals to "rethink the unthinkable." Bush placed Capitol Hill and foreign capitals on notice that the ABM Treaty prohibiting national missile defenses would be replaced with "a new framework."[3] Within this new strategic framework, formalized and lengthy treaty texts would play a much smaller part, while unilateral or parallel steps would gain new prominence.

One key element of the new strategic framework clearly involved significant reductions in deployed strategic forces. After much back and forth with the Pentagon, Bush publicly committed the United States to reduce deployed strategic forces to between 1,700 and 2,200 warheads over a ten-year period. These were notable cuts, but they still fell short of Bush's promised "clean" break with the past. Much continuity remained with nuclear targeting plans, as creative accounting methods were employed by the Pentagon to protect

U.S. force levels. As a result, the Bush administration's much-heralded strategic arms reductions were hardly different from those agreed four years earlier by Clinton and Boris Yeltsin in a projected START III accord. In one respect, Bush's proposed cuts are inferior, since they permit the retention of quick-strike, land-based missiles carrying multiple warheads.

Even with Bush's promised reductions, thousands of nuclear weapons would remain in place over the first decade of the twenty-first century, either on deployed forces or in storage, where they could be reconstituted, if deemed necessary. This hardly qualified as a radical break from Cold War concepts of nuclear deterrence, since residual nuclear capabilities remained so high. A wide range of military, political, and economic targets could be struck in the event of a nuclear war with devastating effect. In other words, the downsized nuclear deterrence posture envisioned by the Clinton and Bush administrations still maintained coverage of the Russian and Chinese target sets. None of the adaptations endorsed by Bush fundamentally altered the punishing character of the threat.

While there was much continuity to the Bush administration's strategic offensive posture, the most notable changes involved the rejection of treaties, the inclusion of non-nuclear strike capabilities to war-fighting plans, and the projected overlay of missile defenses. The net result of these changes can hardly be reassuring to Moscow and Beijing. Their discomfort could also become Washington's, since deterrence without reassurance can be a dangerous condition between major powers. Moscow, and especially Beijing, might be forgiven for wondering whether Mutual Assured Destruction had now been replaced by Unilateral Assured Destruction in the Bush administration's plans.[4] This conjecture will be confirmed or undercut by subsequent U.S. decisions regarding nuclear testing, space warfare, and the design and scope of national missile defenses.

If the void created by treaty trashing is filled by U.S. efforts to devalue or negate the nuclear deterrents of Russia and China, we are in for a very difficult passage, indeed. Is this what President Bush had in mind when he called for a "clear and clean break from the past"? Or will subsequent steps by the Bush administration reflect the promise of his National Defense University speech of May 1, 2001, in which he declared that, "Today's Russia is not our enemy," and called for a "new cooperative relationship" with Moscow, one that "should look to the future, not to the past. It should be reassuring, rather than threatening. It should be premised on openness, mutual confidence and real opportunities for cooperation."[5]

The Bush administration's plans will become clearer in due course. In the meantime, it is incumbent upon its critics to conceptualize a positive construct to fill the void created by the weakened state of strategic arms control and non-proliferation treaties. What alternatives do critics of new nuclear weapon testing, space warfare, and oversized national missile defenses propose? The demise of MAD and the ABM Treaty has left a significant void. This void must be filled with a positive construct, one that is pragmatic and yet visionary. It must generate hope, forward direction, and an increased sense of reassurance in difficult times.

The positive complement to nuclear deterrence during the Cold War was strategic arms control accords that bounded and reduced threats posed by ocean-spanning nuclear strike forces. These accords continue to have utility, but they are now peripheral to the primary security threats of asymmetric warfare, which mandate the safeguarding, reduction, and elimination of dangerous weapons and materials.

President Bush's proposed deep cuts did not begin to fill this void, since residual nuclear capabilities would remain so high. Nor could Bush's vaguely defined mix of missile defenses and nuclear deterrence fill this void, since the eventual mix might diminish international cooperation and fuel proliferation. For example, if Russia and China—the states whose help is needed most to control, reduce, and eliminate dangers in troubled regions—feel threatened by the U.S. mix of missile defense and nuclear offense, they will surely withhold or limit the scope of their cooperation.

Put another way, the deployment of national missile defenses or weapons in space that could devalue or negate the Russian and Chinese nuclear deterrents would be conducive to joint cooperation *against* the United States. Different missile defense architectures could, however, have positive net effects. There is little doubt but that missile defenses have become essential for U.S. engagement in military operations in tense regions where potential adversaries can threaten allies and U.S. forward-deployed troops with missile attacks. A ballistic missile defense of the United States is far less pressing, since this is among the least likely threats America now faces. Nonetheless, a modest insurance policy in the form of limited national missile defense deployments need not be unwise or incompatible with cooperative threat reduction—if the insurance premiums remain consonant with the modesty of the threat.

Uncontested U.S. strategic superiority is a fact of life in the post-Cold War era. This surprising gift must be applied wisely against a new constellation of threats to national, regional, and international security. There is little debate in the United States over the utility of improved power projection, unconventional warfare, and intelligence capabilities. The asymmetric threats to U.S. national security require such tools. Rather, the emerging debate centers around how much America should rely upon diplomatic or military instruments, how fast and how far to prosecute offenders, and whether to add robust national missile defenses and the weaponization of space to the existing panoply of U.S. strengths. There will be intense debate over initiatives that seek to extend U.S. military superiority in ways that weaken American diplomacy, arms control norms, and alliance ties. The arguments ahead are not about the extension of U.S. military superiority; they are about the most useful instruments to combat proliferation, bad actors, and unconventional threats.

Unconventional threats are unlikely to be deterred by the introduction of national missile defenses and the weaponization of space. Moreover, Moscow and Beijing would view these initiatives as war-fighting adjuncts to deterrence, or as instruments of U.S. compellance. Adding many hundreds of national missile defense interceptors and the weaponization of space to the thousands of deployed or deployable nuclear weapons would be akin to putting U.S. nuclear deterrence on steroids. Opponents of the ABM Treaty have long sought these initiatives, but were blocked during the Cold War by Soviet military power. The Soviet Union's demise is an insufficient reason to pursue such capabilities now, especially when to do so would accelerate the further unraveling of non-proliferation treaties and the accentuation of domestic and international political divides.

The replacement of MAD with national ballistic missile defenses sized to devalue or negate the Russian and Chinese nuclear deterrents is bound to backfire, as will U.S. "leadership" in weaponizing space. Instead, the successful extension and application of U.S. strategic superiority requires a positive and collaborative complement to deterrence, power projection capabilities, and preventive diplomacy. This new strategic concept is in plain view, because the United States has practiced it successfully, albeit in an overly bureaucratic and segmented way, over the past decade. It is called cooperative threat reduction.

The time is ripe to elevate the varied practices of cooperative threat reduction to a central organizing principle for dealing with the combined dangers associated with the demise of the Soviet Union and the rise of asymmetric warfare. Cooperative threat reduction programs provide the positive construct needed to meet the top-most security challenge facing the United States—to keep dangerous weapons and materials out of the hands of those ready to use them. The shift from a MAD-based structure of strategic arms control to one based on cooperative threat reduction is already well underway. The need for this transition, and the difficulty of achieving it, has become more apparent after the tragic events of September 11.

The concept of cooperative threat reduction is far too important and useful to be confined to the former Soviet Union. Instead, CTR-related activities can and should be employed in other troubled regions, wherever dangerous weapons and materials are being held by states that are willing to forgo them in return for economic or security assistance. The practical application of cooperative threat reduction to contain, reduce, and eliminate dangerous weapons and materials should extend as far as political adroitness and financial backing will allow.

Cooperative threat reduction is a full-service concept, covering the entire spectrum of post-Cold War dangers ranging from the control of dangerous materials at the source to the dismantlement of deployed strategic weapon systems. As such, these programs provide direct and effective linkages between strategic arms control and non-proliferation accords. During the Cold War, CTR programs were an adjunct to strategic arms control treaties; now these accords will struggle to maintain co-equal status with cooperative threat reduction. The two work best in concert: CTR initiatives are easiest to implement when backed up by treaty-based obligations for transparency and arms reduction. A cavalier approach to treaties make CTR initiatives more essential, but also more difficult to implement.

Strengthening deterrence with missile defenses still leaves a dangerous void in U.S. national security policy. Deterrence, however defined and reinforced, does not progressively reduce and eliminate dangerous weapons and materials; CTR programs do. Cooperative threat reduction, writ large, is therefore as central a component of U.S. national security policy as deterrence or preventive diplomacy.

The elevation of cooperative threat reduction to a central organizing principle for reducing dangers associated with weapons of mass destruction can also clarify missteps in the pursuit of deterrence. Successful cooperative threat reduction requires the progressive diminishment of the salience given to weapons of mass destruction. If the strongest nation on the planet needs to fine tune nuclear weapons to fight proliferation, the fight against proliferation will be lost. Consequently, the low-profile maintenance of the U.S. nuclear deterrent facilitates cooperative threat reduction; the design of new nuclear weapons and the resumption of underground tests will produce quite different and pernicious effects. Likewise, successful cooperative threat reduction requires collaboration with Russia and China. The development of rules of the road to prevent the weaponization of space is likely to expand the scope of cooperative threat reduction; the impulse to deploy anti-satellite weapons on earth or weapons in space will surely curtail the scope of Russian and Chinese cooperation.

Cooperative threat reduction techniques can also facilitate collective steps by states that wish to set higher standards for implementing treaty obligations. Multilateral accords governing nuclear, chemical, and biological weapons were painstakingly constructed during the Cold War. These accords aimed for universality at the cost of rigorous enforcement. Universality is a critically important principle for strengthening global norms and for isolating miscreants who seek or use weapons of mass destruction. But these treaties are not very helpful in dealing with member states that use treaties as a cover to covertly develop and produce prohibited weapons. Nor do universal treaty regimes lend themselves to strengthening measures, because some joiners are unwilling to accept tighter controls. Even when many states are willing to tighten standards, procedural hurdles make it virtually impossible to do so. With the exception of the Comprehensive Test Ban Treaty, universal treaty regimes apply lax monitoring standards to stringent obligations.

Voluntary associations of member states that wish to strengthen multilateral treaty regimes would do so by agreeing to implement CTR initiatives. These voluntary associations would be open to any state that wishes to join. The only requirement for being a member of this club would be a willingness to accept higher standards of demonstrating good faith. In return, members of the club could provide each other with certain benefits that are withheld from non-members, such as trade in "dual-use" items that could have both civilian and military applications. Such preferential trading arrangements are often characterized as "discriminatory" and harmful to treaty regimes by states unwilling to accept higher standards. But there is nothing discriminatory about membership in a voluntary association that is open to every state. Abstainers harm treaty regimes far more than joiners to these voluntary associations.

Bilateral treaty regimes between the United States and the Russian Federation could also benefit from CTR techniques. Deep reductions that are pursued alongside treaty obligations are one form of CTR. As reductions proceed, transparency measures and comprehensive cradle-to-grave monitoring of fissile material become more essential. At least in the near term, these arrangements are more likely to be realized through CTR techniques and voluntary associations than through new treaty obligations. Over time, a broad web of CTR initiatives could become intertwined with treaty regimes, if both states wish to translate higher standards into formal obligations.

The scope of bilateral CTR activities will depend on many factors, not the least of which is the degree of comfort each party has with the strategic objectives of the other. In this context, reassurance and transparency matter no less than deterrence. The value of bilateral accords, negotiated with heroic effort over many decades of Cold War strife, rests now, in vastly altered circumstances, primarily in the reassurance they provide to the weaker party, whose cooperation is needed for CTR to expand and deepen.

Unilateral steps to withdraw from treaties make cooperative threat reduction harder to accomplish. Conversely, CTR measures are easiest to implement as adjuncts, rather than as alternatives, to treaty regimes. For example, the steps taken by Presidents George H.W. Bush and Mikhail Gorbachev removing from the field the least safe and secure nuclear weapon designs followed just two months after completion of the first Strategic Arms Reduction Treaty in 1991. It would be difficult to imagine the successful choreography of these extraordinary moves to reduce nuclear dangers in the absence of a reassuring network of treaty constraints.

The demise of the Soviet Union and the rise of asymmetric threats present a welcome new opportunity to reconceptualize strategic arms control. The quest to replace MAD-based treaty regimes with a more positive construct was sidelined during the Cold War, when treaties codified national vulnerabilities. One of the founding fathers of strategic arms control, Donald G. Brennan, quit the community over this circumstance, arguing that defenses should run free and offenses be tightly controlled.[6] Brennan's vision of a defense-dominant strategic posture was foiled by technical limitations, the abundance of strategic offensive forces, and long memories of the Maginot Line's fate. With the Cold War's passing, alternative conceptions to (or variations of) MAD, based on a mix of nuclear offense and missile defense, again began to surface. For example, President Clinton's second Secretary of Defense, William J. Perry, floated the idea of replacing MAD with Mutual Assured Safety.[7]

The elevation of cooperative threat reduction to a strategic concept can succeed and flourish alongside the deployment of missile defenses as long as defenses are reassuring to major powers. If, however, the deployment of missile defenses is threatening rather than reassuring, the scope of cooperative threat reduction initiatives will be reduced to those programs that are in the economic interest of the weaker party—and no more.

Unlike MAD, the strategic concept of cooperative threat reduction is affirmative, providing clarity and concreteness to constructive national purposes. The practice of nuclear deterrence often distances the United States from non-proliferation treaty regimes, whereas the practice of CTR bridges strategic arms reduction with these treaty regimes. Cooperative threat reduction is much broader than traditional strategic arms control and non-proliferation accords—broad enough to encompass the varied threats posed by a new era of asymmetric warfare. CTR is not a solution to all security dilemmas or a substitute for the use of force, when necessary. Instead, these programs can reduce security dilemmas and diminish threats facing the United States and the international community.

Elevating and expanding the practice of cooperative threat reduction to a strategic concept would reflect and connect the duality of contemporary conditions, where strength does not necessarily provide protection. Conception and practice must be flexible enough to adapt to fluid circumstances, and yet fixed on broad goals that enable international cooperation as well as domestic support.

One purpose of this book is to introduce a more balanced approach to achieve U.S. national security objectives at a time when the pendulum has swung away from treaties. Another is to help those who believe in arms control to fill the void created by the withdrawal from the ABM Treaty and the sidelining of MAD in a new era of asymmetric warfare. This book has been written to generate new thinking about a positive strategic concept to accompany deterrence, diplomacy, and superior U.S. military capabilities. The argument presented here is that cooperative threat reduction has far greater utility than our limited conceptions of it. Just as Schelling, Halperin, and their colleagues sought to "broaden the term" of disarmament to encompass arms control, we now need to broaden the concept of arms control to include cooperative threat reduction.[8]

CHAPTER 1

The Paradigm Shifts

S hifts happen. Soon after the collapse of the Soviet Union, U.S. national confidence might well have been at an all-time high. The United States had defeated an ideological foe, not by force of arms, but on the battlefield of ideas and markets. Reluctant allies of the former Soviet Union now scrambled to place themselves under America's protective umbrella by seeking to join the North Atlantic Treaty Organization (NATO). U.S. culture and the English language ranged to all azimuths. A new age of information technology further solidified U.S. global leadership while fueling an unprecedented decade of economic growth and wealth creation. American military might was unchallenged. A U.S.-led coalition pushed back Saddam Hussein's attempt to control the oil fields of the Persian Gulf, strengthening the rule of law and non-proliferation norms. Stock market indexes reached dizzying heights, reflecting U.S. primacy and good fortune.

This era of good feeling was short-lived. Within a decade, the self-congratulatory mood that dominated earlier political commentary had begun to ring hollow. By the end of the Clinton administration, the dominant images of the United States projected in foreign capitals were, to be sure, American primacy in economic strength, entrepreneurship, military might, and continued leadership in the information revolution. But other images of the United States also reverberated across the globe—images that badly corroded U.S. standing as the "indispensable nation," to use one of Secretary of State Madeleine Albright's favorite phrases. These images included extended haggling over a reduction of U.S. dues to the United Nations during an era of unprecedented national prosperity; carrying out military campaigns or punitive acts by remote control; and the defeat of the Comprehensive

Test Ban Treaty by Senate Republicans, who argued, to an incredulous international community, that the world's pre-eminent conventional and nuclear power could be disadvantaged by giving up testing indefinitely.

At decade's end, allied military actions in the Balkans, which were so wrenching politically to NATO, resulted in qualified successes and extended peacekeeping operations. The Clinton administration's most consequential decision in Europe, the expansion of NATO to include former states of the Warsaw Pact, set in motion repeated dilemmas about inclusion and exclusion. Every addition raised the prospects of further weakening the utility of NATO as a military alliance and fueling retrograde tendencies in the Russian Federation.

Meanwhile, the bull market finally turned bearish. Free markets were not a panacea for many countries suffering from severe economic distress. Globalization turned out to be a distinctly regional phenomenon. The American political system continued to have admirers around the world, but the champion of democracy suffered embarrassing voting irregularities in the 2000 presidential election. Friendly foreign governments worried increasingly about the distractions, partisanship, and insularity of U.S. politics. Nor was the clear, continuing pre-eminence of U.S. military might very helpful in dealing with many of the international security problems facing the United States in the post-Cold War period—especially problems relating to weapons of mass destruction.

The cross-cutting effects of the information and military revolutions became increasingly apparent as the first post-Cold War decade progressed. Integrative and entropic effects proceeded concurrently. Some sought higher consciousness while others sought refuge in fundamentalism. Gaps between rich and poor grew. The selective benefits of globalization resulted in opportunities for the favored and seething resentments among the unfortunate. Synthesis and antithesis ground against each other along the fault lines of international politics. The pervasiveness of U.S. popular culture, the dominance of the U.S. economy, and the extension of American power projection capabilities grated on friends as well as potential adversaries. The computer's lines of code, software, and hardware were instruments of uplifting for some, while others chose truck bombs or strapped themselves with explosives. Separate wiring diagrams formed for the upwardly mobile in this lifetime and those heavenly bound in the next.

The primary beneficiary and target of these dichotomies was clearly the United States, the place where upward mobility, entrepreneurship, and wealth accumulation were most advanced and democratic. As America became increasingly advantaged, critics began to caricature Washington as a capital that could play by its own rules, wave off the world's complaints, enjoy the benefits of global interactions, yet be protected from many of its infectious diseases. The punitive power of the U.S. military was both envied and feared. It was remote, yet lethal, able to strike from long distance with precision—at least most of the time. Conspicuous failures were the result of intelligence, mechanical, and human errors. The Chinese embassy in Belgrade was struck in the high-altitude war against Serbia. A pharmaceutical plant in Sudan was targeted in a cruise missile attack. Without apology, aspirin production in a very poor country became collateral damage in the war against Islamic extremism.

Asymmetries in military capabilities bred further resentment. The more the United States sought—and was able—to carry out military strikes while protecting American soldiers, the more adversaries sought to turn the tables through unconventional means. No one could compete with the United States militarily after the Cold War ended; it was foolish to think of doing so. America's adversaries understood the meaning of the twin revolutions in information and military affairs, having watched its effects on television in the Gulf War and in Serbia. They reacted in predictable ways. Adversaries chose to use surrogates on the front lines of the war between the fortunate and the aggrieved. Suicide bombers were more effective in producing U.S. casualties than tank armies. A pontoon boat laden with conventional explosives crippled a U.S. destroyer refueling in Aden harbor. The face of the new enemy was not a sclerotic communist ruler, but a bearded man with a turban, posing with an automatic weapon. He had scorned the privileges of birth, and his name was known the world over: Osama bin Laden became the modern-day Ché Guevara, a hero for the perpetually aggrieved, the dispossessed, and the nimble blame shifters. In less than a decade, the Cold War was replaced by asymmetric warfare.

Post-war Contrasts

After the end of World War II, the United States engaged in a burst of diplomatic creativity. Those "present at the creation" of a new world, to use Dean Acheson's phrase, designed NATO and the United Nations, the Bretton Woods agreement, and the beginnings of international institutions to support global development. This was a time of governmental activism and unbridled engagement in the international arena. The end of the Cold War was marked, in stark contrast, by soaring rhetoric but a poverty of ambition, a lack of creativity, an aversion to institution building. American engagement abroad was highly selective. The indispensable nation was extremely cost conscious.

The economic resources to lend a new, sustained, and positive impetus to the post-Cold War world existed in abundance; the political resources did not. At the end of the Cold War, the downsizing of the U.S. military and a huge economic surge produced large budget surpluses, some of which could have been applied to constructive international engagement. This time, however, there was no Communist menace to impel U.S. action, and this time, the victors chose to adjust existing institutions rather to build new ones. In 1948, a time of grave domestic dislocation, the Congress authorized 1.2 percent of the gross national product to help with Europe's reconstruction. In contemporary terms, that would amount to an annual appropriation of approximately $100 billion. In stark contrast, the end of the Cold War was accompanied by the slashing of foreign assistance. Foreign affairs-related funding declined from 4 percent of the federal budget in the 1960s to 1 percent in the 1990s.

In the crucial period of constructive U.S. engagement after World War II, a bicameral, bipartisan congressional delegation led by Foreign Affairs Committee Chairman Charles A. Eaton and Representative Christian A. Herter, sailed to Europe and spent six weeks in the summer of 1947 preparing a legislative response to Europe's dire needs. As one observer of this effort recounted, "First hand study—focused on realities abroad rather than on divisions at home—resulted not in confusion but in greater harmony of outlook and a release of constructive energy."[1] Previously, in the waning months of the war, Senate Foreign Relations Committee Chairman Tom Connolly and Republican Leader Arthur H. Vandenberg spent two long months in San Francisco, helping to draft the new UN Charter. The most junior member of their congressional delegation was the former president of the University of Arkansas, J. William Fulbright.

Members of Congress do not now have the leisure time to spend weeks, let alone months, gaining first hand experience in dealing with the world's most consequential problems. The demands of constituent service and fund raising have crowded out foreign relations—except after tragedy strikes. After World War II, members of Congress also had many reasons to attend to the home front, where millions of families had been separated for three years, domestic agenda items had been deferred by war, and the reconversion of a wartime economy was eagerly anticipated. Back then, the global challenge of Communism kept the United States engaged abroad. After winning the Cold War, foreign relations did not weigh heavily on the legislative and executive branches. Presidential candidate Bill Clinton bested George H.W. Bush by focusing on domestic policy. "It's the economy, stupid!" was the rallying cry of his successful campaign.

After winning the Cold War, America turned inward. Engagement was episodic and primarily keyed to markets, not to traditional security concerns. There was also a vast difference in outlook in 1945 and in 1990 among Republicans on Capitol Hill. The Party's insular wing was routed by the outbreak of World War II; it was given a new lease on life with the end of the Cold War. One out of eight members of the House of Representatives voted in 1997 for the United States to withdraw from the United Nations. One in four House members—and nearly half of the Republican caucus—supported a resolution calling for the United Nations to get out of the United States. That same year only a bare majority of Republican Senators supported the Chemical Weapons Convention, a treaty largely negotiated under the auspices of Presidents Ronald Reagan and George H.W. Bush. Naysayers included the second- and third-ranking Republican leaders, as well as the Republican chairmen of the Foreign Relations, Armed Services, and Intelligence committees. Two years later, Senate Republicans voted overwhelmingly to defeat ratification of the Comprehensive Test Ban Treaty.

Democrats on Capitol Hill sought insularity in different ways. Only 20 percent of President Bill Clinton's fellow Democrats in the House of Representatives were prepared to support granting him "fast track" authority to negotiate trade deals in 1997. The opposition was led by the two highest-ranking House Democrats, at a time when U.S. unemployment was at a twenty-four-year low, industrial employment was up by 7 percent, and inflation was at a rock-bottom 2 percent. Even with such shallow support from his own party, Clinton could have won fast track authority, had it not been for the defection of twenty-five Republicans who withheld their support because the President refused to eliminate family planning funds to Third World countries in a pending foreign assistance bill.

In stark contrast, the post–World War II mood on Capitol Hill constituted a triumph of the larger view. Members of Congress who championed constructive U.S. engagement were profoundly influenced by travel and military service abroad. Vandenberg was an ardent isolationist in the years prior to World War II. In 1942, during a visit to London, he experienced an air raid. Later he became a key Republican architect of the Marshall Plan to rebuild war-torn Europe. Fulbright received a Rhodes fellowship to study at Oxford, returning to the United States after four years abroad a fervent internationalist. He later became Chairman of the Foreign Relations Committee. As a young man, Mike Mansfield left the mining fields of Montana to join the Marines, serve his country, and see the world. He was stationed in the Philippines and China. Mansfield later became the Senate's

Majority Leader and resident expert on Asia, subsequently serving with great distinction as the U.S. Ambassador to Japan.

After winning the Cold War, key Republican leaders traveled abroad little, and regretted it less. In his last decade of service on Capitol Hill, Chairman of the Foreign Relations Committee Jesse Helms briefly traveled once to Israel to attend the funeral of Prime Minister Yitzhak Rabin and once to Mexico to hold a hearing. International experience on Capitol Hill declined steeply as the ranks of congressional veterans dwindled. During the 1970s, as many as 70 percent of the membership in Congress had served in the armed forces. By the mid-1990s, this percentage was halved, and fell further with every subsequent election. The America First contingent on Capitol Hill took aim at the State Department's budget, U.S. foreign assistance, and treaties constraining missile defenses and nuclear testing. Chairman Helms of the Foreign Relations Committee defined his accomplishments in negative, rather than positive, terms. He counted as victories the whittling of U.S. dues to the United Nations and the blocking of ambassadorial appointments. Everyone on Capitol Hill was for stronger American leadership, but not enough were willing to provide the resources to back this up.

It is not surprising that the parallel integrative and entropic trends of international affairs produced a diffuse, unfocused response on Capitol Hill. After all, the United States had no compelling global challenger to keep the Congress engaged internationally after the Cold War ended. The electorate's natural instinct to focus on domestic matters after the Cold War ended, was reinforced not only by the Clinton administration's posture, but also by a new profusion of media outlets. During the Cold War, Americans learned about the world from essentially three television networks. News programs were quite short, but they provided a national basis of understanding of world events.

Victory in the Cold War was accompanied by the profusion of media outlets. Some Americans used the new powers of information access to become extremely well-versed on international issues. At the same time, expertise became increasingly narrow banded. Increasing numbers of Americans stayed away from hard news, preferring endless options of infotainment or other diversions. There were, as Bruce Springsteen deftly observed, fifty-seven channels to watch, but nothing was on television.[2] Major media outlets chose not to compete with specialized information channels over the coverage of hard news. Commercial news coverage gravitated along with most newspapers to human-interest stories and crime. Foreign news coverage on ABC News declined by 51 percent from 1989 to 1996. At NBC, the decline was 65 percent over the same period.[3]

The post–Cold War generation of politicians became bound up with e-mails, fax machines, cell phones, fund raising chores, and the continuous thirty-minute news cycle—phenomena that earlier generations of politicians never knew. The influence of advocacy groups and deceptive political advertising has shaped foreign as well as domestic policy. This blurring is most evident in the pursuit of well-funded advocacy groups with equities in U.S. foreign policy. Members of Congress cast votes with the clear understanding that massive media buys with simplistic, negative messages could trump well-reasoned, but difficult-to-defend positions. The repetition of polarizing debates, the negative tone of national politics, and the pervasive influence of large campaign contributions added to public cynicism and insularity. This dynamic was aptly captured in a perceptive book's subtitle, *How Attack Ads Shrink and Polarize the Electorate.*[4]

Most of the electorate continued to hold moderate views, but on Capitol Hill, single-issue advocacy groups increasingly defined policy choices, while those most strongly committed to narrow agendas employed procedural delays with greater frequency. The triumph of narrow agendas could be measured by a vast increase in delaying tactics on Capitol Hill. There were twenty-one Senate filibusters in the entire nineteenth century, and thirty-four in the 102nd Congress alone.[5] International treaties, which are required by the Constitution to garner the support of two-thirds of the Senate, were particularly susceptible to blocking action.

After the Cold War ended, committed internationalists on Capitol Hill could be found in both political parties. The most creative and far-sighted initiative of the post-Cold War period was largely the handiwork of two Senators, Sam Nunn and Richard Lugar, who conceived of and shaped the cooperative threat reduction program to reduce nuclear dangers in the former Soviet Union. Other Senators, such as Carl Levin, Pete Domenici, and Chuck Hagel worked tirelessly to promote constructive U.S. engagement abroad, as did senior members of the House of Representatives, such as Lee Hamilton. These members of Congress, however, did not control the congressional agenda. During much of the first decade after the Cold War ended, the Senate Foreign Relations Committee was led by the insular Jesse Helms, while the Senate Armed Services Committee was chaired by an aged Strom Thurmond. The shift in the Republican Party's perspective was symbolized when the highly decorated World War II veteran Bob Dole handed the baton of Senate Republican leadership in 1996 to Trent Lott, a man who rarely traveled abroad and who focused hard on domestic issues.

Committed internationalists faced an additional constraint: the absence of a new and compelling strategic concept to shape how a revitalized U.S.

international engagement might be pursued. U.S. national security policy during the Cold War was defined by the imperatives of containing the Soviet Union without sparking a nuclear war. The safety net behind the policy of containment was the doctrine of Mutual Assured Destruction, or MAD. The U.S.–Soviet competition was intense and unyielding, but offsetting and omnipresent nuclear capabilities bounded the competition for global supremacy.

After the Cold War ended in the demise of America's ideological foe, the linked rationales for containment and international engagement disappeared. Assured destruction continued to be a fact of life owing to the size of the U.S. and Russian nuclear arsenals, but MAD's embellishments, including high alert rates, long targeting lists, and strict limits on missile defenses, seemed disconnected from post-Cold War realities. A decade passed without a serious national debate over what might replace containment and MAD. The Clinton administration's primary argument for continued engagement—international trade and economic growth—had cross-cutting domestic effects. This was hardly a sufficiently broad foundation upon which to construct an effective policy of global engagement.

Moreover, the fear factor was missing. President Harry S. Truman and Secretary of State Dean Acheson rallied America to meet the Soviet threat by casting this challenge in terms that were "clearer than the truth." A compelling strategy of post-Cold War international engagement could not be based on troubling global trends, because virtually everything in the early 1990s seemed to be going America's way. After winning the Cold War, the United States reigned supreme. Worrisome trend lines were evolving quite slowly and almost imperceptibly, like global warming and the growth of Osama bin Laden's al-Qaeda network. The shift from the Cold War to asymmetric warfare was real enough, as were specific acts of terror directed at U.S. targets abroad. But the United States did not wake up to this challenge until September 11, 2001. Once aroused by the attacks on the World Trade Center and Pentagon, Americans discovered that much of the Third World—especially the Muslim world—was deeply alienated by the arrogance and insularity of U.S. power.

The terrorist acts of September 11 stunned America, but they paled in comparison to the shocks absorbed by the Truman administration soon after celebrating victory in World War II. During his embattled presidency, Harry S. Truman faced no less than the outbreak of war in Korea, the test of a Soviet atomic bomb, and the solidification of communist rule in Eastern Europe. The Truman administration met these challenges by giving shape to a new conceptualization of America's role in the world. The policy of containment was shored up by new institutions that offered hope as well as protection against Soviet might. The Marshall Plan to help rebuild Europe was of equal importance to NATO. Diplomatic, economic, and military initiatives were pursued in unison.

The difficulties facing newly elected President Bill Clinton were of an entirely different order of magnitude. After America's victory in the Cold War, Clinton focused, as promised, on economic and domestic matters. Creative energy and political capital were applied to new international trade mechanisms, not to a new conceptualization of America's role in the world. For the most part, the Clinton administration's approach to deal with radically new circumstances was to make marginal adaptations of Cold War institutions. A promising Partnership for Peace concept to make Europe "whole and free" took a back seat to the expansion of NATO. Cold War treaties governing nuclear arsenals were downsized, while the severe constraints of the Anti-Ballistic Missile Treaty were loosened somewhat. No serious effort was made by the Clinton administration to propound a new strategic concept to guide U.S. foreign relations in a new era. During his first term, President Clinton focused on national security challenges primarily when mandated by deadlines, such as the time-sensitive need to help Russia retrieve the nuclear weapons left behind in former Soviet republics, or when an international conference was scheduled to decide whether the Non-Proliferation Treaty should be extended indefinitely.

In the absence of deadline-driven challenges, Clinton's natural inclinations gravitated to domestic issues. Throughout his tenure, Clinton was quite averse to defining America's role in the world beyond glancing rhetorical themes. (The phraseology of "enlargement and engagement" was briefly attempted and then shelved.) He never really connected the dots between programming initiatives, whether at home or abroad. Clinton's first major national address on dealing with nuclear dangers was given in the eighth year of his presidency. His empathy and energy levels were boundless, and during his second term Clinton applied both more intensively to foreign policy concerns. But given his wide-ranging interests, and his tactical rather than strategic orientation, Clinton's imprint was usually episodic and short lasting. For a president with such extraordinary political skills, it is remarkable how much the terms of debate on foreign and national security policies were set by his political opponents. The Clinton administration's foreign policies in these areas were easily caricatured as highly energetic but *ad hoc* and surface layered.

In defense of President Clinton, it would have been exceptionally difficult to propound a compelling concept of U.S. global engagement during the 1990s beyond pushing for expanded trade and democracy. The world was very much in flux. References to the "post-Cold War" period were apt: it was easier to characterize this new era in terms of what it was not than by what it truly represented. The dangers posed by proliferation and international terrorism were worrisome but not politically compelling. Moreover, had Clinton tried to conceptualize and sell a basis for America's global engagement beyond trade and democracy promotion, he would have encountered stiff resistance on Capitol Hill. His ties with the largely insular, highly partisan, and penny-pinching Republican caucus on Capitol Hill were abysmal, especially in his second term.

This defense of the Clinton administration would be more convincing if the President and his senior officials had made a sustained effort to redefine the security challenges requiring renewed American engagement abroad. Instead, Washington talked a great deal during the 1990s about global leadership and the advancement of democracy and free markets, but deeds and resources rarely matched words. Hortatory diplomacy simply did not do justice to the changing valences of international affairs at the century's end. The variability and capriciousness of events were sobering; political fortunes seemed to rise and fall like the stock market. Washington was clearly preeminent, but oddly shaky. The century ended with several worrisome tremors, but with no rousing shocks to American complacency.

A decade after America's victory in the Cold War, the global strategic environment had become quite fluid, shifting perceptibly in troubling directions. Reliable strategic concepts during the fight against communism had no bearing in dealing with a Russia in decline. Containment was beside the point. The paradigm governing nuclear weapons, arms control, and missile defenses during the Cold War—Mutual Assured Destruction—now seemed archaic, an ancient language rarely spoken and barely understood. The string of successes in reducing nuclear dangers at the end of the Cold War and soon thereafter were exhilarating, but were overtaken by concerns over "loose nukes" and weak oversight of fissile material. The security gained from victory in the Cold War—as with the triumph of defeating Germany and Japan in World War II—proved to be short lived.

First, the Good News

The last fifteen years of the Cold War produced extraordinary accomplishments in reducing dangers associated with weapons of mass destruction. These breakthroughs began with Presidents Ronald Reagan and Mikhail Gorbachev who pledged that a nuclear war must never be fought and could not be won. Subsequently, they lent credence to this proclamation by concluding the 1987

Intermediate-Range Nuclear Forces (INF) Treaty, which eliminated entire classes of nuclear weapon-launchers from Europe. In so doing, Reagan and Gorbachev grievously damaged nuclear war-fighting plans, targeting requirements, and hard-liners in both Washington and Moscow. The INF Treaty also paved the way for a free fall in deployed strategic nuclear forces. This odd couple effectively broke the back of the strategic arms race.

In 1991, President George H.W. Bush and Gorbachev completed the first-ever Strategic Arms Reduction Treaty (START). This accord obligated each country to deploy no more than 6,000 nuclear weapons on intercontinental ballistic missiles, submarine-launched ballistic missiles, and strategic bombers. Six thousand potential mushroom clouds on each side seems like an absurdly high number. But at the time, reductions to this level were considered quite risky by custodians of the U.S. and Soviet nuclear arsenals.

Also in 1991, a coalition led by the United States routed Saddam Hussein's forces from Kuwait. Saddam received no help from the Kremlin in this power grab. In the aftermath of his reckless invasion, the international community gained access to most of Saddam's holdings of weapons of mass destruction and missiles. United Nations observers uncovered chemical warheads for ballistic missiles, a surprisingly advanced nuclear weapons program, and an expansive infrastructure for biological weapons. Some stocks presumably escaped detection. Nevertheless, the control, dismantlement, and destruction of the bulk of Saddam's deadly weapons and missiles, together with his massive conventional defeat, constituted a huge boost for regional security and non-proliferation. After being embarrassed by failing to detect Iraq's nuclear holdings, the International Atomic Energy Agency resolved to strengthen its inspection procedures, another plus.

In September and October of 1991, just as the Cold War was ending, Presidents Bush and Gorbachev took unilateral and reciprocal initiatives to further reduce nuclear dangers. Both Presidents ordered weapons that posed special problems of nuclear safety or command and control to be removed from naval vessels, air bases, and army units. Thousands of nuclear-tipped demolition mines, anti-submarine depth bombs and rockets, artillery shells, and short-range missiles were destroyed or placed in storage. These creative steps were long overdue, but were especially welcome at a time when the Soviet Union was coming apart and when command and control over the immense Soviet nuclear arsenal was of great concern.

Presidents Bush and Boris Yeltsin built on the foundation laid by their predecessors by completing the second Strategic Arms Reduction Treaty in 1993. The START II accord reduced deployed U.S. and Russian weapons to between 3,000–3,500 per side. President Bill Clinton built on this extraordinary record of accomplishment by successfully persuading three states of the former Soviet Union—Belarus, Ukraine, and Kazakhstan—to voluntarily give up their inheritance of nuclear weapons and to join the Non-Proliferation Treaty. Given the historic friction between Moscow and Kiev, and the possibility for clashes over territory, naval assets, as well as nuclear weapons, the denuclearization agreement was an historic accomplishment. It also facilitated Russian ratification of the first START accord in 1994.

During this period, the Non-Proliferation Treaty was further strengthened by the accession of South Africa, Brazil, Argentina, and Algeria—states with nuclear infrastructure that could provide the base for nuclear weapons programs. Indeed, South Africa's departing apartheid government announced that it had destroyed a small, covert nuclear arsenal before handing over the reigns of power to Nelson Mandela. The advent of democratic governments in Brasilia and Buenos Aires ended military-led programs in the missile and nuclear fields. Non-proliferation efforts received yet another boost when, in 1994, a troubling and unsafeguarded nuclear program in North Korea was frozen by agreement with the Clinton administration. In return, the communist government in Pyongyang received pledges for assistance from the United States, Japan, and South Korea for the construction of nuclear power plants and the provision of fuel oil. Then, in 1995, the Non-Proliferation Treaty—the cornerstone of global efforts to reduce nuclear dangers stemming from proliferation—was extended indefinitely at a conference held at the United Nations.

One year later, the Comprehensive Test Ban Treaty was negotiated. The culmination of decades of effort, the Test Ban Treaty obligated its 150 signatories not to test nuclear weapons at any time, or in any place. No other measure—dubbed the "longest sought, hardest fought" arms control accord by the Clinton administration—held greater promise to reduce the salience of nuclear weapons. Since every underground test constituted a declaration of power and utility for nuclear weapons, the stoppage of tests was intended to signal a far different course. Without new testing, new weapon designs were unlikely to be certified, at least in states with advanced nuclear arsenals.

In 1997, Presidents Clinton and Yeltsin reached an agreed framework at Helsinki, Finland for a third strategic arms reduction treaty, setting a new ceiling between 2,000 and 2,500 deployed warheads. If fully implemented, the three START accords promised to reduce deployed Cold War arsenals by 80 percent from peak levels. The Helsinki framework endorsed transparency measures for the verified dismantlement of many thousands of non-deployed nuclear weapons that were in storage—an important new and complex area for negotiations.

The negotiation of deeper cuts in nuclear arsenals was accompanied by the development of novel forms of cooperative threat reduction between the U.S. and Russian defense establishments and nuclear weapon laboratories. These programs helped an economically stressed Russia dismantle its large Cold War nuclear force structure, improve safeguards on dangerous materials, and tighten export controls.

Progress on another front was achieved in April 1997, when the Chemical Weapons Convention entered into force. This accord, which bans the possession, acquisition, and use of poison gas, received the consent of two-thirds of the U.S. Senate following lengthy and contentious debate. Quickly after the Senate acted, China and Russia joined the Convention. An international inspectorate began its work, visiting not only military facilities, but also chemical industry plants.

This record of achievement was unprecedented by any measure of merit in the history of arms control. By the end of 1997, treaty regimes governing strategic arms control and non-proliferation appeared to be in excellent shape. But appearances were deceptive. The tide turned quickly and unexpectedly in the latter part of the decade. Difficulties first became apparent with the fine print of treaties, spreading rapidly to the political realm.

The Tide Turns

The momentum behind efforts to reduce dangers posed by weapons of mass destruction is not self-generating: progress comes only with sustained and concerted efforts from the top down. Nor do these dangers remain in a state of equilibrium. If forward progress is not forthcoming, backsliding is likely to result. The absence of sustained presidential leadership in reducing nuclear dangers therefore invites trouble. President Clinton accomplished much for arms control during his first four years in office, but he lost considerable ground in his second term.

The momentum behind efforts to reduce nuclear dangers was already dangerously depleted by 1996, when the Comprehensive Test Ban Treaty was finally concluded. Indeed, states reluctant to stop testing, led by Russia and China, attached a provision to the Treaty conditioning its entry-into-force with the unprecedented requirement that all forty-four "nuclear-capable" states—states with overt nuclear weapon programs, nuclear power plants or infrastructure that would enable a country to build a bomb—ratify the accord before formal implementation could begin. This provision, requiring the consent of countries such as North Korea, India, and Pakistan, was nominally supposed to capture reluctant parties without singling them out.

Instead, the Test Ban Treaty's fine print on entry into force effectively kept the treaty hostage to the most reluctant states, while backfiring on the Clinton administration and treaty supporters in the United States.

Other accords had quite simple entry-into-force provisions. The Non-Proliferation Treaty, for example, required only three states—the United States, Great Britain, and the Soviet Union—to deposit their instruments of ratification. The Chemical Weapons Convention employed another useful model: This treaty would take effect when sixty-five states, regardless of size or military capability, had ratified. Another provision penalized states economically for delaying ratification. Those lagging behind would not be allowed to engage in the commerce of chemicals subject to scrutiny under the Convention. By contrast, the Comprehensive Test Ban Treaty elevated the requirements for entry into force to a much higher level, indicating the reluctance of nuclear powers to finalize this accord's flat prohibition on testing.

The fine print of a treaty's entry into force is not a mobilizing issue at the grass roots, on Capitol Hill, or elsewhere. Nor does this subject lend itself to lobbying efforts. Bureaucracies deal with such matters, and the U.S. bureaucratic imperative in 1996 was to complete the treaty, keep the Chinese on board and the Indians from torpedoing a negotiating end game. China, Russia, Great Britain, and France all supported this tortuous entry-into-force provision: If India decided to play the spoiler (New Delhi viewed this provision as a thinly disguised effort to force its inclusion) and if the treaty's provisions were never actuated, their nuclear weapons establishments would shed few tears. Entreaties by non-governmental organizations that the Treaty's entry-into-force provision would create serious trouble downstream lacked effect. By the time President Clinton belatedly picked up the phone to coax flexibility from London and Paris on this matter, time was already running out on the negotiations at the Conference on Disarmament in Geneva. Immediately after succeeding with London and Paris, Clinton deferred to the strongly held views of Moscow and Beijing. India then rejected the resulting treaty, but at least it had emerged from Geneva for a triumphant signing ceremony at the United Nations.

The immediate spoiler turned out to be Senate Republicans, not India. Strong supporters of the Test Ban Treaty in the Senate believed that an up-or-down vote would succeed, assuming that Republicans would not wish to accept the onus of voting against a popular treaty during an election year. Polls showed overwhelming majorities in support of the Test Ban Treaty among Republican and independent voters, but these polls did not measure the intensity of popular views, nor the intensity of Republican antipathy to President Clinton. The Clinton administration did not make the Senate

Republican leadership a partner in the treaty negotiations; had the effort been made, divisions over the test ban would only have become more apparent. Instead, the Clinton team attempted to present Senate Republicans with a *fait accompli.*

No treaty of this magnitude has ever carried the necessary two-thirds vote without the support of the Republican leader in the Senate. Henry Cabot Lodge's opposition doomed the League of Nations, and Howard Baker's negative stance helped kill chances for the second Strategic Arms Limitation Treaty months before the Soviet invasion of Afghanistan.[6] Senate Republican Leader Trent Lott was viscerally uncomfortable with treaties and with Clinton. Lott and most of his fellow Republicans opposed the test ban on substance and did not fear the political fallout. Polls indicated that support for nuclear deterrence was as strong as support for the test ban. If opposition to the Treaty were couched as support for a strong U.S. nuclear deterrent, the political fallout was manageable.

By the time the administration's head counters in the Senate had made it clear to the White House that the test ban would be rejected by all but a handful of Senate Republicans, the trap planned by staunch foes was clamping shut. Sixty-two senators (including twenty-four Republicans) signed a letter asking that a vote not be taken, given the grave international consequences of the Senate's rejection. Clinton privately urged his advisors to find additional senators willing to sign the letter, while continuing his belated efforts to rally public opinion behind the Treaty. With defeat staring him in the face, Clinton subsequently wrote Senator Lott requesting that the Senate postpone consideration of the Treaty.

Normally, this would be sufficient, but congressional–executive relations during the Clinton administration were anything but normal. Clinton rejected Lott's stipulation that the President not resubmit the Treaty during the last year of his presidency. To do so would have undercut presidential prerogatives—or so Clinton's advisors successfully argued—even though an eleventh-hour re-submission by a deeply wounded president of a treaty bitterly opposed by Republican leaders would surely have invited the same, devastating result. By asserting presidential prerogatives on this matter for the remaining year of his term, Clinton provided the pretext for Republican hard-liners to insist on a vote driving a stake into the Comprehensive Test Ban Treaty. To save the United States from a serious diplomatic embarrassment (and President Clinton from a stinging defeat), Lott would have had to swallow his own deep misgivings about the test ban and convince Republican irreconcilables to stand down. Lott's calculus led to a predictable result: On October 13, 1999, the roll was called. Forty-eight senators voted in support of the Test Ban Treaty, and fifty-one against. The test ban failed even to garner a simple majority, let alone the two-thirds necessary for ratification.[7]

The Treaty's defeat was a painful blow not only to global efforts for a permanent ban on nuclear testing, but also to arms control and non-proliferation agenda items across the board. By voting down the test ban, Republican Senators also killed whatever chance the Clinton administration had of securing India's (and Pakistan's) accession—even after they carried out nuclear tests in 1998. As intended by treaty foes, Clinton's standing to seek the ratification of other accords in the Senate was nullified, as was his ability to negotiate new provisions governing nuclear offense and missile defense. Republican majorities on Capitol Hill underlined this point by refusing to give Clinton the authority to adjust downward strategic nuclear force levels below the first Strategic Arms Reduction Treaty's high level of 6,000 deployed nuclear weapons.

The health of the Non-Proliferation Treaty—extended indefinitely in the first Clinton term—was jeopardized by the test ban's defeat. The strength of the Non-Proliferation Treaty depends, in large measure, on the strength of its bargain between the nuclear-weapon states and more than 170 other states adhering to the Treaty that have foresworn nuclear weapons. In return for this abstinence, the Non-Proliferation Treaty's "grand bargain" requires the five recognized nuclear-weapon states to negotiate in good faith toward disarmament. The demise of the Comprehensive Test Ban Treaty—and the subsequent resumption of nuclear testing—would loosen constraints on proliferation.

The Clinton administration's troubles soon multiplied. The March 1997 meeting between Clinton and Yeltsin to adopt a framework for a third strategic arms reduction accord made positive headlines with the promise of further nuclear reductions, but the reality was that START was bogged down in executive–legislative wrangling in both capitals. Rather than seek to jump start the process with parallel initiatives, the Clinton administration never wavered from a step-by-step approach, with each step requiring ratification in Washington and Moscow.[8] Neither Clinton nor Yeltsin could deliver on this work plan. Clinton was checked by Republicans angling to embarrass him and to kill the Anti-Ballistic Missile Treaty, while nationalist and communist deputies were more than a match for a distracted and erratic Yeltsin.

The Clinton administration's cautious strategy was erroneously predicated on leveraging Yeltsin and the Russian Duma to accept ratification of the START II accord. The Clinton team convinced themselves that Russia's economic duress and the Kremlin's inability to match U.S. force levels would mandate this rational choice, because START II provided for a fictional equality with the United States. But rational choices are made through the prism of domestic politics, and START II was deeply disliked in Russia. It disestablished Russia's lone remaining nuclear trump card, land-based missiles carrying multiple warheads, and it was negotiated during the brief honeymoon period of U.S.–Russian relations by a Russian Foreign Minister and President who had lost the confidence of their country. The Clinton administration hoped in vain that the Kremlin would swallow the bitter medicine of START II in order to secure a third accord, where the disparities in nuclear force levels would be reduced.

From 1996 through 1998, President Clinton declined to enter new negotiations with Russia, seeking instead an up-or-down vote in the Duma on START II. With the benefit of hindsight, this cautious strategy was clearly ill advised. The Russian Duma's incentives to ratify this treaty diminished as Clinton's standing fell and as plans for U.S. missile defenses picked up steam. By the fall of 1998, the momentum behind U.S.–Russian strategic arms reductions had virtually ground to a halt. Yeltsin never delivered, and the Duma never voted to do business with the Clinton administration on deep cuts. Yeltsin's handpicked successor, Vladimir Putin, succeeded in engineering a highly conditional Russian ratification of START II in April 2000, linking entry into force to the U.S. Senate's approval of ABM Treaty-related accords that were anathema to many Senate Republicans.

This gambit proved to be as unsuccessful as the Clinton's administration's maneuvering to secure the entry into force of START II. After eight years of jousting, the Clinton administration and Republicans in the Senate produced a twisted ball of yarn knotting together the implementation of deep cuts and the deployment of missile defenses. Republicans on Capitol Hill held the scissors, but they were interested only in cutting up the ABM Treaty. After two terms, President Clinton left a much-weakened enterprise of arms control to his successor.

Further evidence of the Clinton administration's weaknesses and Republican predilections were on display during the ratification debate over the Chemical Weapons Convention. Many of the key provisions of the Convention were negotiated in the Reagan and Bush administrations, a clear plus for prospects of successful Senate consideration. This accord also had the strong support of the Chemical Manufacturers Association, which organized phone calls and private visits with Republican senators by industry leaders. The Majority Leader, Senator Lott, held strong reservations, and his Republican ranks were painfully divided. Nearly half of the Senate Republican caucus believed that multilateral treaties tied U.S. hands and protected cheaters. But this accord also facilitated global commerce in chemicals, and had Republican parentage. At the end of the debate, the Convention limped through—but not before being vitiated with conditions. One condition prevented treaty inspectors from removing soil samples from the United States. Another condition granted the President veto authority over mandatory treaty inspections.

Both provisions were championed by staunch treaty opponents on the grounds that industry and national security secrets would be compromised by foreign inspectors. The Chemical Manufacturers Association and the Pentagon did not object to the treaty's strenuous inspection provisions, so the Clinton administration was on firm political ground to fight these conditions which, if adopted by other states, would badly impair the Convention's intrusive challenge inspection provisions. The staunchest backers of the vitiating conditions were not going to support the accord in any event. Nonetheless, the Clinton administration chose not to protect tough standards of compliance.

Immediately upon entering into force, the Convention began to experience more difficulties. Some countries, including the United States, were slow to pay their dues, making it difficult to sustain a proper pace of routine inspections. The international organization in The Hague, created to draw up implementation procedures, began to whittle away further at the Convention's intrusive monitoring provisions. This effort was led by an awkward but effective combination of highly industrialized countries, including Germany and Japan, that feared industrial espionage; Iran, Egypt, China, and other states suspected of possessing illicit stocks of chemical weapons; and Israel, concerned about prospective challenge inspections by Arab states of the Dimona nuclear facility. For the remainder of the Clinton administration, no country issued a challenge inspection that would test the fragile regime and establish weak inspection standards against suspect states.[9]

Then, in May 1998, international efforts to reduce nuclear dangers were set back by the testing of nuclear weapons by India and Pakistan. These tests violated no treaty commitments, since both countries refused to sign the Comprehensive Test Ban and Non-Proliferation treaties. Nonetheless, nuclear testing on the Subcontinent constituted a severe blow to global norms against acquiring nuclear weapons, since every nuclear test demonstrated national conviction of their military and political utility. The acquisition of nuclear or other weapons of mass destruction also increased the valuation of ballistic missiles that could reach deep into enemy territory. India and Pakistan proceeded down this path as well. Every new entrant into this field requires some external sources of assistance. In this instance, India received help primarily from Russia; Pakistan succeeded in obtaining support from China and North Korea.

Proliferation lowers barriers and tends to beget more proliferation. As the decade ended, weapons of mass destruction and missile programs in Iraq and Iran gained momentum. Saddam Hussein expelled UN inspectors, outlasted the coalition that was created to punish him, and demonstrated the ineffectuality of the Clinton administration's occasional air strikes. Freedom from inspection, increased oil revenues, and the unraveling of diplomatic isolation meant renewed opportunities for Saddam to reconstruct deadly weapons. Next door, Iran was the active beneficiary of Russian nuclear and military assistance. Tehran's presumed requirements for deterrence extended beyond Iraqi contingencies to those involving Israel and the United States.

The combined effects of overt proliferation in South Asia and the Persian Gulf could well exceed the tolerances of existing non-proliferation regimes. Proliferation in the Gulf region, following on the heels of nuclear testing on the Subcontinent, could lead other states to hedge their bets or invite new entrants into the field, particularly in the Middle East. Further impetus to this momentum was provided by the rollback of intrusive monitoring arrangements negotiated for the Chemical Weapons Convention, the U.S. rejection of strengthening measures for the Biological Weapons Convention, and the Senate's rejection of the Comprehensive Test Ban Treaty.

To make matters still worse, export controls were becoming more lax after the demise of the Soviet Union. The Clinton administration's effort to shore up trans-Atlantic export controls met with very limited success. North Korea presented a particularly egregious problem, marketing its extended-range ballistic missiles by a flight test over Japanese territory. Even more problematic was the lax state of export controls in Russia and China, as politically well-connected suppliers continued to make lucrative transactions. "Brain drain" from the vast Soviet nuclear, chemical, and biological weapon and missile production complexes remained a serious concern, with many predicting a new wave of terror from biological warfare, whether home grown or export-assisted.[10]

By the end of the Clinton administration, early negotiating gains had been eclipsed by losses on many fronts, domestic as well as foreign. Two significant successes appeared to be enduring—the denuclearization of Russia's neighbors and the implementation of CTR programs in the former Soviet Union. In addition, a critically important freeze on the North Korean nuclear program remained tenuously in effect. On the negative side of the ledger, no new strategic arms reduction treaty with the Kremlin was formalized, the formidable monitoring provisions of the Chemical Weapons Convention were gutted during ratification and treaty implementation, and the Comprehensive Test Ban Treaty was rejected by Senate Republicans.

Moreover, the ABM Treaty hung by a slender thread, which the incoming Bush administration was eager to cut.

Stuck on MAD

The Clinton administration's travails stemmed from many well-chronicled sources. One lesser-noted reason for the administration's difficulties was its decision to proceed within a Cold War conceptual framework, rather than to articulate a new strategic concept attuned to vastly different circumstances. After the Soviet Union died, the Clinton team set about to trim (in the case of START) or loosen (in the case of the ABM Treaty) treaties grounded in the twin constructs of nuclear overkill and national vulnerability. Deeper reductions were defended domestically as being consistent with nuclear targeting plans that would reduce to rubble what remained of the old Soviet military, leadership, and economic targets. Limited missile defense deployments were defended on the grounds that they would not undercut national vulnerability upon which stability and even deeper cuts were predicated.

There were many reasons for the Clinton team to couch its treaty activities in old-fashioned terms. The post-Cold War strategic environment was very muddled. In the early Clinton years, it felt safer to hedge against the resurrection of old threats than to reconceptualize policies that retained the support of allies, Russia, and China. In addition, the administration inherited two exceptional, but unratified, START accords, and rightly felt the urgency to secure this inheritance. Moreover, presidents do not benefit politically from taking on the Pentagon's guardians of nuclear orthodoxy. Had President Clinton tried to do so, he would have raised the ire of Republicans on Capitol Hill, whose support was necessary for the treaties Clinton sought.

While the Clinton administration's reasons for adhering to orthodoxy were understandable, its "safe" strategy proved to be exceedingly risky. Arguments that were serviceable during the Cold War were unpersuasive at a time when Russian strategic forces were no match for the United States, when deep cuts in the Kremlin's obsolescent arsenal were inevitable, and when making a virtue of national vulnerability appeared to be increasingly nonsensical. The Clinton administration's dogged defense of orthodoxy failed not only because Republicans were intent on pursuing another agenda, but also because most Americans were ready to move beyond MAD.

When U.S. concerns shifted from Soviet strength to Russian weakness, the rationale for START also shifted in important ways that the Clinton administration failed to articulate. As initially conceived, strategic arms reduction accords were primarily about downsizing bloated arsenals and preventing the resumption of an arms race. These goals became easily achievable without treaties when the Soviet Union died. In the post-Cold War era, START and the ABM accords became important for very different reasons. For Moscow, these accords reduced disparities in U.S. and Russian force levels, while allowing the maintenance of nuclear deterrence in a greatly disadvantaged position. For Washington, reductions in oversized Cold War arsenals remained useful, but they began to take a back seat in importance to safeguarding dangerous weapons and materials in the former Soviet Union from potential buyers such as Saddam Hussein and Osama bin Laden. Before the fall of the Soviet Union, mutual reassurance based on strategic vulnerability was essential. After the fall of the Soviet Union, a different kind of mutual reassurance was needed to facilitate access for cooperative threat reduction. The intrusive inspections and patterns of cooperation established by treaties could become baselines for more ambitious arrangements to control "loose nukes," chemical weapon stocks, and fissile material. The Kremlin's receptivity to this new agenda would be proportional to its perception of the United States as a partner rather than as a threat.

The Clinton administration's proposed changes to START and the ABM Treaty failed to gain traction in part because they were couched in Cold War abstractions of assured destruction and strategic stability. In contrast, the administration's implementation of CTR initiatives achieved traction because they addressed easily understood and pressing threats to national security. Cooperative threat reduction was about reducing dangers emanating from Russia's weakness. This forward-leaning agenda stood in stark contrast to strategic arms control treaties situated in Cold War equations of strategic offense and missile defense.

By compartmentalizing strategic arms control and cooperative threat reduction, the Clinton administration contributed to its own undoing. The administration's foes had an open field to argue that the new security agenda was disconnected from strategic arms control and, worse, that old treaties prevented progress in countering new threats. This case was disingenuous in many respects, but it stacked up well against the Clinton team's defense of strategic arms control orthodoxy. After all, the collapse of the Soviet challenge clearly produced a new set of dangers, completely unrelated to the anxieties that preoccupied many during the Cold War. National security threats generated by proliferation-related economic transactions, destabilized economies, humanitarian crises, and weak central governments were utterly different from contingency planning against Soviet tank armies ranging across the German plain. Dangerously unpredictable national leaders in tension-plagued regions like Saddam Hussein or North Korea's Kim Jong Il, now preoccupied U.S. defense planning, not a collectivized and stultified Kremlin leadership. A dynamic China also needed to be watched closely.

To adapt to this new world, Pentagon leaders reacted by conceptualizing and implementing a "Revolution in Military Affairs," in which information age technologies were applied to the battlefield.[11] Beginning in the Clinton administration, the most effective and powerful armed forces in the world set out to make themselves better, smarter, and more agile. Complacency was not a viable option; new thinking was required. On nuclear matters, the picture was quite different. The core Cold War strategic concept underpinning nuclear offense and missile defense, MAD, remained unchallenged during the Clinton years. Under MAD, the best defense was a strong offense, and a strong defense weakened deterrence. Strategic arms control based on MAD sanctioned and regulated massive nuclear arsenals, but tightly controlled missile defenses. This equation, established in a bipolar, global competition with a peer competitor, progressively lost popular support and strategic relevance.

Large nuclear arsenals and strict constraints on missile defenses were not terribly applicable to post-Cold War circumstances. Nuclear weapons had less utility than laser-guided bombs when dealing with far weaker states possessing deadly weapons or dangerously unpredictable national leaders. Nuclear overkill was not a credible rejoinder to global commerce in missiles and lax controls over deadly materials. Indeed, the more salience the United States gave to nuclear weapons under these changed circumstances, the more disadvantaged the United States became. A Gulliver beset by Lilliputians would find it futile and counterproductive to use a blunderbuss. Asymmetric warfare was the counterpoint to nuclear dominance.

While the paradigm governing nuclear weapons and missile defenses shifted when the Cold War ended, MAD remained central to the Clinton administration's strategic calculations. Deep cuts in bloated nuclear arsenals were predicated on the continued viability of the ABM Treaty. Substantial nuclear forces would remain on alert, and a wide range of nuclear targeting options could be maintained. MAD was more important to Moscow, constituting a security blanket against a rapidly growing disparity of fortunes with Washington. As Russian conventional might dissipated, and as its nuclear arsenal aged, mutual defenselessness against nuclear attack became the Kremlin's insurance policy. Protecting the ABM Treaty became the cornerstone of Russian treaty diplomacy. Beijing used different calculations to arrive at the same bottom line. China's conventional and nuclear forces were dwarfed by U.S. capabilities in any protracted conflict over Taiwan. For China to protect itself against nuclear blackmail and to gain some footing in any future clash over Taiwan, Beijing needed both the ABM Treaty and a survivable capability to deliver a few nuclear weapons on U.S. cities. London and Paris were no less committed to MAD, given the limited nature of their nuclear deterrents.

The Clinton administration understood that MAD was a hard sell, and shied away from publicly defending it except when pressed by critics. A nuclear posture review carried out in the first two years of the Clinton presidency flirted briefly with new ideas, and then retreated to safe ground.[12] The nuclear forces needed to implement MAD's precepts were downsized somewhat—Cold War nuclear targeting plans could always be pruned—but the need for three separate means of delivering devastating nuclear strikes and the requirement to keep a few thousand nuclear weapons on high alert were reaffirmed. This approach was justified on the grounds that it was too soon to forecast Russia's future course. Pentagon planners postulated that bilateral relations could again sour, Moscow could quickly rebound, and the maintenance of thousands of deployed warheads on strategic nuclear forces might again be necessary. Indeed, reductions to the level of a few thousand deployed warheads were deemed so risky that a comparably sized number of warheads were to be maintained in ready reserve, in the event of a reconstituted Russian deterrent.

The Pentagon characterized the resulting nuclear posture as a "lead and hedge" strategy.[13] The United States would push for new strategic arms accords, while maintaining a hedge against negative developments in Russia. As for missile defenses, the Clinton administration funded research and development programs, while killing the expansive deployment plans inherited from the Bush administration. During the second Clinton term, this "lead and hedge" posture morphed into a "wait and hedge" policy, as Clinton sought to leverage Moscow to ratify treaties negotiated by his predecessor. Deeper cuts than those negotiated in the Bush administration—reductions that the Kremlin would need to make in any event, and that Moscow would want to make bilaterally—were placed on hold until the Russian Duma swallowed the bitter pill of ratifying START II. As domestic criticism grew over its betwixt and between choices, the Clinton administration circled the wagons around old verities. MAD did not require radical changes in nuclear offenses (which avoided pitched battles with the Pentagon and with Republicans on Capitol Hill). MAD also avoided fights with Democrats and allies wedded to the ABM Treaty as the "cornerstone of strategic stability."

In the decade of accomplishment bookmarked by the negotiation of the INF Treaty and the indefinite extension of the Non-Proliferation Treaty, there was no evident need to rethink MAD. When nuclear and proliferation dangers started to grow in the latter part of the 1990s, its obsolescence became more apparent and meaningful. During the Cold War, MAD provided necessary cohesion for diplomatic and nuclear strategies. After the Cold War ended, it generated dissonance and partisan division. Republicans held strong attachments to nuclear weapons and a growing aversion to treaties, undercutting the U.S. non-proliferation agenda. Meanwhile, Democrats found it increasingly difficult to explain the central support structures of MAD, weakening strategic arms control accords. Vulnerability to nuclear danger remained a fact of life after the Cold War ended, but it was no longer possible to enshrine vulnerability as the cornerstone of strategic stability. MAD's days—and those of the ABM Treaty—were numbered.

After MAD, What?

MAD was an easy target for the incoming Bush administration. Killing the ABM Treaty was supposed to be a harder trophy, but this was pulled off with very few immediate perturbations by President George W. Bush in December 2001. Media reports during the fall latched on to the possibility of a U.S.–Russian deal to postpone contentious treaty issues and to allow for considerable latitude in U.S. testing in return for a non-withdrawal pledge. The alacrity with which the Bush team switched gears suggested that the window for this opportunity was either exceedingly brief or never really open. The timing of Bush's decision was propitious for treaty foes. The news was dominated in mid-December by the successful prosecution of the war on terrorism in Afghanistan, and the President's popularity hovered around 90 percent. Earlier on the day of the White House announcement to withdraw from the ABM Treaty, extremists linked to Pakistan attacked the Indian Parliament building in New Delhi, another potential *casus belli* linked to terrorism.

President Bush framed his decision to withdraw in terms that were well suited to the temper of the times: "I have concluded," he said in a brief announcement, "the ABM Treaty hinders our government's ability to develop ways to protect our people from future terrorist or rogue-state missile attacks."[14] The *Washington Post* editorial page, previously a defender of the Treaty, offered a mild endorsement; the *Wall Street Journal*'s editorial was titled, "Out with a Whimper."[15] Bush's decision was received in low-key fashion abroad. Putin termed it "erroneous," while calling for discussions "to work out the new framework of a strategic relationship as soon as possible."[16] Beijing's response was similarly muted. The Chinese Foreign Ministry dropped all previous bombast, issuing a statement "taking note" and "expressing concern" over Bush's decision, then adding, "It is of crucial importance to maintain the international disarmament and arms control efforts." Beijing, like Moscow, welcomed talks with the Bush administration over its proposed "new strategic framework."[17] U.S. allies in Europe and Japan swallowed hard and moved on to damage limitation strategies.

Russia and China were far from alone in wishing to learn more about the Bush administration's plans. The much-heralded new strategic framework remained a work in progress, partly owing to the administration's lack of knowledge about what missile defense technologies would shine or falter in subsequent tests. The Bush administration was also hesitant to fill in the blanks, perhaps because if the ambitions of the administration's missile defense enthusiasts were clarified, they would deeply trouble skeptics at home and abroad.

President Bush and his top lieutenants couched their opposition to the ABM Treaty by saying repeatedly that the Cold War was over, and that the United States and Russia were no longer adversaries. A domestic and foreign backlash would surely be generated if the administration's preferred architecture for missile defenses harkened back to the days when Washington and Moscow were strategic competitors. The crux of Cold War debates over national missile defenses had to do with efforts by one side or the other to achieve strategic superiority and the likely adverse consequences of this pursuit. It would be ironic, but hardly surprising, if missile defense enthusiasts continued to press for favored programs on the grounds that U.S. superiority was now incontestable. If, during the Cold War, peace through strength was the objective, now that the Cold War was over, peace through superiority in nuclear offense and missile defense could be realized.

A window into the Bush administration's thinking was provided in a collaborative effort published in January 2001 by a group that included several individuals who subsequently became key staff members at the National Security Council and Pentagon. The strategic framework advocated by this report issued by the National Institute for Public Policy made a virtue of flexibility and "adaptive deterrence" in lieu of treaties. Among this report's findings:

> Because the international environment and operational considerations are dynamic ... the ability to adjust the U.S. offensive and defensive force posture to a changing strategic environment is crucial ...
>
> Adaptability also requires a capacity to design and build new [nuclear] weapons ...
>
> The codification of deep reductions now, according to the traditional Cold War approach to arms control, would preclude the U.S. *de jure* prerogative and *de facto* capability to adjust forces as necessary to fit a changing strategic environment. It would render the U.S. vulnerable to the highly questionable assumption that the international environment is and will continue to be relatively benign ...

Further adjustments to the U.S. strategic forces must not be rendered practically or legally "irreversible" via codification in the traditional arms control process ...

Given the post-Cold War diversity of potential opponents and crises Washington will want to deter, the value of "superiority" ... may again be important.[18]

There is nothing intrinsically wrong with, and many advantages to, U.S. strategic superiority. While there are risks of overreaching and of becoming a more attractive target because of American strength, these risks are far better to run than those associated with national weakness. In any event, U.S. superiority will be a fact of international relations for the foreseeable future. No U.S. administration will give these advantages away, and no peer competitor will exist for a decade or more that could contest U.S. primacy. So the question at hand is not whether superiority as a strategic concept for the United States is a good or a bad idea. Instead, the relevant question is how best to apply U.S. superiority against potential threats facing America and America's friends and allies.

Because of U.S. superiority, those threats will be asymmetric in nature. As discussed in Chapter 2, the most probable threats are likely to be delivered by unconventional means. The most severe threats to U.S. national security are posed by weapons of mass destruction. The utility of U.S. strategic superiority against such threats is bounded partly by how much and where proliferation occurs, how often American political leaders are willing to place U.S. military forces in harm's way, and how much help Washington receives to block and, if necessary, to combat proliferation. Other factors could be added to this complex equation. Any combination of factors adds up to a single, essential truth: The successful battle against unconventional warfare, asymmetric threats, and proliferation requires cooperation on many fronts. Domestic cooperation is needed for homeland defense. A consensus at home is needed to prosecute successfully enemies abroad. International cooperation is needed to safeguard dangerous materials and weapons at the source. Cooperation from permanent members of the U.N. Security Council might be needed to authorize politically sensitive missions. There will be occasions when coalition warfare makes more sense than unilateral action, and there will be times when multilateral peacekeeping or enforcement operations might be required.

Those who seek the strength to act unilaterally are not always willing to go it alone. Indeed, for some who seek the strongest possible protections, the use of force is deemed essential in very few cases. The challenges of proliferation and asymmetric warfare facing the United States, however, are likely to be multiple and multi-directional. Forward-leaning U.S. engagement and preventive diplomacy can reduce the necessity to use force, and can make the use of force, when necessary, more effective. International cooperation is required to dry up sources of supply and proliferation. International cooperation can also lift some burdens from U.S. fighting forces.

How the United States goes about extending strategic superiority will help define how much cooperation Washington can expect from others in difficult cases. Reassurance was the handmaiden of deterrence during the Cold War. The object of reassurance then, as Michael Howard has written, was "to persuade one's own people, and those of one's allies, that the benefits of military action, or preparation for it, will outweigh the costs."[19] Reassurance is also a necessary complement to U.S. strategic superiority in future diplomatic and military campaigns against asymmetric threats. Friends and allies in troubled regions where weapons of mass destruction and ballistic missiles are present will need the reassurance of U.S. protection, otherwise they will be more likely to fight fire with fire. Russia will want reassurance that U.S. strategic superiority will not be employed to its disadvantage, or else the extent of its assistance will be constrained in cases where Moscow's interests are not aligned closely with Washington. The same holds true for China.

The National Institute for Public Policy report acknowledges this point in its critique of MAD which, it argued, "now contributes to U.S.–Russian enmity.... There is an inherent contradiction in attempting to improve U.S.–Russian political relations by remaining committed to the Cold War approach to arms control, an approach designed to perpetuate MAD."[20] This line of argument, which was used with such political adeptness in the run-up to the withdrawal from the ABM Treaty, would be more persuasive if its proponents rejected other U.S. initiatives that would sour ties with Russia. Indeed, the combined pursuit of the ideas embedded in the National Institute for Public Policy report are quite likely to worsen U.S.–Russian political relations, such as the need for "significant numbers of nuclear weapons, particularly against a hostile China or Russia—or worse yet, a Sino-Russian alliance;" counterforce targeting that "will entail more targets, including many that are harder to find and better protected;" capabilities to destroy hardened, underground targets or mobile missile launchers; the need for a robust nuclear reserve force; and precision-guided munitions for some nuclear attack scenarios.[21]

This list of nuclear war-fighting capabilities is entirely familiar from the Cold War. When the enthusiasm for missile defense deployments is added to this mix, one is hard pressed to distinguish between the ambitions of anti-Soviet nuclear strategists and those who now profess to want a new, friendly relationship with Russia. Indeed, the study director of this report co-authored an article on nuclear strategy in 1980 entitled "Victory is Possible." The thesis of this article was that "Nuclear war is possible," and that "the West needs to devise ways in which it can employ strategic nuclear forces coercively, while minimizing the potentially paralyzing impact of self-deterrence."[22] There is, in other words, clear compatibility between prescriptions offered before and after the collapse of the Soviet empire. Arms controllers readily connected these dots. They understood clearly where the twin assaults on MAD and the ABM Treaty were headed, but they did not have the arguments or the troops needed to defend the ramparts. By enshrining national vulnerability in the form of the ABM Treaty and defending MAD, arms controllers lost their domestic audience.

With President Bush's decision to withdraw from the ABM Treaty, some missile defense enthusiasts looked forward to deploying robust missile defenses and to testing refinements in nuclear deterrence. By rejecting MAD and the ABM Treaty, the way was now open to move from deterrence to dominance and compellance. The pursuit of such an agenda, along with the rejection of treaties, would be profoundly divisive at home and unsettling to Russia, China, and U.S. allies. The more deterrence is traded in for compellance, the stronger the backlash that will result. Should this matter to the sole remaining superpower? Absolutely. Because strategic superiority in the absence of reassurance and key partnerships generates coalition building against U.S. interests, more regional proliferation, and more asymmetric warfare.

American strategic superiority can be wisely or foolishly extended. Reassurance comes not only from superior U.S. military capabilities, but also from the perceived wisdom of U.S. diplomatic and military initiatives. An America that walks away from treaties while arrogating to itself the right to reject international norms against testing nuclear weapons and weaponizing space will become a very lonely, muscle-bound superpower. The rejoinders to U.S. supremacy will take many forms, ranging from embarrassingly lopsided votes in the United Nations to the far more serious matter of proliferation. The Lilliputians will not fight Gulliver fairly.

Paradox is woven deeply into the narrative thread of any history of nuclear weapons, arms control, and missile defenses. Newtonian laws of physics apply: For every action, there is an equal and opposite reaction. Arms control triumphs beget backlashes, and the triumphs of weapon strategists or the killing of arms control treaties generate new protective mechanisms. With the withdrawal from the ABM Treaty and the fashioning of a "new strategic framework," opportunities abound for a wise, new strategic synthesis that is both protective and reassuring. There is also ample opportunity for overreaching.

CHAPTER 2

Prioritizing Threats and Responses

The paradigm shift from Cold War to asymmetric warfare was widely predicted prior to the terrorist attacks on the World Trade Center and Pentagon. Many prescient assessments by government agencies, non-governmental organizations (NGOs) and advisory panels drawing on senior Republican and Democratic figures all warned of serious trouble ahead. This body of work concluded, with remarkably little variation, that the primary threats facing the United States after the Cold War were posed by weak foes that would exploit the vulnerabilities of a modern society while seeking to skirt U.S. military strengths. Terrorism—especially acts of terror utilizing weapons of mass destruction—was at the top of nearly every one of these threat assessments. Cold War-era dangers posed by ocean-spanning ballistic missiles were at or very near the bottom.

Washington responded sluggishly to these warnings until the nightmarish events of September 11, 2001. Domestic political debate, bureaucratic preferences, and U.S. diplomatic and defense postures continued to dwell on familiar agendas rather than new ones. Some budgetary adjustments were made to focus more on asymmetric threats, but the modesty of this effort is evident when measured against the funding increases after September 11. The U.S. intelligence community forecast in general terms the coming threat, but multiple warning signs of impending national trauma still went unheeded. National guardians were asleep at the switch when the nightmare became real. From the fall of the Berlin Wall to the collapse of the World Trade Center, Washington operated far too much on pretense. Washington's political class made chest-thumping speeches. Denunciations, diversions, and congratulations filled the airwaves. Trivia ruled. International obligations were short-changed. Attentiveness to domestic concerns paid evident dividends, but the pursuit of tax cuts, educational reform, and economic growth left America woefully unprepared for asymmetric warfare.

As the U.S. economy became far stronger during the 1990s, it also became more vulnerable to unconventional intrusions. During this decade of national congratulation and diversion, resource allocations conformed more to old habits than to emerging threats. Calls for a realignment of national strategy went unheeded. President Bill Clinton did not have the standing, inclination, or tenacity to try to move a largely disinterested public toward new definitions of threat and response. And even if he had tried to lead, it is unlikely that Republicans on Capitol Hill would have followed.

A Post–Cold War Consensus Emerges

After the attacks on the World Trade Center and Pentagon, it was unmistakably clear that acts of terror belonged at the very top of the post-Cold War threat hierarchy. As bad as these attacks were, the trauma could have been far worse had the perpetrators used biological, nuclear, radiological, or chemical means to produce mass casualties. After the collapse of the Soviet Union, many experts warned that attacks with such weapons of mass destruction were far more likely. These dangerous materials were now more available as a result of weakened controls in the former Soviet Union. Materials not illicitly traded might be indigenously produced by "rogue" states or small terrorist cells.

A plethora of studies appeared on this deeply troubling prospect, which was dubbed "megaterrorism."[1] It is not easy, however, to produce mass death by chemical or biological weapons. The batching and dissemination of these weapons require multiple skills that are not easily acquired or integrated by loners, as the Aum Shinrikyo cult in Japan discovered. Their attempts to infuse the Tokyo subway system with the nerve agent Sarin proved ineffectual. Similarly, the dissemination of anthrax to cause mass death is extraordinarily difficult to do. But very small fatality counts can still seriously wound the national psyche, as was evident by the use of the U.S. mail to send anthrax spores to Capitol Hill offices and news media personalities in the wake of the September 11 attacks.

The generation of casualties by weapons of mass destruction in the hands of terrorist groups remains a looming threat that has, so far, produced very few fatalities. The overwhelming incidence of terrorism and fatalities during the first decade after the Soviet Union's demise resulted from conventional explosives delivered by unconventional means. During the Cold War, fears of surprise attack centered around the "bolt-out-of-the-blue" launch of ballistic missiles. In asymmetric warfare, acts of terror—whether involving weapons of mass destruction or conventional explosives—are most likely to be carried out by means of innocent-looking messengers, trucks, boats, or planes.

In the ten years after the demise of the Soviet Union, terrorists that used conventional explosives produced far more fatalities and casualties than terrorists trying to use weapons of mass destruction. From 1990 to 2000, the U.S. Department of State recorded 4,247 acts of terror. In the year 2000 alone, the State Department lists 423 terrorist attacks—up 8 percent from 1999. During this decade, there was only one significant terrorist act using a weapon of mass destruction—the release of Sarin nerve agent by the Aum Shinrikyo cult into the Tokyo subway system. Of the 1,038 individuals categorized by Tokyo hospitals as suffering the symptoms of Sarin gas exposure, 980 suffered minor symptoms such as vision impairment and headache, fifty-four were critically or severely injured, and, of those, twelve died as a result. The subsequent use of anthrax as an agent of terror through the U.S. mail system resulted in twenty-three cases of infection reported to the Centers for Disease Control and five fatalities. In contrast, the terrorist attacks using jet fuel and airplanes as incendiary devices on September 11, 2001 resulted in 3,019 fatalities. This single day of infamy also eclipsed the number of fatalities recorded by the State Department over the previous decade for acts of terror using conventional explosives.[2]

Before the attacks on September 11, an inordinate amount of attention was focused on the threats posed by ballistic missiles possessed by maverick states and undeterrable leaders. The use of missiles to terrorize population centers dates back to World War II, when Nazi Germany struck London and other cities with crude ballistic as well as cruise missiles, then called "buzz bombs." Short-range ballistic missiles were used during the Iran–Iraq war in the 1980s; several score more were used by Saddam Hussein against Israel and Saudi Arabia in the war between Iraq and coalition forces led by the United States. This record of ballistic missile use is discussed in more detail below.

There is no available evidence that any of these missiles carried unconventional weapons. Typically, short-range missiles are armed with conventional explosives, in part because it is difficult to miniaturize or disperse more deadly payloads. In addition, short-range ballistic missiles are deployed at the forward edge of the battlefield, where they could be overrun, or where weapons' effects could harm the side firing the missile as well as an adversary's forces. States that have ballistic missiles are, however, keenly interested in extending their reach. Some of these states are also intent on acquiring weapons of mass destruction, if they have not done so already. The longer the range of the ballistic missile, the more it is presumed to carry unconventional payloads.

Otherwise, the large expense and the deterrent message attached to the missile would be vitiated.

Ocean- or continent-spanning missiles are expected to carry weapons of mass destruction. Over the first fifty years of their existence, these weapons have not been used in war, making them the least problematic but most consequential threat facing the United States. The launch of a long-range ballistic missile provides an unmistakable return address, simplifying a prompt, devastating response. There are other, less traceable, and therefore more likely ways to package deadly weapons and to convey them long distances, such as by merchant or container shipping. As a consequence, a broad spectrum of informed opinion has concluded that, while the use of ballistic missiles to attack American soil cannot be dismissed, this threat is unlikely, compared with other nightmare scenarios. In an era of asymmetric warfare, Gulliver carries the blunderbuss, not the Lilliputians.

This hierarchy of asymmetric threats was reflected in the conclusions of the Commission on America's National Interests, a bipartisan assessment released in July 2000. Co-chaired by Robert Ellsworth, Andrew Goodpaster, and Rita Hauser, the members of the Commission, including Condoleezza Rice (soon to become President George W. Bush's national security adviser), Brent Scowcroft, and Senator John McCain, identified six "cardinal challenges" for the next U.S. president. Three of the challenges identified concerned strengthening U.S. alliances, maintaining U.S. leadership, and promoting freedom, peace, and prosperity. The other three cardinal challenges are of direct relevance to post-Cold War threats:

- facilitate China's entry onto the world stage without disruption;
- prevent loss of control of nuclear weapons and nuclear weapons-usable materials, and contain the proliferation of biological and chemical weapons;
- prevent Russia's reversion to authoritarianism or disintegration into chaos.

The members of the Commission then defined and rank-ordered U.S. national interests. "Vital" interests were defined as "conditions that are strictly necessary to safeguard and enhance Americans' survival and well-being in a free and secure nation." The very first vital national interest identified was to "prevent, deter, and reduce the threat of nuclear, biological, and chemical weapons attacks on the United States or its military forces abroad." Other vital national interests were listed as ensuring the survival of U.S. allies and their active cooperation; preventing the emergence of hostile major powers or failed states on U.S. borders; ensuring the viability and stability of major global trade, financial, energy, and environmental systems; and establishing productive relations with China and Russia.

The Commission defined "extremely important" national interests as "conditions that, if compromised, would severely prejudice, but not strictly imperil the ability of the U.S. government to safeguard and enhance the well-being of Americans in a free and secure nation." The first two (of eleven) extremely important national interests were to "prevent, deter, and reduce the threat of the use of nuclear, biological, or chemical weapons anywhere," and to "prevent the regional proliferation of weapons of mass destruction and delivery systems." The report then goes on to list ten "important" and four "less important" U.S. national interests. The deployment of national missile defenses against ocean-spanning threats is not identified as a vital interest.[3]

Another bipartisan effort, the United States Commission on National Security/21st Century, was co-chaired by former U.S. senators Gary Hart and Warren B. Rudman. Its members included former Speaker of the House of Representatives Newt Gingrich, former Secretary of Defense James Schlesinger, and Leslie H. Gelb, head of the Council on Foreign Relations. The Commission predicted that, "The combination of unconventional weapons proliferation with the persistence of international terrorism will end the relative invulnerability of the U.S. homeland to catastrophic attack. A direct attack against American citizens on American soil is likely over the next quarter century."[4] Thus, the first recommendation of the Commission was to reorganize and combine the Federal Emergency Management Agency, the Coast Guard, the Customs Service and the Border Patrol into a National Homeland Security Agency. President George W. Bush directed the creation of such an agency after the September 11 attacks. The Hart–Rudman Commission defined this agenda item as urgent and essential, but did not accord a similar status to the deployment of a national missile defense. Instead, the Commission concluded that, "A ballistic missile defense system would be a useful addition and should be developed to the extent technically feasible, fiscally prudent, and politically sustainable."[5]

An earlier report by the Hart–Rudman Commission defined American national security interests in terms very similar to those identified by the Commission on America's National Interests. The top-most interest was labeled "survival" and defined as "safety from direct attack, especially involving weapons of mass destruction, by either states or terrorists." This panel concluded that, "Non-proliferation of weapons of mass destruction is of the highest priority in U.S. national security policy in the next quarter century." While offering the same, qualified endorsement of national missile defenses, the earlier Hart–Rudman report provided an unqualified endorsement "to build comprehensive theater missile defense capabilities."[6]

Yet another high-level assessment of post-Cold War challenges was co-chaired by former senator Howard Baker and Lloyd Cutler. This report focused on the unprecedented challenges associated with the "dissolution of an empire having over 40,000 nuclear weapons, over a thousand metric tons of nuclear materials, vast quantities of chemical and biological weapons materials, and thousands of missiles." The central conclusion of the Baker–Cutler panel was as follows:

> The most urgent unmet national security threat to the United States today is the danger that weapons of mass destruction or weapons-usable material in Russia could be stolen and sold to terrorists or hostile nation states and used against American troops abroad or citizens at home.[7]

U.S. government and intelligence community assessments reflected a similar understanding of the new panoply of threats to U.S. national security in the years prior to the September 11 attacks. During the Cold War, the Pentagon was preoccupied by Soviet nuclear capabilities and strategic modernization programs. In marked contrast, outgoing Secretary of Defense William Cohen characterized the threat in the following way:

> In virtually every corner of the globe, the United States and its allies face a growing threat from the proliferation and possible use of nuclear, biological, and chemical (NBC) weapons and their delivery systems. In some cases, our chief concern is indigenous weapons development programs; in others it is transfer of hardware or know-how across international borders. Broadly, however, we have become increasingly concerned in recent years that NBC weapons, delivery systems, and technology may all be "for sale" to the highest bidder.[8]

The spectacular success of U.S.-led forces in the Gulf War against Saddam Hussein followed by a decade of dynamic U.S. economic growth and improved conventional military capabilities clarified to potential foes that any battlefield campaign against U.S. military forces would be a very unfair fight. However, the economic indicators of American strength, especially U.S. technological advancement and connectivity, were also potential vulnerabilities. As a collaborative effort by the National Intelligence Council and non-governmental experts concluded:

> [M]ost adversaries will recognize the information advantage and military superiority of the United States in 2015. Rather than acquiesce to any

potential U.S. military domination, they will try to circumvent or mini-mize U.S. strengths and exploit perceived weaknesses. Information technology-driven globalization will significantly increase interaction among terrorists, narcotraffickers, weapons proliferators, and organized criminals, who in a networked world will have greater access to informa-tion, to technology, to finance, to sophisticated deception-and-denial techniques and to each other. Such asymmetric approaches—whether undertaken by states or non-state actors—will become the dominant characteristic of most threats to the U.S. homeland.[9]

During the Clinton administration, the Joint Staff of the Joint Chiefs of Staff conveyed a similar message to help congressional staff understand the hierarchy of threats facing America's men and women in uniform. Their unclassified briefing chart, titled "The Threat Spectrum," represented poten-tial damage to U.S. vital interests on one axis; the other axis represented drain on U.S. military capability. The Pentagon's internal assessment con-cluded that the most threatening event—a strategic military attack by Russian or Chinese nuclear forces—was also the least likely. The Pentagon's "threat continuum" rose from humanitarian crises, the war on drugs, and peacekeeping operations at the bottom to the top-most threats of major the-ater wars, a rogue missile attack, and a nuclear war with Russia or China. As the threat continuum rose, the Pentagon judged that the probability of occurrence would decrease.

The Pentagon's working assumptions were entirely consistent with the threat assessments noted above. Well before the attacks on the World Trade Center and Pentagon, there was an uncommonly broad agreement among experts that, in a world of U.S. military dominance, Americans could expect the unexpected. The unpleasant surprises in store for U.S. citizens and mili-tary forces would be asymmetric in nature. There was already a long and tragic number of incidents in which conventional explosives had been used with fatal effect by unconventional means. Still, America was stunned on the morning of September 11. After absorbing these shocks, another realization settled in, that acts of terror could be far worse. They could involve weapons of mass destruction.

Do Defenses Deter?

In the wake of the World Trade Center attacks, supporters of national ballis-tic missile defenses reaffirmed their commitment to prompt deployments, while skeptics placed this need at or near the bottom of their hierarchy of responses to international terrorism. With the end of the Cold War and the steady contraction of Soviet ballistic missile deployments, advocates of national missile defenses shifted gears, resting their case on rogue state threats, the impermanence of deterrence, the constancy of surprise, and the laxness of missile export controls. If Osama bin Laden or his ilk could gain access to ballistic missiles and weapons of mass destruction, they argued, would there be any doubt that such weapons would be used?

The fear of surprise attack is certainly justified by historical example and by the events of September 11. But would future unpleasant surprises include a ballistic missile attack on the U.S. homeland, either by a terrorist cell or by a rogue state? Terrorists would be hard-pressed to acquire, transport, hide, and launch ballistic missiles. National leaders, unlike terrorists, did not welcome death, appearing instead to place the highest priority on maintaining power. Would it not be suicidal for a rogue leader of a small state to take on a giant by means of ballistic missiles, where the origin of attack would be so unambiguously traceable? Asymmetric warfare is fought under different rules. The stronger adversary is challenged in unorthodox ways that are inexpensive, unsophisticated, unexpected, and highly damaging. The Lilliputians used threads to tie down Gulliver.

National missile defense advocates argue that some practitioners of asymmetric warfare—leaders with megalomaniacal personalities, such as Iraq's Saddam Hussein or perhaps North Korea's Kim Jong Il—are undeterrable.[10] Without question, U.S. officials have not always understood their calculus of decision, and have therefore been caught off guard by their actions. Saddam certainly surprised Washington by invading Kuwait, and was then surprised with the purposefulness of President George H. W. Bush's response. Saddam subsequently suffered a grievous defeat, an outcome that he did not seek to alter with missiles carrying weapons of mass destruction. After this defeat, Saddam managed to retain power, which suggests that despots who are capable of surprise and misjudgment usually place retention of power above all other priorities. Those who wish to retain power as long as possible seem to understand that attacking U.S. soil with ballistic missiles provides a fast track to oblivion.

National missile defenses might have some deterrent value in persuading a hostile government not to spend scarce defense resources on ocean-spanning missiles or, if this decision has already been made, to raise the opportunity costs of this decision by increasing the number of missiles required to penetrate U.S. defenses. Other allocations of resources, however, might have far more deterrent value, such as greater investment in power projection capabilities. Alternatively, the United States could invest more heavily in theater missile defenses against the plethora of short- and medium-range missiles that cannot threaten American soil but that pose a threat to forward-deployed forces, friends, and allies. There are also far more cost-effective responses to proliferation threats, such as safeguarding dangerous materials and weapons from potential export.

These choices are certainly not mutually exclusive. If there were an unlimited amount of resources to apply to defense needs, and if the diplomatic and political costs of pursuing vigorously national missile defenses were modest, then the United States could seek defenses of all kinds to deal with a wide range of threats. In the aftermath of the September 11 attacks, far more resources have been applied to these tasks, beginning with much neglected aspects of homeland defense against terrorism. Even so, the Pentagon has not been given a blank check, and the varied costs of national missile defenses are considerable. Under these circumstances—and even in the context of a global war against terrorism—prioritization is mandatory.

In setting priorities, the United States has had the luxury of being able to distinguish between national and theater ballistic missile defenses. National defenses protect the U.S. homeland against ocean-spanning missiles. Theater missile defenses are keyed to shorter-range missiles, which are increasingly available in regions of tension. Washington and Moscow established this dividing line in the first strategic arms limitation accords, signed in 1972. The SALT accords covered land-based missiles with ranges greater than 5,500 kilometers—the approximate distance to reach the continental United States from Mother Russia. The Anti-Ballistic Missile Treaty strictly limited missile defenses against such fast-flying, long-distance threats, while permitting defenses against short-range missiles. Subsequent negotiations worked out permissive clarifications of this boundary to address missiles of increasing range under development in North Korea and Iran. Treaty adaptation was necessary because the protective oceanic distances that separate the United States from "states of concern" were being shortened.

Another conceivable missile threat to U.S. shores would entail hiding a missile on board a ship, operating that ship close enough for the missile to be within range of its intended target, and then firing the missile. This scenario, which was included in the January 2002 unclassified threat assessment of the Central Intelligence Agency, blurs the distinction between national and theater missile defenses. However, theater missile defense systems would continue to be the most effective means to counter close-in, ship-borne missile threats. U.S. intelligence community assessments continued to conclude, quite reasonably, that other threats of weapons of mass destruction conveyed by sea—such as container ships—would be far more likely, as they "can be used without attribution, and would avoid missile defenses."[11] Of all the new asymmetric threats facing the United States, ballistic missiles remained far, far down on the list, thanks to the protective expanses of the Atlantic and Pacific oceans.

States in tension-filled regions cannot rely on geography for protection. When neighbors possess short- and medium-range ballistic missiles as well as unconventional weapons, threatened states can seek safety in matching military capabilities, the protection of a strong patron, and missile defenses. Small states have the option of using theater missile defenses to secure national coverage, depending on the location and reach of deployed missile defenses. National coverage, however, might well not provide national protection, because leak-proof missile defenses require 100 percent effectiveness in the fog of war. The distinction between theater and national missile defenses re-emerges for large states in troubled regions. India or China could seek to protect regions with theater missile defenses, or could choose to invest in national coverage. Since both countries have an expansive landmass to defend and since both face missile threats with widely varying ranges, nominal national protection could be provided only by multi-tiered and extraordinarily expensive missile defenses. The United States is pursuing this path, which is likely to be out of the technical and financial reach of other states. Countries that seek partial protection by means of missile defenses could collaborate with the United States, rely on U.S. capabilities, or seek purchases and technical assistance from Russia or Israel.

Many theater missile defense programs are now in development and field-testing. Some, like the U.S. Patriot or the Russian S-300, began as air defense systems that were subsequently modified to counter short-range ballistic missiles as well as hostile aircraft. "Lower-tier" defenses are designed to protect against the plethora of short-range missiles now in existence. Many of these missiles are derivatives of the Soviet SCUD, which was exported, reverse engineered, and re-exported to nations in the Middle East, Persian Gulf, and Asia. These short-range missiles never leave the earth's atmosphere. By adding a second stage to the SCUD, countries could achieve added range. Medium-range ballistic missiles are classified as those able to strike targets between 1,000 and 3,000 kilometers from their launch point. More advanced ballistic missiles are classified as intermediate-range, with a reach of between 3,000 and 5,500 kilometers. Medium- and intermediate-range ballistic missiles reach their apogee above the earth's atmosphere, where "upper-tier" theater missile defense systems can carry out intercepts. The U.S. Army and the U.S. Navy each have their own lower- and upper-tier missile defense systems in development.

From Gunboat to Missile Defense Diplomacy

Frederick the Great is reputed to have said, "Diplomacy without armaments is like music without instruments." The first armaments to travel long distances to project military power were naval combatants. "Sea power," as Alfred Thayer Mahan noted in 1900, "is but the handmaiden of expansion, its begetter and preserver." Raymond Aron updated these aphorisms for the nuclear age, concluding that, "In the interstate system, one counts divisions, missiles, and the will to use them."[12] In post-Cold War circumstances, sea power and U.S. diplomacy in troubled regions must now be backed up by theater missile defenses. Proliferation mandates theater missile defenses to strengthen deterrence, protect, reassure, and maintain allied cohesion. During the Cold War, the U.S. Navy steamed into harm's way with nuclear weapons; in future crises, Washington will convey political resolve to come to the aid of threatened allies by deploying theater missile defenses. Regional diplomacy in the future without theater missile defenses will be like music without instruments.

The extent to which missile defenses will complement gunboats in future campaigns became clear in the Gulf War against Saddam Hussein. Saddam's limited inventories of ballistic missiles threatened U.S. allies and killed U.S. troops. Those living in Tel Aviv, Dhahran, and Riyadh now felt the terror that Londoners experienced in 1944. Iraq's missiles were deployed on mobile launchers that were exceedingly difficult to find. The United States carried out 1,500 sorties to search and destroy Saddam's SCUDs. These operations complicated Saddam's missile strikes, but no SCUDs were destroyed.[13] The rationale behind Saddam's purchasing habits became manifestly clear. The implied and actual threats posed by ballistic missiles could affect the psychology of, and exact punishment on, foes. Missiles carrying weapons of mass destruction might not prevent defeat against a stronger foe, but they might dissuade a more powerful adversary from overthrowing you. The value of ballistic missiles was duly noted elsewhere. These missiles have become central to the military planning of states as diverse as China, Iran, North Korea, Egypt, Saudi Arabia, India, and Pakistan.

Contingency planning in troubled regions must now deal with the psychological and military implications of ballistic missile attacks of uncertain accuracy and payloads. Individual theater missile defense intercepts are not easy to accomplish, and saturation attacks constitute a serious threat. Theater missile defense intercepts are, however, easier to accomplish than defending against the very high re-entry speeds and the technical countermeasures presumed to accompany ocean-spanning attacks. Flight tests of theater missile defenses were troubled early in the Clinton administration, but then began to demonstrate promise. At the same time, the Clinton team successfully negotiated with the Kremlin a relaxation of the Anti-Ballistic Missile Treaty's strictures to expressly permit the flight-testing and deployment of more capable theater missile defenses. Treaty defenders initially fought against these moves, fearing that high performance, theater missile defenses would undermine the ABM Treaty.

Toward the end of the Clinton administration, even vocal critics of missile defenses came to acknowledge the utility of advanced theater defenses. Skeptics granted that the technical challenges of demonstrating military effectiveness were not as daunting as anticipated, and that well-positioned, advanced theater missile defenses might even substitute for national missile defenses.[14] For example, stationed off the Korean peninsula, theater missile defenses could intercept threatening missiles in their boost or ascent phase, when they are easy targets, rising slowly and emanating heat exhaust that could serve as a beacon for interception. Shooting down a rising missile body is far, far preferable to trying to intercept a warhead and its accompanying countermeasures midway to their target, where discrimination between real warheads and decoys is a huge challenge. While protectors of the ABM Treaty relaxed their opposition to advanced theater missile defenses, staunch treaty opponents threatened to vote down the Clinton administration's relaxation of Treaty constraints, so as not to give the accord renewed meaning.

As theater missile defenses improve, adversaries are likely to supplement their inventories of SCUD derivatives with cruise missiles. Indeed, some analysts believe that in the second decade of the twenty-first century cruise missiles will eclipse ballistic missiles as the most worrisome missile threat.[15] Cruise missile attacks hug the earth's surface, posing a very different defensive challenge than intercepting ballistic missile trajectories, and making a combined defense against cruise and ballistic missiles extraordinarily challenging. The classic arms control dilemma of offense begetting defense and defense begetting more offense—what former Secretary of Defense Robert McNamara and others called the action–reaction phenomenon—is destined to play out far more with theater missile defenses than with national missile defense deployments.

Missile Defenses and Regional Warfare

Unlike ocean-spanning missiles, shorter-range ballistic and cruise missiles have an extensive track record in warfare, ranging from the earliest use of missiles by Nazi Germany to the cruise missile attacks that have become a staple of U.S. warfare. Many thousands of these missiles have already been fired for psychological, military, and political effect. Consequently, the cost-benefit calculations for deploying theater missile defenses are quite different than for ballistic missile defenses of the U.S. homeland.

The first and most concerted use of "buzz" bombs and ballistic missiles was the German bombardment of London, Antwerp, and other cities during World War II. The German missile attacks were carried out for psychological warfare, not military effectiveness. The German V-1, first launched in June 1944, was a lumbering cruise missile with an average range of 240 kilometers. Germany launched approximately 21,000 V-1s, against allied cities. In London and environs, V-1 attacks killed more than 6,000 civilians and seriously injured another 18,000. A more advanced "weapon of vengeance," the V-2, was the world's first ballistic missile. Approximately 3,000 V-2s were launched, one-third of which fell on the United Kingdom, beginning in September 1944. Approximately 500 V-2s hit London and the surrounding area, resulting in almost 3,000 fatalities. *In toto*, V-2 launches caused 5,400 fatalities in the United Kingdom and continental Europe, as well as 22,000 serious injuries. Over time, the Royal Air Force developed an effective counter to the slow-flying V-1, with an ultimate intercept rate of 79 percent; the British had no counter to the V-2.[16]

Short-range ballistic missiles have also figured prominently in recent wars, with a significant twist, as combatants have had to consider the possibility that missiles might be used to deliver weapons of mass destruction. (Inspections of and belated acknowledgments by a defeated Iraq revealed the existence of chemical and biological warheads for its ballistic missile inventory.[17]) During the Gulf War, Saddam Hussein's missile attacks against Israel were widely believed to serve political, rather than military purposes. Secretary of State James A. Baker viewed Iraq's missile strikes as an invitation for Israeli retaliation, which would be "a potentially catastrophic escalation." National security adviser Brent Scowcroft later described the SCUD attacks as "a shrewd attempt to split the Arab allies from the coalition," thereby ending Iraq's political isolation in the Arab world created by the invasion of Kuwait.[18]

Saddam's tactics and the dilemmas of coalition warfare so evident in this case provide glimpses into the future of regional conflict. Had Israel responded to the forty missiles launched by Saddam by entering the war, Arab coalition partners against Iraq, so painstakingly cobbled together by Washington, would likely have peeled away. Saddam launched more ballistic missiles (forty-eight) against Saudi Arabia than at Israel. These missile strikes appear to have been designed to weaken Saudi support for coalition warfare, and to punish the House of Saud for providing bases for its U.S. protectors. Three missiles were also launched against Bahrain, the home base of U.S. naval forces for the Gulf region. Long after the war ended, Saddam's missile strikes provided a lingering reminder of future Iraqi power projection capabilities.[19]

Ballistic missiles have also been used in a war between evenly matched foes. In the lengthy conflict between Iran and Iraq, both countries were politically isolated. (Henry Kissinger quipped that, ideally, both would lose.) Baghdad and Tehran were financially and militarily drained by this eight-year-long war, with neither seemingly able to secure a breakthrough. The pattern of ballistic missile use during the Iran–Iraq war began with short-range battlefield missiles, escalating to the use of longer-range missiles when they became available. Each side launched in excess of 400 missiles. While chemical weapons were used during the war, mostly by Iraq, their means of delivery was apparently by aircraft and artillery, rather than by missiles.

Ballistic missiles were often targeted against Iranian and Iraqi cities. This "war of the cities" began in limited fashion when Iraq used short-range ballistic missiles against the nearest Iranian towns of Ahvaz and Dezful, in November 1980, just two months after the war began. When Saddam Hussein was able to purchase longer-range SCUD missiles in 1983, he began using them, in the words of one of his commanders, "to bring the Iranian people into the front lines of the war."[20] According to one account, as the SCUDs began falling on Tehran, nearly one-quarter of the city's population left the city in fear. Iran scrambled to develop and purchase missiles that could reach Baghdad. At the conflict's end, the war of the cities was carried out to the maximum allowed by modest inventories. In 1988, Iraq fired over 200 ballistic missiles at Iranian cities, while Iran retaliated with seventy-six missiles. Given Iraq's tactics, the short distance between the Iranian border and Baghdad—130 kilometers—and Iran's vastly weakened air force, counter-city attacks by 300 kilometer-range missiles with 1,000 kilogram payloads were Tehran's only way to give Baghdad a taste of its own medicine.[21]

The Primacy of Theater over National Missile Defenses

In the current era of asymmetric warfare, Gulliver relies heavily on air power while the Lilliputians prize their short- and medium-range ballistic missiles. Missile attacks cannot seize and hold territory, but they can still be militarily effective by shaking an adversary's will to fight, creating wedges in coalition warfare, and degrading the enemy's war effort. During World War II, the United States used air power with these objectives in mind, carrying out indiscriminate bombing of German and Japanese cities. Aerial attacks on cities remained a staple of U.S. war fighting in the Balkan wars of the 1990s, reinforced both by Washington's aversion to ground combat and by "smart" bombs that reduced collateral damage in built-up areas. Debates over the political and military efficacy of aerial bombardment campaigns in the Balkans were reminiscent of post-World War II evaluations of air power.

With the advent of asymmetric warfare, city strikes have become feared by the strong as well as by the weak. Terrorists have demonstrated many times that "soft" targets, such as office buildings (Oklahoma City and New York), embassies (Dar es-Salaam and Nairobi), subway systems (Tokyo), or stock exchanges (Bombay), are far easier to attack than heavily protected military installations. As John C. Reppert has wisely observed, "You don't rob Fort Knox. You rob the local 7-11 store." Striking soft targets also creates much greater psychological and economic trauma. Similarly, in conventional military campaigns, nations that are overmatched or exhausted on the battlefield can hope to achieve political or punitive objectives by striking nearby cities with ballistic missiles.

Theater ballistic missiles have clearly become very important pieces on regional chessboards. Another war on the Korean peninsula would surely result in ballistic missile attacks from the North Korean inventory of perhaps 500 SCUD derivatives and Nodong missiles.[22] Even in future combat where missiles are not used, they will preoccupy political and military leaders, as was the case in the 1999 high-altitude war between India and Pakistan. In this limited war, Pakistan had the advantage of tactical surprise and possession of the high ground, but India had superior conventional capabilities and widespread diplomatic support. In this case, both adversaries possessed overt nuclear weapon capabilities, and at least one of the combatants (Pakistan) had the ability to place a compact warhead atop its ballistic missiles. As the Indian Army began to regain lost ground, and as New Delhi signaled its consideration of cross-border conventional military options, the shadow of nuclear confrontation grew darker.

The status of both sides' nuclear-capable forces became of intense interest, within and outside the region. Rumors of impending nuclear danger are staples of South Asian crises, as are nuclear threats from the weaker party, Pakistan, whose missiles and nuclear-capable aircraft are susceptible to preemption. The rumored movement of nuclear-capable forces by Pakistan during the 1999 crisis was a very disquieting development, since this could have been interpreted by India as preparation for launch as well as a purely precautionary measure. Given the lack of trust and poor communication between the parties, nuclear signaling on the Subcontinent is a dangerously opaque exercise, at best. In this case, the importance of ballistic missiles grew as the war progressed, even though they were not used. Well-sourced reports indicate that both Pakistan and India increased the readiness of nuclear-capable missiles during this short but intense war.[23] In a subsequent crisis sparked by a December 2001 terrorist attack on the Indian Parliament building in New Delhi, the deployment of short-range ballistic missiles was leaked to the media by government officials. Ballistic missiles on the Subcontinent have become symbols of national resolve.

Post-Cold War trend lines in missile production and dismantlement confirm the rising importance of missiles in regional warfare and the diminishing profile of ocean-spanning ballistic missiles. The 1987 Intermediate-Range Nuclear Forces Treaty mandated the complete elimination of Soviet missiles with ranges between 500 and 5,500 kilometers. This Treaty's implementation was completed on May 31, 2001. In addition, Russia's inventory of ocean-spanning missiles is dropping significantly. The Kremlin has been able to produce approximately ten new such missiles annually—one-tenth the annual production rate during the 1980s. Soviet missile production rates were higher still in previous years. In 1977, the U.S. intelligence community estimated an annual production rate of 300 intercontinental ballistic missiles, dropping to 200 annually from 1978 to 1981. In addition, during this period the CIA estimated an annual production run of 175 submarine-launched ballistic missiles.[24] The disparity between Cold War and post-Cold War production rates for missiles able to reach the United States is quite stark: Russia produced one missile in the year 2000 for every thirty produced annually during the 1970s.

As a result of these trend lines and the difficulties Russia faces in greatly increasing missile production rates, the Kremlin will likely decommission four out of every five Cold War-vintage missiles that could reach the United States over the next fifteen years. By abrogating the Intermediate-Range Nuclear Forces Treaty, Russia could partially compensate for this draw-down, but this would entail significant diplomatic as well as financial costs. The stratagem of threatening Berlin, Paris, and London with Euro-missiles failed during the Cold War; it would be an odd way to attempt to increase Russian influence in European capitals in the post-Cold War era. More likely, the Kremlin could accept the financial burden of increasing the production rate for ocean-spanning missiles. But the opportunity costs of this choice would fall on greatly weakened conventional forces, and the resulting increase in missiles would be quite marginal.

The threat posed by China's ocean-spanning missiles has not begun to replace that of Russia. Instead, Beijing's deployed strategic nuclear forces remained paltry in the 1990s. During this period, U.S. estimates of Beijing's intercontinental ballistic missiles remained static, at perhaps two dozen in number, while China appeared to be adding fifty shorter-range ballistic missiles annually to its arsenal.[25] This allocation of effort provided a fair representation of how Beijing perceived the military utility of Armageddon weapon systems and battlefield missiles. China's inventory of long-range missiles could certainly grow, however. As one well-informed study concluded:

> How big China's nuclear force becomes is largely a matter of will, not capability. Beijing certainly has more than enough fissile material for a substantial increase in its nuclear arsenal. It can also afford a major expansion of its missile force ... and some reports indicate a Chinese capability to produce ten to twelve new long-range intercontinental ballistic missiles per year.[26]

Non-governmental experts predict that the U.S. deployment of a limited homeland defense against ballistic missiles will generate an increase by China of its long-range missile launchers from a few tens to perhaps 100–200 deployed missiles.[27] The January 2002 estimate by the Central Intelligence Agency predicts that Beijing's future intercontinental missile force will number "around 75 to 100 warheads" by 2015.[28] Over time, as one Pentagon assessment has concluded, "China probably will have the industrial capacity, though not necessarily the intent, to produce a large number, perhaps as many as a thousand, new missiles within the next decade."[29] The vast majority of these missiles will have ranges sufficient to cross the Taiwan Strait, not the Pacific Ocean.

After Russia and China, the roster of states that might acquire ocean-spanning missiles, thus threatening U.S. cities, is rather limited. Three friendly countries—Japan, India, and Israel—have space launch capabilities that could be converted to produce missiles with intercontinental reach. Missile defense advocates warn that North Korea, Iran, and eventually Iraq might seek the capability to reach the periphery of the United States with a few missiles thinly disguised as satellite launchers. These threat assessments are evaluated below. Even if such worst-case scenarios are realized, the combined ocean-spanning ballistic missile threat to the U.S. homeland—from Russia, China and rogue states—would constitute a 75 percent reduction from Cold War norms.[30]

The probability of use associated with theater ballistic missiles and ocean-spanning missiles correlates with inventory trend lines. In the event of a future clash between the United States and China over Taiwan, the odds of a single launch of an intercontinental ballistic missile are extremely low, while the odds of multiple launches of theater ballistic missiles are high. China watchers fully expect Beijing to launch ballistic missile attacks against Taiwan in any war across the Taiwan Strait, since Beijing's missile inventories constitute the mainland's most effective power projection capability. Missile attacks would likely be employed in an effort to demoralize Taiwan's population and create a severe economic crisis. Beijing's presumed hope is that missile attacks would prompt a quick capitulation before U.S. forces could be mobilized to come to Taipei's aid.[31]

Likewise, in the event of renewed regional warfare in the Middle East or the Persian Gulf, the pattern of theater ballistic missile strikes against cities has been well established and is very likely to be repeated. With good reason, Israel has worked closely with the United States on the Arrow, a theater missile defense system with the advertised capability of being able to detect and track up to fourteen incoming missiles from a distance of 500 kilometers.[32] Other states in troubled regions with the resources to acquire theater missile defenses are also moving in this direction. Tokyo, in particular, received a rude wake-up call to ballistic missile threats when North Korea launched a missile over Japanese soil in 1998, ostensibly to deploy a broadcast satellite in low earth orbit.

As regional missile threats grow, so does the political and military utility of theater missile defenses. Many U.S. allies and friends have a clear need for protection against theater ballistic missiles, and few have the resources and technical capabilities to respond adequately to this requirement. The United States could reap diplomatic benefits, strengthen alliances, and address serious threats to regional security by placing a high priority on the deployment of effective theater missile defenses. In contrast, the requirements for and benefits accruing from missile defenses of the U.S. homeland are rather modest.

During the Cold War, the military utility of nuclear weapons was very low, while the political salience of these fearsome weapons was high. The U.S. nuclear umbrella played an important part in maintaining alliance cohesion, retarding proliferation, and signaling U.S. resolve to the Soviet Union. In a similar fashion, many question the military effectiveness of theater missile defenses. Successful intercepts under highly controlled circumstances do not ensure success on a chaotic battlefield where missiles are launched in large salvos. Nonetheless, the provision or forward deployment by the United States of theater missile defenses could have significant political value in demonstrating Washington's resolve to come to the aid of a beleaguered friend or ally. And, over time, theater missile defenses are likely to become more effective.

While the Pentagon will be challenged over the next decade to prove the effectiveness of theater missile defenses, the State Department will be challenged to include these defenses in collaborative regional security arrangements. The design of theater missile defenses can be quite varied and agile. While poorly configured and clumsily advanced missile defense deployments could add strain to alliance ties, theater missile defenses could also have great up-side potential—if they are pursued in ways that alleviate political sensitivities while configured to counter real military threats. In contrast, prospective deployments of U.S. defenses against ocean-spanning missile threats are dominated by downside risks and diplomatic damage control.

The diplomatic and military utility of theater missile defenses are quite evident in the case of Israel, which faces prospective missile attacks from Iraq, Iran, Syria, and Egypt—states that are widely acknowledged to have weapons of mass destruction that could be packaged atop missiles. Israeli acquisition and deployment of theater missile defenses has already occurred; supplementary deployments by the United States in the event of another outbreak of fighting in the Middle East are not in doubt. In such contingencies, the absence of theater missile defenses, rather than their deployment, would have significant, negative ramifications. Similarly, in the event of another threat by Iraq to Saudi Arabia, Kuwait, or other Gulf states, the forward deployment of U.S. theater missile defenses would be widely anticipated.

Theater Missile Defenses in East Asia

Previous debates over national missile defenses have roiled Europe. New debates on theater missile defenses generate the strongest ripples in East Asia.[33] North Korea has the capacity to flight test ballistic missiles that could carry weapons of mass destruction (WMD). China's growing inventories of theater ballistic missiles cast a lengthening shadow over South as well as East Asia. Japan, South Korea, and Taiwan are all troubled by missiles that could carry WMD, but different mixes of political, diplomatic, geographic, and military factors make theater missile defense deployments anything but straightforward or uniform. In East Asia, ill-conceived missile defense architectures could alienate friends as well as potential adversaries. They could also greatly stimulate the very proliferation that missile defense deployments seek to counter. On the other hand, a too lax approach could weaken alliance ties, raise questions about U.S. security guarantees, and have deleterious consequences for proliferation. Because theater missile defenses will be available at sea or on land, deployments could be designed to meet unique geographical and regional circumstances.

If the United States were perceived as not responding purposefully enough to threatening ballistic missile programs, allies and friends in the Asia-Pacific region could seek to acquire theater missile defenses from Russia or Israel, or they could seek greater reliance on alternative means to provide for their security. One alternative to theater missile defenses might be heavier reliance on strike aircraft to destroy missile launch sites and nearby production facilities. (In most military playbooks, a good offense beats a good defense.) Another alternative might be to fight fire with fire—to deter threats posed by WMD and ballistic missiles by responding in kind. Collaborative theater missile defense deployments are certainly preferable to these alternatives.

Great care is therefore required to realize the benefits and minimize the risks associated with theater missile defense deployments in East Asia. The great diversity of regional security issues and geography in East Asia forecloses a "one size fits all" approach to missile defenses. Burden sharing will vary from case to case. The architecture and missions for theater missile defenses are shaped primarily by geographical, political, diplomatic, and technical circumstances. In the case of South Korea, missile defense calculations are dominated by the close proximity of Seoul, home to more than 25 percent of the South's population, to the demilitarized zone. Consequently, South Korea's capital is within range of North Korean artillery as well as short-range ballistic missiles. In addition, the geography of the Korean peninsula facilitates close access by U.S. naval combatants that could provide some protection against longer-range missile attacks. A third critical consideration is the U.S. military requirement to protect ports and military bases that are essential to the defense and resupply of an ally in the event of another war on the peninsula.

South Korea initially contemplated the purchase of theater missile defenses from Russia. Consultations began in 1992 over a joint licensing agreement to produce the S-300 air defense system. This deal might have been initiated, in part, to help Russia pay off debts for the import of South Korean goods. Washington lobbied Seoul not to go through with this transaction, urging instead the purchase of U.S. systems. At the same time, Washington urged South Korea not to breach the Missile Technology Control Regime's guidelines, which seek to constrain missiles to ranges below 180 kilometers and payloads to less than 500 kilograms.

Seoul held discussions with both Washington and Moscow from 1993 to 1996, after which the Russian option was dropped. Three years later, Seoul also decided against the purchase of U.S. missile defenses, citing the high cost, political sensitivity, and limited military effectiveness of missile defenses against the North Korean threat. Theater missile defenses, as a former South Korean Defense Minister noted, would "only provoke China and North Korea without [providing] any military advantage" as well as "harm the present policy of reconciliation and cooperation with the North."[34]

All of these factors combine to make theater missile defenses a low priority for South Korea and a high priority for the United States. Missile defenses do not help in the defense of Seoul, but they are essential to help protect South Korean ports and U.S. military bases needed to counter military actions undertaken by the North. Moreover, flexibly deployed missile defenses on U.S. naval platforms off the North Korean coast could help provide protection against Pyongyang's medium-range missiles that could threaten Japan. In this case, a clear division of labor and burden sharing is warranted by the special responsibilities of South Korean and U.S. military forces in the event of conflict.

The division of labor and complications associated with theater missile defenses are quite different in the case of Japan.[35] Japanese officials worry about North Korean and Chinese missile holdings. Passive defenses such as civil defense or hardening have not been carried out and might be politically difficult to do in the future. Active defense at the lower-tier consists of an early version of the Patriot, which was designed to protect national territory against aircraft and which has only a limited capability against ballistic missile threats. Japanese forces began receiving twenty-four second generation Patriot batteries (or PAC-2) in 1998. These units have a total of 192 launch stations, for which Japan has purchased 768 missiles. The mission of these Patriot batteries is to protect military installations and urban areas throughout Japan. Japan decided in 1999 to upgrade its Patriot force to the PAC-3 configuration, as the United States is doing, enabling units to engage longer range ballistic missiles as well as aircraft. The estimated cost of adding sixteen PAC-3 missiles to each of the twenty-four Patriot fire units and making requisite changes to fire control hardware and software is $1.7–2.3 billion. Even with the PAC-3 upgrade, however, the Patriot system alone will not be adequate to defend Japan against ballistic missile attack.

An upper tier must be added to provide a more capable, layered national missile defense system for Japan. Tokyo is giving serious consideration to equipping four Kongo-class Aegis-equipped destroyers with upper-tier capabilities. Two additional destroyers could be procured. In December 1998, Japan agreed to engage in joint research with the United States on upper-tier missile defenses, beginning with a $10 million contribution. A joint development program on ship-based missile defenses would be politically sensitive, but would serve Japan's interests in acquiring advanced defense technologies which, in turn, could provide possible spin-off benefits to the commercial sector.

Unlike the case in South Korea, the U.S.–Japan alliance gives to the Japanese Self-Defense Forces the responsibility to protect U.S. facilities on Japanese soil. Consequently, U.S. military forces do not have any Patriot air defense units deployed in Japan. Significant changes in assigned responsibilities for U.S. and

Japanese forces, and the introduction of more advanced theater missile defenses—especially upper-tier defenses—would raise sensitive political, constitutional, diplomatic, and military questions, including the division of roles and missions between U.S. and Japanese forces. Under the "sword and shield" framework governing the U.S.–Japan alliance, Japan's Self-Defense Forces concentrate on protecting Japanese territory, including U.S. bases, while U.S. forces focus on offensive missions. Since missile intercepts are by definition a defensive mission, this might fit comfortably within Japan's sphere of responsibility—at least at the lower tier. The United States could also engage in defenses of those ports, bases, and facilities essential to U.S. defense commitments to Japan, but basing sensitivities could suggest that missile defenses be deployed at sea rather than on land.

Upper-tier missile defense for Japan is a tricky business. These defenses are costly, and burden sharing could be a contentious issue with the United States. Japan's air defense infrastructure is inadequate to support an upper-tier missile defense system, and there appears to be little enthusiasm for upgrading these radar and command and control facilities. Neither is Japan's air defense system inter-netted with U.S. military capabilities, making coordination of an upper-tier missile defense for Japan quite difficult. Interoperability is a problem for other reasons, as well. Japan's constitution and post-war military doctrine calls for "exclusively defensive defense." Missile defense engagements by U.S. forces, on the other hand, could well be accompanied by offensive military operations. It would be awkward and difficult for Japan to be interoperable in one sphere but not another. In addition, upper-tier missile defense deployments by Japan could raise questions concerning its "remilitarization," both at home and along Japan's periphery.

For the near term, Japan's interest in missile defenses appears limited to upgrading its lower-tier, land-based Patriot batteries, and exploring with the United States an upper-tier, sea-based missile defense system. It makes little sense for the United States to push this envelope further, unless external drivers change the dynamics of Japanese domestic politics. Instead of prodding Tokyo to expand the scope of these efforts, it makes more sense for Washington to strengthen the alliance through U.S. naval deployments of advanced missile defenses to respond to contingencies involving regional missile threats. Defenses deployed on U.S. naval surface combatants offer the most utility and flexibility which more than offset the political sensitivities and costs associated with home porting these ships in Japan.

The command and control arrangements for upper-tier missile defenses are likely to pose the greatest sensitivity for the U.S.–Japan alliance and for Japanese civil–military relations. There is no easy or optimal choice for the command and control of upper-tier theater missile defenses. If Japan opts to deploy its own naval missile defenses, its neighbors in the Asia-Pacific region would feel uncomfortable. But there is also discomfort—especially in China—from an inter-netted missile defense network involving Japan, the United States, and perhaps others. If Japan were to forgo upper-tier missile defenses because of cost or regional sensitivities, national defense against missile attacks would become the responsibility of the United States, prompting another set of discomforts. One hedge against negative repercussions would be for Japan to invest in a command and control system that could be fully integrated with U.S. forces, but also capable of operating independently, as needed. But this effort would require considerable expense, and has not been a high priority for Tokyo.

The varied complications and sensitivities associated with upper-tier defenses for Japan suggest that Tokyo be given breathing room to sort out its priorities, while the United States moves ahead smartly on equipping naval surface combatants with effective theater missile defense capabilities. Tokyo's decisions will hinge on Japanese defense needs, budgetary constraints, and security imperatives. U.S. foreign policy and military deployments will need to work in tandem, if the alliance ties are to be strengthened while countering missile dangers.

Taiwan presents an even more complicated case for theater missile defense deployments. Taiwan's most significant vulnerability, according to Pentagon assessments, is from Beijing's ample and growing inventories of short-range ballistic missiles. China's missiles do not pose a threat to hardened military targets on Taiwan, but they could create great political and psychological distress, while creating havoc with daily commerce and economic transactions.

Taiwan's missile defense dilemma is defined by geography. The distance across the Taiwan Strait is a mere 175 kilometers, within range of China's plentiful inventories of short-range ballistic missiles. These missiles arc within the intercept envelope of lower-tier theater missile defenses, but below that of upper-tier defense systems. Beijing could supplement these attacks with longer-range missiles launched from interior locations that could only be intercepted by upper-tier defenses. A 1999 Pentagon assessment of Taiwan's vulnerabilities to missile attack concluded that both lower- and upper-tier defenses would be required, in addition to an extensive program to harden critical assets. The report refrained from addressing the political or economic feasibility of such an undertaking, or the diplomatic and regional security consequences of helping Taiwan to counter Beijing's missile buildup.[36]

In 1993—three years after Beijing began to deploy new short-range ballistic missiles opposite Taiwan—Taipei ordered three PAC-2 fire control units and 200 missiles from the United States. Deliveries began arriving in Taiwan in 1997, and were subsequently deployed around Taipei. As with the PAC-2s delivered to Japan, these Patriot batteries are primarily for air defense, with only limited capabilities against short-range ballistic missiles. They are likely to be very high priority targets in the event of an attack by the mainland on Taiwan.[37]

In 1998, Taiwan began laying the groundwork to upgrade the PAC-2s and to investigate acquiring a sea-based, lower-tier complement to the Patriot. Taiwan's defense minister estimated that it would cost over 9 billion dollars to deploy lower-tier defenses—roughly half the cost of Taiwan's entire military purchases from 1991 to 1999.[38] After internal debates on how best to proceed with modernizing its navy, Taiwan formally requested permission to buy four Aegis-equipped destroyers for missile defense in 1999, at an estimated cost of $6.5 billion. Given Taiwan's pressing defense needs, the long lead times involved in ship delivery (perhaps five years), and the political sensitivity of transmitting Aegis ships to Taipei, the Clinton administration deferred a decision on this request in April 2000. The Bush administration reaffirmed this decision a year later, while leaving open the option to include Aegis destroyers in a subsequent arms package.

Taipei has several reasons to seek lower-tier missile defenses. First, Beijing's missile threat is quite evident, and the upgraded Patriot system and Aegis-equipped ships would provide Taiwan with a limited capability against this threat. Second, the deployment of missile defenses would provide psychological reassurance to the people of Taiwan. Passive defense measures, such as hardening command and control bunkers, would not provide the same degree of psychological reassurance as would missile defense purchases from the United States. Third, the political utility of missile defense purchases far outweighs their military effectiveness.[39]

Taiwan's leaders fully understand that missile defenses cannot provide a protective, leak-proof umbrella against China's ballistic missiles. As is evident from Beijing's production rates for short-range ballistic missiles, China has the capacity and intention to swamp any missile defenses Taiwan deploys. Missile defenses for Taiwan, however, have important political symbolism, especially with respect to bilateral ties with the United States. The acquisition of U.S. missile defenses would, from Taipei's perspective, provide tangible evidence of U.S. support for the defense of Taiwan. The purchase of upper-tier defenses would raise the question of interoperability with U.S. systems—prior to and during any future conflict across the Strait. Taiwan would naturally seek interoperability and the resumption of U.S.–Taiwan defense ties, severed when the United States established formal diplomatic relations with the People's Republic of China in January 1979. To be sure, Washington could re-establish defense ties with Taipei without transferring missile defenses, if circumstances warrant. The transfer of complex missile defense systems, however, provides an opening to transform U.S.–Taiwan relations.

Such transfers would be in conformity with the Taiwan Relations Act, which became public law when the United States established diplomatic relations with the People's Republic of China. It states:

> It is the policy of the United States ... to provide Taiwan with arms of a defensive character. The United States will make available to Taiwan such defense articles and defense services in such quantity as may be necessary to enable Taiwan to maintain a sufficient self-defense capability. The President and the Congress shall determine the nature and quantity of such defense articles and services based solely upon their judgment of the needs of Taiwan, in accordance with procedures established by law.[40]

Beijing strenuously opposes missile defense transfers to Taiwan for many reasons. Missile defense assistance is viewed as an intrusion into Chinese internal affairs; a violation of joint U.S.–Chinese communiqués; a harbinger of a regional network to counter Chinese missiles; and a complication to Beijing's military plans. Moreover, missile defense transfers might encourage those seeking independence on Taiwan, while the technology gained could also help Taiwan to eventually produce its own ballistic missiles. In the near term, however, Beijing's primary concern is that missile defense transfers could become the leading edge of renewed military cooperation and coordination between Washington and Taipei.[41]

The repercussions of such a shift could be profound, including the increased likelihood of another war across the Taiwan Strait. There could also be negative repercussions, however, in responding with blanket refusals to Taipei's requests for missile defense assistance. Some military and political leaders in Taiwan are less enthusiastic about purchasing missile defenses. They would prefer the alternative of developing offensive missiles or other strike capabilities. For example, in a December 1999 speech on national security, Vice President (and subsequent presidential candidate) Lien Chan said, "Our country must establish effective deterrent forces so that Communist China won't dare take on Taiwan, including the attacking potential of long-distance surface-to-surface missiles."[42] Strike aircraft could also be used to attack missile bases and other military targets on the mainland. Acquiring conventional strike capabilities would be far more cost-effective than purchasing theater missile defenses.

The ultimate deterrent to a Chinese attack would be for Taiwan to develop nuclear weapons. Taipei has explored this avenue in the past, and if its perceived vulnerabilities and sense of isolation grow, might do so again.[43] The pursuit by Taipei of a nuclear deterrent could prompt a more vigorous reaction by Beijing than the transfer of upgraded Patriots or Aegis destroyers. In addition, Taiwan's pursuit of missiles and nuclear weapons would do further damage to global non-proliferation regimes.

The transfer of upgraded Patriots and Aegis destroyers to Taiwan could also produce a wide range of negative consequences for cross-Strait and U.S.–China relations. Of particular concern to Beijing would be the transfer to Taiwan of theater missile defenses that are interoperable and linked with U.S. military forces. Such transfers would suggest to Beijing the restoration of the U.S.–Taiwan Mutual Defense Treaty, thus seriously contravening the letter and spirit of the 1979 communiqué on normalization of diplomatic relations. Providing Taiwan with interoperable and linked TMD systems could therefore precipitate a severe diplomatic crisis in U.S.–China relations as well as new tensions in the Taiwan Strait.

How should the United States balance the risks associated with helping Taipei to respond to the Chinese buildup of ballistic missiles opposite Taiwan? The overriding U.S. foreign and national security policy interest— as well as the overriding regional security interest—in cross-Strait relations is the peaceful resolution of issues that can produce conflict between China and Taiwan. U.S. choices on theater missile defenses should reflect this overriding policy objective. Taiwan has the legitimate right to defend itself against China's growing arsenal of ballistic missiles, many of which are deployed directly across from the island. The transfer of lower-tier theater missile defenses clearly falls within the guidelines of the Taiwan Relations Act. This is not to suggest that open-ended sales of lower-tier missile defenses to Taiwan would be either cost-effective or wise. Instead, it suggests the need to address Taiwan's missile defense needs on a case-by-case basis, taking into account Beijing's missile programs and its overall posture toward Taipei.

If the mainland's approach to Taiwan becomes increasingly bellicose, favorable consideration might first be given to providing Taipei with more and more sophisticated Patriots. Even a significant purchase of new Patriot missiles would be insufficient to provide adequate coverage against a concerted ballistic missile attack. Nonetheless, these transfers would signal stronger U.S. opposition by Beijing's coercive missile diplomacy. Improved Patriots that are sold to Taiwan, like those already transferred, should be controlled and operated by Taiwan, and should not be interoperable with U.S. systems. This would signal Washington's intention not to resume close defense cooperation with Taipei.

If Beijing continues to adopt coercive strategies toward Taipei, pressures would grow in the United States to transfer Aegis destroyers equipped with lower-tier missile defenses. It would be unwise to place too high a priority on such transfers, given the long time lag before the ships could be constructed, and given the multiple deficiencies in Taipei's defense capabilities that could be addressed in the meantime. Moreover, an Aegis-equipped ship operated by the U.S. Navy would have far more utility than Aegis-equipped ships operated by Taiwan's Navy. Theater missile defenses on U.S. ships would serve as a better response to Beijing's missile buildup and enhance regional stability; theater missile defenses on Taiwan's ships would add little military capability and could precipitate political and military crises the United States seeks to avoid. The rationale for providing Taipei with upper-tier theater missile defenses is even less persuasive: Taiwan has not expressed an interest in acquiring these capabilities, they are far from ready for deployment, and they do not address the vast majority of ballistic missile threats facing the island.

Taipei could demonstrate the seriousness with which it views the missile threat by hardening critical facilities and improving rapid runway repair capabilities. These steps would increase its ability to withstand and respond to a ballistic missile attack. Taiwan also needs to better integrate and harden its command and control networks. These measures would be more cost-effective and more quickly implemented than Taiwan's deployment of island-wide missile defenses. While these "passive" defense measures might not have the same psychological or political impact as would new military transfers of "active" defenses, they would provide more military effectiveness at less cost.

The diplomacy of theater missile defenses does not get any harder—and the stakes do not get any higher—than when dealing with Beijing and Taipei. U.S. policy choices toward defenses must be acutely mindful of the pitfalls associated with deployments, but they must also be responsive to the growing ballistic missile threats in the Asia-Pacific region. Theater missile defense deployments would likely result in a further increase in China's tactical missile inventories, but abstaining completely from military counter-moves would also be as unwise as overreacting. As former Secretary of Defense William J. Perry has noted, "I share the Chinese concern over the deleterious affect of an arms race in the region, but I believe that if an arms race does get underway, it will have been stimulated by the extensive deployment of missiles, not the deployment of missile defenses."[44]

The middle path outlined here will hardly suit those who prefer black and white policy options, but the diplomatic and military minefields associated with theater missile defenses mandate mixed messages. The surrogate use of theater missile defense initiatives to support Taiwan's independence or to confront the People's Republic of China could easily backfire. Instead, the overriding U.S. policy interest in this context is the peaceful resolution of differences across the Taiwan Strait. The use of force by Beijing or a declaration of independence by Taipei would have profoundly negative ramifications for the entire Asia-Pacific region. U.S. decisions regarding theater missile defenses ought to reinforce these messages rather than encourage them.

From Theater to Ocean-spanning Missiles?

Given the primacy of theater missile threats over ocean-spanning missiles, and given the revised threat spectrum associated with asymmetric warfare, what accounts for the zeal with which some have pursued a homeland defense of the United States against ballistic missile attack? After decades of effort, the campaign against the Anti-Ballistic Missile (ABM) Treaty reached fruition with the Bush administration's decision to withdraw from the Treaty in December 2001. One possible explanation for this successful campaign is the belief that U.S. strategic superiority requires maximum freedom of action which cannot be pursued within treaty constraints predicated on equal security. A corollary presumption is that the extension of U.S. strategic superiority requires national missile defenses to reinforce U.S. offensive capabilities. Another possible explanation might be constituent service, both with respect to defense contractors and to activists within the Republican Party. The high priority attached to national missile defenses could also rest on strong presumptions of technical feasibility and the prospective acquisition by maverick states of missiles that could threaten U.S. shores. The mix of reasons for casting aside the ABM Treaty and vigorously pursuing homeland missile defenses no doubt vary from one supporter to the next, but the public rationale for giving national missile defenses an urgent priority requires a clear and present danger.

This case was set forth by a commission chaired by Donald H. Rumsfeld before his selection as George W. Bush's Secretary of Defense. The Rumsfeld Commission's alarming report on ballistic missile threats to the U.S. homeland concluded that North Korea and Iran could manage to make the leap from theater to ocean-spanning missiles, and thus "would be able to inflict major destruction on the U.S. within about five years of a decision to acquire such a capability (10 years in the case of Iraq)." Moreover, the Commission found that, "During several of those [five] years, the U.S. might not be aware that such a decision had been made. The threat to the U.S. posed by these emerging capabilities is broader, more mature and evolving more rapidly than has been reported in estimates and reports by the Intelligence Community." Even worse, the Rumsfeld Commission concluded that,

"Under some plausible scenarios—including re-basing or transfer of operational missiles, sea- and air-launch options, shortened development programs that might include testing in a third country, or some combination of these—the U.S. might well have little or no warning before operational deployment."[45]

Members of the Commission included pro- as well as anti-arms control analysts. While their report did not suggest remedies, by laying out the worst case for a surprise ocean-spanning missile deployment, they paved the way for the Bush administration's subsequent withdrawal from the ABM Treaty. Since the time line for initial deployment of national defenses against ballistic missile attack would normally take longer than five years, one clear inference from the Rumsfeld Commission report was the need to give this task priority status and funding.

There is ample evidence to confirm the pursuit of longer- and longer-range ballistic missiles by worrisome states. North Korea, Iran, Iraq, and Pakistan all started with short-range SCUD missiles, and then worked (or purchased) diligently to extend the range of these missiles to reach more distant targets within their regions. Iran seeks to target Baghdad and Tel Aviv. If or when Iraq is able to reconstitute its missile inventories, it will likely seek comparable strike capabilities against Tehran and Tel Aviv. This trend is also evident in South Asia. India is developing medium- and intermediate-range missiles capable of reaching Beijing and Shanghai, while Pakistan seeks to place Bombay and other cities in India's south at risk. Why wouldn't these states seek to take the next leap, to ocean-spanning missiles? Over time, might not states of concern acquire the means and apply the resources to develop missiles that could directly threaten U.S. population centers?

This argument is critical to backers of national missile defenses, who postulate that maverick leaders would not be deterred by U.S. conventional military and nuclear superiority, but would seek to deter the United States by deploying intercontinental-range ballistic missiles (ICBMs). In other words, the "undeterrables" will engage in the canonical form of deterrence in the nuclear age by acquiring the most prestigious and threatening means of striking distant targets quickly. Alternatively, these states could acquire thinly disguised "space launch vehicles" instead of ICBMs. The real purpose of such "satellite" launchers would be to reach distant U.S. targets. A case in point was the launch of North Korea's Taepo Dong-1 "space vehicle launch" in August 1998. This 5,500-kilometer missile barely qualifies as having intercontinental reach, since it placed the outermost islands of Hawaii and the Aleutian chain within range—assuming that everything worked properly and that North Korea could learn how to develop a weapon for the missile that could survive the rigors of re-entry. If one assumed all this, as well as the will to challenge

Gulliver in this most dramatic way, then one could readily take the next leap and assume a still-longer range missile aimed at U.S. population centers.

Critics of worst-case missile threat analysis counter that the furthest extent to which states of concern could scale up SCUD-based technologies and missile bodies might extend to Alaska and Hawaii, but not to the continental United States. In this event, it would be wiser to deploy missile defenses near the Korean peninsula than on the continental United States. Skeptics received the support of the Central Intelligence Agency—until the release of the Rumsfeld Commission's report in 1998. For example, the National Intelligence Estimate prepared on "Emerging Missile Threats to North America During the Next 15 Years" in 1995 flatly concluded that:

> North Korea is unlikely to obtain the technological capability to develop a longer range operational ICBM. North Korea would have to overcome significant hurdles to complete such a program, particularly given the political and economic uncertainties and technological challenges it faces. For such an ICBM, North Korea would have to develop new propulsion and improved guidance and control systems and conduct a flight test program. We have no evidence that Pyongyang has begun or intends to begin such a program, and we think we would detect propulsion system development.[46]

Prior to the issuance of the Rumsfeld Commission report, the CIA reached similar judgments for Iran and Iraq, concluding in 1995 that, "We have no evidence Iran wants to develop an ICBM. Even if Tehran wanted to, we assess that it would not be able to do so before 2010 because it lacks the economic resources and technological infrastructure." As for Iraq, the CIA estimated that, with the demise of sanctions and United Nations inspections, Baghdad "could develop the technology and infrastructure necessary for an ICBM program. But even with substantial foreign assistance, it would require at least 15 years to develop an operational ICBM." The CIA acknowledged that foreign assistance was the "wild card" in such estimates, since a country seeking an ocean-spanning missile could circumvent the significant technological hurdles involved in missile stage separation, propulsion, guidance and control systems with illicit transactions. Nevertheless, the intelligence community flatly asserted that "countries that currently have ICBMs will not sell them."[47]

This reasoning—based on the assumption that Russia and China, which have the most to fear from a U.S. national missile defense program, would presumably control ICBM transfers—should also apply to the export of key components essential for the upscaling of ballistic missiles to ocean-spanning distances. With good reason, Richard N. Cooper, then-Chairman of the National Intelligence Council, testified:

> Nearly a dozen states other than Russia and China have ballistic missile development programs. In the view of the Intelligence Community, these programs are to serve regional goals. Making the change from a short or medium range missile—that may pose a threat to U.S. troops located abroad—to a long range ICBM capable of threatening our citizens at home, is a major technological leap.[48]

Missile Scares

The Rumsfeld Commission report savaged this analysis, and was given immediate credence by the surprising launch of North Korea's Taepo Dong-1. There was much to critique in the CIA's reassuring estimate, particularly its focus on missile threats to the continental United States, excluding Alaska and Hawaii. This estimate was not appreciated by the senior senators representing these states, through whose hands passed all defense appropriations. The Rumsfeld Commission also took issue with the compartmented and mechanistic way in which the intelligence community pieced together its threat assessments, which did not adequately cover the ingenious ways in which states seeking to acquire missiles and weapons of mass destruction went about their business—especially the short cuts that could result from covert transactions. In addition, the Rumsfeld Commission report noted correctly that mavericks used different standards than nuclear powers in judging the success of their efforts. They were not, for example, much interested in a lengthy and expensive missile flight test program that would provide ample notice and warning time for U.S. responses.

One can accept the validity of the Rumsfeld Commission's critique without accepting its alarmist estimates. The basic conclusions of the CIA's threat assessments of the mid-1990s appear sound. After all, the third stage of the surprising North Korean Taepo Dong-1 launch failed, and its ability to deliver WMD to U.S. soil was suspect. Even the chastened, post-Rumsfeld Commission CIA estimates concluded that two-thirds of the Taepo Dong-1's payload mass would be taken up by the re-entry vehicle. The remaining mass, according to the Agency, would be "probably too light for an early generation nuclear weapon but could deliver biological or chemical warfare agent"—if, somehow, Pyongyang could master the difficult arts of delivering such agents intact after the enormous stresses and heat of re-entry.[49] Moreover, Russia and China subsequently prevailed upon the North Korean regime to suspend missile flight tests so as not to provoke the deployment of national missile defenses in the United States.

CIA missile threat estimates were heavily hedged after the release of the Rumsfeld Commission, providing assessments of what maverick states *could* do, while noting parenthetically that, "Some analysts believe that the prominence given to missiles countries 'could' develop gives more credence than is warranted to developments that may prove implausible."[50] Particularly worrisome in these revised estimates was an improved, longer-range version of the Taepo Dong, which the intelligence community predicted would probably be launched in 1999, "unless delayed for political reasons." There was no such launch during the remainder of the Clinton administration, which was striving for a breakthrough with North Korea. In addition, the post-Rumsfeld Commission CIA estimated that Iran "could test an ICBM that could deliver a several-hundred kilogram payload to many parts of the United States in the latter half of the next decade, using Russian technology and assistance," and that Iran is "likely to test" a space launch vehicle by 2020. Some analysts even predicted such a launch "within the next few years." Assessments of an Iraqi ICBM threat were similarly varied, ranging from "likely before 2005, possibly before 2010 (foreign assistance would affect capability and timing) to unlikely before 2015."[51]

Missile threat estimates, as Albert Wohlstetter documented a quarter-century ago, are notoriously difficult to assess properly. Official U.S. estimates of Soviet ICBM programs were far too high in the late 1950s, the era of the "missile gap," and then, as Wohlstetter detailed, too low from the period of 1962 to 1972.[52] Wohlstetter's critique was but one swell in a succession of heavy waves that washed over the intelligence community in the 1970s, resulting in a significant revision upwards of the Soviet threat. The biggest wave was created by the assembly of "Team B" by President Gerald Ford and then-CIA Director George H. W. Bush. Team B consisted of analysts deeply skeptical of Soviet intentions, whose worst-case threat assessment made deep inroads in official estimates, much like the Rumsfeld Commission.[53] Not surprisingly, the intelligence community then proceeded to overestimate the Soviet missile threat.

Missile scares are a recurring phenomenon in American strategic debates. The first scare came immediately after the Soviet Union launched Sputnik in 1959. The sudden, graphically demonstrated U.S. inferiority in this case had immense strategic consequences, since a huge rocket that could send a satellite into space could also be used to send nuclear bombs hurtling toward U.S. cities and bomber bases. Worst-case scenarios generated by the Sputnik launch spread easily, since Soviet leaders verbalized hostile intent and avowedly viewed nuclear war as entirely possible. Moreover, military technology was then moving at a dizzying pace, and U.S. monitoring capabilities of Soviet missile and bomber programs were extremely limited.

According to press reports, post-Sputnik intelligence projections of Soviet ICBM deployments by the U.S. Air Force ballooned to 500 by 1961, jumping to 1,000 by 1962 and 2,000 by 1964. By comparison, the Eisenhower administration had approved a total of 130 Atlas and Titan missiles during this time line.[54] The projected imbalance in missile striking power was not subject to debate at the end of the Eisenhower administration. As Henry A. Kissinger wrote in 1961, "[T]here is no dispute about the missile gap as such. ... The disagreement concerns the significance of this state of affairs."[55] Democrats on Capitol Hill with presidential ambitions convened blistering hearings on the "missile gap." In 1958, Senator Lyndon Baines Johnson direly predicted that the Soviet Union was not only leading in missile production, but that "we may be behind them in all phases of military capabilities very shortly."[56] Albert Wohlstetter published a powerful critique of complacency entitled "The Delicate Balance of Terror," itemizing false hopes of stable nuclear deterrence and near-term vulnerabilities to surprise Soviet attack. The strategic balance, declared Wohlstetter, was, "precarious," and could be remedied only through quite sustained and broad-gauged effort.[57] Presidential candidate John F. Kennedy upped the ante, worrying in public that "the deterrent ratio might well shift to the Soviets so heavily, during the years of the gap, as to open to them a new shortcut to world domination."[58]

A blue ribbon panel convened by President Eisenhower, headed by H. Rowan Gaither, added fuel to the fire. Reading the Gaither Report, transmitted to Eisenhower one month after the launch of Sputnik, "was like looking into the abyss and seeing Hell at the bottom."[59] The report concluded that in just two years, "by 1959, the U.S.S.R. may be able to launch an attack with ICBMs carrying megaton warheads, against which SAC [the Strategic Air Command] will be almost completely vulnerable under present programs."[60]

Against this withering fire, President Eisenhower and Secretary of Defense Thomas Gates held their ground, countering worst-case Air Force intelligence projections by predicting, at the very worst, only "a moderate numerical superiority" for the Soviet Union during a brief three-year period.[61] Even this estimate proved to be overdramatized. With advancements in U.S. satellite surveillance capabilities, the Kennedy administration soon discovered that there was no crash Soviet missile production program, and that the United States might even be leading this particular competition.[62]

The next great campaign to popularize a dire missile threat picked up steam during the presidency of Gerald R. Ford and reached full throttle during the administration of Jimmy Carter. In the view of Paul Nitze, Richard Pipes, and other members of Team B, Soviet advantages in ICBMs created an alarming "window of vulnerability," a central theme in attacks against the second Strategic Arms Limitation Treaty (SALT II) spearheaded by the newly created Committee on the Present Danger. The Senate Armed Services Committee's negative report on SALT II concluded that, "The United States now faces the near certainty that a significant element of its strategic deterrent will be vulnerable to preemptive attack … [T]he Soviet Union will have the capability to destroy virtually the entire U.S. land-based missile force."[63]

On the eve of signing the treaty, Democratic Senator Henry M. Jackson, a powerhouse on the Armed Services Committee, labeled the SALT negotiations as a decade of appeasement and retreat.[64] Nitze warned that the growth of Soviet strategic power and adventurism constituted "the gravest [threat] that the United States and the West have faced at least since the Soviet threat to Berlin in 1958–1962 and possibly at any time since the end of World War II."[65] Pipes, a Soviet historian and the convener of Team B, argued that the Kremlin's advantages in ICBMs reflected a broader truth: "There is something innately destabilizing in the very fact that we consider nuclear war unfeasible and suicidal for both, and our chief adversary views it as feasible and winnable for himself."[66]

With the benefit of hindsight and from declassified assessments of the Central Intelligence Agency, we now know that, at the very time that the members of Team B and their colleagues on the Committee on the Present Danger were trumpeting the Soviet drive for strategic superiority and a nuclear war-winning posture, the Kremlin was actually retrenching. Facing withering scrutiny for too-low estimates subsequent to the Missile Gap, the Agency calculated a troubling 4–5 percent annual growth in Soviet military spending during the Ford/Carter years. In actuality, Moscow's defense spending in general was virtually flat from 1976 to 1983, and Soviet investment in strategic offensive forces declined by 40 percent.[67]

Unlike President Eisenhower, Jimmy Carter was poorly situated to deflate concerns over another missile gap and impending Soviet strategic superiority. When the treaty was signed, his popularity had dwindled to 29 percent, and plummeted further with the Iranian hostage crisis and the Soviet invasion of Afghanistan. During the presidency of Ronald Reagan, this window of vulnerability was quietly shut when no acceptable political means could be found to redress the vulnerability of U.S. land-based missiles.[68] Nonetheless, the Soviet threat remained heavily inflated throughout the tenure of Secretary of Defense Caspar Weinberger. During the first Reagan administration, when the Pentagon and CIA were issuing worried estimates of a confident Soviet adversary seeking to secure nuclear advantage, the Kremlin's paranoid intelligence agencies were watching blood banks in the United States for preparatory signs of a surprise attack.[69]

Missile scares lingered even after it was clearly evident that Mikhail Gorbachev was in the process of changing the Soviet Union beyond recognition. During the U.S. presidential campaign in 1988, Jeane Kirkpatrick declared that, "The vulnerability of the United States is *the* most important fact of our times. Most Americans do not understand that improvements in the accuracy and speed of Soviet missiles and the silencing of Soviet submarines have rendered the United States more vulnerable that at any time in its history."[70] As late as November 1989, Frank J. Gaffney Jr. argued that U.S. arms control agreements with Gorbachev "may well" make the country "more vulnerable to a Soviet first strike than it is today."[71]

The Rumsfeld Commission's dark warning of impending ocean-spanning missile threats from rogue states, therefore, has ample precedent. This threat, however, is even less compelling than earlier missile scares. In previous cases there were more justifiable reasons for concern. In the 1950s, the U.S. strategic deterrent was poorly deployed, placing too many eggs in too few baskets. In the 1970s, Soviet missile production rates and the Kremlin's activism in sensitive regions were very worrisome. In contrast, the quest by maverick states to acquire ocean-spanning ballistic missiles—assuming it materializes—comes from Lilliputians, not a peer competitor.

Maverick states are stockpiling theater missiles for use in regional warfare. It may well be possible for them to construct an ocean-spanning missile, but the extrapolation from theater to intercontinental range is far from simple. They must acquire the skills needed for missile stage separation, compact warhead design, and re-entry vehicle design. The expense, difficulty, and foreign assistance required to master these tasks all suggest that cheaper alternative means will be found to damage Gulliver. After the unconventional attacks on the World Trade Center and Pentagon, the CIA's unclassified estimates of foreign ballistic missile programs finally placed this threat into a broader context. The CIA concluded that:

U.S. territory is more likely to be attacked by weapons of mass destruction using nonmissile means, primarily because such means:

- Are less expensive than developing and producing ICBMs.
- Can be covertly developed and employed; the source of the weapon could be masked in an attempt to evade retaliation.
- Probably would be more reliable than ICBMs that have not completed rigorous testing and validation programs.

- Probably would be much more accurate than emerging ICBMs over the next 15 years.
- Probably would be more effective for disseminating biological warfare agent than a ballistic missile.
- Would avoid missile defenses.[72]

There is, in sum, a world of difference between possibilities and probabilities in estimating ballistic missile threats. Public policies based on the worst that could happen tend to be costly in political, diplomatic, and financial terms. On the other hand, being unprepared for the unexpected can also be quite costly. Insurance policies will be needed. Their cost should be commensurate with the probability of need, while taking into account downside risks and unintended negative consequences. Insurance policies are, after all, monetary calculations, not exercises in willful belief or disbelief.

The need for an insurance policy grew when North Korea surprised the U.S. intelligence community by launching a three-stage rocket with a "satellite" aboard. Since North Korea's need to utilize space for commercial or economic purposes is rather slight, it has been universally assumed that Pyongyang was getting the attention of potential aid-givers and missile purchasers. If the price is right, and if the United States, Japan, and other countries pursue an astute mix of carrots and sticks, the North Korean "space launch vehicle" will not become a new product line. If, however, U.S. diplomacy fails, the best missile defense against this particular threat is likely to consist of forward-deployed, sea-based, theater missile defenses to destroy Pyongyang's missiles in the boost or ascent phase, when they are most susceptible to successful interception. An extremely modest national missile defense of the U.S. homeland could also be added for additional insurance against an unlikely, but not completely inconceivable North Korean missile attack.

Other states, most notably Iran and Iraq, are also pursuing longer-range missiles. Their basing options do not include silos protected against blast effects, which have the decided disadvantage of presenting fixed targets to potential adversaries. Instead, the preferred basing mode for these states is mobility on land. Pyongyang's product lines have the unfortunate attribute, however, of being liquid-fueled, which mandates a cumbersome and time-consuming process to prepare missiles for launch. During this dangerous fueling process, which could take several hours, crews in the field present an obvious and attractive target to an adversary with the capability of learning their whereabouts in real time. The road networks in states seeking longer-range missiles might also be inhospitable to the rapid movement of liquid-fueled missiles.

Missile-hungry states therefore have many reasons to prefer solid-fueled missiles, but these are not easy to acquire covertly. China has supplied short-range, solid-fueled missiles to Pakistan in the past, and might extend such assistance in the future to assist Islamabad and to keep India off balance. It is not in Beijing's interest, however, to fuel the deployment of missile defenses, either in India or the United States. Countries that seek longer-range, solid-fueled missiles could also acquire these capabilities indigenously, through black markets, or through expertise hired from Russia. Indigenous development takes time, however. Acquisitions on black markets provide tip-offs, intercept opportunities, and the product might be of uncertain quality. The short cut of buying Russian expertise is not as easy as it sounds, given the reluctance of Russian scientists to enter this market.[73] Nonetheless, the extension of Iranian, Indian, and Pakistani missiles to ranges of approximately 2,500–3,500 kilometers is widely expected. Range extensions of this kind could be extrapolated from existing programs and purchases, from indigenous developments, and from subterranean assistance. Range extensions to intercontinental reach pose much greater technical and financial difficulties.

The Primacy of Theater over National Missile Defenses

The insurance policies associated with the paradigm shift from Cold War to asymmetric warfare are now beginning to be paid. After the terror attacks of September 11, new sums have been added for homeland defense. Airport security and public health infrastructure are being beefed up. U.S. seaports will receive greater protection. Visa applications will receive greater scrutiny. Funding for cooperative threat reduction programs in the former Soviet Union will be beefed up. All of this and more is long overdue. Some discontinuities between post-Cold War threats and responses have lingered, however, especially with regard to missile defense priorities.

The most time-critical missile threats and pressing diplomatic dilemmas relate to theater, and not ocean-spanning missiles. The high priority given to national missile defenses is therefore misplaced. The threats posed by theater ballistic missiles to forward-deployed U.S. forces, friends, and allies far outstrip improbable threats posed by ocean-spanning missiles. National missile defense deployments add little to U.S. strength and protection; theater missile defenses add greatly to a forward-deployed U.S. military presence as well as to U.S. diplomacy.

Henceforth, national leaders and military commanders in troubled regions will expect the use of theater ballistic missiles in wars between aspiring regional hegemons, by rising regional powers against weaker neighbors, and in asymmetric warfare, where the weaker party seeks to keep a bigger power off-balance or out of the fray. These missiles could carry conventional explosives or WMD to terrorize city-dwellers. They could be used to seek a quick and decisive outcome to conflict, or as a substitute for power projection capabilities that might otherwise be lacking. Alternatively, they could be used as an adjunct to conventional military campaigns, whether to tear up runways or to inflict casualties on armies massing in the field. The perceived value and versatility of missiles in regional warfare are too great to expect states to abstain from using them. In contrast, the penalties of the use of ocean-spanning missiles carrying WMD far exceed prospective benefits.

The potential use of ballistic missiles carrying deadly weapons has political utility; their actual use would trigger horrifying retaliation. As with nuclear weapons that are tested underground but not used on the battlefield, the flight tests of missiles that could carry WMD have become powerful message senders. This was most evident in North Korea's missile launch over Japanese soil in August 1998 and China's missile-firing exercises close to Taiwan's two major port cities in conjunction with Taiwan's national elections in March 1996. North Korea's missile tests were advertisements for export earnings; warnings to Seoul, Tokyo, and Washington; and invitations for deal making, given Pyongyang's hard-currency needs. China's missile flight tests were warnings to politicians in Taipei not to go too far towards independence, and to politicians in Washington of the risks of going too far to help Taiwan. Less dramatically (and more regularly), the Kremlin carries out periodic missile flight tests as a reminder that Moscow's deterrent still matters.

States seeking regional hegemony, or seeking to prevent another from achieving it, are acquiring theater ballistic missiles. Weak states in need of an insurance policy against strong power projection capabilities are acquiring missiles. China is building up theater ballistic missile inventories, anticipating that they will play a prominent role in contingencies relating to Taiwan. In addition, China has used missile transfers to secure ties with an "old friend," Pakistan, to counter-balance India, a regional rival, and to retaliate for Washington's arms transfers to Taiwan. Russia helps Iranian and Indian missile programs to gain hard currency and to maintain friendly ties. North Korea sells theater ballistic missiles for hard currency, and has intimated it would refrain from selling missiles in exchange for more money.

For quite varied reasons, the threats posed by theater ballistic missiles in states of concern are growing, while the number of ocean-spanning ballistic missiles that could threaten the U.S. homeland is declining markedly. China, the aspiring peer competitor, is predicted to acquire perhaps 75 to 100 warheads on its intercontinental ballistic missiles through 2015, if U.S. intelligence community estimates are to be believed, a rather modest number by major power standards.[74] China is a rising power, no doubt, but a rising weak and brittle power, judging by its domestic political sensitivities and structural economic difficulties. Meanwhile, Russian deployments face block obsolescence. With the shift from Cold War to asymmetric warfare, the threat posed by ocean-spanning ballistic missiles has dropped considerably. As former Senator Sam Nunn has noted, "The likeliest nuclear attack against the United States would come not from a nuclear missile launched by a rogue state but from a warhead in the belly of a ship or the back of a truck delivered by a group with no return address."[75]

If the missile threat to U.S. national security interests is probability-based rather than possibility-oriented, what might an appropriate U.S. missile defense posture look like? A prudent insurance policy would focus heavily on theater missile defenses. The cases reviewed here all strongly suggest that theater missile defenses have become a necessity, regardless of cost. By comparison, ballistic missile defenses of the U.S. homeland are a luxury, depending on cost. Since the risk of a globe-spanning attack by ballistic missiles continues to be low, and since the opportunity, political, and diplomatic costs of deploying national missile defenses could be high, the insurance premium paid for homeland defenses against missile attack ought to be relatively modest. In contrast, theater missile attacks constitute a clear and present danger, not just to U.S. forward-deployed forces, but also to friends and allies.

As noted above, deployments of theater missile defenses are far from a routine matter. In a few cases, theater missile defense deployments by the United States could cause perturbations with allies, most notably with Japan. Nondeployment of missile defenses, however, could create greater difficulties in the U.S.–Japan alliance if perceived regional missile threats from North Korea and China grow. Most U.S. allies would welcome theater missile defense deployments, especially if the basing is offshore and if the financial burden is borne primarily by Washington. In contrast, allies view the high priority given to homeland missile defenses in the United States as driven by domestic politics, technological optimism, or the drive for continued, unfettered strategic superiority, rather than by missile threats. If U.S. national missile defenses are given a higher priority than theater missile defenses, the former could promote alliance dissension by conveying an "America First" posture abroad.

The misalignment of missile threat and national response was quite apparent in the Clinton administration, where spending on national missile defenses against the least probable threat was approximately equal to that for theater defenses, where threats were burgeoning.[76] The outgoing Clinton administration presented Congress with a budget that allocated to missile defense programs 80 percent of the entire State Department budget. Put another way, for every dollar proposed for preventive diplomacy, 80 cents were to be spent on missile defenses. Moreover, during the Clinton administration, 5 taxpayer dollars were spent on the care of the U.S. nuclear stockpile for every dollar spent on controlling "loose nukes" and other CTR efforts in the former Soviet Union. During this period, less than 1 percent of the annual Department of Defense appropriations were allocated to CTR efforts.

These distortions became even more accentuated at the outset of the administration of President George W. Bush. Changes in the Bush administration's defense budgeting made it difficult to compare allocations between theater and national missile defenses, but the sum total of these programs now equaled that of the Department of State's entire budget. The Bush administration's budget priorities were also more skewed toward nuclear stockpile "stewardship" and away from programs to control proliferation at the source. Bush's first budget allocated $5.50 for stockpile stewardship for every 75 cents spent for cooperative threat reduction.

After the attacks on the World Trade Center and the Pentagon, some budgetary distortions were corrected. Spending for homeland defense rose precipitously, and the Bush administration's initial cuts in cooperative threat reduction programs were reversed. Other distortions remained. The State Department and preventive diplomacy continued to be short-changed, while funding for cooperative threat reductions lagged far behind spending for U.S. nuclear stockpile stewardship. In addition, the paradigm shift in the threat spectrum from the Cold War to asymmetric warfare did not deflect the Bush administration from its avid pursuit of national missile defenses.

Domestic political and bureaucratic factors help explain these disconnects. After all, the Department of State has few advocates on Capitol Hill, and military expenditures have far stronger constituencies than CTR initiatives. The greatest disconnect between threat and response continued to revolve around national missile defense deployments, a core belief that held intact after the fall of the Soviet Union. Core beliefs do not bend before cost-benefit analysis, and they are impervious to the transformation of the threat spectrum generated by the Cold War's sudden and surprising end. A new hierarchy of threats has come to the fore, on which there is widespread domestic agreement. And yet the pursuit of national missile defenses continues to draw funding away from higher priorities. Every important battle has its proper time and place, but the battle over national missile defenses never ends.

CHAPTER 3

Missile Defense from the Cold War to Asymmetric Warfare

G overnment officials, military strategists, and the general public generally reacted to the atomic bomb by concluding that a defense against this fearsome weapon would be utterly futile. While other European and Japanese cities were leveled by air campaigns during the war, the economical means by which Hiroshima and Nagasaki were destroyed came as a great shock. Tokyo was incinerated by 279 planes and 1,667 tons of bombs; a single plane carrying one atomic bomb wreaked complete destruction on Hiroshima and three days later at Nagasaki.[1] Few took issue with the sentiment expressed in Bernard Brodie's influential collection of essays, *The Absolute Weapon:* "No adequate defense against the bomb exists, and the possibilities of its existence in the future are exceedingly remote."[2]

No less of an authority than Albert Einstein concluded, in a *New York Times Magazine* interview, "Rifle bullets kill men, but atomic bombs kill cities. A tank is a defense against a bullet but there is no defense in science against a weapon which can destroy civilization."[3] Leo Szilard, the scientist who helped Einstein gain President Franklin Delano Roosevelt's ear about the potential of nuclear weapons, warned in March 1945 that, "Even if we assume that we could keep ahead [in an arms competition] ... this may neither offer us protection from attack nor give us substantial advantage in the case of war."[4] These sentiments evolved into the doctrine of "Mutual Assured Destruction," or MAD: The best way to avoid a nuclear war would be to realize and accept its destructive consequences.

The seeming impossibility of protection against nuclear attack initially led U.S. officials to seek abolition and international control over atomic energy after World War II. The ambitious Acheson–Lilienthal Plan, for example, which advocated that dangerous aspects of atomic energy be "taken out of national hands," was predicated on the assumption that the Soviet Union would eventually discover the deadly secrets behind the bomb. Consequently, either this devastating weapon would be effectively caged, or the mushroom cloud would forever shadow national survival.[5] Bernard Baruch offered a modified version of the Acheson–Lilienthal Plan to the United Nations, where it was rebuffed by a Soviet Union unwilling to relinquish its veto power.

The failure of the Acheson–Lilienthal and Baruch plans to achieve international control, followed by the steady accretion of atomic weapons during the first decade of nuclear danger, eventually led to a reopening of the question of defending against nuclear danger. As early as 1953, the head of the Manhattan Project, J. Robert Oppenheimer, mused about a transition strategy:

> A more effective defense could even be of great relevance should the time come for serious discussion of the regulation of armaments. There will have been by then a vast accumulation of materials for atomic weapons and a troublesome margin of uncertainty with regard to its accounting— very troublesome indeed if we still live with vestiges of the suspicion, hostility, and secretiveness of the world today. This will call for a very broad and robust regulation of armaments, in which … steps of evasion will be either far too vast to conceal or far too small to have, in view of then-existing measures of defense, a decisive strategic effect. Defense and regulation may thus be necessary complements. And here, too, all that we do effectively to contribute to our own immunity will be helpful in giving us some measure of an increased freedom of action.[6]

Sentinel

Oppenheimer, as usual, was several steps ahead of his contemporaries. The "serious discussion of armaments" he anticipated began in the Lyndon Baines Johnson administration under considerably less than ideal conditions. Consumed by the war in Vietnam and ever mindful of the concerns of powerful hawks on Capitol Hill, LBJ was nonetheless eager to begin talks with the Kremlin on nuclear offensive and defensive forces. Fashioning a U.S. negotiating position wasn't easy, as President Johnson was torn between the political imperatives of competing with Moscow over missile defenses and the warnings of key advisors that defensive deployments would consign the forthcoming talks to failure.

In a private letter to Soviet Premier Aleksey N. Kosygin delivered in January 1967, LBJ attempted to lay out "the possibilities of reaching an understanding between us which would curb the strategic arms race." The note continued:

> I think you must realize that following the deployment by you of an anti-ballistic missile system I face great pressures from members of Congress and from public opinion not only to deploy defensive systems in this country, but also to increase greatly our capabilities to penetrate any defensive systems which you might establish. If we should feel compelled to make such major increases in our strategic weapons capabilities, I have no doubt that you would in turn feel under compulsion to do likewise.[7]

LBJ's solution to this quandary was to propose building a "thin" national missile defense system ostensibly directed against China rather than the Soviet Union. A secondary rationale was to counter accidental missile launches. The proposed "Sentinel" system was, however, quite substantial, consisting of no less than fourteen Anti-Ballistic Missile (ABM) bases across the country.[8] Moreover, Secretary of Defense Robert McNamara's estimates that the Chinese missile threat would arrive in the "early 1970s," growing to a "modest force" by the mid-1970s were off by a decade.[9] In actuality, the first Chinese ballistic missiles with ranges sufficient to reach the continental United States were not deployed until 1981.[10] Needless to say, few in the United States or the Soviet Union believed the Johnson administration's public rationale, which was grounded in domestic and bureaucratic politics rather than in serious strategic analysis.[11]

McNamara's public rationale for LBJ's tortured compromise was delivered to a gathering of United Press International editors and publishers in September 1967. This speech is probably best known for its dire warning about the "action–reaction" phenomenon inherent in U.S.–Soviet nuclear rivalry. "If we ... opt for heavy ABM deployment, at whatever price," McNamara argued, "we can be certain that the Soviets will react to offset the advantage we would hope to gain."[12] Defenses, in other words, would breed offenses, and offenses would render defenses ineffectual. To avoid this syndrome, McNamara counseled restraint. If the Kremlin unwisely expanded its modest missile defense effort, the Secretary of Defense advised, "our response must be realistic. There is no point whatever in our responding by going to a massive ABM deployment to protect our population, when such a system would be ineffective against a sophisticated Soviet offense."[13]

LBJ and McNamara faced the daunting challenge of trying to convince Kosygin at the 1967 Glassboro, New Jersey summit that a defense of the

Soviet Union was a bad idea. Not surprisingly, as Raymond L. Garthoff has chronicled, there was "no real meeting of the minds" on the dangers of missile defenses, which sounded even more counter-intuitive to Russian than to American ears.[14] The Johnson administration's plans for the Sentinel system and for strategic arms limitation talks were both stillborn. The Soviet occupation of Czechoslovakia and LBJ's decision not to seek re-election left these matters in the hands of the incoming Nixon administration.

Safeguard

President Richard M. Nixon's reworking of the Sentinel program was unveiled just two months after assuming office. The rationales for deployment against a limited Chinese attack and against accidental launch were retained, but the primary task of nation-wide defenses was now to protect U.S. nuclear-tipped intercontinental ballistic missiles (ICBMs) against a preemptive Soviet strike. Despite the addition of this mission, the architecture of the new "Safeguard" system was quite similar to Sentinel, one principal change being a modest reduction in ABM sites, from fourteen to twelve in number. In another change, Nixon proposed moving nuclear-tipped missile interceptors away from cities. Unlike the Johnson administration's approach, President Nixon offered no apologia of missile defenses. "The modified system has been designed so that its defensive intent is unmistakable," he announced, adding that U.S. missile defense deployments would be "subject to modification as the threat changes, either through negotiations or through unilateral actions." His speech to the nation in March 1969 seized the political high ground: "No President with the responsibility for the lives and security for the American people could fail to provide this protection."[15]

Secretary of Defense Melvin Laird then traveled to Capitol Hill to provide his former colleagues with a hair-raising Top Secret threat analysis depicting a precipitous rise in Soviet nuclear war-fighting capabilities that endangered the U.S. nuclear deterrent. The specter of a new Soviet "orbiting bombardment system" was raised. The prospective deployment by the Soviet Union of multiple independently targetable reentry vehicles (MIRVs) meant that the chances of U.S. land-based missiles surviving a first strike past the mid- to late-1970s were "virtually nil." No one could "preclude the possibility that the Soviets in the next few years may devise some weapon technique or tactic which might increase the vulnerability of our submarines."[16] The almost 3:1 lead in deployed strategic nuclear weapons then enjoyed by the United States seemed to be in extraordinary danger of nullification.[17] Laird's chilling testimony was unclassified upon its delivery to the Congress.

The debate over missile defenses was sharply drawn, with proponents and opponents employing arguments that continue to have wide currency. Herman Kahn of the RAND Corporation and Donald G. Brennan of the Hudson Institute weighed in with trenchant criticism of MAD—"a strategic posture that appears to favor dead Russians over live Americans."[18] Kahn offered ten reasons to support limited defenses: to stabilize the arms race; to prepare for a deterioration in U.S.–Soviet relations; to be open to the possibility that defenses might work unexpectedly well; to exploit new technological discoveries; to protect against new proliferants; to guard against accidental launch; to advance and protect against psychological warfare; to introduce uncertainty in the minds of a potential attacker; to protect some assets for postwar reconstruction; and to raise the price for an attacker.[19] Brennan split with his fellow arms controllers over missile defenses. "The American body politic," he concluded, "is unlikely to judge that pursuit of 'Assured Vulnerability' is a proper objective of the Department of Defense."[20] Unlike most of his fellow debaters, Brennan was thinking about transition strategies: "If we accept a MAD posture as an interim solution, we should be looking for ways out of it, not ways to enshrine it."[21]

Opposition to the Safeguard system was led by highly credentialed scientists and former government officials such as Jerome B. Weisner, President John F. Kennedy's science advisor. Weisner and others argued that ABMs would not work reliably, could be easily overwhelmed, could not be tested properly, and would prompt negative countermoves by Moscow. "Its deployment," he reasoned, "would be a move in the wrong direction. Safeguard is more likely to reduce our security than enhance it and represents a complicating step in the arms race."[22] McNamara's earlier warning about the action–reaction syndrome weighed heavily in the Safeguard debate, as plans for national missile defenses and MIRVs were proceeding in parallel. Even before the advent of MIRVs, skeptics of national missile defenses such as Herbert York, the first director of Lawrence Livermore National Laboratory, had concluded that, "In any development race between antiballistic missiles and ballistic missiles, I believe the offense will always, and by a wide margin, have the advantage over the defense."[23] With MIRVs now clearly on the horizon, this argument took on added force.

Missile defense opponents also fought against MIRVs, but their success in blocking the former proved insufficient to stop the latter. Critics did not argue that missile defenses were intrinsically bad, but that defenses would be terribly ineffectual and costly. Proponents countered that technological challenges could be surmounted, but their claims of "well over ninety percent kill probability" and of Safeguard "not be[ing] seriously limited" by nuclear detonations stretched credulity.[24] In a public debate defined by competing rhetorical questions, "Why should the United States remain undefended?" lost ground over time to "How can defenses possibly protect against nuclear weapons?" As Bernard Brodie observed, missile defense advocates "assumed that an extraordinarily complicated system that could never be fully tested in peacetime would work perfectly in the first hour of a nuclear war."[25]

The Strategic Arms Limitation Talks (SALT) allowed MIRVs to run free while limiting national defenses to two sites of 100 interceptor missiles each. Brennan concluded that the "ABM treaty does the wrong thing well and the Interim Agreement [limiting offensive forces] does the right thing badly."[26] Most commentators and members of Congress, however, supported the accords negotiated by President Nixon and national security adviser Henry Kissinger, albeit with considerable misgivings. The Senate consented to the ABM Treaty and the SALT I accord with just two opposing votes.

The debate over Safeguard offered no insight as to how the United States and the Soviet Union might change the mix of nuclear offenses and missile defenses. Since the debate was cast in absolutist terms, transition strategies had little relevance. On one side were analysts such as William Schneider, Jr., who claimed before joining the Reagan administration that, "Over the long term, no foreign policy can be effective without the capacity for homeland defense."[27] On the other side were men like Marshall Shulman, a Soviet expert who subsequently joined the Carter administration. "I would argue," he said, "that every level of antiballistic missile deployment under every circumstance is necessarily destabilizing."[28] In the early 1970s, transition strategies were besides the point: both the United States and the Soviet Union were positioning themselves to compete fully in an offensive build up to ensure bargaining leverage in the next round of SALT negotiations.

After the ratification vote, domestic battles resumed without let-up. Critics of ballistic missile defense succeeded in mothballing one deployed, ineffectual, Safeguard site no sooner than it had become operational; the other was negotiated away by the Nixon administration in a 1974 Protocol to the ABM Treaty. On the other side of the ledger, U.S. and Soviet offensive forces began to rise steeply as the impact of MIRVs began to be felt. The Pentagon's preferences—a "passionate" attachment to MIRVs and a lukewarm embrace of ABMs—were thus realized.[29] Brennan seemed increasingly prescient with the passage of time; the combination of nuclear overkill and defenselessness meant that, sooner or later, the issue of ballistic missile defense would resurface. The issue was rejoined suddenly and surprisingly in March 1983, by the most anti-nuclear and anti-communist U.S. president of the Cold War.

The Strategic Defense Initiative

Anti-communism and anti-nuclear sentiment were usually a null set during the Cold War, but Ronald Reagan repeatedly defied expectation and Washington convention. In a surprise insert to a Pentagon budget speech, Reagan spoke from the heart, over the reservations of his closest advisors: "I've become more and more deeply convinced that the human spirit must be capable of rising above dealing with other nations and human beings by threatening their existence." The Strategic Defense Initiative (SDI) that followed came as a shock to official Washington, U.S. friends, allies, and adversaries alike. "Wouldn't it be better to save lives than to avenge them," Reagan asked? His answer was in the form of a "vision of the future which offers hope"—and which sought to overturn four decades of strategic doctrine, superpower relations, and technological reality:

> It is that we embark on a program to counter the awesome Soviet missile threat with measures that are defensive. Let us turn to the very strengths in technology that spawned our great industrial base and that have given us the quality of life we enjoy today.
>
> What if free people could live secure in the knowledge that their security did not rest upon the threat of instant U.S. retaliation to deter a Soviet attack, that we could intercept and destroy strategic ballistic missiles before they reached our own soil or that of our allies?

President Reagan asked nothing less of the Pentagon and the U.S. defense science community than "to give us the means of rendering these nuclear weapons impotent and obsolete."[30] In one bold stroke, the debate over nuclear weapons and missile defenses was back to square one. There was a brief acknowledgment in the President's speech that SDI could pose grave difficulties for a stable U.S.–Soviet relationship. "If paired with offensive systems," Reagan noted, strategic defenses "can be viewed as fostering an aggressive policy; and no-one wants that."[31] The catch was that a defense designed to realize Reagan's dream would have to hover over the Soviet Union at all times, with an ability to destroy ballistic missiles within seconds of their launch.

Unlike earlier debates, this time there was an explicit acknowledgment that a transition from offense to defense was required; indeed the SDI could not possibly succeed without one. A transition strategy required cooperation, whether willing or reluctant. The Kremlin, however, was then under the paranoid and sickly leadership of Yuri Andropov. During this time, the Kremlin's intelligence agents had fanned out in key western capitals to watch for signs of an impending U.S. nuclear attack.[32] SDI could hardly serve as a balm to the Kremlin's paranoia about the Reagan team's strategic objectives. This initiative was, after all, the brainchild of a president dedicated to place communism on the "ash heap of history." Not surprisingly, Andropov's initial reaction to SDI was to label it "a bid to disarm the Soviet Union."[33]

To American critics, the SDI was a flight of fancy. To the Kremlin, it constituted a grave strategic threat and technological challenge. To some Reagan administration negotiators, the SDI program provided powerful leverage to achieve deep cuts in Soviet nuclear forces—as long as space-based missile defenses remained a serious prospect rather than a reality. To arms controllers, the ABM Treaty was necessary protection against a free-fall in superpower relations. Retention of the Treaty immediately became the focus of Soviet diplomatic strategy and subject of a fierce, extended debate in the United States. Media chroniclers pitted Hawks vs. Doves and, within the Reagan administration, "hard-liners" against pragmatists.

The arguments for and against SDI were a virtual rerun of the Sentinel and Safeguard debates. True believers and cynics lined up against arms controllers and skeptics. No one projected more true belief after President Reagan's speech than Secretary of Defense Caspar Weinberger. Weinberger abhorred shades of gray, arguing, "It's a matter of whether it's better to destroy people or to destroy weapons."[34] In addition to the moral imperative of trying to protect lives, supporters of SDI stressed the need for leverage against the Soviet Union's huge nuclear arsenal and the imperative to shift the competition to an area of U.S. technological advantage. Opponents quickly dubbed SDI "Star Wars," focusing on the program's escapist and unreal features, as well as the damage likely to accrue from its unfettered pursuit. Arms control stalwarts McGeorge Bundy, George Kennan, Robert McNamara, and Gerard Smith summed up the opposition by borrowing an aphorism from Arthur Vandenberg: "The end is unattainable, the means hare-brained, and the cost staggering."[35]

On a rhetorical plane, supporters of SDI held their own, but practical considerations adversely shifted the terrain. Weinberger confidently asserted that "I don't see any reasons why that [thoroughly reliable] defense can't be done,"[36] but a panel of defense scientists convened by the Reagan administration to assess SDI's feasibility had a somewhat different message, cautioning that, "The computers ... should be designed to be maintenance free for ten years ... In addition, the computers must be able to operate in a nuclear environment." Moreover, software for nuclear battle management would require "an enormous and error-free program, on the order of ten million lines of code."[37] Once surmounting these challenges, SDI would have to deal with an adversary determined to defeat it.

During the SDI debate, proponents benefited from a great infusion of new spending for missile defenses, strengthening defense contractor and congressional support. The absence of visual results from this largesse, however, diminished popular support. The ranks of critics were swelled by prominent defense strategists, including many with solid Republican credentials. Former Secretary of Defense James Schlesinger concluded, "There is no realistic hope that we shall ever again be able to protect American cities. There is no leak-proof defense."[38] Another former Secretary of Defense, Harold Brown, concurred:

> [A]n imperfect defense could not be expected to reduce significantly the damage to the United States if deterrence failed through a deliberate and major attack. To protect the United States against even a small missile attack, the U.S. would still need to deploy a substantial and extensive ABM system. And the risks of deploying such a system outweigh its potential for saving some American lives. There are therefore strong reasons to oppose moving to abrogate or modify the ABM Treaty.[39]

While skeptics dwelled on the issues of technical feasibility, cost, and the relative ease of Soviet countermeasures, proponents of SDI found themselves divided over which missile defense architecture to pursue. Every change in architecture, from space-based lasers to space-based kinetic kill vehicles to prosaic land-based interceptor missiles, conveyed trouble within the program. There was the added burden of explaining credibly how SDI would lead to the transition to nuclear safety in light of implacable Soviet hostility. Without an answer to the transition question, SDI would become just another phase of the nuclear competition it was designed to stop. Arms controllers hemmed in SDI advocates by demanding concrete proof of feasibility, while constraining tests to parameters established by the ABM Treaty. Missile defenses that were technically feasible, they argued, were also easily overwhelmed. Bernard Brodie's conclusion, reached in 1959, still seemed apt: "[T]here is not much solace in raising the enemy's requirements if he is still able to meet them."[40]

During the Reagan administration, staunch supporters of SDI were hard-pressed to argue that the Soviet Union would be unable to meet the challenge of countering their efforts, since they were also highlighting the Soviet threat. Indeed, Pentagon publications during this period drew an unrelenting portrait of Russian military might. The frightening details were depicted in an annual Pentagon publication, *Soviet Military Power.* The 1983 edition—the year that Andropov deemed it necessary to watch American blood banks for signs of a U.S. surprise attack—warned that, "As a result of the 20-year buildup of the USSR's armed forces, the global military balance has been shifting steadily against the United States and its Allies."[41] Moreover:

> Doctrine, structure and offensive posture combine to constitute a threat of direct military action that is of unprecedented proportions... Thus the main operative role of that formidable war machine is to undergird, by its very presence, the step-by-step extension of Soviet influence and control by instilling fear and promoting paralysis, by sapping the vitality of collective security arrangements, by subversion, by coercive political actions of every genre.[42]

The SDI was not only a counter to the Soviet military build up; it was a catch-up exercise against unconventional Soviet missile defense deployments. The Defense Intelligence Agency predicted that, by the early 1990s, the Soviets could proceed with large-scale SDI-like deployments of their own.[43] The U.S. intelligence community projected a similarly worrisome picture with respect to Soviet offensive nuclear forces, estimating in 1984 that the Kremlin could expand its forces for intercontinental attack from approximately 8,500 deployed warheads to between 16,000 and 19,000, absent arms control restraints. "Nor do we believe," the intelligence community concluded, "that domestic economic difficulties will bear significantly on the size and composition of future Soviet strategic forces because of the high priority the Soviets place on such forces."[44] These heightened threat estimates placed the Reagan administration in a bind: The SDI was deemed essential to counter the Kremlin's quest for strategic superiority, but SDI could easily be overwhelmed by Soviet military power, foiling the cooperative transition the administration ostensibly sought.

The task of creating a workable negotiating strategy out of this morass fell to Secretary of State George Shultz and his arms control adviser, Paul Nitze. In a speech before the Philadelphia World Affairs Council in February 1985, Nitze outlined three criteria for defensive systems. First, they had to be effective. Second, defenses must be survivable, "if not, the defenses would themselves be tempting targets for a first strike. This would decrease rather than enhance stability." Third, defenses must be cost effective at the margin—"they must be cheap enough to add additional defensive capability so that the other side has no incentive to add additional offensive capability to overcome the defense." Otherwise, Nitze asserted, defenses would breed more offense instead of "a redirection of effort from offense to defense."

Nitze then proposed an ambitious strategic concept for a cooperative transition, calling for "radical reductions in the power of existing and planned offensive nuclear arms, as well as the stabilization of the relationship between offensive and defensive arms." Defenses would be deployed "at a measured pace," in a transition period that could last for decades, leading eventually to a world without nuclear weapons and with widespread deployments of effective, non-nuclear defenses.[45]

Had Nitze not been the architect of this plan, he and other Reagan administration officials would have skewered it without mercy as being hopelessly naive. His criteria for SDI, however, were politically unobjectionable,[46] and Nitze had at least managed to situate President Reagan's ambitious goals for denuclearization and strategic defenses under the same tent. His motivating purposes, however, were not to demonstrate his vaunted powers of strategic analysis, but to affix sensible guidelines to the SDI development program and to coax the Kremlin into a serious negotiation to reduce strategic arms. As Strobe Talbott observed, "It was part of Nitze's effort to make a silk purse out of the sow's ear of SDI."[47]

The battle between hard-liners and pragmatists in the Reagan administration has been chronicled extensively.[48] By the close of the Reagan administration, SDI had been wrestled to the ground by the combined weight of technological constraints, cost, congressional opposition, and a more sophisticated negotiating strategy pursued by the Kremlin. Under the new management of Mikhail Gorbachev, the Kremlin subsequently decided to adopt an indirect approach to grounding SDI, accepting deep cuts in strategic forces and relying on ABM Treaty supporters on Capitol Hill to keep this safety net in place. The 50 percent reductions mandated by the first strategic arms reduction accord in 1991 clarified that nuclear threat reduction by treaty was far simpler, safer and less costly than by the pursuit of "thoroughly effective" strategic defenses. The resulting improvement in bilateral relations further marginalized SDI advocates.

During the Reagan administration, the twin visions of a world in which nuclear weapons were dramatically devalued and strategic defenses were championed coexisted almost exclusively in the mind of the President. The fractious collection of negotiators and ideologues around him jousted over which objective to pursue, with SDI ultimately losing out to strategic arms reductions. The victory engineered by Shultz and Nitze still owed much to Reagan administration's ideologues who helped the Kremlin see the wisdom of accepting deep cuts. With SDI remaining a distant quest, a mix of strategic offense and missile defense would have to wait another day.

Global Protection against Limited Strikes

In January 1991, George H. W. Bush became the fourth president to propose a major initiative on national missile defenses. Following on the heels of the Gulf War against Saddam Hussein, Bush proposed a "limited" system to counter missile attacks from developing countries as well as accidental or unauthorized strikes from nuclear powers. Once again, the architecture for the missile defense initiative, now called Global Protection Against Limited Strikes, or GPALS, seemed to belie its stated objectives. The Bush plan called for no less than a three-tiered defense consisting of mobile, theater missile defenses, a national defense consisting of 750 interceptor missiles deployed at six sites, and a space-based tier encompassing 1,000 interceptors. The principal utility of GPALS was keyed to regional conflicts against "rogue" states, but the system's architecture seemed far too extensive for this purpose.

Just six months later, Gorbachev signed the first strategic arms reduction accord, a clear indicator of the Kremlin's confidence that Democratic majorities in the House and Senate would not give up their allegiance to the ABM Treaty. Indeed, congressional views on space-based interceptors, now dubbed "brilliant pebbles" by advocates, had changed little from the Reagan administration. Missile defense enthusiasts now rested their hopes on the much-heralded successes of the Patriot missile in the Gulf War. If jerry-rigged Patriots, which were originally designed to be used against hostile aircraft, could also shoot down Saddam Hussein's SCUD missiles, skepticism over more ambitious missile defenses might be diminished. Subsequent analysis, however, suggested that the Patriots fared poorly on the battlefield.[49]

The vast changes underway in the Soviet Union and the negotiation of extraordinary nuclear arms reduction treaties by the Reagan and Bush administrations appeared to have little impact on the terms of debate over GPALS. On one side, Edward Teller predicted that, "In the absence of space-based defense, attack missiles will continue to proliferate around the world."[50] On the other, Robert McNamara countered, "A partial defense designed to protect against accidents and one aimed at complicating a Soviet attack do have one thing in common. They threaten the viability of the ABM Treaty, which in turn undermines the chances for achieving reductions in strategic arms."[51]

The combined impact of continued success in negotiating strategic arms reductions with Gorbachev and his successor, Boris Yeltsin, continued congressional resistance to space-based interceptors, and the demise of the Soviet Union took the steam out of the Bush administration's three-tiered approach to missile defenses. Under the leadership of Senator Sam Nunn, a moderate alternative to GPALS was constructed around the less ambitious goals of improved theater missile defenses and modest adjustments to the ABM Treaty to permit limited national missile defense against accidental or unauthorized launch.[52] This middle ground received little support. ABM Treaty protectors continued to argue that limited national missile defenses were unnecessary and destabilizing, while SDI supporters accepted Nunn's minimalism only as a way station to more robust defenses.

Clinton's Hedge Strategy

The administration of President Bill Clinton quickly shelved the GPALS architecture, believing it to be unnecessary as well as an impediment to deeper strategic arms reductions. President Clinton inherited two strategic arms reduction treaties that were signed, but not ratified. Consequently, the first order of business for administration officials was the time-sensitive task of convincing the newly independent states of Ukraine, Kazakhstan, and Belarus to give up their nuclear inheritance—a Russian condition to ratifying the first strategic arms reduction treaty.

National missile defenses did not figure high in the Clinton administration's priorities. During President Clinton's first term, the Pentagon kept advocates at arm's length by pursing a "technology readiness" program. In February 1996, Secretary of Defense William J. Perry shifted these efforts to a "deployment readiness" mode, with the objective of being able to field a national missile defense three years after presidential authorization to do so.[53] This posture served as a hedge against Republican advocates of national missile defenses as well as emerging missile threats. The steadfastness of the Clinton administration's deployment readiness posture was predicated, however, on two critical— and questionable—assumptions. First, the U.S. intelligence community would need to be able to confirm the covert acquisition of long-range missile threats in sufficient time for the administration to take appropriate responses. Second, the Pentagon and its defense contractors would need to be able to fast-track national missile defense programs to be in a position to respond with deployments within three years of confirmed threats. The initial readiness date set by the Clinton administration for national missile defense deployments was 2003.

Republican majorities on Capitol Hill took strong exception to both of these assumptions as well as to the Clinton administration's overall commitment to national missile defenses. The first pillar of the administration's deployment readiness program—having sufficient intelligence warning of impending missile threats—was attacked in familiar fashion, by mandating the appointment of an advisory panel of experts to critique overly sanguine intelligence community findings. A similar mechanism was utilized to dramatize the Soviet threat during the Carter administration.

The subsequent report by a commission headed by Donald H. Rumsfeld found easy targets in the intelligence community's central finding that,

"No country, other than the major declared nuclear powers, will develop or otherwise acquire a ballistic missile in the next fifteen years that could threaten the contiguous 48 states." The Rumsfeld Commission noted that the Republic's two non-contiguous states also mattered, and that covert acquisition of critical missile components was a regular occurrence. It was simply not possible to assert categorically that a back-door transaction or series of transactions resulting in a missile threat to the United States would not occur. Moreover, new states might have very different and far more relaxed standards regarding missile development and flight-testing programs. Consequently, the lengthy time lines of overt missile preparation might not be evident. [54] The Rumsfeld Commission's critique of the intelligence community's methodology was given immediate confirmation when Pyongyang flight tested a crude three-stage missile advertised as a satellite launcher, much to the surprise of the Central Intelligence Agency's analysts. The intelligence community subsequently shortened its fairly relaxed time lines of a missile attack capability against the continental United States by a rogue state from "at least 15 years" to less than ten years.[55]

The second pillar of the Clinton administration's readiness program—the initial operational deployment date of 2003—was clearly unrealistic even with a vastly accelerated national missile defense program, which was certainly not part of the Pentagon's plans. The earliest deployment date was subsequently pushed back to 2005 by Perry's successor, William S. Cohen.

With pressure from the Republican right and proliferation woes increasing, the Clinton administration began to consider limited missile defenses as an adjunct to deep cuts in order to counter "rogue" states, later renamed "states of proliferation concern." The Clinton team's enthusiasm for this mix was deeply suspect, as became evident once leaving office, when key Clinton advisers published unequivocal critiques of a deployment decision that, just a few months earlier, was supposedly under serious consideration.[56]

The Clinton team's hedging and hesitant missile defense strategy finally reached the unavoidable juncture of choice at the particularly inauspicious time of the run-up to the 2000 presidential election. The Democratic standard bearer, Vice President Al Gore, hewed to the administration line that nuclear deterrence and limited missile defenses could be combined, while expressing caution about serious revision of U.S. nuclear doctrine. Republican presidential candidate George W. Bush promised a new mix of offenses and defenses, less ambitious on both counts than the President Reagan's construct of abolition plus SDI, but quite explicit in its rejection of Cold War constructs.

In order to meet the 2005 initial operational deployment date, President Clinton was faced at the end of his term with a decision to start construction of a new radar on a rock outcropping in the Bering Sea, ostensibly to deal with a limited missile attack from North Korea, a rationale that many at home and abroad found deeply suspect. Not surprisingly, President Clinton announced his decision to put off a missile defense deployment decision in September 2000.

The issues of ballistic missile defense and nuclear strategy did not figure prominently in the election of 2000, unlike the previous three presidential contests. A new Bush administration took office in deeply contested circumstances, with no popular mandate for significant change. Nevertheless, for the first time since 1980, a new U.S. administration announced its intention to do just that toward Cold War constructs of arms control and missile defenses.

George W. Bush's Defense against Evil

President George W. Bush and his national security team quickly made the deployment of national missile defenses and the replacement of the ABM Treaty with a new "strategic framework" centerpieces of their foreign and national security policies. In his first address on missile defenses, Bush challenged listeners to "rethink the unthinkable and find new ways to keep the peace." The ABM Treaty, he asserted, "does not recognize the present, or point us to the future. It enshrines the past." Deterrence, he argued, needed to be strengthened with a mix of offensive and defensive forces.[57]

The Bush administration's national missile defense plans were said to be quite limited, but undefined. Tactical and political considerations militated toward moving quickly, and in projecting a sense of inevitability regarding the ABM Treaty's impending obituary. The Treaty was hopelessly antiquated and restricting, according to administration officials. A wide range of technologies needed to be tested in order to champion the right missile defense architecture, and these tests would need to extend far beyond treaty constraints. Hardened treaty critics within the administration now argued that it was better to jettison the ABM Treaty than to curtail testing or be charged with violating solemn obligations. A sounder course, they argued, was reaching a bilateral agreement with Moscow on a new strategic framework and, failing that, extrication. Moscow, needless to say, would have a greater incentive to reach a new strategic framework if the United States withdrew from the ABM Treaty. In July 2001, the State Department issued guidance to embassies abroad advising them to tell foreign governments that the administration's ambitious test programs would violate the ABM Treaty "in months, not years."[58]

The administration's haste might well have been linked to the weaknesses of its syllogism. If U.S. missile defense ambitions were so limited, why did the administration seek treaty nullification rather than change? And what accounted for the breakneck speed with which the administration sought the demise of a treaty when its preferred architecture for missile defenses could neither be proposed nor vetted on Capitol Hill? The Bush administration's rejoinders were that the eventual design and scope of missile defenses could be known only after extensive and lengthy field tests. All possibilities needed to be explored, including those prohibited by the ABM Treaty.

Other reasons for the administration's haste to dispose of the ABM Treaty were not hard to divine. Previous missile defense debates suggested the necessity for pre-emptive executive branch moves, since the longer advocates lingered over treaty withdrawal, the more Capitol Hill and U.S. allies rallied to the treaty's defense. Also, exacting missile defense tests often ended in failure—at least at the outset of the test series. Not surprisingly, the Bush administration argued that, while it could not clarify the details of its limited national missile defense, it was entirely sure that whatever resulted from internal reviews and test programs could not possibly be accommodated by amendments to the ABM Treaty. Newly confirmed Secretary of Defense Rumsfeld angled for an initial operational capability in 2004, while boosting missile defense funding to a level equal to the State Department's entire budget.[59]

After initial parrying between the Bush administration and the Kremlin, the bare outlines of a tradeoff involving extensive freedom for U.S. testing in return for non-withdrawal from the ABM Treaty surfaced in media reports.[60] After meeting President Bush in Shanghai in October 2001, President Putin announced at a joint press conference that, in addition to their mutual intention to reduce strategic offensive forces, he and Bush "made some progress, at least, I believe we do have understanding that we can reach agreements, taking into account national interests of Russia, United States, and taking into account the necessity to strengthen international stability in this very important area."[61]

Within two months, prospects for a trade off nose-dived and President Bush notified foreign capitals of his intention to withdraw from the ABM Treaty. Press accounts suggested that this breakdown resulted from Russian efforts to attach conditions to U.S. missile defense tests alongside American demands for a completely unfettered test program.[62] While these accounts were plausible, they did not explain the basis for Putin's earlier optimism or the abruptness of Bush's decision. Perhaps the Russian side was playing for time, and was given an object lesson in the President's temperament. If so, the Kremlin's standard negotiating tactics of aiming high and then accepting the middle ground ill fitted the Bush team's insistence on a blank check. The official White House statement ending nearly three decades of treaty constraints was issued on December 13, 2001. "I have concluded the ABM Treaty hinders our government's ability to develop ways to protect our people from future terrorist or rogue-state missile attacks," Bush announced. Putin somberly characterized this move as "mistaken," and called for prompt talks on Bush's "new strategic framework."[63]

The old strategic framework was built around mutual assured destruction (MAD). Now the Kremlin faced the possibility that a triumphant United States, freed from the shackles of the ABM Treaty, would seek unilateral assured destruction.[64] The deep reductions subsequently promised by the Bush administration remained quite sufficient to cover a shrinking list of targets in Russia. Moreover, deployed U.S. nuclear forces could be adjusted upward, as necessary, with the retention of a warhead stockpile at least twice the size of U.S. deployed forces. The Bush team's Nuclear Posture Review, announced one month after the withdrawal from the ABM Treaty, provided little comfort to Moscow, and less to Beijing, with the addition of non-nuclear strike capabilities and "limited," but open-ended missile defenses to U.S. nuclear war plans.[65]

Looking Ahead

The Bush administration's much-ballyhooed "clear and clean break from the past, and especially from the adversarial legacy of the Cold War" was incontestable. But where, exactly, was the Bush administration heading? President Bush's call for a decisive break in Cold War thinking was embedded in his first major address on nuclear issues and missile defenses. In that speech, he declared that, "Today's Russia is not our enemy," and called for a "new cooperative relationship" with Moscow, one that "should look to the future, not to the past. It should be reassuring, rather than threatening. It should be premised on openness, mutual confidence and real opportunities for cooperation."[66]

The Bush administration's Nuclear Posture Review did, indeed, call for a significant reduction in deployed warheads atop U.S. strategic forces, as well as a much-reduced alert rate. The resulting posture, however, was hardly reassuring. Nor was Bush's withdrawal from the ABM Treaty suggestive of a "new cooperative relationship." Meanwhile, drumbeats could be heard in the distance calling for a resumption of nuclear testing and the weaponization of space. Was unfettered U.S. strategic superiority the "clear and clean break" from Cold War thinking what the Bush administration had in mind? Or would other initiatives follow that would clarify non-threatening and cooperative intent? The answers to these questions would become evident only in subsequent policy choices, especially the design and scope of U.S. missile defenses.

CHAPTER 4

Vulnerability, Risk, and Missile Defense

T he Cold War strategy of containment was designed, in George Kennan's original game plan, to hold the fort until Democracy ultimately triumphed over Communism.[1] Mutual Assured Destruction, or MAD, was another vestige of the Cold War. It, too, was meant to check Soviet expansionism by clarifying that the use of force to change boundaries or allegiances in sensitive areas would entail intolerable risks. With the demise of the Soviet Union, containment became unnecessary and MAD lost its underpinnings. Vulnerability remains a post-Cold War fact of life, however, not simply from the destructive power of still-bloated nuclear arsenals, but also from new threats that are asymmetric in nature. Indeed, these two sets of vulnerabilities are intertwined, since asymmetric warriors could gain immense new powers from illicit transfers of weapons or dangerous materials out of the former Soviet Union.

How would the United States deal with these vulnerabilities as the world's sole superpower with no strategic competitor in sight for at least a decade and probably more? Having jettisoned the Anti-Ballistic Missile (ABM) Treaty, would Washington continue to accept vulnerability in its dealings with Moscow and Beijing, the only "near peer competitor" (to use the Pentagon's term) on the horizon? Or would the United States seek to reinforce its unparalleled superiority in conventional and nuclear forces with missile defenses sufficiently sized and structured to take on all comers? What strategic objectives should missile defenses serve? To counter "rogue" states? China? Or all potential foes, including Russia? Should Washington accept a mutual deterrence relationship with any other capital? Where exactly do missile defenses fit into a world of U.S. military predominance?

During the Cold War, Hawks and Doves battled continuously over nuclear weapons and arms control. One side sought primacy; the other valued balance. With the end of the Cold War, American primacy was so great that it could not be balanced by opposing coalitions or by ill-fitting treaties premised on equality. U.S. strategic superiority could only be weakened by overreaching and challenged by unconventional means. At the outset of the twenty-first century, those fearing and loathing American power sought deterrence through weapons of mass destruction (WMD) and the means to deliver them.

Tribunes of American primacy were unapologetic about the exercise of U.S. power. "The new unilateralism," wrote Charles Krauthammer, was all about asserting "American freedom of action and the primacy of American national interests."[2] A new administration headed by President George W. Bush came to Washington singing this refrain, following eight years of tentative multilateralism under President Bill Clinton. Unilateralism is, however, a course of last resort, and one to be used sparingly. Proliferation, on the other hand, proceeds on multiple fronts led by the "axis of evil" as characterized by President Bush. Public enemies number 1, 2 and 3 were Iraq, Iran, and North Korea.[3]

Success in countering proliferation requires far more than U.S. strategic superiority. Success requires cooperation from the permanent members of the United Nations Security Council; from regional partners that could provide necessary forward bases; from foreign intelligence services; from strengthened treaty norms and export controls against proliferation; and in dozens of other ways.

Missile defenses, like U.S. conventional military superiority, could be part of the solution. They also could be part of the problem. Since the deployment of missile defenses would reinforce American primacy, the likely response by states fearing U.S. power projection capabilities would be to redouble their efforts to acquire missiles and WMD. The design and scope of missile defenses therefore need to be aligned with diplomatic strategies as well as military contingencies. Unilateral military action happens rarely; multilateral cooperation against proliferation is required on a daily basis. Much therefore depends on whether proposed missile defenses facilitate collaborative action against proliferation as well as protection in the event of hostilities. The ideal missile defense architecture would combine political appeal with military utility. Unfortunately, successful missile intercepts in the fog of war are quite difficult to pull off. Unless technological optimists are finally proven correct, the political utility of missile defenses is likely to exceed military utility. And if skeptics are proven right, the United States could find itself deploying missile defenses with high political liabilities and low military effectiveness.

President George W. Bush's decision to withdraw from the ABM Treaty shifted the terms of America's debate over missile defenses. The presumption of deployment now made questions of design and scope paramount. Different purposes for ballistic missile defense require different architectures. Missile defenses sized and structured to devalue the Russian nuclear arsenal would look very different from defenses designed to counter potential missile threats to the United States from maverick states like North Korea, Iran or Iraq. Similarly, missile defenses designed to negate a Chinese nuclear deterrent would be more robust than a defense against a small country with very few nuclear warheads and long-range missiles. The architecture chosen for ballistic missile defense matters greatly, since the financial, diplomatic, and arms control consequences of seeking to devalue or negate the nuclear deterrents of major powers would be quite different from the consequences of defenses configured against regional troublemakers.

Friends and potential foes will try to discern which national objectives the United States seeks in large measure by its chosen architecture for ballistic missile defense. Does the United States seek to become the national equivalent of a "gated community," protected from the world's ills?[4] Or do missile defenses fit coherently into a broader strategy of international engagement and cooperation? Down-sizing U.S. nuclear forces was not, by itself, indicative of a cooperative approach, since the reductions endorsed by President Bush would still cover an extensive range of targets in Russia. The addition of conventional strike and space warfare capabilities as well as "limited" missile defenses to the U.S. nuclear posture could thus be construed by the Kremlin as a thinly disguised effort to greatly devalue, if not negate, its deterrent.

Similarly, cooperative threat reduction programs could be construed as being truly cooperative in nature, or as thinly veiled efforts to further weaken the Kremlin's nuclear posture—depending on the larger strategic context in which they are pursued. After all, the identification of every additional ramshackle nuclear weapons storage site in Russia allows the United States to provide needed safety and security, while adding an exact location to the U.S. targeting lists. As war planners like to say, intentions can change quickly, so assessing military capabilities is of paramount importance. Washington might talk a good game about a new era of cooperation, but its missile defense deployments would speak louder than words.

Beijing's concerns are far greater than Moscow's because its nuclear deterrent is so modest and because of the Taiwan issue, over which a military confrontation with Washington could occur. The more America is perceived by both Moscow and Beijing as utilizing missile defenses to devalue or negate their deterrents, the less inclined they will be to cooperate with Washington against troublemakers. And because the maverick states that Washington worries about most have long-standing ties with either Russia or China, successful campaigns against proliferation in troubled regions require their help. During a time of unchallenged U.S. power projection capabilities, their veto power in the United Nations Security Council is usually more relevant than their military capabilities. A military alliance between Russia and China still would not balance American power. Proliferation, on the other hand, would preoccupy, and perhaps seriously complicate, U.S. military options.

Dominators vs. Conciliators

The changing of the guard from Bill Clinton and Vice President Al Gore to the team of George W. Bush, Vice President Dick Cheney, and Secretary of Defense Donald H. Rumsfeld resulted in a new assertiveness in U.S. national security policy. The outgoing Democrats were conciliators by nature. They were uncomfortable with military options, which they exercised hesitantly. The new team was selective but unapologetic about the use of force. The old Cold War typology of Hawks vs. Doves was history; Dominators now clashed with Conciliators, and after the disputed 2000 presidential election, the Dominators ruled. For Dominators, unilateral action is to be used sparingly, but decisively. Maximum freedom of action is required for the unilateral use of force. Treaties are ineffectual, especially treaties that enshrine vulnerability and formalize a fictional strategic equality. Treaties that constrain military flexibility need to be sloughed off.

Both Conciliators and Dominators worry primarily about proliferation and asymmetric warfare, but their preferred remedies vary greatly. Conciliators believe strongly in reassurance. They rely heavily on diplomatic suasion and preventive diplomacy. Stopping and reversing proliferation requires strong international norms. Treaties are therefore essential, providing a basis to isolate transgressors, build coalitions against them and, if necessary, take military action against states that seek or use deadly weapons and missiles. Conciliators are treaty protectors by nature. They seek to devalue weapons of mass destruction by example, by multilateral diplomacy, and by strengthening treaty regimes. They worry that by placing a high value on missile defenses, nuclear weapons, and seizing the high ground of space, the United States would separate itself from its allies, cement adversarial political alliances, unravel or hollow out nonproliferation treaties, and accelerate worrisome proliferation trend lines.

Conciliators seek to reduce the salience of U.S. nuclear forces and rely instead on strong conventional military capabilities to supplement treaty regimes. They view the weaponization of space with alarm. Missile defenses would be pursued with caution, so as not to impair the cooperation needed to counter proliferation. Theater missile defenses deployed in or around troubled regions where short-range missiles could threaten U.S. forces, friends, and allies are viewed as essential. On the other hand, national missile defenses are viewed with considerable skepticism, since the threat to American soil by means of ocean-spanning North Korean, Iranian, or Iraqi missiles is believed to be remote. Conciliators do not seek to devalue or negate the Russian and Chinese nuclear deterrents, since their help would be needed to contain and roll back proliferation.

Dominators do not discount the utility of cooperation, but they believe that it can be elicited most effectively from a position of strength and the willingness to use it. The most well articulated, closely reasoned presentation of this argument appeared just before the Bush administration took office in a report issued by the National Institute for Public Policy. Several contributors to this report, *Rationale and Requirements for U.S. Nuclear Forces and Arms Control,* subsequently were given key staff positions at the Pentagon and National Security Council. The central conclusion in *Rationale and Requirements for U.S. Nuclear Forces and Arms Control* was that the future was difficult to predict. And since it was not possible to predict accurately future deterrence requirements, the United States should seek maximum flexibility.

In this view, treaties should be avoided, because they are inherently difficult to amend or adapt. In addition, "Given the post-Cold War diversity of potential opponents and crises Washington will want to deter, the value of 'superiority' … may again be important." Unilateral reductions in U.S. nuclear forces to promote "mutual reassurance" were preferable to treaties. Unilateral increases might also be necessary: "[I]t would be wise for the United States to maintain the *de jure* prerogative to adjust its nuclear force structure to coincide with changes in strategic requirements. Legal flexibility alone, however, is of little value if the U.S. production infrastructure does not allow Washington to design and build new types of weapons as necessary in a timely fashion."[5] Left unstated was that new types of nuclear weapons would require a resumption of nuclear testing.

These guideposts were subsequently reflected in the Bush administration's Nuclear Posture Review, unveiled in January 2002. Indeed, the Pentagon's outside review board for this exercise was led by Keith Payne, the convener of the National Institute for Public Policy study. As advertised, President Bush announced the withdrawal from the ABM Treaty which he previously declared as irrelevant. Unilateral reductions in U.S. nuclear forces were announced. The moratorium on nuclear weapon testing was continued, with the hint that this would not be of indefinite duration, and steps were proposed to reduce the time line for resuming tests. Few words were spoken about the weaponization of space, amid a widespread presumption of classified activities in this sphere.

The typology of Dominators drawn to unilateral initiatives and Conciliators inclined to multilateralism is, of course, overdrawn, much like the Cold War caricatures of Hawks and Doves.[6] Stark divisions are useful for ordering chaos, but the two camps also had much in common. They both support superior U.S. conventional military and power projection capabilities, and provide generous funding to the Pentagon for these purposes. Conciliators and Dominators support improvements in U.S. intelligence-gathering capabilities, recognize the value of reducing deployed nuclear forces, and seek the earliest possible deployment of effective theater missile defenses. The two camps also agree that asymmetric threats and proliferation challenges are now paramount. Both camps support cooperative threat reduction efforts in Russia, although Conciliators are prepared to be more generous in this regard. Both camps favor preventive diplomacy, and both champion American values. They often agree on specific policy ends while disagreeing on means.

In addition, both camps have internal schisms.[7] The question of whether or not to seek nullification of the Chinese nuclear deterrent is an important fault line within the pro-national missile defense camp, as is whether to weaponize space. Conciliators are split between whether to hold the line completely against national missile defense or to endorse limited deployments. There are also contradictions aplenty in both camps. Dominators place a high priority on freedom of action, but typically impose many criteria to the use of force that would greatly reduce the number of instances when force would actually be used. Conciliators tend to be more inclined toward the use of force than Dominators in humanitarian interventions. Paradoxically, the more freedom of action Dominators seek, the more likely they are to be corralled by Conciliators. And the more hesitant Conciliators are to use military power decisively, the more susceptible they are to displacement by Dominators.

Dominators have rhetorical advantages in domestic political debates by offering simple and compelling messages, such as "defending America," or "keeping America strong," while remaining circumspect about their central strategic concept. Conciliators also have powerful messages to convey about the need for cooperation and international engagement. Conciliators failed to articulate their preferred strategic concept during the eight years of the Clinton administration. Conciliators also were unable to articulate a compelling case for the extension of treaties governing strategic offenses and missile defenses once the Cold War ended. Instead, they fell back upon a defense of MAD, which made little sense.

While the two camps have much in common, they remain well defined by their differences. Dominators and Conciliators diverge most on the value they place on treaties, diplomacy, nuclear weapons, national missile defenses, and the weaponization of space. In a pinch, Dominators expect little help from alliances, diplomacy, and treaties, which is why they place a premium on freedom of maneuver, flexibility, and superior military capabilities. As Senator Jon Kyl, a leading Republican treaty foe, has said, the United States needs "a different approach to national security issues... [one] that begins with the premise that the United States must be able to act unilaterally in its own best interests."[8] Republicans "will ask Americans to face this increasingly dangerous world without illusions," opined William Kristol and Robert Kagan. "They will argue that American dominance can be sustained for many decades to come, not by arms agreements, but by augmenting America's power, and, therefore, its ability to lead."[9] Charles Krauthammer rejoiced at President Bush's disdain for the ABM Treaty, declaring a new "Bush Doctrine":

> The new Bush Doctrine holds that, when it comes to designing our nuclear forces, we build to suit. We will build defensive missiles to suit our needs. We will build offensive missiles to suit our needs... For reasons of delicacy, Bush spoke of the need to "replace" rather than abrogate the treaty, which remains the Linus blanket of an entire generation of arms controllers. No matter. He made it clear that we will blithely ignore it... Sure, to placate the critics we will be consulting and assuaging and schmoozing everyone from Tokyo to Moscow. But in the end, we will build a defense to meet the challenge of the missile era. If others don't like it, too bad.[10]

Dominators see considerable value in extending "full spectrum dominance" from conventional military forces to nuclear weapons, national missile defenses, and space. They value nuclear weapons highly and consequently, they are very uncomfortable with an extended moratorium on nuclear testing. Dominators worry about covert Russian testing of nuclear weapons—but not enough to ratify the Comprehensive Test Ban Treaty and to implement its intrusive monitoring arrangements, including challenge inspections at the Russian test site. Some Dominators are attracted to a new nuclear weapon design that could be employed against underground bunkers housing evil leaders or hidden caches of deadly weapons. Reductions from bloated Cold War levels are acceptable, as long as they do not conflict with targeting requirements and as long as the United States maintains a large, ready reserve of nuclear warheads that could be deployed, when needed.

Dominators view the weaponization of space as a force multiplier. They expect other states not to abide by negotiated restraints or "rules of the road" against space warfare, and thus prefer to compete to win in this realm. As a Commission headed by Donald H. Rumsfeld concluded in January 2001, "[W]e know from history that every medium—air, land and sea—has seen conflict. Reality indicates that space will be no different." The Rumsfeld Commission called for "superior space capabilities," including the ability to "negate the hostile use of space against U.S. interests." A robust deterrence strategy for space would require "power projection in, from and through space." Moreover, senior political and military leadership "needs to test these capabilities in exercises on a regular basis."[11]

Conciliators have a much higher regard for non-military instruments to deal with proliferation threats. In this view, unilateral military "solutions" against proliferation threats usually breed new problems. As Senator Carl Levin, a leader of the pro-treaty ranks, said in response to Bush's announcement of the ABM Treaty's "irrelevance," "I have great concerns about a unilateral decision, because I believe that it could risk a second cold war." Senate Democratic Leader Tom Daschle added, "A missile defense system that undermines our nation politically, economically and strategically—without providing any real security—is no defense at all."[12]

Conciliators seek to strengthen multilateral treaties such as the Chemical Weapons Convention and the Biological Weapons Convention, accords that Dominators view as hopelessly hollow and, for some, not worth paying the dues owed by the United States. The decades-long battle between Conciliators and Dominators over the Comprehensive Test Ban Treaty (CTBT) was, in part, a contest over the salience of nuclear weapons in U.S. national security policy. For Conciliators, the CTBT's indefinite ban on testing was central to a broader campaign to devalue nuclear weapons. The goal for Dominators was to devalue the nuclear weapons of other countries, not the United States. Having lost the battle over ratification, Conciliators took solace in the Clinton administration's signature on the CTBT which, under international law, constitutes a solemn U.S. commitment not to test again, while Dominators began to plan extrication strategies.

In addition to the resumption of nuclear testing, Dominators looked forward to extending U.S. dominance into space. Military-related satellites have been orbiting the earth for four decades, but the weaponization of space was avoided even during the roughest stretches of the Cold War. Placing weapons in space or weapons on the ground to destroy or disable objects in space would set in motion a very purposeful competition in technologically feasible and affordable satellite killers, a competition that Conciliators dreaded. Dominators believe that weaponization of space is in the process of occurring, and aim to win this competition. The ABM Treaty was the most serious obstacle to weaponization, as it expressly prohibited interference with monitoring satellites as well as the flight-testing and deployment of space-based interceptors. By withdrawing from the ABM Treaty, the Bush administration removed these obstacles, mandating new blocking strategies by Conciliators.

Another major division between Conciliators and Dominators relates to the design and scope of national missile defenses. Dominators seek very robust strategic missile defenses to devalue the Kremlin's nuclear deterrent and to seek to nullify Beijing's modest holdings. These objectives could ostensibly be pursued under the rubric of defending against a possible North Korean, Iraqi, or Iranian missile attack. Conciliators are deeply skeptical of the need and wisdom of national missile defenses, but could accept, if need be, interceptors on U.S. soil as long as they were designed and sized not to jeopardize cooperation with Moscow and Beijing.

Stale Debates, New Circumstances

The demise of the Soviet Union liberated Dominators to pursue their objectives, while challenging Conciliators to re-conceptualize how their favored outcomes best served U.S. interests. Both camps, however, continued to debate missile defenses in terms that were utterly familiar. One sage participant in past debates characterized the second half of the twentieth century as the "golden age of nuclear scholastics."[13] Favored outcomes did not change in the first post-Cold War decade. After the demise of the Soviet Union, however, Americans tuned out of those debates. Another important change was that the principal cause of prior American restraint—the Kremlin's ability to effectively compete with the United States—was missing.

Notwithstanding these differences, Conciliators continued to maintain that the costs associated with even limited national missile defenses (NMD) would far exceed prospective benefits. Thus, Eugene Carroll of the Center for Defense Information asserted, "NMD will certainly be a bar to progress on future arms control agreements, which are essential to achieve genuine reductions in still bloated nuclear arsenals."[14] This assertion assumed that treaties, and not unilateral or reciprocal initiatives, would remain the primary mechanism for future reductions, a construct that was not shared by many in the Bush administration. How, then, would Dominators secure the cooperation of Moscow and Beijing against evildoers? As a study released by the Union of Concerned Scientists argued, missile defenses would "impede cooperation by these countries in international efforts to control the proliferation of long-range ballistic missiles and weapons of mass destruction."[15] In the short hand of public debate, even limited NMD deployments would inevitably lead to instability and proliferation.

The new Bush administration was strongly averse to fence-sitting. Not so the Clinton administration, which was drawn to the treacherous middle ground of triangulation. In this instance, the Clinton team agreed with the Kremlin that the ABM Treaty, which expressly prohibited NMD, remained the "cornerstone of strategic stability," while proposing amendments to the Treaty allowing limited homeland defenses against ballistic missiles. President Clinton was never able to extricate himself from endorsing both views. If the ABM Treaty truly remained the cornerstone of strategic stability, its central prohibition should logically remain in force. As a report issued by the Lawyers Alliance for World Security concluded, "It is not possible to 'amend' the ABM Treaty to permit full deployment of the proposed U.S. NMD program without totally gutting the agreement."[16]

The administration of President George W. Bush heartily endorsed this argument, and subsequently acted upon it. Dominators viewed bilateral arms control treaties as unnecessary constraints, and multilateral non-proliferation accords as ineffectual. During his confirmation hearings on January 11, 2001 for a second tour as Secretary of Defense, Donald H. Rumsfeld foreshadowed the administration's nuclear posture review by calling the ABM Treaty "ancient history." Of particular concern to Rumsfeld was the lengthening reach of ballistic missiles, which determined proliferators sought to keep the United States at arm's length and to influence neighbors. To Rumsfeld, ballistic missiles worked "without being fired; they alter behavior."[17] In this view, the ABM Treaty tied U.S. hands against asymmetric threats and missile proliferation.

For Dominators, arms control was an illusion that needed to end.[18] Reality was reflected in a commission report bearing Rumsfeld's name, which concluded that ballistic missile threats were "evolving more rapidly" than estimated by the U.S. intelligence community. Worse, "the U.S. might well have little or no warning before operational deployment" of missiles able to reach American soil.[19] Consequently, it would be far better to rely on the primacy of U.S. power than on treaties. Allied concerns over prospective missile defense deployments could largely be assuaged by determined American leadership. Moscow and Beijing would grouse, and then learn to live with missile defenses. Negative responses would be far outweighed by prospective benefits. Conciliators predicted dire consequences if the United States turned away from treaties, including strained alliances, renewed arms races, and accelerated proliferation.

The negative consequences of missile defenses are likely to come true in direct proportion to the ambitions of advocates. For example, prior to the Bush administration's withdrawal from the ABM Treaty, Daniel Gouré argued that the accord needed to be amended to "negate" a Chinese nuclear war-fighting posture and "deter Russian 'backsliding.'"[20] These were extremely ambitious goals to place on any treaty—or to pursue in the absence of treaties. Without a transformation in major power relations, ambitious U.S. missile defense deployments are likely to produce uncooperative behavior by Moscow and Beijing. Conversely, the more ambitious the deployment of U.S. missile defenses, the less likely a transformation in great power relations would become.

The Bush administration's withdrawal from the ABM Treaty mandated fresh thinking about the countervailing risks of deploying or not deploying missile defenses of varying kinds. Repetition of the old Cold War arguments for and against NMD no longer served useful purposes. Missile defenses are no longer about the wisdom or folly of maintaining safety through MAD. Instead, the utility or disutility of missile defenses must now relate to a new era of asymmetric warfare.

Rethinking Missile Defenses in Asymmetric Warfare

Saddam Hussein made the extraordinary blunder of inviting desert warfare against the United States and allied expeditionary forces. Osama bin Laden made the mistake of thinking his al-Qaeda fighters could match up well against American forces in the mountains and caves of Afghanistan. These futile exercises became object lessons in how not to fight the United States in an era of pronounced and growing U.S. conventional military supremacy. Future adversaries will try to avoid fighting the United States on Washington's terms. Like Osama bin Laden, they will engage in asymmetric warfare. After Osama's defeat, their methods are likely to be more deadly and/or harder to trace back to their source.

The Pentagon defines asymmetric warfare as "countering an adversary's strengths by focusing on its weaknesses," or leveling the playing field by using a very different set of rules of engagement against vastly superior firepower.[21] While the practice of asymmetric warfare is not new, its instruments are.

The delivery vehicles of death by unconventional means now include truck bombs, pontoon boats, container ships, subway cars, hijacked airliners, and letters. Maverick states and terrorist groups might now be able to use weapons of mass destruction in attack plans. Ballistic missiles that could deliver deadly weapons need not be of sufficient range to hit North America to sway U.S. choices; they need only reach close friends and allies of the United States, or nearby military bases in order to hamper coalition building or keep U.S. forces at a distance. In this way, the leadership of a rogue state might hope to deter the strongest nation on earth from toppling it.

The Central Intelligence Agency's National Intelligence Officer for Strategic and Nuclear Programs characterized the problem this way:

> Acquiring long-range ballistic missiles with a weapon of mass destruction will enable weaker countries to do three things that they might otherwise not be able to do: deter, constrain, and harm the United States. To achieve these objectives, the missiles need not be deployed in large numbers; even with a few weapons, these countries would judge that they had the capability to threaten at least politically significant damage to the United States or its allies. They need not be highly accurate; the ability to target a large urban area is sufficient. They need not be highly reliable, because their strategic value is derived primarily for the implicit or explicit threat of their use, not the certain outcome of such use.[22]

After the destruction of the U.S. embassies in Kenya and Tanzania, the attack of the *USS Cole* by a pontoon boat in Aden's harbor, the truck-bombing and subsequent demolition by hijacked airliners of the World Trade Center, there is widespread public understanding of the reality, challenges, and dangers of asymmetric warfare. It is far easier for rogue states to use these means than to build or acquire an ocean-spanning missile. States like North Korea, Iran, and Iraq do have shorter-range missiles, however, and they are working on extending their range. As a result, there is a strong consensus in the United States that theater missile defenses are essential. As their name implies, theater missile defenses are designed for use within a particular theater of military operations where they could counter missiles that threaten forward-deployed U.S. forces, essential military bases, friends and allies.

The Clinton administration proposed changes to the ABM Treaty to expressly permit advanced theater ballistic missile defenses. At first, these treaty amendments were strenuously opposed by the Kremlin and by many Conciliators, but subsequently negotiated. Ironically, missile defense enthusiasts opposed these amendments, since making the ABM Treaty more relevant was not what they had in mind. Instead, Dominators sought to leverage public support for theater missile defenses into the ABM Treaty's demise. If, they argued, defenses against ballistic missile attacks were necessary to protect allies, friends, forward-deployed forces, and Americans living in troubled regions, why should the U.S. government continue to forgo all such protection for its citizens living at home?

In rhetorical terms, this was an appealing argument: Protection that is offered to others should not be denied to U.S. citizens. In strategic and political terms, the answer was not so simple. The threats posed by ocean-spanning missiles were very low, while those generated by shorter-range missiles were high. Russia still maintained many intercontinental ballistic missiles, but was very unlikely to use them unless there were a breakdown in the Kremlin's command and control system. China was slowly increasing its capabilities in this area, but it, too, would face a devastating response-in-kind to a missile attack on U.S. soil. A few worrisome states were ostensibly developing space launch capabilities that could also be used as long-distance weapon carriers. But would they be so crazed as to attack America in this way—unless attacked first by U.S. forces?

Dominators argued that the United States might well find it necessary some day to use force against rogue states possessing long-range ballistic missiles. Conciliators argued that the value of homeland defense against such missiles depended on whether prospective benefits exceeded downside risks. Where does NMD fit in an age of truck bombs and anthrax-laced letters? A poll of perceived national concerns and priorities taken at the outset of President George W. Bush's administration ranked the deployment of a national missile defense as the eighteenth priority out of twenty issues, bracketed between strengthening gun control laws and reforming the campaign finance system.[23]

Similarly, the Joint Chiefs of Staff placed globe-spanning missiles last in terms of the hierarchy of threats facing U.S. troops and citizens, but first in terms of potential damage to vital national interests. The Joint Chiefs worried more about involvement in humanitarian crises, the war on drugs, peacekeeping operations, regional conflicts and internal instability, terrorist attacks on the United States, and cyberwar than strategic missile attacks.[24] Public views generally reflected these priorities, favoring missile defenses, but not if this meant tearing up treaties.[25] The Bush administration dealt decisively with this duality by withdrawal from the ABM Treaty in the context of a war against terrorism claiming—notwithstanding the Clinton administration's treaty modifications expressly permitting advanced theater missile defenses—that the ABM Treaty precluded effective missile defenses against rogue states.[26]

Classical Arms Control and Deterrence Theory Revisited

In the first decade after the demise of the Soviet Union, Conciliators continued to base their opposition to missile defenses on "classical" arms control theories of arms race and crisis stability. In classical arms control theory, arms race instability results when one side deploys defenses, and then another side deploys compensating offenses, leading to what former Secretary of Defense Robert McNamara and others called the action–reaction syndrome.[27] President Jimmy Carter's arms control negotiator, Paul C. Warnke, likened this phenomenon to a treadmill that neither party could get off, resulting in the amassing of nuclear weapons "in quantities and varieties inexplicable to any military basis."[28]

While arms control theorists and practitioners were skeptical about missile defenses, they could not entirely reject them. After all, the 1972 ABM Treaty permitted 200 missile interceptors, a number subsequently halved in 1974 by the Nixon administration. Limited missile defenses were not destabilizing, as Carl Kaysen wrote, as long as they did not reduce "in any important way" one side's capability to inflict "unacceptable damage" on the other in a retaliatory strike.[29] Limited defenses therefore could be accommodated in Cold War-era treaties; defenses to achieve strategic superiority could not.

In classical arms control reasoning, the architecture and extent of missile defenses mattered during the Cold War because they could prompt crisis instability, making it more likely that one of the two scorpions in the bottle would strike first during periods of excruciating tension. In 1961, Thomas C. Schelling and Morton H. Halperin wrote, "The most mischievous character of today's strategic weapons is that they may provide an enormous advantage, in the event that war occurs, to the side that starts it."[30] "The essential criterion for equilibrium," as Glenn Snyder noted, "is mutual capacity to inflict intolerable damage in retaliation."[31] If the deployment of missile defenses alongside strategic offenses accentuated perceptions of advantage or disadvantage, they could also accentuate danger and risk in crises.

How do these postulates of arms race and crisis stability relate to the shift from Cold War to asymmetric warfare? To begin with, worst-case projections of arms racing and instability no longer appear relevant. While Russia and China would seek to compensate for U.S. deployments of national missile defenses, their ability or interest to engage in an arms race appear unlikely. Even the deployment of thick national missile defenses by the United States would not stimulate a new Russian nuclear buildup, since the Kremlin is unlikely to devote the resources required to replace Soviet-era warheads and strategic forces facing block obsolescence.

A decade and more hence, when the Kremlin could begin to reverse the decline in its deployed nuclear forces, it might resort to an arms buildup if Dominators seek to devalue Russia's deterrent through defenses. The Kremlin could also choose other options to counter these designs, since asymmetric warfare need not be confined to small states or terrorist groups. While Moscow's course over the next decade cannot be confidently predicted, it is nonetheless reasonably clear that, in the first ten–fifteen years of the twenty-first century, arms racing by Moscow is not in the cards.

Alternatively, if the United States seeks an architecture for missile defenses that does not devalue Moscow's deterrent, the Kremlin would have one less reason to reverse the steep decline in its nuclear forces. Other factors could point in the opposite direction. The conventional imbalance of U.S. and Russian forces would weigh heavily on Moscow's choices. The future military potential and cohesion of NATO, as well as the extent of its expansion eastward would also have a direct bearing on the Kremlin's nuclear force posture, as would the salience future U.S. administrations give to nuclear weapons. Under some circumstances, it is conceivable that the Kremlin would eventually seek to reverse the decline in its nuclear capabilities even if U.S. national missile defense deployments are unthreatening. Domestic political, bureaucratic, and institutional constituencies could again impel Russia's leaders to increase reliance on nuclear forces to stimulate employment, for reasons of status, or to influence nearby states.

Above all, Russia's future nuclear force requirements would depend on whether relations between Washington and Moscow are largely cooperative or competitive. The more Dominators succeed in sidelining treaties, weaponizing space, and pursuing steps perceived by the Kremlin as a devaluation of its deterrent, the more Moscow will seek refuge in asymmetric responses. One predictable response would be to strengthen ties with China. Another would be to seek low-cost counters to U.S. space warfare capabilities. Still another would be to explore and deploy more sophisticated penetration aids atop its missiles to foil U.S. defenses. Kremlin officials will do what is necessary to maintain at least a minimal deterrent capability against the United States. In private discussion, Russian strategic analysts express concern that asymmetries in nuclear offense and missile defense would provide Washington with troubling leverage over Moscow's choices. Devaluation—not negation—of Russia's strategic posture is what most worries Moscow's strategic analysts.

Beijing, on the other hand, worries about negation. China possesses antiquated conventional forces, limited power projection capabilities, and a minimal, vulnerable nuclear deterrent. Beijing is now devoting far greater resources to address its military vulnerabilities and to respond to prospective missile defense deployments by the United States, but it faces technical challenges that Russia has mastered, such as the techniques needed to deploy multiple warheads atop mobile missiles.[32] Some Dominators are eager to run this race, believing that the United States could win a direct offense–defense interaction with China, or win indirectly by accelerating the economic demise of another communist megastate. As Eliot A. Cohen has written, "NMD will make sense only if it offers protection not only against the odd missile from North Korea, Iraq, or Iran, but against America's main rival— China."[33] Kim Holmes concurs, arguing:

> The addition of a U.S. missile defense system would not give a first-strike capability against China since, in reality, it already has one. However, the inclusion of Taiwan under a U.S. global protection system would degrade China's capability to intimidate Taiwan. … [I]t could, because of China's relatively small ICBM force, effectively neutralize China's nuclear capability to threaten the U.S. mainland directly if Washington should ever come to Taiwan's aid in the event of an attack.[34]

China's strategic modernization efforts do not fit into the classical arms control construct of arms racing. During the Cold War, the United States and the Soviet Union habitually produced several hundred globe-spanning missiles annually, as well as comparable numbers of new nuclear weapons.[35] China's projected nuclear buildup is of a far different order of magnitude. The U.S. intelligence community predicts that China would deploy, on average, only about six intercontinental ballistic missiles annually over the next fifteen years.[36] Some China watchers estimate that Beijing will raise its production rate to perhaps ten to twelve intercontinental ballistic missiles per year.[37] It seems unlikely that China's leadership would submit to perceived U.S. efforts to negate its deterrent. Beijing's options in response include increasing its nuclear capacity to strike U.S. bases and allies along its periphery, developing space warfare capabilities, devoting greater resources to further expand its ocean-spanning missile forces, and seeking to induce Russia to part with the technology required to place multiple warheads atop its new mobile missiles.

These rejoinders would not constitute arms racing by Cold War standards. Beijing has many compelling reasons to avoid the costs and regional repercussions of a high-octane arms race—including the Soviet example, which China's leaders are determined not to emulate. Nonetheless, even modest increases in China's nuclear capabilities could still have cascade effects along its periphery, as discussed in Chapter 5. If one assumes that

Beijing is determined to avoid nuclear blackmail in the future—an assumption that is widely held by those who study China—then the extent of the cascade depends in large measure upon the extent to which Dominators override Conciliators in the United States.

If the classical arms control concern of arms racing is overdrawn in an era of asymmetric warfare, what about the conundrum of instability in crisis situations? Would missile defenses designed and sized to threaten a major power's nuclear deterrent prompt a momentous crossing of the nuclear threshold? Arms control theory holds that, as Bernard Brodie observed, "Stability is achieved when each nation believes that the strategic advantage of striking first is overshadowed by the tremendous cost of doing so."[38] To be sure, the introduction of U.S. missile defenses would worry Moscow and, to a greater extent, Beijing. But would NMD deployments make any easier or more likely fateful decisions by Russian or Chinese leaders to cross this Rubicon?

Nuclear powers have not hesitated to use conventional firepower on a number of occasions when the presumed risks were low. They have also engaged in risky uses of military force when national security interests were presumed to be high, and they have engaged in proxy wars against other nuclear powers. There have even been two occasions—the Soviet–Chinese clash along the Ussuri River in 1969 and the 1999 Indian–Pakistani high-altitude war in Kashmir—when states possessing nuclear weapons engaged in direct conventional clashes. The most well documented and nerve-wracking case of contemplated nuclear weapons' use remains, of course, the Cuban missile crisis.

In this case, national leaders exercised extreme care not to cross the nuclear threshold. To do so in any circumstance other than a matter of the most extreme national emergency would result in unimaginable loss for less than absolutely necessary reasons. In this context, Nikita Khrushchev once said, "No sound-minded man would start a war."[39] Another veteran of the Cuban missile crisis, McGeorge Bundy, arrived at precisely the same conclusion: "In light of the certain prospect of retaliation there has been literally no chance at all that any sane political authority, in either the United States or the Soviet Union, would consciously choose to start a nuclear war." In the real world of political leaders, Bundy added, "a decision that would bring even one hydrogen bomb on one city of one's own country would be recognized in advance as a catastrophic blunder ... Political leaders, whether here or in Russia, are cut from a very different mold than strategic planners. They see cities and people as part of what they are trying to help—not as targets."[40]

How much do the harrowing experiences of the Cold War, which did not result in nuclear weapons' use, shed light on crisis stability considerations in asymmetric warfare? A rogue state leadership that possesses weapons of mass destruction, facing expulsion or worse at the hands of U.S. expeditionary forces, might well resort to their use. The acquisition of weapons of mass destruction could have been viewed, in part, as an insurance policy against this eventuality. An embittered leader might conclude that there was nothing to lose for exacting revenge on the United States. But what about major powers with much to lose that are not facing the prospect of a conventional war against superior U.S. forces? It is one thing to launch a diplomatic offensive; it is something else entirely to launch a nuclear-tipped missile. In the depths of a crisis, would Russia or China be more inclined to use nuclear weapons because of the deployment of U.S. missile defenses?

In some instances, the deployment of theater missile defenses could make the use of force less likely if, as a result, the belligerent state backs off or if the resolve of a threatened ally or friend of the United States is strengthened. Conversely, missile defense deployments could sour relations between Washington and Moscow or Beijing, coloring the political context of a future crisis, perhaps making it more intense and harder to resolve. Whatever the net effect of missile defense deployments, would an agonizing decision to cross the nuclear threshold become any easier, or more likely, for the leadership of a major power?

Any future military confrontation between the United States and Russia or China, especially one that could place at risk Russian or Chinese supreme national interests, would position leaders at the knife's edge of nuclear deterrence theory. To make the case that U.S. missile defense deployments would prompt a dreaded crossing of the nuclear threshold by a deliberate leadership decision, one would first have to assume extraordinarily reckless behavior that would threaten the supreme national interests of a major power. Second, one would need to assume either extreme confidence or fear in the efficacy of missile defenses.

For some deterrence theorists, such as Kenneth Waltz, this combination of circumstances would never occur. First, Waltz presumes that offsetting nuclear weapons are stabilizing: "Because catastrophic outcomes of nuclear exchanges are easy to imagine, leaders of states will shrink in horror from initiating them."[41] Second, Waltz contends that defenses against nuclear weapons are ineffective: "That a perfect defense against nuclear weapons could be deployed and sustained is inconceivable. This is so for two reasons: (1) it is impossible, and (2) if it were possible, it wouldn't last."[42]

Waltz and his fellow "realists" disagree completely with classical arms control theorists about the value of nuclear weapons, but both schools agree on Waltz's contention that missile defenses will fail. Nonetheless, many arms controllers argued during the Cold War that penetrable missile defenses could still be destabilizing if they prompted actions to guard against worst cases. Consequently, Richard L. Garwin argued that the Nixon administration's plans for missile defenses were unwise because "large investments in strategic forces may be provoked by a very small ABM system."[43] The first director of the U.S. Arms Control and Disarmament Agency, William Foster, made the classical case for crisis instability associated with missile defenses, concluding that, "A power confronting an adversary with a large-scale BMD might in a crisis situation feel impelled to strike first because a sudden, massive first strike with unimpaired offensive forces would have a better chance of penetrating missile defenses than would a retaliatory strike with a partially destroyed offensive force." Not everyone in the arms control community concurred with this assessment. During the debate over President Ronald Reagan's Strategic Defense Initiative (SDI), George Rathjens and Jack Ruina concluded otherwise, asserting that crisis instability fears "can be almost totally discounted given the offense-dominant nature of nuclear weapons, and the technical realities facing strategic defenses."[44]

If the addition of missile defenses into the strategic equation was unlikely to prompt a crossing of the nuclear threshold during an intense, Cold War crisis, would this also be true in an era of asymmetric warfare? Would the addition of missile defenses to U.S. nuclear and conventional military dominance make a major power more likely to resort to the first use of nuclear weapons? Cold reason suggests that a major power far weaker than the United States would seek other means of retribution if its national security interests were threatened. While breakdowns in command and control cannot be discounted in deep crisis, the deliberate use of nuclear weapons by a major power not threatened with regime change appears remote.

Some deterrence theorists have suggested that, while offsetting nuclear capabilities are likely to make a central strategic war remote, they could prompt the use of violence at lower levels. Glenn Snyder and Robert Jervis mapped this terrain, finding in it the "stability–instability paradox."[45] According to Jervis, "[I]f an uncontrolled war would lead to mutual destruction, then neither side would ever start one. But this very stability allows either side to use limited violence because the other's threat to respond by all-out retaliation cannot be very credible."[46] In this view, stability is far from assured, and a resort to violence remains a real possibility. Nonetheless, the consequences of a deliberate leadership decision to cross the nuclear threshold would be so devastating as to be irrational and unlikely. These dynamics would seem equally, if not more applicable to asymmetric warfare than was the case during the Cold War.

Another school of deterrence theorists argues that any future crossing of the nuclear threshold is most likely to result from organizational, bureaucratic, or institutional mishaps, rather than a calculated act of national policy. In this view, aptly summarized by Bruce Blair, nuclear postures are "accidents waiting to happen."[47] After reviewing a series of harrowing Cold War cases, Scott Sagan has concluded that, "Nuclear weapons may have made *deliberate* war less likely, but the complex and tightly coupled nuclear arsenals we have constructed has simultaneously made *accidental* war more likely."[48] This school of deterrence theorists give added meaning to the stability–instability paradox.

Analytical calculations of deterrence theory, crisis stability, and missile defenses could play out over the Taiwan issue. Beijing believes it must have a credible nuclear deterrent in the event of a future crisis across the Taiwan Strait, while Washington believes it must have effective theater missile defenses to counter Chinese coercive missile diplomacy. National missile defenses could also have some political or military utility in the event of a clash over Taiwan. Indeed, Dominators who seek national missile defenses sufficiently sized to negate the Chinese nuclear deterrent or to provide escalation dominance in a crisis appear to have this contingency in mind. Many China watchers have concluded that Beijing would use military force if Taipei declares or is moving inexorably toward independence.[49]

In this troubling case, would nuclear deterrence be more likely to break down, deliberately or inadvertently, because of the introduction of U.S. missile defenses? On the American side of the equation, would the faith of a future U.S. president in deployed national missile defenses be so great as to prompt actions so provocative that they could push a confrontation across this radioactive threshold? Even if Dominators are given significant leeway, it seems most unlikely that a future U.S. president could count on the impenetrability of theater and national missile shields. President John F. Kennedy, who enjoyed nuclear superiority over the Soviet Union during the 1962 Cuban missile crisis, still rejected the counsel of those who wished to conduct pre-emptive strikes that could lead to a crossing of the nuclear threshold. Nonetheless, Kennedy authorized a naval embargo around Cuba, and appeared quite willing to commit U.S. conventional forces if the crisis erupted into conflict.

Similarly, one can readily imagine a future U.S. president, despite enjoying conventional and nuclear superiority, being unwilling to count on a leakproof missile defense umbrella in any confrontation with China over Taiwan. Even if China's small nuclear deterrent remained vulnerable to pre-emption by U.S. conventional and nuclear forces, the thought of losing a single American city in a retaliatory strike would be a powerful inhibiting factor. The acknowledgment of vulnerability to nuclear danger in deep crisis, however, does not translate into passivity when stakes are high. As in the case of the Cuban missile crisis, one can well imagine that a future president would place U.S. forces in harm's way in a confrontation across the Taiwan Strait. If Beijing takes military action against Taiwan, Washington is likely to enter this dangerous fray, while seeking to avoid military actions that could lead to the use of nuclear weapons by China.

What about the other side of this equation? Would China be more likely to cross the nuclear threshold in a Taiwan crisis because of U.S. missile defenses? As long as Washington refrains from crossing China's presumed "red lines"—and as long as Washington understands where these critical thresholds lie—Beijing has powerful incentives to avoid crossing the nuclear threshold. The United States maintains overwhelming nuclear and conventional superiority over China. A first strike by Chinese strategic nuclear forces against the only targets Beijing's intercontinental ballistic missiles could reliably hit—urban areas—would result in devastating retaliation.

This brief exposition does not do justice to the complexities inherent in the event of a future confrontation over Taiwan, including the role of U.S. misperception with regard to Beijing's tolerances. While there is much we cannot foresee in the event of another Taiwan crisis, the most salient conclusion we might reasonably draw from this scenario—besides the inherent dangers of another confrontation—is the degree of caution over crossing the nuclear threshold that U.S. and Chinese leaders are likely to exhibit. In a possible clash with the United States, China's leaders must ask whether it is worth risking the mainland in order not to lose Taiwan. A long unconventional war would remain a better outcome for Beijing's leadership than a short nuclear exchange. This calculation would reinforce the People's Liberation Army (PLA) nuclear doctrine that values nuclear weapons as a counter to U.S. nuclear threats, not as a means to escalate a conflict.[50] As long as Beijing's command and control over its nuclear forces holds, and as long as Washington refrains from escalatory actions, the nuclear threshold is likely to remain extremely high in a crisis over Taiwan.

Offsetting nuclear capabilities make crises more harrowing, but missile defenses do not make them inherently more dangerous, as long as each side perceives that it retains the ability to destroy what the other holds dear. Thus, in a U.S.–Chinese context, Washington's missile defenses would increase Beijing's nuclear arsenal and exacerbate tensions, but not lower the nuclear threshold. A deliberate, top-down decision to cross the nuclear threshold for the first time since 1945 would be no easier for China than for any other powerful state.

The most critical assumptions here are that the United States understands Beijing's tolerances and will avoid dangerous "red lines," that there will be no break down of command and control, and that popular pressures over Taiwan would not push the Chinese leadership across the nuclear threshold. Popular pressures did not have this effect on presidents Truman, Eisenhower, and Johnson, who never resorted to nuclear weapons' use while bogged down in unpopular wars. But what about the key assumption that command and control will hold?

The "Murphy's Law" school of deterrence theory argues that dangerous, accident-prone weapons could create terrible events at any time, and that inadvertent, accidental, or unauthorized use are especially worrisome in crisis or in conflict. The overlay of missile defenses sized to devalue or negate the nuclear deterrent of a major power would presumably force that adversary to heighten the readiness of its deterrent. In so doing, Washington could inadvertently trigger Murphy's Law in a confrontation with China. On the other hand, Communist China, like the Soviet Union, maintains redundant, reliable command and control over its nuclear forces. If China implodes like the Soviet Union, then command and control concerns would obviously become far more worrisome.

The point of this analytical excursion is not to promote brinksmanship over the Taiwan question, but to reassess the application of classical arms control and deterrence theory to a new era of asymmetric warfare. The shadow of nuclear weapons would certainly darken any clash between the United States and China over Taiwan. In any crisis over stakes this high, effective diplomacy would be far more consequential than deployed missile defenses. And if diplomacy fails, conventional military calculations are likely to remain paramount.

Classical arms control theory has some validity in asymmetric warfare, but a number of qualifications are now in order. To begin with, missile defense deployments are likely to trigger compensating steps, but these will fall well below the traditional meaning of an arms race. Classical arms control concerns that missile defense deployments could facilitate a decision by a major power to cross the nuclear threshold appear overdrawn in the context of great disparities in conventional military and strategic power. Considerations of arms race stability also need rethinking. Even the deployment of missile defenses sized to devalue or negate the nuclear deterrents of major powers are unlikely over the next decade or more to generate a Cold War-type arms competition. Ill-advised missile defenses could, nonetheless, generate a host of negative consequences in bilateral relations.

While the Kremlin would not be able to build up its nuclear forces over the next ten–fifteen years in response to U.S. missile defenses, it could try to maintain dangerously aging nuclear forces in the field. Aging solid-fueled missiles or poorly maintained aircraft and submarines could have catastrophic accidents that could result in the release of radioactive material. Alternatively, Russia could partly seek to counter U.S. missile defenses by maintaining dangerous operational practices for its nuclear forces, especially by retaining strategic forces on alert.

A decade after the end of the Cold War, the Kremlin still maintained more than 3,000 warheads on globe-spanning missiles, ready to fire. (The Clinton administration maintained 2,000 warheads on alert.)[51] The command and control over Russian nuclear forces is less robust and reliable than was previously the case. There are many good reasons to work with the Kremlin to reduce the alert rate of its nuclear forces. This would be much harder to do if the United States deploys a combination of missile defenses and strategic offensive capabilities that sow doubt in the Kremlin about the viability of its nuclear deterrent.

Missile defense deployments that devalue or negate the Russian and Chinese nuclear deterrents could have many other deleterious consequences. They could freeze U.S. relations with China, prompt greater strategic cooperation between Moscow and Beijing, and less cooperation from both capitals on proliferation concerns. Even modest increases in China's nuclear forces as a result of U.S. missile defense deployments could accelerate cascade effects around its periphery.

Weighing Countervailing Risks

The obvious risks associated with U.S. deployments of ballistic missile defenses must be weighted against the countervailing risks associated with not deploying defenses. Allies and friends that feel threatened by missiles will look for other options if help is not forthcoming from the United States. As a consequence, U.S. restraint could contribute to proliferation, just as American deployments of missile defenses could produce a similar result. In the event of a regional conflict involving missile attacks, the absence of effective missile defenses could have profound consequences, but deployments are no guarantee against missile volleys, as was evident in the 1991 Gulf War against Saddam Hussein.

How might countervailing risks be weighed? One set of risks relates to the design and scope of ballistic missile defenses. The negative consequences associated with national missile defense deployments are quite likely to grow in proportion to U.S. deployments. The more Washington seeks to devalue or negate the nuclear deterrents of Russia and China, the more likely these countries are to resist U.S. leverage. Another set of risks is keyed to American restraint, even from deploying minimal national missile defenses against a rogue state threat.

One might begin with a simple exercise of identifying developments that could have far more deleterious consequences for proliferation or for national and regional security than would the minimal deployment of missile defenses. For example, the launch of a single ballistic missile carrying a weapon of mass destruction would be a seminal event. If that ballistic missile were aimed at the United States and the detonation occurred on American soil, the immediate devastation and long-term effects would be compounded by recriminations over the absence of an effective homeland defense. The further demise of treaty regimes would surely follow, creating new proliferation impulses in several regions. Surely, the negative consequences resulting from the use of a single ballistic missile carrying a weapon of mass destruction could far exceed the likely repercussions associated with minimal national missile defense deployments.

A deadly missile attack on U.S. soil could result from unauthorized actions abetted by a breakdown of command and control, a deliberate or desperate decision on the part of a national leader, or conceivably by a terrorist group with successful purchasing power. While the probability of each of these events is low, none can be discounted. After all, other low-probability, highly damaging events have occurred throughout modern history. Unpleasant surprises, which are so evident in all walks of life as well as in international relations, might also apply to ballistic missiles carrying deadly weapons.

The probability of a ballistic missile launch carrying a weapon of mass destruction is far greater in tense regions of the globe where U.S. friends and allies reside. If just one such ballistic missile causes heavy loss of life and lasting damage, it would have far-reaching consequences for proliferation, alliance ties, and regional security. This catastrophe would doubtless trigger new or accelerated efforts to produce ballistic missiles and weapons of mass destruction, as well as missile defense programs to counter heightened threats.

Negative consequences of this magnitude could also be triggered by other dreadful events. Any renewed crossing of the nuclear threshold after more than fifty years of restraint, by whatever means of delivery, would have profoundly negative consequences. More broadly speaking, new instances of chemical and/or biological weapons' use would increase the salience and acquisition of such weapons while diminishing existing barriers against subsequent use. Depending on the extent, location, and user(s) of weapons of mass destruction, the fabric of non-proliferation and disarmament treaties would either be weakened greatly or unravel completely. If victimized states happen to be allies of the United States, proliferation consequences could be compounded by loosened alliance ties. States in troubled regions that have relied upon treaties and alliance protection in lieu of their own weapons of mass destruction and missile programs would certainly think twice about continued abstinence.

Nuclear proliferation in the Persian Gulf region would also have profoundly negative consequences. Iran and Iraq have many reasons to acquire weapons of mass destruction and missiles of increased range: to counter each other's efforts, to counter American and Israeli power projection capabilities, and to become the pre-eminent power in the Gulf region. The acquisition of nuclear weapons by one or both states, following on the heels of the 1998 nuclear tests in South Asia, would generate extensive damage to non-proliferation regimes and norms. Proliferation by Iran and Iraq would reverberate in Israel, Egypt, Saudi Arabia, and elsewhere in the Middle East. In contrast, the negative repercussions associated with U.S. deployments of missile defenses keyed to rogue states would appear to be rather modest.

The use of weapons of mass destruction by terrorist groups in the Middle East or in other regions would have profoundly negative consequences. If and when terrorists acquire and use super-toxic weapons, proliferation problems would take on a whole new dimension. Treaty regimes would consequently lose considerable relevance. In addition, renewed outbreaks of conventional conflict in the Middle East, Persian Gulf, and along China's periphery could have negative consequences far beyond those generated by limited national missile defense programs. If these conflicts prompt the further use of conventionally armed ballistic missiles to demoralize city dwellers, missile defenses as well as new missile programs would receive a considerable boost.

Other worrisome scenarios could be added to this list. The leakage of weapons of mass destruction or deadly materials from Russia could destabilize regions, directly threaten U.S. national security, and create escalatory spirals in tense regions. Even in the absence of such dramatic events, creeping proliferation in troubled regions could lead to a hedging of national bets that hollows out non-proliferation treaties. Additional proliferation along the periphery of Asia, in the Middle East, and the Persian Gulf could generate negative consequences that far exceed those associated with limited national missile defense deployments.

In addition, the resumption of deeply strained relations between the United States and Russia and/or China could have grave consequences for proliferation and regional security. Factors disconnected from national missile defenses could also produce these negative effects, such as a conflict between Taiwan and the mainland. In the event of a deep freeze in U.S. relations with Russia and/or China, Washington might expect little help on proliferation emanating from a state friendly to Moscow or Beijing. Regional crises or conflicts could become harder to resolve, and strengthening measures for non-proliferation regimes would become more remote. In sum, many plausible scenarios could produce negative consequences that far exceed those generated by minimal national missile defense deployments.

Missile Defenses and Risk Reduction

Most of the threats listed above fall most heavily on America's friends and allies in tense regions where short-range ballistic missiles are prevalent and proliferation has already begun. In contrast, the threat that a ballistic missile carrying a weapon of mass destruction would fall on the fifty American states is very low. This exercise suggests that a compelling case can be made for theater missile defense deployments in strategically sensitive areas where U.S. allies and friends face growing threats. While great care must be exercised in the architecture chosen for theater missile defenses to address national sensitivities as well as neighboring threats, well-designed, forward-deployed theater missile defenses could alleviate allied concerns, signal U.S. resolve for friends in need, and possibly intercept missiles carrying lethal weapons. The downside risks of having forward-deployed theater missile defenses near or in troubled regions are far lower than the risks of abstention.

How, then, might Washington assess the countervailing risks associated with national missile defenses? While the likelihood of a globe-spanning ballistic missile attack on U.S. soil is very low, its consequences are very high. At the same time, the political, diplomatic, and opportunity costs of national missile defense deployments could be substantial or modest, depending on how much of an insurance policy Washington wishes to buy. The cost-benefit calculus surrounding NMD rests, in addition, on whether two slippery slopes often associated with missile defenses can be avoided.

The first slippery slope is situated on the assumption that even limited NMD leads inexorably to expanded deployments. The second slippery slope assumes that missile defense plans eventually and inexorably lead to the weaponization of space. Many Conciliators assume that both slippery slopes are quite likely. Their view is shared by Dominators who contend that the United States could remain at least one step ahead of adversarial reactions. Much is therefore riding on whether limited NMD deployments inevitably lead to steep slippery slopes, or whether safety ledges could be found to brake the momentum of deployments. If the two slippery slopes are real, then even minimal NMD would pose far reaching, negative consequences. If the assumption of slippery slopes is faulty, it is incumbent upon Conciliators to identify safety ledges and to hold this ground.

Both of these slippery slopes were notably avoided during the Cold War. The 200 interceptors permitted under the ABM Treaty were never deployed. After building 100, President Gerald R. Ford (and his Secretary of Defense, Donald H. Rumsfeld) recognized that this protection was neither cost-effective nor essential. After all, maintaining 100 interceptors would, at maximum effectiveness, have defended only 10 percent or less of the U.S. land-based missile force. Congressional majorities were also inclined to dismantle these interceptors, even though the Kremlin maintained a similarly modest deployment around Moscow. During the Cold War, the possession of thousands of warheads on globe-spanning missiles and bombers substituted for national missile defenses. Nor was there a perceived need to defend against lesser threats. A breakdown in Soviet command and control, for example, seemed inconceivable.

In matters of national missile defense, as Donald G. Brennan argued during the Safeguard debate, it was possible to remain "a little bit pregnant." On matters of national protection against nuclear danger, there was simply no strong domestic push for more or better protection, as was amply evident from the shrinking of U.S. funding and deployments of both air and civil defenses.[52] In other words, during the Cold War, the slippery slope applied to offensive nuclear forces, not national missile defenses. Nuclear offense bred more offense, while ambitious plans for national missile defenses were progressively downsized.

Nor was a slippery slope in evidence during the Cold War regarding the weaponization of space. True, space was used for many military purposes, and both countries tested anti-satellite weapons in an episodic and minimal way. Neither superpower, however, deployed weapons in space, and the occasional impulse to do so—most notably President Ronald Reagan's SDI—was met with formidable political, diplomatic, technical and budgetary roadblocks. For a variety of reasons, public opinion remained very protective of outer space. This barrier will again be tested in an era of asymmetric warfare, when Washington views space as a force multiplier and when weaker capitals view it as a way to neutralize U.S. power. Militating against these impulses is the far greater commercial utilization of space than was the case during the Cold War. Global commerce is, to put it mildly, incompatible with space warfare.

The slippery slopes often associated with NMD deployments are therefore not as slippery nor as steep as often suggested. The greater the ambitions that missile defense enthusiasts have, the more they are likely to encounter friction at home and abroad. To avoid friction in conjunction with his decision to withdraw from the ABM Treaty, President Bush's stated ambitions were muted.

The proffered reason for this decision was extremely limited—to help defend the United States against terror attacks utilizing ballistic missiles. If this were the only rationale for NMD, deployments would remain minimal. If more ambitious plans are waiting in the wings, they would become apparent over time.

Conciliators and Dominators have more rounds to fight over missile defenses. In principle, however, thin national missile defenses need not lead inexorably to thick missile deployments. The downside risks of deploying NMD could be minimized if three conditions are met. First, by sizing and structuring missile defenses to counter proliferation threats rather than to devalue or negate the Russian and Chinese nuclear deterrents. Second, by pursuing missile defenses through a process of consultation and transparency. This course of action is now essential since the safety mechanism of managing deployments within a process of treaty adaptation rather than demolition was unilaterally abandoned by the Bush administration. Third, by avoiding the weaponization of space, both by means of terrestrially based anti-satellite weapons or space-based programs. If these three key boundaries are honored, the chances of limiting downside associated with NMD deployments increase. If any of these boundaries are crossed, the management of downside risks will become problematic. Relations between Washington and both Moscow and Beijing will become strained, proliferation problems will grow more acute, coalition building against proliferation threats will become harder, and the demise of non-proliferation treaties will become more likely.

CHAPTER 5

Missile Defense and the Asian Cascade

With the end of the Cold War, Asia has replaced Europe as the region most likely to be roiled by prospective U.S. missile defense deployments. While European capitals remain uncomfortable with American impulses to construct a national missile shield, these concerns pale in comparison to the 1980s, when Moscow employed intense coercive diplomacy and military bluster trying to block President Ronald Reagan's Strategic Defense Initiative (SDI). Back then, hundreds of thousands of street demonstrators rallied across Europe against the "Star Wars" program. In contrast, President George W. Bush's decisions to withdraw from the Anti-Ballistic Missile Treaty and fast-track national missile defenses produced a muted response in Europe. This time around, Moscow's diplomatic and military options were quite limited, with the Kremlin's defense budget in 2002 barely one-twelfth that of the United States. If European misgivings rise again, the most likely cause will be overreaching by Washington rather than posturing by Moscow.

Washington's missile defense decisions now matter far more around the periphery of Asia and along its most consequential fault lines. Abstract debates in European capitals over the utility or disutility of missile defenses have concrete meaning for Beijing, Taipei, Tokyo, New Delhi, Islamabad, Seoul, and Pyongyang. Taipei views missile defense deployments as an opportunity to reconnect with the U.S. military establishment and as a symbolic counter to China's missile build up. Beijing is the most vocal opponent of ballistic missile defenses and, unlike Moscow, has the capacity to increase its nuclear capabilities in reaction to U.S. programs. New Delhi does not oppose U.S. missile defense plans, hoping to solidify military and diplomatic ties to Washington. Privately, however, Indian officials worry about the wisdom of Washington's moves and Beijing's likely reactions to them, including renewed missile or nuclear assistance to Pakistan. Islamabad is plainly concerned about military technology transfers between India and the United States, and has lined up with China in opposition to ballistic missile defenses. Tokyo has mixed emotions, worrying both about U.S. belligerency and Beijing's growing arsenal of theater ballistic missiles. Japanese concerns shift seamlessly between not being enmeshed in unwise American policies and not being properly defended by Washington. A thaw between Seoul and Pyongyang depends in good measure on the outcome of U.S. diplomacy and missile defense deployments.

India, Pakistan, and China all have near-term, growing nuclear potential, in contrast to the Russian Federation, whose nuclear capabilities will be trending downwards over the next ten–fifteen years. In addition, Beijing, New Delhi, and Islamabad all have new and malleable strategic doctrines. Their missile and nuclear interactions could result in shifts from minimal to open-ended requirements for nuclear deterrence. Consequently, U.S. missile defense deployments and transfers could prompt cascading military requirements in China and around the periphery of Asia. Cascade effects could include accelerated growth in nuclear stockpiles, missile inventories, and conventional military capabilities.

In some ways, missile defenses appear to be like nuclear weapons. Their military utility is likely to be questionable in times of war. Even so, missile defenses, like nuclear weapons, are likely to have very high political salience. And like nuclear weapons, missile defenses could have either political utility or disutility, depending on how others react to them. The political salience and presumed utility of nuclear weapons remain high even though they have not been used on the battlefield in over five decades. This prolonged period of non-use could reflect questionable military utility or the efficacy of nuclear deterrence. Either way, political dimensions dominate. Even in the absence of battlefield use, every nuclear weapon test, every flight test of a missile designed to carry nuclear weapons, and every nuclear modernization program sends powerful messages to neighbors and potential adversaries. States on the receiving end of these messages can react quietly, seek the shelter of powerful allies, or respond in kind.

These dynamics could also apply to missile defenses, albeit with important variations. Theater missile defenses are likely to be deployed on the battlefield, even though they could be overwhelmed by large inventories of short-range ballistic missiles, such as those possessed by China and North

Korea. Similarly, national missile defenses cannot be relied upon, but they have drawn considerable interest. The political salience of missile defenses, both national and theater, is extremely high in Asia. Washington's decisions regarding missile defenses could improve some bilateral ties, while causing significant deterioration in others. Missile defense deployments or transfers in Asia could cause serious spikes in regional tensions or help defuse crises. Few U.S. defense modernization programs have more varied political ramifications than missile defenses.

Asian Triangulation

With the demise of the Soviet Union, nuclear signaling has shifted to Asia, becoming most pronounced in triangular interactions among China, India, and Pakistan. While other nations were signing and ratifying the Comprehensive Test Ban Treaty, India and Pakistan tested nuclear weapons. Prior to the Treaty's completion, China carried out a hurried and perhaps incomplete series of tests. All three states have active production lines for short-, medium-, and intermediate-range ballistic missiles. The testing of nuclear weapons and ballistic missiles demonstrates national resolve for these countries, whose modern history includes periods of humbling subservience. Testing demonstrates that Beijing, New Delhi, and Islamabad will not accept dictation. Nor will they seek refuge in formal alliances. Leaders in all three countries view nuclear weapons and missiles as instruments of independence, power, status, and protection against stronger competitors.

Consequently, China, India, and Pakistan are enmeshed in a three-cornered interaction that will not be easy to stabilize. It was hard enough during the Cold War to maintain strategic stability in a two-power equation, when both Washington and Moscow acknowledged that stability required acceptance of rough numerical parity, meaningful changes in the nuclear balance were readily observable, both superpowers acknowledged the need for intrusive monitoring, and when the implementation of treaty obligations was verifiable. Southern Asia presents a far more complex model. Leaders in Beijing, New Delhi, and Islamabad all say that minimum deterrence will serve as their guide, and that they will avoid the competitive drives leading to ever-larger nuclear arsenals. But national leaders in all three countries have also acknowledged that deterrence is not a static concept. The requirements of each state will depend, in some measure, on what the others are doing or might seek to do.

Accepting—let alone codifying—a hierarchical, triangular relationship will be extraordinarily difficult for these proud nations. No two sides of the triangle in southern Asia are equal, and within the triangle, there are two competing dyads. There is nothing inherently stable about a triangle consisting of three unequal sides. India clashes with Pakistan over a disputed border and jockeys with China over contested areas. India and Pakistan are enmeshed in a deadly dispute over Kashmir. India and China are acutely sensitive over Tibet and anticipate a competition between "blue water" navies. All three countries worry about Islamic extremism. Nuclear weapons and missile programs now overlay these neuralgic issues, making it even harder for national leaders in China, India, and Pakistan to create and sustain a stable strategic environment.

The close triangular interactions involving China, India, and Pakistan magnify nuclear message sending, within and beyond the confines of southern Asia. Prospective U.S. missile defense deployments will undoubtedly compound these tympanum effects. To complicate matters further, the regional effects of U.S. missile defense deployments are invariably crosscutting around the periphery of Asia. Harmony in one sphere produces dissonance in the next. Take, for example, the case of Japan. Deployments that soothe Japanese concerns could easily rub Chinese sensibilities raw. Conversely, voluntary restraint by Washington in the face of Chinese or North Korean missile threats could be as unsettling to Japan as ill-conceived transfers. Whatever deployment choice is agreed upon by Washington and Tokyo will likely raise sensitive constitutional, civil–military, and burden sharing questions in Japan.

The United States and the Soviet Union engaged in an extended strategic dialogue to establish rules of their nuclear competition. Severe crises were followed by bilateral arrangements to improve communication lines and mutual understanding. Triangular interactions in southern Asia follow different patterns. Crises and wars are usually followed either by deep freezes or poorly implemented confidence-building measures. Beijing and New Delhi have begun a strategic dialogue, but their interactions on nuclear matters have initially dwelled on China's displeasure at being obliquely named as a reason for India's nuclear tests in 1998, and New Delhi's concerns over China's support for Pakistan's nuclear and missile capabilities. China has been reluctant to discuss mechanisms to stabilize the Sino–Indian nuclear relationship in a context that presumes equality.

Relations between India and Pakistan have oscillated wildly, marked by nuclear testing in 1998, a Lahore summit in 1999 that suggested the possibility of a paradigm shift in bilateral relations, only to be followed by a Pakistan Army-led and planned military probe to seize high ground on the Indian side of divided Kashmir. The ensuing high-altitude combat over the summer of 1999 generated increased readiness in nuclear capabilities, but did not have the chastening effects produced by other nuclear scares, such as the Cuban missile crisis. The Kremlin lied blatantly before and during the Cuban missile crisis. Nonetheless, this hair-raising brush with nuclear disaster led the Kennedy administration to pursue nuclear risk-reduction arrangements with the Kremlin, which took immediate form in the Hot Line agreement establishing direct and reliable communications between national leaders. In contrast, New Delhi reacted to Pakistan's dissimulations about the high-altitude war by seeking to isolate its nuclear neighbor. The Indian government's policy of containment reflected domestic political imperatives as well as official calculations that isolating Pakistan would yield greater benefit than formalizing nuclear risk-reduction arrangements with an unreliable negotiating partner.

India's containment policy toward Pakistan lasted for two years, after which Prime Minister Atal Bihari Vajpayee invited the "architect" of the 1999 war, General Pervez Musharraf, to Agra for an unscripted summit. The July 2001 Agra summit failed to achieve an agreed structure for subsequent dialogue, breaking down in public wrangling over the Kashmir dispute. Then came the September 2001 demolition of the twin towers of the World Trade Center. The ensuing U.S. war against the al-Qaeda terrorist network added new layers of complication to nuclear risk-reduction efforts on the Subcontinent. Pakistan suddenly became a front line state in the war against terrorism, distancing itself from groups that used to do its bidding in Kashmir, without altering its "principled" stand in this dispute. Backlash predictably followed. When a band of terrorists attacked the Indian Parliament building in December 2001, South Asia witnessed another mobilization of two huge standing armies, as nuclear capabilities were again readied for use.

Supporters of nuclear weapons in India and Pakistan casually predicted that the 1998 tests would usher in a period of stability on the Subcontinent. Instead, India and Pakistan immediately became deeper enmeshed in crises and border clashes. South Asia's roller coaster ride provided little time or space to put in place nuclear risk-reduction measures like those employed by Washington and Moscow to stabilize their Cold War pursuits. Instead, nuclear dangers remained inter-twined with the Kashmir dispute. Crises became more frequent, and more dangerous.

Deterrence theorists in the West have a name for this phenomenon: the "stability–instability paradox."[1] The essence of this paradox is that, while offsetting nuclear capabilities might foreclose a central strategic exchange, they might also increase provocations and risk taking at lower levels–whether to remedy perceived weaknesses or to press territorial claims. Nuclear weapons can generate risk taking because they presumably provide an insurance policy against escalation. The most dangerous time to control escalation usually comes in the years immediately after both adversaries initially possess nuclear capabilities. During this awkward period, tolerance levels or "red lines" have not been clarified, the nuclear balance is unclear, and risk-reduction arrangements have not been implemented. At the earliest stages of offsetting nuclear capabilities, new weapon developments add to threat perceptions and uncertainties. India and Pakistan are now proceeding through this difficult passage.

The prospective deployment of ballistic missile defenses by the United States will surely complicate the nuclear risk-reduction agenda in southern Asia. Leaders in China, India, and Pakistan have time before national and advanced theater missile defenses are deployed to take serious steps to reduce negative consequences and nuclear risks. The sooner they attend to these tasks, the better. In the meantime, Washington must also attend to the downside risks and unintended consequences in Asia of deploying missile defenses.

Missile Defenses and Nuclear Risk Reduction

Cold War models of nuclear risk reduction are only partly relevant to Asia. The Hot Line agreement and other accords to prevent dangerous military practices could certainly be adapted to meet Asian circumstances. But the stabilizing aspects of strategic arms limitation and reduction accords, especially their codification of equality and intrusive monitoring provisions, are unlikely to be applicable to this region.

To begin with, national leaders in China, India, and Pakistan have publicly rejected equality and opted instead for "minimum" deterrence. The quasi-official "draft" Indian nuclear doctrine is characterized as "a dynamic concept related to the strategic environment, technological imperatives and the needs of national security. The actual size components, deployment and employment of nuclear forces will be decided in the light of these factors."[2] The nuclear postures adopted by China and Pakistan will also be sensitive to external factors. All three countries are unlikely to accept a codification of inequality at a time of great uncertainty about the requirements of nuclear deterrence against more powerful competitors. Moreover, all three are extremely leery of the degree of transparency for nuclear forces that would facilitate treaties or the stabilization of nuclear requirements. In China, subterfuge is an integral aspect of military art and strategic culture. As David Shambaugh has observed, China's military leaders have been

> socialized in a military institution and political culture that prizes discipline and secrecy—thus they do not appreciate the importance of defense

transparency as a security-enhancing measure, and view foreign requests to improve it with suspicion. They refuse to join alliances or participate in joint military exercises with other nations, are reticent to institutionalize military cooperation beyond a superficial level, and are leery of multilateral security cooperation.[3]

India and Pakistan, like China, rely on opacity to cover military weakness or to increase force survivability. The acceptance of transparency to reduce nuclear danger usually comes much later, after states possessing nuclear weapons gain confidence in their deterrent. The United States and the Soviet Union did not accept on-site inspections of each other's nuclear forces until 1986, nearly three decades after first broaching the subject.

In the early stages of a nuclear competition, there are few verifiable data points to measure stability or asymmetry. Paradoxically, the inclination by India and Pakistan to foster stability by not maintaining nuclear forces at high states of readiness could make it harder to clarify baselines. To complicate matters further, technical monitoring capabilities in southern Asia are limited, making it difficult to verify in a timely and repetitive fashion nuclear developments across borders. China and India have invested in "national technical means" to observe military developments from space. Not to be left too far behind, Islamabad has used the launch services of Russia to loft a rudimentary observation satellite.[4] All three states will presumably rely, as well, on imagery purchases from commercial observation satellites to monitor developments of interest.

China, India, and Pakistan will also rely on domestic intelligence assessments, espionage, declassified U.S. assessments or leaks of classified material in the American media, non-governmental reports, or some combination thereof to produce national estimates. These sources might well produce a confusing picture, or reinforce worst-case analysis. National intelligence assessments might well be wide of the mark, producing unpleasant surprises. Strategic surprise is not uncommon in southern Asia: India surprised China with its nuclear tests in 1998; China surprised India by going to war in 1962; and Pakistan surprised India by crossing the Line of Control dividing Kashmir after the 1999 Lahore summit. Future surprises may also be in store.

Taken together, the imbalanced triangular relationship in southern Asia, the lack of hard information and redundant monitoring capabilities, and the perceived necessity for opacity could inflate force-sizing requirements in China, India, and Pakistan—even in the absence of missile defense deployments by the United States. National leaders will certainly be hard pressed to maintain strict limits on their nuclear deterrents when domestic political, institutional, and technological pulls reinforce external drivers pointing toward more and better nuclear capabilities.

China and Cascading Nuclear Requirements

Beijing's calculations of nuclear sufficiency will reverberate in New Delhi, and India's recalibrated nuclear requirements will reverberate in Islamabad. At the top of this cascade, Beijing's calculations will be affected by U.S. deployments of national and advanced theater missile defenses. Whatever additional requirements Beijing feels are warranted to counter U.S. missile defense programs are likely to be relatively inconsequential in terms of the U.S.–China nuclear equation, but could provide grounds for further modernization on the Subcontinent. The potential for cascading nuclear requirements would exist, however, even in the absence of U.S. missile defense programs, since China's military and strategic modernization programs are driven in part by the Taiwan issue.

After the normalization of U.S.–China relations begun in the Nixon administration, stability across the Taiwan strait rested on three pillars: Beijing's inability to project military power, Taipei's lack of interest in distancing itself further from the mainland, and Washington's acceptance of the status quo relationship between Taiwan and China. These pillars began to wobble well before the Clinton administration began to consider seriously national missile defense deployments. As political and demographic trends in Taiwan created greater distance from China's orbit, Beijing countered by improving its power projection capabilities.

Missiles were a relatively quick, inexpensive, and highly symbolic way to demonstrate cross-strait military capabilities. Predictably, China's missile programs prompted more support for missile defenses in the United States, more interest in Taiwan for transfers of new missile defense systems, and stronger drum beats on Capitol Hill in support of Taiwan's fledgling democracy. Beijing's leadership was willing to accept these consequences, given its inability to project military power in any way other than by ballistic missiles, and given its perceived need to "send a message" to Taiwan.

The growing distance between Taipei and Beijing, the multiple weaknesses of the People's Liberation Army, Navy, and Air Force, as well as new uncertainties about Washington's future course, meant that China required not only a demonstrable increase in missiles that could span the Taiwan Strait, but also modernized missiles that could range over intercontinental distances. These programs preceded the administration of President George W. Bush, but were given added impetus after its arrival. In the event of a future crisis over Taiwan, Beijing's leadership is resolved never again to be subject to coercive U.S. nuclear diplomacy, as was the case during the 1950s, especially during the Korean War.[5]

The lesson learned by Mao Tsetung from U.S. nuclear threats was clear: "If we are not to be bullied in the present day world, we cannot do without the [atomic] bomb."[6] This lesson has been internalized by China's military leaders. Marshall Nie Rongzen wrote, "To get rid of imperialist bullying which China had suffered for more than a century, we had to develop these sophisticated [nuclear] weapons. At least then, we could effectively counter-attack if China were subject to imperialist nuclear attack."[7] Major General Yuan Huan wrote in a similar vein: "China's strategic nuclear weapons were developed because of the belief that hegemonic power will continue to use nuclear threats and nuclear blackmail."[8]

The most cost-effective way for China to prevent coercive U.S. nuclear diplomacy is to be able to destroy American cities, a requirement that is far easier to meet in the absence of American missile defenses. Beijing's puzzling laxity during the Cold War regarding the survivability of its nuclear deterrent was less acceptable in changed circumstances. In an environment marked by missile defense deployments and growing drift with Taiwan, more attention needed to be paid to nuclear deterrence. Modern intercontinental ballistic missiles were required—solid-fueled missiles that are mobile, hard to find and target. If Washington deploys national missile defenses, Beijing's deterrent must be able to penetrate them. Warheads must be accompanied by countermeasures that can confuse and foil U.S. intercepts.

Beijing previously assumed a rather relaxed view about nuclear deterrence. Throughout the Cold War, China's strategic nuclear forces were both negligible and surprisingly vulnerable. Beijing was content to possess perhaps twenty intercontinental ballistic missiles that took many hours to become operational, one non-operational submarine carrying missiles that could not reach the United States, and no strategic bombers. Whether China's leaders realized it or not, they were vulnerable to a U.S. first strike.[9] The vulnerability of Beijing's strategic nuclear forces and the enormous asymmetry between Chinese and U.S. nuclear capabilities didn't matter as long as the status quo on Taiwan held firm, and as long as both countries—as well as Taiwan—were content not to change it.

These central determinants of strategic stability are in flux. The combination of Taiwan's drift from the mainland, the acquisition of advanced conventional capabilities by U.S. forces, and Washington's renewed interest in ballistic missile defenses poses a triple threat to China. Beijing's vulnerable strategic deterrent is now clearly insufficient in the event of a confrontation over Taiwan, its ability to coerce Taiwan is being challenged, and its economic development is being taxed, since extra funding for conventional and nuclear forces comes at the expense of domestic priorities, which are essential for economic growth and social cohesion. Nonetheless, Chinese leaders are prepared to direct unprecedented funding increases to the military, reflecting the importance they attach to the Taiwan issue and the concerns they feel about growing asymmetries in Chinese and U.S. military capabilities.[10] As a consequence, one close China watcher believes that:

> From the late 1980s, on Chinese strategists have developed a concept of "limited deterrence" (*you xian wei she*) to describe the kind of deterrent China ought to have. While the concept is still evolving, limited deterrence, according to Chinese strategists, requires sufficient counterforce and countervalue tactical, theater, and strategic nuclear forces to deter the escalation of conventional or nuclear war. If deterrence fails, this capability should be sufficient to control and to compel the enemy to back down. [11]

Not surprisingly, Beijing's opposition to U.S. missile defense programs is more strongly felt than in Moscow. Pakistani leaders have also reacted quite negatively to prospective missile defenses, not simply in support of Beijing, but also out of concern that New Delhi will eventually deploy its own defenses, acquiring useful technology even if it does not negate Islamabad's investment in missiles. New Delhi's diplomatic posture toward missile defenses has shifted from negative to neutral. Early in the Clinton administration, when ties were strained, Indian diplomats derided missile defenses as yet another ill-conceived strategic initiative by an insular and unilateralist Washington. As Indo–U.S. relations improved, criticism toward missile defenses became greatly muted, with some even contemplating active bilateral cooperation in this sphere.[12] At the outset of the administration of George W. Bush, New Delhi's response to presidential pronouncements on strategic policy was far more appreciative than official responses from European capitals.

While New Delhi's views toward missile defenses shifted, Beijing's opposition deepened. Prospective U.S. missile defense deployments reinforced anxieties over the future of Taiwan and the "revolution in military affairs" which has hollowed out the People's Liberation Army's oversized and out-dated conventional forces. To the extent that these concerns are reflected by China's strategic modernization effort, they will then have cascading impacts on Indian threat perceptions and force requirements. The extent of the resulting cascade would depend, in part, on how China's leaders define the requirements of deterrence against the United States (and lesser cases), how U.S. leaders define the extent and architecture of ballistic missile defenses, and how much India's leaders feel compelled to respond to Chinese moves.

There is broad agreement in the United States regarding China's presumed requirements for deterrence. This near-consensus view was stated in the Pentagon's 2001 review of proliferation dangers: "China's stated doctrine reportedly calls for a survivable long-range missile force that can hold a significant portion of the U.S. population at risk in a retaliatory strike."[13] Some who support missile defenses would seek to negate this capability; those who seek a cooperative relationship with Beijing would accept a mutual deterrence relationship. If negation of the Chinese deterrent is either sought or perceived, China's strategic modernization programs are likely to expand accordingly, as will their cascade effects on the Subcontinent.

Given the low priority China's leaders have attached to nuclear deterrence in the past and the higher priority given to conventional force modernization and to economic development, Beijing will seek to fulfill the requirement of targeting U.S. cities at least cost. China's minimalist requirements continue to be reflected in official American projections of Beijing's strategic modernization plans. According to estimates offered by the Pentagon and Central Intelligence Agency, China will likely have "tens to several tens of missiles" capable of reaching the United States by 2015.[14] Acknowledging the linkages between U.S. missile defense plans and Chinese reactions, a January 2002 CIA estimate revised upward China's requirements, predicting between 75 and 100 warheads on ocean-spanning missiles by 2015. Moreover, the U.S. intelligence community estimated that Beijing would "encounter significant technical hurdles" as well as financial costs trying to place multiple warheads atop its mobile missiles.[15] In other words, Beijing would deploy, on average, only six warheads atop intercontinental ballistic missiles per year in response to U.S. national missile defense deployments. This is an extraordinarily low estimate for government agencies that have not been known to deflate the military potential of a prospective strategic competitor.

Depending on the scope of "limited" U.S. national missile defenses that are ostensibly oriented against North Korea, Iran, and Iraq, Washington's deployments could also "capture" China's quite modest nuclear deterrent. If the prospective size of "limited" U.S. missile defense deployments exceeds the intelligence community's estimates of the Chinese strategic nuclear deterrent in 2015, then Beijing could well presume that China is the real object of U.S. defense planning. Beijing is unlikely to sit still if Washington seeks to neutralize its nuclear deterrent. As a consequence, the pace and extent of China's strategic modernization effort are likely to increase alongside the breadth of prospective U.S. missile defense deployments. Several non-governmental studies are less sanguine than the U.S. intelligence community about Beijing's missile plans, predicting force increases from tens to hundreds of missiles.[16] An increase by China of this magnitude could have significant cascade effects in India and Pakistan. It would also create perturbations in Japan and Taiwan. Thus, the prospective size of the "limited" U.S. national missile defense system matters greatly.

With the removal of treaty constraints against missile defenses, these limits will be bounded primarily by U.S. executive branch and legislative interactions. Beijing will unwillingly become a party to American choices, since its responses to U.S. deployments will establish a feedback loop for missile defense enthusiasts and skeptics. If ambitious U.S. missile defense plans alienate Beijing, Moscow, and allied capitals, while appearing to be linked to the resumption of nuclear testing and the weaponization of space, domestic blocking action is likely to be taken. If, on the other hand, China again resorts to the use of ballistic missiles for coercive diplomacy or, worse, initiates a military campaign against Taiwan, missile defenses of all kinds will receive a significant boost. Even if Washington makes wise decisions regarding ballistic missile defense deployments, Beijing could make poor ones resulting in increased tensions, instability, and armament around its periphery.

Given the importance Beijing's leaders attach to the Taiwan issue and still-raw memories of U.S. nuclear coercion, China has already begun a strategic modernization program, albeit one that has proceeded very slowly. A trickle-down effect on South Asia is already underway, but it has yet to become a cascade. The extent of acceleration will depend, in the first instance, on decisions taken in Washington and Beijing. Beijing cannot be given a veto over national missile defenses or for advanced theater defenses provided to friends and allies, but neither should Washington be given encouragement to make bad decisions. The dilemmas associated with missile defense deployments are inescapable, and they have as much to do with minimizing downside risks and unintended consequences as with pursuing favorable outcomes.

India's Nuclear Choices

New Delhi's nuclear choices are different from those driving Beijing, but they are also susceptible to reverberations generated from missile defense deployments. India's nuclear requirements flow from two colluding nuclear neighbors, considerations of status and domestic politics, and the prompting of a well-connected "strategic enclave."[17] The Indian nuclear program has its own biorhythms, however, which are extremely relaxed by western standards.

The most extraordinary data point in this regard is the twenty-four-year hiatus between India's nuclear detonations.

Several reasons could be posited for this elongated time line for developing a nuclear arsenal, including the high priority Indian leaders have given to economic concerns; their past susceptibility to U.S. pressure; a strong aversion by Indian political leaders to make difficult choices; the absence of an indigenous national security consciousness and support structure in New Delhi; and the powerful lassitude and risk aversion of the Indian bureaucracy. To these must be added a unique duality among Indian elites toward the Bomb, in which status-consciousness and anti-colonialism point in one direction, while moral superiority and anti-nuclear Gandhianism point in the other. One chronicler of India's bomb program, George Perkovich, characterizes this odd mix as "defiant assertiveness and diffident timidity."[18]

Indian singularity could comfortably support both pro- and anti-nuclear postures, since either path made India special. As a proud Third World state speaking from uncommon moral authority, New Delhi relished leading international campaigns for nuclear disarmament. But India also privately longed to be a member of this exclusive club. Ongoing nuclear and missile programs in China and Pakistan, the indefinite extension of the Nuclear Non-Proliferation Treaty in 1995, and the 1996 negotiation of the Comprehensive Test Ban Treaty all served to clarify the necessity for choice. The divide between nuclear and non-nuclear-weapon states was now clearer than ever. A newly elected government led by the Hindu nationalist Bharatiya Janata Party, operating with a bare parliamentary majority, definitively resolved India's ambivalence with five nuclear weapon tests in May 1998.[19]

The Prime Minister of this coalition government, Atal Bihari Vajpayee, has spoken few words about India's nuclear ambitions since announcing the tests. Official pronouncements dwell on the guiding principles of minimalism with respect to the requirements of nuclear deterrence and a pledge of no first use that appears to be unconditional.[20] In lieu of more elaborate statements regarding the requirements of nuclear deterrence, the Vajpayee government assembled an eclectic group of advisors to draft a non-official, but officially sanctioned statement of India's nuclear needs. The August 1999 report by the National Security Advisory Board conveys authoritativeness, since it asserts, rather than recommends doctrine (e.g. "India's nuclear forces will be effective, enduring, diverse, flexible, and responsive").

This semi-official and yet quasi-deniable report is certainly unique in national efforts to fashion a nuclear doctrine. The report's release was accompanied by a government invitation for public engagement, furthering the consensus-building effort begun with the diversity of the report's drafting group.

The drafters appeared to have built internal consensus by endorsing a wide range of initiatives, including the need for a nuclear triad of capabilities held by India's Army, Navy, and Air Force. Some of the asserted needs, such as organizing India's deterrent for "rapid punitive response" vitiate India's reassuring principle of no first use, since a force ready to respond quickly would look indistinguishable from one preparing to launch a pre-emptive strike. The core requirement is stated as "credible minimum nuclear deterrence." The demands of credibility, however, can influence the minimum required. A high premium is placed on survivability to lend credence to India's retaliatory force posture.[21]

The advisory board said nothing about the requirement, role, or repercussions of ballistic missile defenses for India's national security. Nor did the advisory board's report provide insight into how India might react to an increase in China's nuclear capabilities as a result of missile defense deployments by the United States. In any event, the incremental requirements resulting from missile defenses would be hard to discern, since the advisory board endorsed such a robust triad of nuclear capabilities. Presumably, however, those advisors who supported a large arsenal would support an even larger one after factoring in the cascade effects of missile defenses.

The absence of official Indian government statements regarding the requirements of nuclear deterrence was not unwelcome to foreign capitals that preferred ambiguity to firmly stated, ambitious estimates of India's nuclear needs. Filling this vacuum were Indian strategic analysts who offered their own unofficial estimates of the requirements of deterrence. One notably hawkish author called for an "escalation dominance" posture against China and at least 300 nuclear weapons.[22] Another hawkish strategist places the stockpile requirement at 132 devices.[23]

The dean of India's strategic analysts, K. Subramanyam, estimated the need for 60 deliverable weapons, but this was before China's strategic modernization program began to take shape.[24] Writing soon after the 1998 nuclear tests, when Western concerns were quite elevated, the head of India's government-supported institute of defense studies, Jasjit Singh, wrote, "it is difficult to visualize an arsenal with anything more than a double-digit quantum of warheads. It may be prudent to even plan on the basis of a lower figure of say, two–three dozen nuclear warheads by the end of ten–fifteen years ... with the passage of time, deterrence decay factors will lead to a smaller arsenal rather than a larger one."[25] This estimate now appears unrealistically low. A subsequent assessment by Raja Menon calculated that India should eventually rely upon a deterrent capability of six submarines, each carrying as many as 96 warheads.[26] Another retired senior military officer, Kapil Kak, called for an initial force for 100 warheads carried by aircraft and land-based missiles.[27]

These unofficial assessments, together with the advisory board's report, suggest some clues as to how the Indian government might translate minimum nuclear deterrence into numbers—at least in the absence of cascade effects. The community of strategic commentators in India that pushed for an overt nuclear capability, and others who have joined them since the 1998 blasts, mostly translate the requirements of nuclear deterrence and the pre requisites of great power status into a thermonuclear weapons capability and a three-digit sized force of nuclear weapons.

The Indian government has also refrained from publicly discussing nuclear targeting, and the National Security Advisory Board provides no elucidation on this subject. Private commentators, mostly with military backgrounds, have again filled this void. Vijay Nair postulates that deterrence against China would translate into strikes against four to five metropolitan areas, nine to ten "strategic industrial centers" and China's submarine bases. As for Pakistan, Nair suggests targeting six to ten cities and a lesser set of communication nodes.[28] Raja Menon promotes a "flexible response" nuclear posture that targets military sites instead of cities.[29] Bharat Karnad advocates striking enemy cities and the development of high-yield thermonuclear weapons.[30]

The targeting of cities poses dilemmas for the stronger state in any nuclear pairing, and Indian government officials are likely to recoil from "counter-value" strikes against Pakistani cities unless Indian urban centers are hit first. In addition, countervalue targeting runs against the grain of Indian strategic culture. India's wars with Pakistan have been quite restrained by western standards, and have almost entirely avoided the targeting of military assets in built-up areas.[31]

To the extent that Indian officials venture beyond the targeting of cities, they expand the parameters of minimal nuclear deterrence. A close U.S. observer of India's evolving nuclear plans, Ashley J. Tellis, believes that New Delhi's requirements are likely to remain limited, following the cardinal principle that nuclear weapons are political, and not war-fighting instruments. Tellis concludes that India will maintain a modest "force in being," a deterrent "consisting of available, but dispersed, components that are constituted into a useable weapon system primarily during a supreme emergency."[32] This sanguine assessment still leaves open the door to increased targeting requirements as India's capabilities grow, providing for "more flexible responses in order to ensure that punishment, whenever inflicted, can be proportional and leads to speedy conflict termination at the most minimal cost."[33] Nuclear strategists in the West know all about this slippery slope and where it can lead.

The "second tier" of nuclear weapon states—China, Great Britain, and France—are assumed to have nuclear weapon stockpiles in the low hundreds, which could set a marker for Indian ambitions. A British expert deeply steeped in western practices of nuclear deterrence, Michael Quinlan, finds it "difficult to believe" that India's requirements "could justifiably reach any higher than the smallest of the five 'NPT' nuclear armouries (the United Kingdom's, at an announced maximum of below 200 operational warheads)."[34] This might be wishful thinking, however, since New Delhi's security dilemmas are far greater than those facing London or Paris. In addition, a status-conscious India might well be averse to establishing a third nuclear tier below Great Britain and France, and might even be inclined to supersede the "colonialist" rung on the nuclear ladder. A three-digit sized Indian nuclear force would be directed mostly against China, while covering the lesser case of deterring Pakistan. The aspiration by India's nuclear hawks for a three-digit sized nuclear capability might well be inflated but, at present, theirs is the dominant discourse in India. Needless to say, these public aspirations help shape Chinese and Pakistani considerations of their own nuclear needs.

Pakistan's Dilemmas

Most scenarios for nuclear danger on the Subcontinent begin at the Line of Control dividing Kashmir. The staging areas for carrying out deadly operations against Indian targets are on Pakistan's side of the Kashmir divide where, for many years, jihadis received logistical, intelligence, fire control, and material support from the Pakistani Army and intelligence services. During the Pakistani-backed Kashmir insurgency, firefights between Indian and Pakistani forces along the Line of Control have been frequent occurrences, sometimes accompanied by the over-running of border posts. The war against terrorism in Afghanistan has greatly complicated Pakistan's Kashmir policy, which relied to a considerable extent on jihadi operations to punish Indian security forces and to draw international attention to its concerns.

Islamabad champions a strategic restraint regime for South Asia alongside its pro-active Kashmir policy. Prior to the U.S. war against terrorism in Afghanistan, the contradictions inherent in the twin pursuits of nuclear risk management and fomenting violence in Kashmir were either not well appreciated at General Headquarters or believed to be manageable. Indeed, during the first decade of offsetting nuclear capabilities in South Asia, Pakistani governments were reluctant to allow too much forward progress on nuclear risk reduction in the absence of satisfaction on Kashmir, viewing one as leverage for the other. Progress in resolving the Kashmir dispute, however, was publicly characterized in zero-sum terms, with the enumeration of Indian wrongs becoming a unifying theme in national life.

Pakistan's parallel pursuit of a strategic restraint regime and a pro-active Kashmir policy became much harder to juggle after September 11, 2001. Prior to this date, Pakistani governments had insisted that their support for militant Islamic groups was limited to moral, diplomatic, and political support. This fiction was exposed during the U.S. military campaign against the Taliban, many of whose ranks received religious and military training from Pakistani mentors. Plausible deniability was now replaced by a presumption of guilt, not only in Afghanistan, but also in Kashmir. Every new act of terror committed by groups that received training and other forms of military assistance from Pakistan became an embarrassment to Islamabad.

By continuing to support jihadi crossings of the Kashmir divide, Pakistan could no longer expect the sympathy of the international community. To the contrary, after September 11, 2001, Islamabad could only expect diplomatic support and protection if it appeared to be moving against jihadi groups. This new dynamic became apparent after a suicide squad of Islamic extremists once backed by Pakistani intelligence outfits attacked the Indian parliament building three months after the World Trade Center collapsed in flames. The government of Pakistani President Pervez Musharraf plausibly argued that it had no role in the attack against the Parliament, but could prove this point only by taking further steps against jihadi groups that previously received official sanction.

Prior to the war against terrorism in Afghanistan, Islamabad's Kashmir diplomacy rested on the expectation that India would be restrained from crossing the Line of Control to retaliate against terrorist acts, owing to concerns over escalation and New Delhi's sensitivity to negative international reaction. After the terrorist attack on the Parliament, the Indian government placed its army on a war footing, announcing that it would not be paralyzed by Pakistan's nuclear deterrent, and that limited war was a viable military option to stop terrorist attacks.[35] The "rules of the game" in the Kashmir dispute are changing, in ways that increase Pakistani and Indian requirements to strengthen deterrence.

During the first decade of offsetting nuclear capabilities in South Asia, Pakistan's nuclear diplomacy was constructed around initiatives offered in the confident expectation of their rejection by India. Indeed, India's acceptance of Pakistan's previous proposals for nuclear abolition, if faithfully and bilaterally implemented, would pose serious dilemmas to Islamabad, the weaker state. Consequently, Pakistani proposals for nuclear disarmament have increasingly been mated to proposals for mutual, disproportionate reductions in conventional military capabilities. As Tanvir Ahmad Khan, a retired senior Pakistani diplomat has noted:

> We are frequently asked by international experts as to what would set Pakistan on the risk-reduction route. Essentially, the answer lies in addressing Pakistan's primary concerns. First, progress towards conflict resolution ... Secondly, the quest for confidence-building measures in the conventional field needs to be intensified. Particularly significant in this regard would be verifiable reduction in the asymmetry of the capability to make pre-emptive strikes.[36]

These proposals are also unlikely to be realized, since India's conventional military requirements must take into account Chinese and as well Pakistani contingencies.

The dance of diplomatic one-upsmanship continued after the 1998 nuclear tests and the 1999 high-altitude war in Kashmir. Pakistan's proposals for nuclear risk-reduction and stabilization measures were explicitly linked to the escalatory potential inherent in the Kashmir dispute. Islamabad's nuclear diplomacy became broader and more nuanced after the nuclear tests, centering around the need for a "nuclear restraint regime" that included prohibitions on deployed nuclear forces and missile defenses.

Michael Quinlan reasoned that India was not "within sight [of a pre-emptive option], or could so render itself for decades ahead, or possessing such an option to a standard which military advisers could recommend to leaders."[37] Pakistan's generals confidently endorse this view. Troubling realities lurk below this surface, however. Pakistan has less than two dozen air-fields from which to operate nuclear-capable aircraft. Its missile production, main operating bases, and nuclear facilities are very few in number, and their geographical coordinates are publicly known. Commercial satellite images of Pakistan's facilities could be found on the internet, along with the particulars of its missile programs.[38]

Quinlan's qualification still has merit. Even if the case for pre-emption were strongly made, it is difficult to envision an Indian Prime Minister believing and acting upon an assurance of complete success. Nonetheless, Pakistan's confidence in the survivability of its nuclear deterrent is likely to degrade in crisis situations, given the quick reach of Indian strike forces. Consequently, there are strong incentives for Pakistani military leaders to increase the readiness of their nuclear deterrent in periods of mounting tension, as they have in the past.[39] The potential for accidents and miscalculations grow when missiles are moved or are placed on heightened alert.

By championing the non-deployment of nuclear forces, Pakistan seeks to protect its deterrent. If faithfully adopted, however, this proposal could increase Islamabad's vulnerability to pre-emption, given the extremely short flight times between northern India and Pakistan's strategic assets. Pakistan's custodians of the nuclear option could, of course, define "non-deployment" in permissive ways. (The oft-used, official Indian idiom of "inducting" nuclear forces lends itself to an equally wide latitude of interpretation.) Because Pakistan lacks strategic depth, it might well "deploy" a portion of its deterrent in unorthodox ways, distant from main operating bases.

There are several precedents for unorthodox basing. China, for example, maintains some of its missiles in caves, where they could be moved surreptitiously to confound targeting. The Soviet Union also used caves blasted out of the shoreline to protect missile-carrying submarines.[40] Pakistan could well resort to similar hide-and-seek practices. But moves to provide safety against a surprise attack could also generate a very different set of dangers, including accidents and breakdowns of command and control. Missiles located at satellite deployment areas away from main operating bases might also require movement in deep crisis, generating alarms (if detected) and prompting dangerous counter-moves if undetected but presumed. The movement of Pakistani missiles operating on poor roadways poses safety concerns, especially if the missiles in transit use highly combustible, liquid fuel. If a nuclear-related accident occurs in a deep crisis, it could trigger unforeseen consequences if enemy action is the presumed cause.

Pakistan faces additional security dilemmas. The Sunni–Shia fault line within Islam is situated along Pakistan's border with Iran. Islamabad has had minor flare-ups with Teheran in the past, which both capitals have chosen not to overemphasize, given their other, more serious security concerns. Iran's quest for nuclear and missile capabilities would complicate regional security matters for Pakistan, creating a two-front nuclear danger—much like that facing India.

Pakistan's border with Afghanistan was supposed to provide strategic depth and a gateway to the markets of Central Asia, but Islamabad's efforts to shape Afghanistan's future by means of the Taliban proved to be a poor choice. What began as a low-cost plan to ensure a friendly border and to facilitate a jihad in Kashmir evolved into diplomatic isolation and domestic woes.[41] A Taliban-led government that President Musharraf deemed essential to Pakistan's well being in March 2001[42] became a huge liability six months later after the demolition of the World Trade Center by Osama bin Laden's recruits. With the U.S. declaration of war against terrorism in Afghanistan, Pakistan was forced to improvise an extrication strategy designed to prevent yet another hostile government along its borders.

Amid these difficulties, Pakistan's friendship with China became increasingly essential to national well being, helping greatly to offset India's strategic advantages and to keep New Delhi off balance. China's ties to Pakistan remained firm despite Beijing's concerns over Islamic militancy along its western borderlands. Pakistan's other major external source of missile-related equipment, North Korea, is decreasing in importance, since Pakistan's clear preference is mobile, solid-fueled missiles, not the liquid models that North Korea has provided. If Pyongyang and Washington reach non-proliferation accords, the missile pipeline from North Korea would close, in any event.

While Pakistan's challenges come from all azimuths, its most serious problems remain social, political and economic in nature. Pakistan's domestic difficulties could lend force to official pronouncements that Islamabad does not intend to engage in a nuclear competition with New Delhi. Nevertheless, Pakistan's army, which oversees nuclear and missile efforts, has invested heavily in these pursuits and is acutely aware of India's growing conventional capabilities. To hold costs and gain greater managerial control over duplicate nuclear and missile laboratories, a reorganization was announced by the Musharraf government in March 2001. Nonetheless, Pakistan is likely to define minimal nuclear deterrence in relative, not minimal, terms. "Pakistan's nuclear policy is," as Samina Ahmed has noted, "reactive in nature, responding to India's nuclear ambitions ... Pakistan's nuclear directions will be determined by India's nuclear choices."[43] If India increases its nuclear and missile capabilities, Pakistan's requirements are likely to be adjusted upward. While India's nuclear infrastructure and financial means are far greater, Pakistan has spared no effort to compete in this realm. With sufficient time and effort, however, New Delhi can pull away from Islamabad, particularly if the combined nuclear threat from China and Pakistan appears to warrant doing so.

Force-sizing Considerations

Nuclear force-sizing calculations between China and India will be determined by the interplay of cross-cutting pressures. Unlike the Cold War competition between the United States and the Soviet Union, domestic factors are, on balance, likely to depress nuclear needs. External drivers point in the opposite direction. On the inflationary side, New Delhi's declared test of a thermonuclear device and its quest for an extended-range missile able to reach Beijing and Shanghai send clear messages to the Chinese leadership. Every flight test of the extended-range Agni III ballistic missile would confirm a Chinese orientation for India's nuclear deterrent. The perceived need for thermonuclear weapons to deter China is relatively new in Indian strategic discourse, and did not play a prominent role in the push for a resumption of nuclear testing in the 1990s. In effect, a debate over thermonuclear weapons was pre-empted by the 1998 test series which, according to Indian government officials, included one such detonation. If additional "China-specific" nuclear tests are required to confirm a thermonuclear weapon design, Beijing's feigned indifference to Indian nuclear and missile programs would become increasingly strained.

Indian nuclear scientists have expressed divided views as to whether the thermonuclear test was a complete success, as asserted by government officials. Outside observers have their doubts.[44] The Government of India has notably declined to sign the Comprehensive Test Ban Treaty, leaving open the possibility of a resumption of tests to confirm a more advanced nuclear capability. China has signed, but not ratified the Test Ban Treaty, a constraining factor for Beijing, both in its dealings with a rising India and with prospective U.S. missile defenses. If China seeks to assert a hierarchical nuclear posture against an India armed with thermonuclear weapons and extended-range missiles, it could do so without testing by ratcheting up its inventories of deployed launchers and nuclear weapons. Or China, along with other states, could resume nuclear testing.

During the Cold War, China was largely uninterested in strategic modernization programs. Rising concerns over Taiwan and U.S. missile defense deployments have given further reinforcement to strategic modernization programs.[45] Chinese calculations are now compounded by India's ambitions and nuclear status-consciousness. If the Government of India appears to be embracing a three-digit sized nuclear capability—either through veiled public statements or through the trajectory of its programs—China is likely to see this bid, and raise it. Doing so would not merely constitute a hierarchical response, but would also reflect China's strategic concerns within and beyond the Subcontinent.

If China and India both appear headed for three-digit sized nuclear capabilities, one key question is what portion of these capabilities would be deployed. Another is what the first integer of the three digits would be for both countries. Non-governmental analysts estimated that, at the turn of the century, China's nuclear arsenal consisted of 300–400 warheads, with very few, if any, deployed on a day-to-day basis.[46] Most of this arsenal appears geared toward regional warfare. These estimates are admittedly sketchy; given Beijing's commitment to nuclear opacity, they could well be wide of the mark.

The first integer of China's three-digit sized nuclear inventory will be determined, in large measure, by the strategic environment around China's periphery, by Beijing's economic circumstances, and by the architecture and extent of U.S. national missile defenses. The more limited the U.S. deployment, the more likely it is to depress China's nuclear needs. If U.S. national missile defense deployments suggest an attempt to negate China's nuclear deterrent, Beijing's nuclear requirements would rise accordingly. In addition, the more extensive the deployment of U.S. national missile defenses, the more Beijing would seek to solve the technical problems associated with placing multiple warheads atop its mobile missiles, perhaps with Russian assistance. The deployment of space-based interceptors that could hover over China as part of the U.S. architecture for ballistic missile defenses would be profoundly disturbing to Beijing, as would other U.S. programs for space warfare. Beijing's options to counter U.S. military dominance might well include the accelerated development of anti-satellite weapons and other asymmetric responses.[47]

Perhaps the most noteworthy aspect of the China–India nuclear equation is the number of significant uncertainties that could affect force-sizing calculations. India would be more sensitive to increases in China's nuclear forces associated with regional targets than with a buildup directed against the United States. One response by Beijing does not necessarily preclude the other, however. Bilateral relations between India and China and between India and Pakistan have oscillated, as have U.S. ties with all three countries. The Taiwan issue and prospective U.S. missile defense deployments add volatility to this mix. There are too many critical variables to predict with confidence how the Chinese–Indian nuclear equation will unfold. If any of these external drivers become more worrisome, nuclear requirements will point upward.

During the Cold War, the United States and the Soviet Union were trapped in determining nuclear force requirements in relative terms. Powerful domestic constituencies mandated that actual or perceived "second place" was unacceptable in the nuclear arms race. The twin impulses of seeking relative advantage and avoiding disadvantage generated huge arsenals and targeting lists. The second rank of nuclear powers during the Cold War avoided this perverse dynamic. For example, the leaders of Great Britain and France concluded that a small number of missile-carrying submarines at sea would suffice to overwhelm the 100 or fewer nuclear-armed missile defense interceptors erected around Moscow.[48]

Similarly, China, India, and Pakistan all retain a strong interest in holding down nuclear force levels. But none of these states will be inclined to establish fixed requirements for minimal nuclear deterrence, given external uncertainties. With external prodding, minimal requirements could be defined in relative ways. This would constitute a dramatic shift for China, which was, by far, the most relaxed nuclear weapon state during the Cold

War. And if Beijing ratchets up its capabilities, domestic pressures and inter-est groups within India will push in a similar direction. Pakistan has the infrastructure to compete with India, as long as nuclear and missile programs remain high budgetary priorities. The more Pakistan's military falls behind Indian conventional capabilities, the more it will be tempted to rely on nuclear weapons as an "equalizer." External drivers could come from the bot-tom up, the top down, or from the status-conscious middle power, India.

A competitive, "tit for tat" dynamic already exists on the Subcontinent, as was evident after India carried out five nuclear tests in 1998, prompting Pakistan to claim a higher number of detonations. Another indicator is Pakistan's decision to extend the reach of its missiles beyond New Delhi. Since India can cover all of its neighbor's cities with missile strikes, Pakistan has decided that it, too, must be able to target urban areas in India's south. The opacity of nuclear and missile programs could prompt national leaders to build in "safety" factors in determining requirements. And, to the extent that nuclear capabilities are equated with status as well as deterrence, further impe-tus to nuclear-related programs could be generated either by the loss of status in non-nuclear domains, or by falling behind in the strategic competition.

Moderating Factors

In South Asia, troubling developments are usually intermixed with hopeful signs. While there is considerable potential for China, India, and Pakistan to become enmeshed in an open-ended nuclear competition, there are also moderating factors within each country that could mitigate negative effects. To begin with, all three states have considerable financial constraints or opportunity costs associated with extensive nuclear modernization. Pakistan's economic forecast is clouded by heavy military expenditures, social needs, and foreign debt. If Pakistan's military leaders seek to keep pace with India's nuclear and missile programs, conventional military capabilities could suffer along with the national economy. While Pakistan's Army leadership strongly supports nuclear and missile programs, that support could wane in the future when such funding competes against the Army's other institutional interests.

Even India and China, which could support increased spending for con-ventional as well as nuclear programs, must seriously consider the opportunity costs of doing so. Although New Delhi's military budgets spiked after the 1999 high-altitude war with Pakistan, sustained growth in Indian defense spending is a rare occurrence. Chinese defense spending also increased signif-icantly in the 1990s, but a growing economy remains the top priority of Beijing's leaders. Without it, they face domestic threats far greater than the external problems posed by U.S. ballistic missile defenses. Much of the added defense spending in both China and India goes to improve the rewards of military service and to replace outmoded tanks, planes, and ships. The expense of strategic modernization programs must be weighed against these priorities.

The Soviet experience of overspending for national defense is clearly within the Chinese field of view. While the scope of China's strategic modernization efforts would depend greatly on the ambitions U.S. officials attach to missile defense programs, Beijing's national security imperative would remain constant—to counter missile defenses and to maintain credible deterrence at least cost. As a leading Chinese arms control official has stated: "We will do whatever possible to ensure that our security will not be compromised, and we are confident that we can succeed without an arms race." The cheapest counter to missile defenses, in this view, is to attack the system's most vulnerable parts.[49]

Beijing has had the good sense to avoid nuclear arms racing in the past, and is not likely to alter this behavior in the future. A significant increase in nuclear capabilities would not only complicate China's relations with India, but also with Japan, Russia, and elsewhere along its periphery. A major build up in nuclear forces would also badly undercut Beijing's diplomatic posture opposing missile defenses, while empowering the missile defense lobby in the United States. Consequently, if future U.S. administrations do not seek the negation of China's strategic deterrent, cascade effects on the Subcontinent could be greatly reduced.

The relaxed biorhythms of Indian nuclear modernization are also not easy to change, although external shocks, such as Pakistan's surprise crossing of the Line of Control in 1999, have done so in the past. Nonetheless, a bureaucratic and political culture that prizes the avoidance of decisive decisions does not change overnight.[50] In the past, powerful Indian civil servants and defense scientists have been loathe to share confidences with military leaders. This, too, has begun to change. Operational and command and control imperatives will require India to confront difficult issues of civil–military relations. Moreover, nuclear issues are politicized in India's hyper-democracy, another constraint on pacing. The Vajpayee government did not take the Congress Party and other opposition groups into confidence before deciding to test nuclear weapons, and they, in turn, do not feel beholden to support all aspects of the Vajpayee government's nuclear agenda. India's relaxed biorhythms have already quickened somewhat, but the deliberative pace of consequential Indian decision making remains an important moderating factor.

The public declarations of national leaders also constrain pacing, at least in a notional fashion. China doesn't deign to compete with India, and India does not deign to compete with Pakistan, at least in official statements. Public pronouncements could well be proven false, but they at least provide an opportunity to realize stability through asymmetry in the difficult passage ahead. Moreover, India's status-consciousness could work in positive as well as negative ways. New Delhi appears determined to demonstrate a far superior wisdom on nuclear matters than that evidenced during the Cold War. In particular, Indian strategists stress the importance of reassurance and affirmation of national pledges not to use nuclear weapons first against nuclear-armed opponents, and not to use them at all against non-nuclear-weapon states. India certainly has the strategic depth to maintain its nuclear holdings in a relaxed status and to take other steps clarifying a non-threatening posture.

New Delhi has already taken positive moves in this regard. Senior Indian officials have publicly rejected "nuclear war-fighting" strategies and requirements. After the release of India's hawkish draft nuclear doctrine, Foreign Minister Jaswant Singh explicitly undercut its stated requirements for prompt retaliatory capabilities, noting: "[W]e would like to convey a sense of assurance in our region, also beyond, so that our deployment posture is not perceived as destabilizing. We have rejected notions of 'launch on warning postures' that lead to maintaining hair trigger alerts, thus increasing the risks of an unauthorized launch."[51] Government officials in India have also repeatedly stated that they intend to demonstrate their commitment to a no-first-use pledge through operational practices. In this regard, some short-range Prithvi missiles were moved from storage cites in central India to the border area near Pakistan in 1997, but were subsequently moved back.[52] This singular step is unlikely to be comforting to Pakistan, given the relative ease with which short-range missiles could be shuttled back to strike locations, as was reported in the war scare following the December 2001 attack on India's Parliament.[53] While crisis stability remains problematic in South Asia, in peacetime New Delhi could provide reassurance to Pakistan, moderating their strategic competition and providing a model for others to follow.

Similarly, China and India could avoid expansive nuclear requirements, if other external drivers remain muted. Both countries have strategic depth and are developing mobile, land-based missiles that neither could locate and destroy. Because pre-emption is not a viable option, "counterforce" targeting or "damage limitation" strategies of nuclear deterrence built around the ability to knock out military capabilities of the other side seem eminently avoidable. These concepts were significant drivers in the expansion of U.S. and Soviet targeting lists.

Alternatively, India and China could adopt a nuclear targeting strategy of placing each other's cities at risk. Both countries have six cities with populations in excess of 5 million. While such a "countervalue" nuclear targeting strategy would not require many warheads, it places national leaders who would prefer more targeting options in a terrible vice.

The United States and Soviet Union "solved" these dilemmas by compiling thousands of targets including military facilities, command and control bunkers, and war-supporting industry that happened to be located within or in close proximity to major metropolitan areas. This allowed national leaders to maintain the moral fiction of not targeting populations *"per se,"* while endorsing nuclear targeting plans that would still produce many millions of collateral deaths.[54] Indian and Chinese leaders might be disinterested in such deadly fictions. If, however, they reject both counterforce and countervalue targeting, what, exactly, would they place on their targeting lists?

The leadership in both countries (as well as in Pakistan) could use a demonstration nuclear detonation to signal the approach of an intolerable threshold, or they could use a nuclear strike against an infrastructure project that could result in devastating economic consequences. It does not take many nuclear weapons for such demonstrative purposes. And if one nuclear detonation leads to a second, what then? Cold War nuclear strategists tried mightily to define multiple escalation rungs and to establish escalation dominance capabilities,[55] but these were not very helpful or convincing to political leaders caught in the crucible of an intense crisis. Indian and Chinese leaders are likely to react no differently in this respect than their American or Soviet counterparts.

Pakistani leaders do not have the luxury of strategic depth. Their lines of communication run perilously close to Indian territory. Lahore is situated just 27 kilometers from the international border, and most of Pakistan's fixed strategic assets could be targeted within minutes of a directive to launch India's strike aircraft. As the gap in conventional military capabilities widens between India and Pakistan, Islamabad's concerns would grow accordingly. As a consequence, Pakistani doctrine apparently holds that a nuclear detonation on national territory carried out by either conventional or nuclear means would constitute grounds for a retaliatory nuclear strike.[56]

The response of Pakistan's military leaders to a disadvantageous order of battle appears to be quite similar to that chosen by other small nuclear powers. "If we have only one bomb left," said one officer, "it will be targeted on New Delhi. If we have two, it will be New Delhi and Bombay." Both Indian cities contain large Muslim populations. Holding them hostage, and exterminating them in response to grave threats to Pakistan's vital national interests, is not viewed as a theological issue by those responsible for Pakistan's nuclear deterrent.[57]

Religion can either moderate or inflame passions. In South Asia, religion has not been a moderating influence. Religious differences can also have a bearing on nuclear postures. For example, clerics affiliated with Pakistan's largest religious party who champion the Bomb cite passages from the Koran to justify the targeting of fellow Muslims residing in India's major cities. One passage reads, "Against them make ready your strength to the utmost of your power, including steeds of war, to strike terror into (the hearts) of the enemies of Allah and your enemies and others besides, whom you may not know." Another passage suggests that if Muslims live voluntarily in the land of a country waging war with Muslims, they too, are subject to the terrible punishments of war. There are also many passages in the Koran that enjoin Muslims not to engage in violence, and certainly not in bloodshed on a scale associated with the use of nuclear weapons.[58] If, however, Pakistan's leaders believe that the country's vital national interests are threatened, they could well target India's major cities.

The bad news in this analysis is that even a modest strategic competition in southern Asia could generate interactive nuclear requirements in a region largely devoid of stabilization measures. Moreover, this region is susceptible to crises, and crises add to perceived nuclear needs. Prospective missile defense deployments add another wild card to this volatile mix. The good news in this analysis is that, while the strategic dynamic among China, India, and Pakistan is quite complex, these interactions are geared toward a modest competition rather than a strategic arms race. All three countries have separate as well as common reasons for dampening their nuclear pursuits. Military and targeting rationales for a nuclear arms buildup are not compelling. Domestic political, bureaucratic and institutional factors pushing for more and better nuclear capabilities are pale shadows of those present in the U.S.–Soviet competition.

Washington's Choices

If change occurs merely through the act of observation, what changes might one expect though the act of deploying U.S. missile defenses? The triangular nuclear arms competition in southern Asia is at a very modest stage, when requirements are small, but amenable to growth. Washington's decisions could accelerate or moderate cascade effects depending on the design and extent of its missile defense deployments. The architecture chosen for U.S. missile defense deployments will speak volumes to Beijing. Sea-based, boost-phase missile defenses would not, by themselves, signal a U.S. intent to negate China's deterrent, which would likely be situated far inland, beyond the reach of these interceptors. Sea-based, boost-phase missile defenses would therefore suggest U.S. readiness for regional contingencies and the protection of friends and allies. Interceptor missiles based on U.S. soil might or might not suggest an attempt by Washington to negate Beijing's nuclear deterrent, depending on the number of interceptors deployed, their presumed capability, and the size of Beijing's ocean-spanning missile forces. Beijing would be most concerned over space-based interceptors that would continually be "on station" overhead. Space-based missile interceptors have the potential to be far more capable than missile defenses on land and at sea that seek intercepts at mid-course or terminal phases. By adding up the elements of U.S. missile defense plans, Beijing will determine Washington's intentions and necessary responses.

The extent of the nuclear cascade in southern Asia will be the sum total of many complex interactions to which the United States is a party. The first integer of China's modernized, three-digit inventory of nuclear weapons—and the mix of tactical and strategic warheads—therefore depends heavily on Washington's choices. If Washington designs and sizes its missile defenses to challenge China's nuclear deterrent, Beijing would react by upping the size and capability of its nuclear forces directed against the U.S. homeland and against America's bases in the region. Alternatively, the choice by Washington not to threaten Beijing's deterrent would help moderate nuclear cascade effects in southern Asia.

It is in the U.S. national security interest, as well as in the interest of America's Asian friends and allies, to deploy highly capable theater missile defenses around China's periphery. Beijing utilizes short- and medium-range ballistic missiles for coercive purposes, and these missiles have already been used as instruments of political coercion. The forward deployment of boost-phase missile defenses, particularly at sea, would signal U.S. resolve to come to the aid of threatened friends and allies. For these and other reasons, U.S. theater missile defenses would not be welcomed by China, but they are nonetheless essential.

Furthermore, it is in the U.S. national security interest, as well as in the interest of India and Pakistan, to depress the size of China's globe-spanning nuclear capability, not to seek its negation. The pursuit of a negation strategy is not only dangerous, but also highly unlikely to succeed, since it would depend on Beijing's inability or unwillingness to maintain a nuclear deterrent against the United States. This quest will fail as long as Beijing has the will and the resources to add to its inventory of long-range missiles.

Washington already enjoys overwhelming superiority over China in strategic offensive forces. Beijing has no national security interest in moving beyond a minimum deterrent unless Washington raises this requirement.

Overwhelming U.S. strategic superiority does not, by itself, generate cascade effects, as long as China could successfully hide a portion of its limited arsenal. The overlay of robust missile defenses atop overwhelming U.S. strategic superiority would force Beijing to adjust upward the requirements of that hidden nuclear arsenal. The extent of this adjustment—and with subsequent steps by India and Pakistan—would depend largely upon the design and extent of U.S. missile defense plans. The resulting cascade effects and Chinese countermoves would be detrimental to regional stability.

The United States could seek to minimize cascade effects by designing and sizing national missile defenses against maverick states such as North Korea, Iran, and Iraq, rather than against China. A defense against the possible acquisition or development of ocean-spanning missiles in maverick states would require a modest insurance policy of a few tens of interceptors on American soil. This number could be adjusted upward or downward depending on the success of U.S. efforts to prevent or limit the deployment of three-stage missiles in maverick states. The primary line of defense against missile inventories in maverick states would continue to be U.S. power projection. It is, after all, far easier and more cost-effective to destroy threatening missiles on the ground with conventional weapons than to intercept an incoming warhead in its final minutes of re-entry. American pre-emptive or preventive military capabilities against missile production capabilities, storage and test sites could be reinforced, in selective cases, by a forward-leaning U.S. declaratory policy warning maverick states against the acquisition, development, or flight testing of missiles that threaten the United States, its friends, and allies.

This approach requires great care, however, in part because questions would naturally arise as to why pre-emption is suitable for and against some states, but not others. The norm to be reinforced is non-proliferation, not pre-emption.[59] In each case, calculations of risk would vary depending on an evaluation of the threat and the likelihood of successful military action. Such calculations, however, would be rare and they would be made with or without a more pointed U.S. declaratory policy regarding proliferation. When the state carrying out pre-emption is itself guilty of proliferation—or of weakening non-proliferation regimes—the overall result would be doubly unfortunate, reinforcing both pre-emption and proliferation.

The diplomatic challenges and potential military consequences of putting into place a forward-leaning U.S. declaratory policy on pre-emption or preventive war would be considerable, requiring much consultation with friends and allies. Diplomatic fall-out could be diminished if a more pointed U.S. declaratory policy were linked to more concerted American efforts to strengthen multilateral non-proliferation accords. A more pointed U.S.

declaratory policy would still need to provide leeway for choice, rather than straightjacketing presidents, but not so much leeway as to vitiate the message. In many, but not all cases, inference might have greater utility than specificity. There could be times, however, when the deterrent value of a more pointed U.S. declaratory policy would be greater than, say, the deployment of an additional one hundred missile defense interceptors on U.S. soil. This tradeoff might be worth making if, for example, the net effect would be to dampen cascade effects in Asia.

If diplomacy and other means fail to prevent Iraq, North Korea and Iran from acquiring missiles able to reach U.S. soil, the number of such missiles is likely to be very low. Conversely, even if the United States succeeds in preventing the spread of missiles with ocean-spanning range, these maverick states would retain many shorter-range missiles that threaten their neighbors and U.S. power projection forces. In every troubling case, priority must be given to theater missile defenses, while great care is required to correlate national missile defenses against modest prospective threats.

U.S. national missile defense plans have a long history of being cast against improbable threats, raising serious doubt of their intended purpose. The first U.S. missile defense plan in the administration of President Lyndon Baines Johnson was ostensibly cast against China, a country that would not acquire ocean-spanning missiles for another fourteen years. The Kremlin dismissed this rationale, rightly figuring that U.S. missile defenses were directed against the Soviet Union. President Richard M. Nixon offered a different rationale for national missile defenses—to protect missile silos—with only modest alterations to his predecessor's architecture. The global protection system against "limited" attack proposed by President George H. W. Bush consisted of almost 2,000 interceptors. Presidents Bill Clinton and George W. Bush proposed quite different architectures for the same declared purpose—a limited defense against mavericks—again generating disbelief in foreign capitals. The Clinton administration asserted that limited defenses could be compatible with the ABM Treaty, while the Bush administration asserted that the treaty was hopelessly outdated, irrelevant, and too constricting, even for limited defenses.

If Washington cannot maintain a straight story on missile defenses from one administration to the next, foreign capitals might be forgiven their skepticism and disbelief of official statements. Foreign governments hoped against hope that the Bush administration's verbal assaults on the ABM Treaty would be a prelude to deal making, but were proven wrong. President Bush's decision to withdraw from the ABM Treaty would appear to be an excessive remedy for the deployment of very limited missile defenses; ambitious deployment plans are likely to prompt Democrats on Capitol Hill to erect new fire breaks to replace those in the Treaty. Judgments as to U.S. strategic objectives will eventually come to rest after much partisan wrangling. In the meantime, foreign governments will proceed with contingency plans.

If the architecture chosen for national missile defense in the United States entails hundreds of missile interceptors to counter rogue missile threats, New Delhi might charitably ascribe such plans to worst-case thinking. Beijing would think and act differently. If U.S. intelligence community projections are correct, and if Beijing deploys only 100 or fewer warheads atop its ocean-spanning missiles by the year 2015, Beijing would likely view a comparable or larger number of U.S. missile interceptors as a concerted effort to negate its nuclear deterrent and to induce stress fractures in the Chinese economy by forcing still-greater defense expenditures. Islamabad would support China and worry about missile defense deployments in India. The deployment of less than 100 interceptor missiles on U.S. soil as an insurance policy against mavericks is still likely to prompt an undesired increase in China's strategic nuclear forces and trickle-down effects on the Subcontinent, but with diminished negative and unintended consequences. The thinner the deployment on U.S. soil the better the chances for limiting cascade effects in southern Asia.

U.S. space warfare programs would generate very little, if any, charitable explanation from foreign capitals. Instead, a U.S. push to weaponize space is likely to promote collaboration between Moscow and Beijing to counter U.S. strategic superiority and space operations at least cost. Responses would be asymmetric in nature, since Beijing and Moscow cannot match Washington's resources or technological advantages. U.S. advantages could nonetheless be dealt with through countermeasures that are relatively inexpensive and that could create havoc with advanced, complex, and vulnerable sensors essential for the military and commercial utilization of space.

The Challenges Ahead

The deployment or transfer of theater missile defenses by the United States could have positive as well as negative repercussions for a country such as Japan. In contrast, prospective U.S. deployments of national missile defenses overwhelmingly point to negative repercussions and downside risks, especially around the periphery of China. Cascade effects in triangular interactions among China, India, and Pakistan have already begun in the form of contingency planning. Washington's decisions could dampen or heighten negative effects. Safety ledges could still be found and slippery slopes avoided if U.S. national missile defenses are demonstrably designed against maverick states rather than China, and if Washington refrains from weaponizing space. These dampening measures could be realized by executive branch forbearance or by congressional control of the purse.

National leaders in India, China, and Pakistan need to find the wisdom to exercise restraint. They also need wise U.S. policy choices, because their own security dilemmas are so complicated. The triangular geometry of regional competition in southern Asia overlays two dyads. In each of the dyads, the stronger of the two antagonists does not outwardly acknowledge its competitor, making formalized nuclear risk reduction extremely difficult. A triangular effort to moderate cascade effects would be plagued by this history, and by the lack of symmetry resulting from three-cornered interactions. Even without the added complications of U.S. missile defenses, formalized bilateral or trilateral arrangements dampening nuclear interactions would be very difficult to negotiate. National or theater missile defense deployments further complicate this picture.

National leaders in China, India, and Pakistan have all declared their firm intention not to repeat the nuclear excesses of the United States and Soviet Union. The only clear benefit of nuclear excess during the Cold War was that large arsenals provided insurance against a surprise attack, making strategic defeats or pre-emption inconceivable. Despite repeated domestic scares, the U.S.–Soviet nuclear balance, as Bernard Brodie noted, was far from "delicate":

> For either superpower to attack the other because of an optimistic guess of the latter's vulnerabilities is obviously to take a risk of cataclysmic proportions. Neither can be seduced into such an error by some apparent shift in the relationship of forces—usually more apparent to technicians than to politicians. Nor will either superpower be seduced by the appearance of some new mechanical contrivance which at best affects only a part of the whole scheme of things, usually a small part. [60]

Small nuclear arsenals provide far less insurance against faulty calculations. Put another way, limited arsenals are more likely to generate risks than to guarantee risk reduction. Indeed, the historical record suggests that security concerns have been particularly worrisome to states possessing small nuclear arsenals. This was certainly true for the U.S.–Soviet experience, when nuclear risks were greatest in the early phases of arsenal building, when vulnerabilities were evident, verification weak, and command and control unsure. Thus, during the formative stages of their nuclear competition, the United States and the Soviet Union faced harrowing crises over Berlin and Cuba. The Korean War was fought under the shadow of the mushroom cloud. Likewise, soon after Beijing acquired a nuclear capability, it fought border skirmishes with Moscow. The brief, crisis-filled record since India and Pakistan acquired offsetting nuclear capabilities, including their high-altitude war in 1999, confirms this pattern.[61]

Nuclear risk reduction in southern Asia will be a far more complex undertaking than was the case for the United States and the Soviet Union, in part because the Cold War risk reduction agenda was not further complicated by open-ended national missile defense deployments. As bad as Cold War nuclear dangers were, bipolarity provided a measure of simplification. The nuclear balance was codified in treaties predicated on equality. These treaties obligated the parties to accept intrusive monitoring. A common understanding of stabilizing and destabilizing activities was negotiated. Competition continued to be pervasive, and yet aspects that were most dangerous were placed off-limits. Berlin and Korea were divided, but Washington and Moscow did not exchange artillery fire across these lines. U.S. and Soviet military planning was not predicated on daily, violent interactions between their armed forces.

India, Pakistan, and China are very distant from these stabilizing conditions. In Central Europe, international boundaries were fixed; not so for India, Pakistan, and China. Even the relatively quiet Line of Actual Control between India and China is the occasional scene of jockeying between military patrols. During the 1990s, ritualized violence in the form of small arms fire and artillery exchanges were a regular occurrence along the Line of Control dividing Kashmir. The geometry of strategic competition in southern Asia makes triangular or bilateral treaty arrangements unlikely, since none of the three parties will accept formalized equality or inequality with another. Consequently, stand-alone nuclear risk reduction arrangements become more essential, but also more difficult, given the absence of trust that verifiable treaty obligations might generate. Cooperative risk reduction in this region is spotty, unreliable, and of unequal interest to the parties.

If New Delhi, Beijing, and Islamabad are to find nuclear safety, they are likely to do so through a combination of bilateral cooperation, unilateral preparation to reduce the risk of accident or miscalculation, as well as unilateral restraint. In the absence of verifiable treaty regimes, nuclear risk reduction is likely to be found—if at all—through an acceptance of bilateral asymmetries in force sizing and deployment readiness. Pakistan, the state with the weakest military posture and most vulnerable nuclear deterrent, would have to refrain from competing with India, while maintaining some nuclear capabilities in a survivable status. New Delhi would need to refrain from competing with China and from posturing its nuclear capabilities so as to threaten Pakistan. Beijing sits atop this cascade. Consequently, the scope of the nuclear competition within southern Asia will be set primarily by China's decisions. The larger China's nuclear arsenal grows—whether in response to U.S. missile defense plans or for other reasons—the more likely it will generate cascade effects elsewhere in the region.

The establishment of hierarchical and stable nuclear postures in southern Asia is an enormously difficult and ambitious agenda. Successful nuclear risk reduction will require finding a unique mixture of transparency and survivability for nuclear capabilities, as well as creative monitoring arrangements that provide reassurance without increased vulnerability. This agenda has barely begun at a time when it can be severely buffeted by prospective U.S. deployments of missile defenses. Perturbations in Asia are insufficient reasons for the United States to forgo a modest insurance policy against the low probability of a ballistic missile attack on the U.S. homeland. Nonetheless, the complex triangular interactions between China, India and Pakistan and the prospect of an Asian nuclear cascade mandate great care in the design and extent of U.S. national missile defenses.

CHAPTER 6

Reassessing Strategic Arms Control

The origins of strategic arms control—broadly defined as the effort to limit the numbers, types, or disposition of weapons[1]—predated the Cold War. During the 1920s and 1930s, the United States, Great Britain, and Japan sought to fix quantitative and qualitative limits on naval combatants, which were the trans-oceanic means of striking targets of that era. The codification of these efforts in the Washington Naval Treaty of 1922 and the London Naval Treaty of 1930 were not central, however, to the geopolitics of the inter-war years. Nor were they very successful.

In contrast, nuclear arms control was a core issue during the Cold War. Nuclear weapons' testing and deployments generated huge street demonstrations. Summit meetings were inextricably linked to nuclear talks, and negotiating gambits were front-page news. Public hopes and fears over the nuclear issue reflected the vagaries of superpower relations. Treaty provisions were driven by, and a reflection of, geopolitical rivalry. "The theory of arms control" itself, as Lawrence Freedman noted, "was a product of a cold war."[2] Emanuel Adler extended this argument, concluding that strategic arms control was "the most important legacy of the Cold War—its enduring contribution to international institutions and order."[3] Nuclear weapons alone, according to Adler, were "unable to bring about peaceful accommodation"; strategic arms control became the forcing mechanism by which the superpowers "invent[ed] ways to institutionalize their joint interest in avoiding war."[4]

The canonical objectives of strategic arms control during the Cold War, as listed in Thomas C. Schelling and Morton H. Halperin's mapping survey, *Strategy and Arms Control*, were first, the avoidance of a war that neither side wanted; second, minimizing the costs and risks of the arms competition; and third, curtailing the scope and violence of war in the event it occurred.[5] The actual record of strategic arms control was decidedly mixed, but success in helping to achieve the first of these objectives overrode failings on the other two. Cold War strategic arms control, unlike naval arms control in the 1920s and 1930s, did not unravel, followed by a global conflagration.

There is considerable room for argument about how much strategic arms control contributed to war avoidance during the Cold War, compared to, say, nuclear deterrence or plain dumb luck. Those who dismiss arms control as a feckless enterprise usually overvalue nuclear deterrence which, during the Cold War, rested on massive numbers of nuclear weapons, thousands of which were on hair-trigger alert or were located on the forward edge of prospective battlefields. These vast, accident-prone underpinnings of nuclear deterrence could not, by themselves, provide the basis of nuclear safety over five decades of intense ideological and geopolitical rivalry. The threat of punishment alone was insufficient to reduce nuclear dangers during the Cold War. A complementary approach was needed, as Adler noted, to "create strengthen, and focus expectations of cooperation." Strategic arms control "helped foster a common understanding that the nuclear situation could be stabilized by human choice."[6] Imagine nuclear deterrence without strategic arms control, and it is far easier to imagine nuclear detonations.

The enterprise of nuclear arms control started slowly. The first decade of strategic arms limitation talks—the SALT process—produced disappointing results in many respects. The first SALT accords reached in 1972—an "Interim Agreement" limiting offensive arms and the Anti-Ballistic Missile (ABM) Treaty—alienated many by leaving the United States "defenseless" while permitting significant growth in offensive forces. This outcome did not reflect the failings of arms control so much as the level of distrust and geopolitical competition between the United States and the Soviet Union during this period, as well as the unwillingness of both leaderships to forgo advances in weapon technology, most notably multiple independently-targetable re-entry vehicles, or MIRVs. The flight testing and deployment of MIRVs produced geometric increases in force levels, ensuring that strategic arms control during this period would be a catch-up exercise.

Demands for reductions, rather than overly generous limitations, first emanated from disaffected arms controllers. These calls became more insistent in the late 1970s, alongside fierce challenges to the SALT process from Hawks who viewed the negotiations as a cover for the Soviet quest for strategic superiority. The SALT process foundered over this domestic divide, becoming completely untenable after the 1979 Soviet invasion of Afghanistan. That year, the second SALT accord, which codified the increased force levels resulting from MIRVs, was shelved. SALT was super-seded by strategic arms reduction talks—START—when the calls by liberal Democrats for deep cuts were seconded by conservative Republicans, the harshest critics of arms control.

The chief spokesperson for this transition in the United States, President Ronald Reagan, was an abolitionist anti-communist, a conjunction that was previously unrecognized in American politics. Reagan's presidential campaign in 1980 cited the permissiveness of SALT (which Hawks had previously insisted upon) as evidence of failure and as grounds for a change in adminis-tration. The Reagan team's initial proposals for deep cuts were so one-sided as to be non-negotiable. This dynamic changed during Reagan's second term. When paired with a similarly unorthodox Soviet leader, Mikhail Gorbachev, pragmatists within the disputatious Reagan administration finally triumphed over obstructionists. The means sought by obstructionists to block treaties—Reagan's cherished Strategic Defense Initiative (SDI)—ultimately became the vehicle for deal makers to secure deep cuts. The odd couple of Reagan and Gorbachev succeeded in breaking the back of the strategic arms race. This accomplishment, in the form of a treaty zeroing out classes of missiles useful for theater nuclear warfare, laid the ground for subsequent and equally extraordinary treaties reducing ocean-spanning missiles.

This transformation needed to be codified in treaty form for many rea-sons. The practice of strategic arms control was still novel, after all, and skep-tics of Soviet motives as well as the process itself demanded specificity. Both superpowers pushed at the margins of their agreed limits; on some occasions, the Soviets cheated outright, while the United States pursued missile defenses that were prospective violations of treaty obligations. Leaders in both coun-tries, therefore, had good reasons to seek commitments in writing. In addi-tion, the time span of treaty implementation extended beyond the political writ of the negotiating partners. There was little debate that the accords signed by national leaders needed to be affirmed by legislatures. Ronald Reagan's nostrum of "trust, but verify," was perfectly pitched to the public mood and a unifying theme for the Republican Party that had become seri-ously divided over the enterprise of strategic arms control. Verification required the fine print of treaties, and the fine print of treaties was necessary for ratification.

The symbolism of treaty signing ceremonies was also helpful in solidify-ing political support behind long-term obligations. Reassurance of domestic and allied audiences was, as Michael Howard observed, no less important than deterrence during the Cold War: "peoples expect their governments to provide them with adequate protection, but they also expect them to seek peace and ensure it, and if they are not seen to be doing so, consensus over defense will crumble."[7] Reassurance required the conduct of serious negotiations, periodic summit meetings, and constructive interventions at the highest level.

Holding Off Disaster

The subliminal messages of the arms control process were easily overlooked by those fixated on numbers, but the function of reassurance was undeniably crucial. Severe critics of arms control warned that negotiations and accords would lull the American public into a false sense of security. Instead, the visceral disrespect for strategic arms control by a new administration generated a quite real sense of public insecurity. Arms control, as Robert Jervis noted, symbolized the successful management of superpower rivalry.[8] Consequently, the fiercest skeptics of arms control could gravely wound treaties negotiated by others, but once assuming public office, they were invariably driven back to the negotiating table by worried Americans and allies. The act of strategic arms control, even in its early, frustrating stages, underscored the essential point that nuclear weapons were, as Thomas C. Schelling argued, "a class apart from conventional weapons. They are under a curse, a taboo, despite the awe in which they are held and the prestige that may go with having them."[9]

Throughout the Cold War, the United States rejected an unequivocal commitment not to use nuclear weapons first. The geography of far-flung allies requiring protection under the extended U.S. nuclear umbrella, as well as Soviet conventional superiority in central Europe, militated against such a pledge. Nevertheless, the process of strategic arms control and the treaties that resulted from it inferentially reinforced Schelling's point that the most fundamental purpose of the exercise was to avoid a nuclear war that neither side wanted. "Holding off disaster," he later wrote, "was what most of us aimed for in 1960."[10]

The bombing of Hiroshima and Nagasaki established a baseline of nuclear weapons' use; a core goal of strategic arms control was to establish a subsequent track record of non-use, to affix the taboo, and to practice forbearance. Year by harrowing year during the course of the Cold War, this objective was achieved. This result was far from assured during the early, crisis-prone phase of the nuclear arms race, when both Hawks and Doves were equally unsure that a nuclear exchange could be avoided. On this score, arms control negotiator Paul Nitze wisely counseled against the long view: "Try to reduce the dangers of nuclear war within the relevant future time period as best you can," he advised others; "you just get depressed if you worry about the long-term future."[11]

Success in avoiding nuclear detonations was ultimately achieved during the Cold War. This extraordinary accomplishment was inconceivable without the conceptualization of nuclear deterrence. It was also inconceivable without the conceptualization of strategic arms control. The two were, after all, joined at the hip. "The purpose of arms control," Schelling wrote in a retrospective assessment, "was to help make certain that deterrence worked."[12] "Basically," wrote Johan Jørgen Holst, a keen Norwegian observer of superpower interactions, "the concept of arms control was a twin sister of the concept of nuclear deterrence."[13]

Strategic arms control was conceptualized by Schelling and Halperin as "a promising, but still only dimly perceived, enlargement of the scope of our military strategy."[14] Its creative premise, forced by the deadly character of the Bomb, was that collaborative effort amid competition with one's adversary was essential. "It is not true," Schelling wrote, " that in the modern world a gain for the Russians is necessarily a loss for us, and *vice versa*. We can both suffer losses, and this fact provides scope for cooperation."[15] Hedley Bull reinforced this point in his mapping text, *The Control of the Arms Race:* "Arms control is significant only among states that are politically opposed and divided, and the existence of political division and tension need not be an obstacle to it."[16] "The key insight," of strategic arms control, wrote Lawrence Freedman in a thirty-year retrospective of the enterprise, "was that when designing strategies it was wise to consider the effect they might have on the adversary."[17] This, in turn, required extended discussion, but discussion alone was insufficient for domestic and allied audiences. The process was rightly expected to produce accords. The codification of obligations became essential, both politically and militarily. "Strategic arms control," as Holst observed, "gradually became a major vehicle for shaping Soviet–American relations."[18]

While strategic arms control helped to prevent a nuclear exchange, it could by no means diminish the competitive pursuits of the two superpowers. As Hedley Bull correctly forecast in *The Control of the Arms Race:* "arms control does not provide a technique of insulating a military situation from the future will of states to change it; it cannot bind, nor settle in advance, the future course of politics."[19] Proxy wars were fought and the jockeying for geopolitical advantage flourished alongside strategic arms negotiations, occasionally making for awkward moments, such as President Richard Nixon's treaty-signing journey to Moscow in 1972 while U.S. combat aircraft were taking aim at targets in North Vietnam that produced Soviet casualties.

Deterrence theorists quickly developed a concept for the phenomena of risk taking within the shadow of the mushroom cloud. The noted British military strategist B. H. Liddell Hart noted in 1954 that, "to the extent that the H[ydrogen]-bomb reduces the likelihood of full-scale war, it increases the possibility of limited war pursued by widespread local aggression."[20] Glenn Snyder reinforced this point at the very time when *Strategy and Arms Control* and *The Control of the Arms Race* were published, warning that the growing U.S. nuclear arsenals and the Eisenhower administration's bellicose declaratory policy of "massive retaliation" would be insufficient to deter the Soviet Union from "a range of minor ventures which they can undertake with impunity, despite the objective existence of some probability of retaliation."[21] The resulting "stability–instability paradox" was neatly summed up by Robert Jervis: "To the extent that the military balance is stable at the level of all-out nuclear war, it will become less stable at lower levels of violence."[22]

Conventional arms control proved to be a very weak reed to ameliorate these competitive pursuits. "Usable" conventional weapons were less subject to constraints than missile-carrying submarines, strategic bombers, and intercontinental ballistic missiles. In the European theater, conventional arms reductions became the subject of serious conversation only at the Cold War's end, shortly after deep cuts in nuclear forces were realized. Earlier "spin offs" from strategic arms control, such as accords designed to reduce and prevent dangerous military practices and to improve superpower communications in periods of crisis, had already proven their worth in whittling down some of the sharp edges of geopolitical competition. Critics of arms control quipped that accords were not possible when they were most needed, and most obtainable when least necessary. It is certainly true that the most far-reaching arms reduction accords—both strategic and conventional—occurred from the mid-1980s onwards. But this ignored the value of preceding steps in eventually securing deep cuts, as well as the role arms control played in keeping the Cold War from becoming hot.

While helping to avoid a war that neither side wanted, arms control during the Cold War fell far short of the other objectives set by Schelling and Halperin. The strategic arms competition continued to impose high economic costs on the United States, which was able to bear them, and on the Soviet Union, which ultimately was not.[23] The arms competition also overshadowed the parallel pursuit of nuclear risk-reduction mechanisms. Critics of the early arms limitation accords asserted that loopholes would be exploited by the Soviet Union and, as a consequence, new U.S. strategic modernization programs would have to be pursued. Supporters of arms control vainly sought to close all loopholes that increased risks of an arms competition. They succeeded in blocking national missile defenses, but not strategic modernization programs.

The Action–Reaction Syndrome

Domestic debates over arms race stability were never conclusive and always overheated. Arms control supporters worried greatly about the "action–reaction phenomenon," a term that gained currency when President Lyndon Baines Johnson and Secretary of Defense Robert McNamara were agonizing over initiating construction of a national missile defense system. McNamara advertised the duality of his thinking by attaching the following warning to his speech announcing this initiative:

> Whatever be their intentions, whatever be our intentions, actions—or even realistically potential actions—on either side relating to the build-up of nuclear forces, be they either offensive or defensive weapons, necessarily trigger reactions from the other side. It is precisely this action–reaction phenomenon that fuels an arms race.[24]

The hoped-for start of strategic arms limitation talks in the Johnson administration came at the very cusp of national missile defenses deployments. As noted in Chapter 3, President Johnson's letter to Soviet Premier Aleksey N. Kosygin spelled out how the presumed action–reaction phenomenon would dash hopes for these talks. The Soviet invasion of Czechoslovakia postponed the initial strategic arms limitation talks to the Nixon administration, which was worried less about the action–reaction syndrome than about the Congress' will to compete with the Soviet Union. This postponement diminished greatly the hopes of arms controllers to forgo the deployment of MIRVs.

Albert Wohlstetter led the charge against this construct of arms racing, labeling McNamara's term a "portentous tautology."[25] Actually, Wohlstetter's analysis did not so much reject the action–reaction syndrome as to point out its lopsidedness: In his view, the United States was insufficiently responsive to Soviet arms racing. And yet the United States continued to surpass the Soviet Union in warhead numbers for deployed strategic forces throughout the Cold War. The concerns of U.S. Hawks were certainly not shared by the Kremlin or the Soviet General Staff, which felt disadvantaged by America's technical adroitness. Wohlstetter was surely right, however, in arguing that McNamara's characterization of the arms competition was far too narrow. This became evident when McNamara's prediction of Soviet restraint in response to his capping U.S. strategic force levels was quickly proven wrong by the Kremlin. Interlocking institutional, ideological, bureaucratic, and domestic political factors drove the competition upward, even after both superpowers agreed to forgo national missile defenses in the 1972 SALT accords. The nuclear arms competition became another form of jockeying for advantage—or at least avoiding disadvantage. The competition was dangerous, but not nearly as hazardous as, say, jockeying over the status of Berlin.

Hawks and Doves had their separate explanations for the arms competition, but both camps could plainly see its effects. By choosing not to stop the flight testing and deployment of MIRVs in the 1972 strategic arms limitation accords, the Nixon administration ensured that the costs and risks of the arms competition would not be minimized. This was, as William Hyland noted, "a truly fateful decision that changed strategic relations, and changed them to the detriment of American security."[26] Hyland's boss, Henry Kissinger, subsequently expressed regret over the decision to let MIRVs run free, but at the crucial juncture of choice he insisted on deploying them as "our counterweight to the growing Soviet numbers."[27] Many Hawks shared Kissinger's view. The action–reaction syndrome applied not just to offense–defense interactions, but to offense–offense dynamics, as well. The failure to make hard decisions banning MIRVs became a cross that defenders of arms control had to bear. Proponents of MIRVing subsequently became arms control's harshest critics.

As for Schelling and Halperin's third criterion for strategic arms control—curtailing the scope and violence in the event war occurs—little needs be said. By working in tandem with nuclear deterrence, strategic arms control helped to strengthen the threshold and affix the taboo against using nuclear weapons, thereby helping to prevent a nuclear war. At the same time, the huge size of MIRVed arsenals meant that, even when U.S. and Soviet political leaders agreed to push the strategic arms competition into reverse gear, any crossing of the nuclear threshold could escalate, resulting in massive destruction. The destructive power codified in arms control treaties that was deemed necessary for deterrence was totally at odds with Schelling and Halperin's third criterion.

Arms Control and Strategic Stability

The most important contribution of arms control in its formative years was the development of specialized and novel communication channels. If nuclear deterrence broke down, for whatever reason, these channels could be employed to try to stop escalation and to limit damage. The size of the arsenals permitted by strategic arms accords and the prominence of deterrence theory obscured the importance of this contribution. Escalation control in the aftermath of a nuclear exchange would have been brutally difficult even with the understandings and communication channels established through prior negotiations. In their absence, escalation control would have been completely hostage to fate.

Limiting the destructive potential of weaponry was cited by Paul Warnke, President Jimmy Carter's SALT negotiator and Director of the Arms Control and Disarmament Agency, as one of the three most important goals of arms control. Warnke's other two criteria were to improve the stability of the strategic nuclear balance and to reduce the prospect of surprise attack.[28] These twin objectives served stability, especially in crises. "The primary goal of any arms control scheme must be to increase stability," wrote Henry Kissinger in 1960.[29] "Stability," as Josef Joffe noted, "is its own reward because it prevents worse arms races, nuclear proliferation, and actual conflicts that might draw in bystanders."[30]

Both Hawks and Doves agreed that arms control must carry the heavy burdens of fostering crisis and strategic stability. Stability, in Kissinger's view, mandated that "the purpose of arms control measures must be to strengthen so far as possible the relative position of the defender, either by enhancing the security of his force or by complicating the calculations of the aggressor."[31] The SALT I accords negotiated by Nixon and Kissinger violated these precepts by foreclosing national missile defenses while letting offenses run free. Theory, in this instance, collided with the reality that missile defenses were technically unsound and politically unpopular, while improvements in nuclear offenses were easily obtainable and cost-effective.

The problem with the Nixon administration's handiwork was not the ABM Treaty's prohibition on national missile defenses, since they were incapable of carrying out intercepts, but entirely capable of generating even more nuclear offense. Rather, the fundamental design flaw in the SALT I accords was the failure to constrain offenses by letting MIRVs run free. This outcome, as well as the secretive and exclusionary manner that Nixon and Kissinger used to reach it, insured a harsh backlash against subsequent arms control efforts. A torrent of criticism accompanied Soviet moves to follow the United States by MIRVing its missile forces. Meanwhile, supporters of arms control rallied to block hawkish remedies, such as increasing the accuracy and destructive power of U.S. warheads or seeking to nullify Soviet moves by deploying missile defenses.

In retrospect, the bitter Cold War debates over the impact of strategic modernization programs and missile defense deployments upon strategic and crisis stability were clearly overdrawn. A keen foreign observer of these supercharged debates, Lawrence Freedman, noted with irony that, "The nuclear balance appeared as a sort of gyroscope upon which the equilibrium of the whole international system depended, thereby exaggerating the importance of every nuance."[32] Beneath the hue and cry over who was ahead, who was falling behind, and which new initiative would have severely damaging implications for the balance of terror, the brutish fact remained that both superpowers retained under every imaginable circumstance the ability to inflict massive damage on the other. During the Cold War, strategic arms control was unable to alter the fundamentals of assured destruction which, perforce, meant that a large measure of stability was built into the equations codified by treaties.

In actuality, the requirement of strategic and crisis stability, Freedman wrote, "was achieved almost as soon as the requirement was stated."[33] The size and composition of nuclear force levels, dutifully codified by treaties, had this effect. As Joseph Nye noted, "The reciprocal vulnerability of strategic forces to a first strike was diminished less by arms control agreements than by the development of ballistic missile submarines in the late 1950s."[34] Hawks kept insisting that the balance of terror was delicate, and Doves bought into this argument; each camp fiercely contested the other's preferences on precisely these grounds. In actuality, damage expectancies would remain intolerably high in the event of a nuclear war. There was no escape from mutual assured destruction during the Cold War. Arms control accords met the objectives of strategic and crisis stability precisely because these criteria were so easy to meet. Arms control could be faulted for being too permissive, but permissiveness served the interests of a nuclear balance that could not be easily tipped.

The stylized battles between Hawks and Doves over strategic arms control exaggerated many things, while obscuring one fundamental point: Each side desperately needed the other—not simply for the purposes of political vilification, but also for the construction of a viable strategic synthesis. Each side had an essential, but partial truth to tell. For Hawks, truth lay in the necessity for vigilance against an evil empire. For Doves, truth lay in the necessity to wall off nuclear weapons from actual use, and to find collaborative accord on at least this one competitive pursuit. The remedies proposed by Hawks provided impetus to the outcomes favored by Doves, while the intellectual constructs championed by Doves could be given successful content only by hawkish administrations.

The Death and Resurrection of Strategic Arms Control

Strategic arms control was declared to be irrelevant, if not dead, many times. At the end of the Carter administration, Leslie Gelb declared that, "[A]rms control has essentially failed. Three decades of U.S.–Soviet competition have done little more than to codify the arms race."[35] At the outset of the Reagan presidency, key portfolios were handed to the sharpest critics of arms control treaties, who gleefully predicted their demise. In 1984, Zbigniew Brzezinski opined that, "A very strong case can be made that we've come to the end of the road with traditional arms control agreements."[36] The rejection of the Comprehensive Test Ban by Senate Republicans toward the end of the Clinton administration appeared to many to be a crippling blow. And at the outset of the presidency of George W. Bush, administration officials called for "a clear and clean break from the past," especially from the ABM Treaty, which was deemed a "relic of the Cold War."[37] Bush's subsequent withdrawal from the Treaty produced another spate of obituaries.

Time and again, these dire predictions proved to be premature. As Paul Warnke liked to say, if arms control were killed, it would have to be resurrected. No president could do without arms control accords, out of strategic as well as political necessity. In the early phases of this enterprise, the sentiment was sometimes expressed that strategic arms control was essential to prevent conflict. In this vein, the science advisor to presidents Eisenhower and Kennedy, George Kistiakowsky, testified, "In the 20th century previous arms races normally ended in wars, not in agreed disarmament."[38] Over time, a more nuanced appreciation of strategic arms control took hold. Contending political relationships and objectives caused wars, not arms races. Nonetheless, arms races added to tensions and created impediments to improved political relations. Conversely, arms control removed impediments to improved political relations and steered the competition into safer channels between states that did not wish a direct clash of arms, especially nuclear arms. The varied channels attendant on strategic arms control also helped to prevent wars by accident or miscalculation.

The value of strategic arms control was repeatedly undersold. Not surprisingly, its potential contributions to extraordinarily positive outcomes were largely unanticipated, even by its keenest academic observers. Michael Mandelbaum wrote in 1979 that nuclear arms control helped to prevent war, but also served to freeze political relations between two opposing camps. Thus blocked, the superpowers shifted the nuclear competition to qualitative dimensions, making the nuclear arms race self-perpetuating.[39] A decade later, Robert Jervis concluded that, "The main purpose of such treaties is to control our expectations and beliefs, not our arms."[40]

Similarly, an even-handed Reagan-era assessment of strategic arms control concluded that:

> without arms control, both U.S. and Soviet force totals probably would be higher than they are now. The arguments suggesting that the United States is worse off [because of arms control] tend to be more theoretical

than real ... it is pointed out that the arms control age has witnessed a shift in the strategic balance toward the Soviet Union. This may indeed be a correct assessment, but to point out that arms control reflects this change is not to hold it responsible.

This assessment was issued shortly before the path-breaking 1987 treaty eliminating intermediate-range nuclear forces, which invalidated the following conclusions:

> What is most striking about the arms control experience ... is what it did not do. Those who hoped arms control would bring about major reductions in existing or planned inventories or slow the introduction of new and more capable technologies have little grounds for satisfaction ... What emerges above all is the modesty of what arms control has wrought. Expectations, for better or for worse, for the most part have not been realized ... If the history reveals anything, it is that arms control has proved neither as promising as some had hoped nor as dangerous as others had feared.[41]

Almost no one anticipated the demise of the Soviet Union and the resulting potential for drastic arms reductions. But advocates of strategic arms control remained optimistic throughout the Cold War that, over time, deep cuts could be realized. One of their most prominent members, George F. Kennan, constructed the strategy of containment on similar grounds—that a holding action would subsequently produce significant gains. (Kennan preceded Ronald Reagan in calling for 50 percent reductions in strategic nuclear forces after the second strategic arms limitation treaty was shelved in 1979.) The deep cuts engineered by Reagan, Gorbachev, and their immediate successors, Presidents George H. W. Bush and Boris Yeltsin, were what the arms control community wanted all along, but could not themselves deliver. The fruits of decades of effort could be marketed only in the conditions produced by conservative Republican administrations and a failing Soviet state. Nonetheless, the prior contributions of strategic arms control were critical to this successful outcome, since the structure of previous accords and long-standing dialogue facilitated quick adaptation and codification of changing political circumstances.

Arms control also made modest, but nonetheless essential, contributions during the most virulent passages of the Cold War. Lawrence Freedman pointed out the obvious but much overlooked point that the process of arms control was "essentially political;" it was "a means of maintaining an active diplomatic relationship at times of tension, providing a forum for dialogue on military issues."[42] Skeptics of arms control focused on the intricacies of the nuclear balance, readily finding the process wanting on crisis stability or arms race stability grounds. But administrations that tried to walk away from the process soon walked back. "The key role of arms control," wrote Joseph Nye, "is political in the sense of creating communication and reassurance."[43] Too much was riding on this process for political leaders to declare it irrelevant or detrimental to national security. President George W. Bush's initial conception of a "clear and clean" break with the past relied heavily on informal, flexible arrangements. But Americans, allies, and the Kremlin preferred to codify obligations. After heroic efforts by previous presidents to secure intrusive monitoring arrangements for strategic arms control, the Bush administration had no effective rejoinder to those repeating President Reagan's admonition, "trust but verify."

Arms control negotiations provided a road map through the security dilemmas of a nuclear-armed competition. Traveling these twisting byways required learning about adversarial perspectives and practices. The initiation of strategic arms limitation talks mandated the exchange of once-classified information. The process began with Soviet military officials chiding U.S. negotiators for providing details of the Kremlin's nuclear force posture, which their civilian counterparts were not privy to. The sacrifice of secrecy for mutual reassurance achieved another milestone in the SALT I accords, which obliged the United States and Soviet Union not to conceal treaty-relevant information from the prying eyes of satellites. Subsequent efforts finally produced Soviet acceptance of intrusive on-site inspections in 1986. In the absence of an arms control process that, in Nye's terminology, "helped change cognitive processes of learning,"[44] these gains were inconceivable, as were the institutions created to routinize cooperation to reduce nuclear danger.

Until the breakthroughs presided over by Mikhail Gorbachev and Ronald Reagan, strategic arms control was maddeningly difficult, reflecting the novelty of the practice, the political divides it engendered, and the stark dichotomies of the U.S.–Soviet contest. Its lead advocates within the political arena swam against strong tides, sometimes at great personal sacrifice. Those arguing for restraint at key junctures—by maintaining hedges but not crossing fateful thresholds first—had their patriotism impugned. J. Robert Oppenheimer had his security clearances lifted after opposing the development of the hydrogen bomb, and Paul Warnke thought it better to resign than to become the Carter administration's lightening rod defending the Second Strategic Arms Limitation Treaty.

These indignities were pursued in a just cause whose most breathtaking gains were realized by others. As Johan Jørgen Holst wrote, despite decades of harsh criticism, "The arms control perspective has taken hold."[45] Deep cuts and on-site inspections were achievable only after decades of concerted effort by successive administrations. Once achieved, they became part of the political landscape. The truth of Holst's assertion is measured best by the accomplishments of professed skeptics. Harsh critics of strategic arms control, men like Ronald Reagan and Paul Nitze, ended up working—and succeeding—within its constructs, building upon the scaffolding erected by rivals. Their seminal accomplishments deconstructed the artifices of nuclear might to which they previously accorded great meaning. The dragon of nuclear arms racing was slain by those who previously provided the beast full nourishment.

The Derailment of Arms Control Strategy

While strategic arms control was falsely declared to be dead many times over, the classic rationales for the process were, indeed, on life support once the Soviet Union came apart. The sudden demise of the sole U.S. strategic competitor made calculations of arms racing and crisis stability largely irrelevant. The fall of the USSR did not, however, make deep cuts and on-site inspections irrelevant. Far from it: When the primary concerns of strategic arms control switched from Soviet strength to Russia's multiple weaknesses, Cold War treaty instruments remained useful, but for reasons far distant from those articulated by Schelling and Halperin. Nuclear arms reduction, intrusive inspections, and mandatory cooperation were now important because they could readily be adapted and expanded to a new kind of threat reduction bearing on potential breakdowns of command and control in Russia or the leakage of lethal weapons and materials from old Soviet stockpiles. Before, the reductions of deployed forces were central; now they became the most visible elements of a far broader set of cooperative endeavors. It turned out that Cold War treaties mandating deep cuts were far more adaptable than anyone envisioned at the time of their negotiation.

While the conflation of strategic arms reduction with cooperative threat reduction was quietly taking place after the fall of the Soviet Union, the old rationales for strategic arms control remained fixed in public discourse, reflecting the concepts and language developed in the 1960s. The "golden age" of conceptualization was from 1959 to 1961, when study groups in Cambridge (Massachusetts), London, and New York helped to formulate ideas that were reflected in *Strategy and Arms Control, The Control of the Arms Race, Arms Control, Disarmament, and National Security* (an influential compilation of essays edited by Donald G. Brennan), and Henry Kissinger's *The Necessity for Choice*. "Development of this new theory was very rapid," wrote Morton H. Halperin. "The next twenty years were to see its extraordinary popularization but virtually no intellectual development."⁴⁶ Thomas C. Schelling later concluded that "the thinking on arms control was on the right track, and was effective, from the late 1950s to the early 1970s, culminating in the Anti-Ballistic Missile Treaty of 1972, but that things have derailed since."⁴⁷

Many conceptualizers of arms control left their academic perches to help translate their ideas into public policy. Their big idea was that the acceptance of mutual vulnerability was essential to prevent nuclear war. This core principle of assured destruction (soon re-labeled as Mutual Assured Destruction, or MAD, by a disaffected Brennan) was more than a fact of Cold War life; it was codified by treaties permitting huge offensive nuclear arsenals while expressly prohibiting national missile defenses.

The derailment of arms control strategy, in Schelling's view, occurred in the post-ABM Treaty period with "the shift in interest from the *character* of weapons to their *numbers*." The fixation with numbers—shared by Hawks as well as Doves—related to treaty limits and sub-limits "having nothing to do with weapon characteristics that most deserve attention." Arms control, Schelling argued, needed to be about reducing lethality and capabilities for pre-emption. The Reagan administration shared this view, but applied it selectively to Soviet forces: strategic arms control during the first Reagan term was about reducing Moscow's pre-emption capabilities while increasing Washington's. This deepened Schelling's alienation, as he watched the Reagan team seek to deploy the silo-busting and extremely vulnerable "Peacekeeper" missile, rather than to shift more of the U.S. nuclear deterrent to sea. When mimicking the most destabilizing Soviet weapons was justified in terms of the permissibility of treaty provisions and the imperative to increase negotiating leverage, Schelling got off the boat. "Who needs arms control," he asked, "if economical and reliable retaliatory weapons are available that are neither susceptible to pre-emption nor capable of pre-emption? ... [A]rms control appears to get in the way of pursuing its own objective."⁴⁸

This critique also proved to be premature, thanks to the efforts of seasoned U.S. negotiators such as Secretary of State George Shultz and his arms control adviser Paul Nitze, who succeeded in paring down significantly land-based missiles and warheads that were most susceptible to, and capable of, pre-emption. These deal makers, in turn, were greatly assisted by obstinate colleagues who failed in their intended goal of blocking agreements. (The most adept treaty blocker, Richard Perle, once noted, "Democracies will not sacrifice to protect their security in the absence of a sense of danger. And every time we create the impression that we and the Soviets are cooperating and moderating the competition, we diminish that sense of apprehension."⁴⁹)

The hard-line tactics of treaty foes ultimately provided deal makers with the leverage needed to reach favorable terms with the Kremlin.

Arms controllers watched these pitched intramural battles in the Reagan administration from the sidelines, their voices of doom later silenced by stunning successes. Another consummate deal maker, Secretary of State James A. Baker III, subsequently seized the opportunities presented by the full-scale retreat of Soviet power and anti-Soviet ideologues in the United States. The strategic arms accords reached in the administration of President George H. W. Bush finally shifted the competition into reverse gear, promising cuts in deployed warheads to pre-MIRV levels. Indeed, the second strategic arms reduction accord finally banned MIRVed land-based missiles, an objective arms controllers tried and failed to achieve in the SALT accords.

The belated realization of the promise of strategic arms control and the achievement of deep cuts did not redound to the credit of the conceptualizers and early practitioners of arms control. The reasons why were plain enough: These accords were negotiated by conservative Republican administrations during a period of stark decline in the Kremlin's fortunes. Credit was therefore given to skeptics of the enterprise who stood fast while the Soviet Union crumbled. This credit was surely due, since skeptics negotiated with far more authority than arms controllers. But there was little doubt that skeptics succeeded by building upon the foundations laid by a community they often scorned. The virtues of deep cuts and getting rid of MIRVed missiles were ideas that originated in the arms control community and were subsequently appropriated by its critics. The cornerstone of this foundation—the acceptance of mutual vulnerability—helped to keep the Cold War from becoming hot, while fostering deep cuts. Conservative Republican administrations railed against the condition of national vulnerability, but their most notable treaty successes depended upon it.

The foundations of strategic arms control rest on paradox—and not just on the paradoxical virtues of vulnerability or the successes of skeptics. In addition to facilitating deep cuts, the demise of the Soviet Union also signaled the demise of mutual vulnerability as a central organizing principle for strategic arms control. MAD was essential company during the Cold War, but times had changed. Skeptics felt free to discard MAD during a new era of U.S. primacy, while the arms control community responded to renewed assaults on the ABM Treaty by finding continued virtue in national vulnerability. By continuing to rally around MAD, arms controllers were unable to explain themselves at a time of unchallenged U.S. superiority, troubling missile proliferation, and the rise of unconventional threats to national security. Paradoxically, soon after the fruition of many decades of effort to achieve deep cuts, the arms control community found itself unable to communicate to the American public.

Arms controllers boxed themselves into a classic defense of the ABM Treaty, linking the Treaty's continued viability to the achievement of still deeper reductions and the avoidance of arms racing. In actuality, deeper cuts would happen with or without the ABM Treaty because of Russia's inability to compete with the United States. Arms racing was no longer the issue; proliferation was central. The true value of the ABM Treaty shifted with the end of the Cold War from the containment of superpower rivalry to the containment of proliferation. By retaining the ABM Treaty at a time when Russia could no longer compete, Washington could offer Moscow needed reassurance, in return for its help on proliferation.

The classic arms control linkage between strategic arms reduction and non-proliferation was explicitly codified in Article VI of the Non-Proliferation Treaty, which tied continued abstinence by non-nuclear-weapon states to disarmament efforts by the nuclear powers. Critics of arms control scoffed at the impracticality of achieving nuclear disarmament. Nevertheless, the goal embedded in Article VI remained for many an essential declaration of intent because an international system predicated on nuclear apartheid was untenable.

While achievement of nuclear disarmament was widely viewed as impractical and dangerous, progress toward it remained essential for many reasons. U.S. and Russian nuclear arsenals were grossly oversized, Cold War-era targeting lists needed to be pared, and costs could be saved. In addition, the Non-Proliferation Treaty needed to be reinforced: The grand bargain contained in Article VI did not disappear just because the Soviet Union dissolved. While these reasons for deep cuts remained valid, the primary utility of mutual reductions after the Cold War ended shifted: Mutual reductions were now essential to facilitate cooperative threat reduction (CTR) programs in the former Soviet Union.

Reassurance had now eclipsed deterrence in dealings with the Russian Federation, and reassurance was now needed to control dangerous materials at the source. The links between reassurance and deterrence were not discussed in public by either Washington or Moscow, but they were mutually understood. Every additional, far-flung, and poorly secured nuclear weapon storage site divulged by Moscow in order to benefit from U.S.-supplied locks, fences, and surveillance equipment would become another target for Pentagon war planners. The divulgence of Moscow's weaknesses therefore correlated with its readings of Washington's intentions. Controls over dangerous weapons and materials in Russia would henceforth depend on Moscow's comfort level as much as on Washington's largesse.

Russia had no choice but to accept deep cuts in its Cold War arsenal, while the United States could maintain artificially high force levels. By pursuing deep cuts in parallel, Washington could reassure Moscow and open up new areas of cooperative endeavor. After the Cold War ended, the ABM Treaty remained an essential instrument of reassurance for the Kremlin because, even with parallel reductions, the United States would retain strategic superiority. The Treaty's codification of mutual vulnerability was Moscow's insurance blanket. The most potent argument for the ABM Treaty's continued viability was that it facilitated cooperative threat reduction programs, not deep cuts.

Russia had plenty of company in seeking to retain the ABM Treaty after the Cold War ended. No foreign capital cheered when President George W. Bush announced his intention to withdraw from the Treaty in December 2001. The international community had come to rely upon the ABM Treaty as the "cornerstone" of strategic stability, a lexicon readily accepted by the Clinton administration. At a time of dominant and ever-growing U.S. power projection capabilities, America's allies as well as its potential adversaries viewed the ABM Treaty as a check against unbridled U.S. unilateralism. Moreover, by removing this cornerstone, they feared that the structures of nuclear deterrence and arms control erected during the Cold War could topple. These concerns were privately shared by allies seeking safety under the U.S. nuclear umbrella or their own national deterrents, and vocalized strenuously by Beijing and Moscow. Sergei Ivanov, then the Secretary of Russian President Vladimir Putin's Security Council, publicly warned in February 2001 that, "[T]he destruction of the ABM Treaty, we are quite confident, will result in the annihilation of the whole structure of strategic stability and create prerequisites for a new arms race."[50]

President George W. Bush called this bluff, engendering only the most tepid responses. Arguments that were powerfully persuasive in the 1960s, 1970s, and 1980s—that missile defenses would prompt arms racing and upset strategic stability—had little bearing at the turn of the century, when Russia and China did not have the means or the inclination to compete in an arms race with the United States. Leaders in both countries would no doubt act to meet the challenges posed by U.S. missile defense deployments, but would be sensible enough to do so through less expensive means.

During the Cold War, it was absolutely necessary to argue the counterintuitive case that national safety rested on vulnerability. This argument stopped making sense when new proliferation threats arose, and when the primary source of strategic vulnerability emanated from Russian weakness rather than Soviet strength. Every time the arms control community rose to defend the ABM Treaty against another Republican onslaught by championing MAD and sounding the alarm of arms racing, its standing diminished. By the time President George W. Bush entered office, arms controllers had essentially lost their domestic audience.

The Clinton administration tried to adapt classic arms control rationales to its plans for limited national missile defenses, but succeeded only in alienating those who wished to confirm MAD as well as those who sought its complete demise. The care with which the Clinton team sought to parse differences between opposing domestic camps was evident with the publication of leaked "talking points" to the Kremlin on how the administration proposed to square MAD with its proposed missile defenses. The Kremlin need not worry about limited national missile defenses, the Clinton administration argued, because Russia would retain "the certain ability to carry out an annihilating counter-attack ... regardless of the conditions under which the war began." To reinforce this point, the Clinton administration noted that Russia would retain strategic forces "on constant alert," so that it had little to fear about U.S. pre-emption.[51]

This case was carefully drawn and analytically defensible. It was also deeply unpersuasive, even among Clinton administration officials, not to mention their domestic critics and foreign audiences. The Clinton team's ambivalence about its own proposals undermined its case, as did the tone-deafness and intellectual narrowness of its argument. By walking a fine analytical line between missile defense enthusiasts and arms controllers, the tight-rope walkers in the Clinton administration lost their balance. One stanchion for the tight rope was removed when missile defense advocates were freed from having to accept MAD by the demise of the Soviet Union. The other was kicked away by staunch defenders of MAD in the arms control community, who sought deep cuts and lowered alert rates in U.S. and Russian nuclear forces as a substitute for missile defenses.

The arms control community's prescriptions for deep cuts and "de-alerting" were not predicated on waiting for the Kremlin to ratify treaties.[52] For some in the arms control community, the threat of an accidental or unauthorized launch "resulting from an error in Russia's warning system or a failure in its command-and-control system" constituted the "greatest" threat facing the United States.[53] This conclusion seemed greatly overdrawn, given the far more evident dangers resulting from loosened controls over dangerous weapons and materials in the former Soviet Union. It was also at variance with U.S. intelligence community assessments that ascribed a low risk of accidental or unauthorized Russian missile launch.[54]

While arms controllers were seeking ways to relieve ratification gridlock, treaty critics sought to tie the Clinton administration's hands. They conditioned deep cuts to Russian consent to ratify the second strategic arms reduction treaty (START II). The Kremlin, in turn, made it known that it could only accept START II, which eliminated its last strategic advantage—MIRVed land-based missiles—with the U.S. Senate's reaffirmation of the ABM Treaty, to which most Republicans were adamantly opposed. Treaties governing strategic offense and missile defense were becoming tied in a Gordian knot.

The Clinton administration tried to untie this knot by walking a tight-rope between deal makers and deal breakers. It colluded with Republicans on Capitol Hill to defer the implementation of deep cuts and de-alerting measures, hoping to leverage the Russian Duma into consenting to ratify START II. At the same time, it offered to compensate for deficiencies in the Kremlin's tattered early warning network by providing assistance on shared notifications of missile launches.[55] These mixed messages leveraged no one and alienated many. By withholding deep cuts and de-alerting, the Clinton administration not only failed to convince the Kremlin to ratify START II, but also encouraged it to maintain dangerously aging nuclear forces in the field. And by arguing that continued high alert rates by Russian forces were an insurance policy against limited U.S. missile defenses, the Clinton administration undermined the case for de-alerting.

Republicans on Capitol Hill waited for a new administration to take office before permitting deep cuts and de-alerting in the absence of—and perhaps as a replacement for—formalized treaty provisions. Presidential candidate George W. Bush's campaign platform on these matters was more forward-leaning than his opponent, Vice President Al Gore, whose defense of classic arms control tenets on the hustings ("nuclear unilateralism will hinder rather than help arms control")[56] alienated supporters while failing to enlist new recruits. Candidate Bush championed deep cuts while bad-mouthing treaties. The Kremlin waited until the Clinton administration's days were numbered to ratify START II, conditioned upon the U.S. Senate's reaffirmation of the ABM Treaty. Moscow again prepared to take its chances on another Republican administration that would presumably talk tough about treaties before settling on a deal.

The Gordian knot tightened over theater ballistic missile defenses designed to help shield forward-deployed U.S. troops and allies from neighboring missile threats. Treaty foes supported the unrestricted flight testing and deployment of these defenses—but not amendments to the ABM Treaty expressly permitting weapon systems in development. To do so, in their view, would only re-validate the ABM Treaty. Many arms controllers took a jaundiced view toward advanced theater missile defenses, since they could encroach upon, or even substitute for, the national missile defenses prohibited under the Treaty. (Missile defenses able to shoot down long-range missiles possessed by maverick states could also have some applicability against ocean-spanning missiles.) Again, the Clinton administration walked the tight-rope between arms controllers and missile defense enthusiasts, loosening the ABM Treaty's constraints to allow more advanced theater missile defenses. This deeply chagrined arms controllers who presumed that treaty opponents would not be content with half a loaf, and that advanced missile defenses could be used to gut the Treaty. Missile defense enthusiasts were not placated. They promised to reject these accords whenever the Clinton administration transmitted them to the Senate. The Clinton White House refrained from doing so.

The concerns of the arms control community were well founded. Missile defense enthusiasts were not satisfied with loosening the bonds of the ABM Treaty; they wished to abrogate, not update, the Treaty. The arms control community's strict constructionist view of the ABM Treaty was therefore understandable, but it was also self-defeating. By adopting an orthodox defense of the Treaty—asserting that vulnerability was an essential condition of successful arms control—arms controllers stopped making sense. They were also guilty of misreading the Treaty. The ABM Treaty did not elevate national vulnerability above all other objectives. To the contrary, it was negotiated, as its preamble stated, to become a means to curb an offensive arms race, to enhance conditions for future progress in negotiations, and to relax tensions. The Treaty itself permitted limited missile defenses, albeit not those that covered the entire national territory. By arguing that the full benefits of the ABM Treaty required the opposition to effective theater missile defenses because the latter could also be employed to defend national territory, staunch defenders of the ABM Treaty boxed themselves into a corner.[57]

President George W. Bush had a clear field when he announced on December 13, 2001 his administration's intention to withdraw from the ABM Treaty six months later. The Treaty's fundamental premise of national vulnerability as a means to achieve broader security objectives no longer correlated to external circumstances. Even if missile attacks against the U.S. homeland were at the bottom of a new threat spectrum marked by Russian weakness and the growth of asymmetric threats, it was no longer possible to enshrine national vulnerability as a cardinal principle of arms control, especially in the wake of terrorist attacks on the U.S. homeland. Treaty supporters failed to offer an alternative construct that could extend the ABM Treaty's viability, while opponents hammered away, seeking its early demise. When Bush announced his decision to withdraw from the treaty, few eulogies were offered.

Born of Cold War necessity, the ABM Treaty survived a frontal challenge during the Reagan administration, and lingered for a decade longer than the Soviet Union. During this transition period, Republicans on Capitol Hill shored up their conservative credentials by opposing the Treaty, whose longevity, no less than its ratification, could be sustained only by bipartisan support. The demise of the ABM Treaty raised many difficult questions for the future of strategic arms control. Would informal arrangements, as initially preferred by the Bush administration, suffice? What mix of offense and defense would best serve U.S. national security interests, and how might the balance between the two be established? Would U.S. primacy facilitate or retard cooperation with Moscow and Beijing? And what strategic concept would now fill the void left by the rejection of MAD and the ABM Treaty?

The withdrawal from the ABM Treaty was a severe blow to the remnants of the arms control community, but it was also an unwelcome gift. Arms controllers were now freed from their own orthodoxy. New recruits could enter the field with new ideas about how best to proceed. Strategic arms control has always been energized by the bad ideas of opponents, two of which—the resumption of nuclear testing and the weaponization of space— were waiting in the wings. The more treaty foes seek to extend their writ, the more they will generate new health and vitality in the arms control community. A new chapter in the history of strategic arms control is waiting to be written.

Blocking actions against unwise initiatives can be energizing, but they are insufficient. The rehabilitation of strategic arms control also requires positive constructs to provide guidelines for the future. The enshrinement of national vulnerability was a negative, apolitical construct. A new conceptualization is now needed, as well as a new road map for the future. What core principles should now guide this enterprise? These principles must reduce dangers posed by weapons of mass destruction in an era of asymmetric warfare. In this new era, proliferation will be the most effective counter to American primacy and power projection capabilities. Success in countering proliferation will require not just U.S. military might, but the cooperation of others. Thus, the void created by the rejection of MAD and the ABM Treaty must be filled in ways that facilitate cooperation with major powers, strengthen relations with friends and allies, while curtailing proliferation. The void created by the rejection of MAD and the ABM Treaty can be filled by elevating cooperative threat reduction from the realm of programmatic initiatives to the status of a strategic concept, alongside military power, nuclear deterrence, preventive diplomacy, and arms control.

CHAPTER 7

From MAD to Cooperative
Threat Reduction

Treaties governing nuclear arms reduction and missile defenses have slipped from their Cold War moorings and now drift in uncharted waters. The Anti-Ballistic Missile (ABM) Treaty and the second Strategic Arms Reduction Treaty (START II) were set aside by President George W. Bush in December 2001. These accords were premised on equality, but the United States and the Russian Federation have become very unequal partners. It is always extremely difficult for arms control treaties to formalize fictional equality or to codify inequality in changing geopolitical circumstances. Durable treaties also require bipartisan political support in the United States, which was non-existent for the ABM Treaty prior to the Bush administration's withdrawal decision.

Bilateral treaties between the United States and Russia remained in limbo for a more fundamental reason. These accords reflected the logic of Mutual Assured Destruction, or MAD, the central organizing principle of strategic arms control during the Cold War. MAD's two most basic tenets, as practiced by the United States and the Soviet Union, were nuclear overkill and vulnerability to missile attack. With the fall of the Soviet Union, these tenets no longer commanded widespread U.S. public or congressional support. A sustainable and bipartisan basis for future U.S. policies geared toward the reduction of nuclear dangers must be built on different terrain.

Nuclear deterrence was separable from MAD. While the latter fell from grace, the former remained essential for U.S. strategic analysts, as well as for major powers and maverick states that feared American military dominance.

Each of these countries pursued nuclear deterrence in quite different ways, however. The demise of the Soviet Union freed some U.S. strategists to seek the replacement of deterrence with compellance. The ten-year plan for a downsized U.S. nuclear posture endorsed by President George W. Bush was compatible with a compellance strategy, since it still permitted coverage of essential targets in Russia and China, maintained large stocks of warheads in reserves, and added conventional strike capabilities to the U.S. nuclear war plan. By overlaying missile defenses atop superior American conventional and nuclear forces, the United States might just be able to replace MAD with unilateral assured destruction against both major powers.[1]

For Russia and China, nuclear deterrence was essential to counter U.S. strategic superiority. In an era of extended and growing American military dominance, the ability to inflict damage on U.S. targets remained their last safeguard against compellance. Having lost an ability to maintain essential equivalence with U.S. nuclear capabilities, Moscow sought fictional numerical parity with Washington, codified in written form. Whatever the numbers agreed to, however, substantial disparities in operational forces and vulnerabilities would remain. The dictates of asymmetric warfare now applied to Russia, since U.S. nuclear capabilities would remain paramount in virtually every respect. Because Washington could exercise escalation dominance (a long-standing superpower ambition during the Cold War, finally realized), henceforth the Kremlin's deterrent would increasingly be measured in terms of its ability to place U.S. metropolitan areas at risk. Beijing faced this problem in far starker terms, given the small size of its intercontinental nuclear forces. For Beijing, the dictates of deterrence might be met by targeting nearby U.S. bases as well as a few American cities. For both major powers, the acronym MAD now stood for "Minimal Assured Destruction."

After watching the United States wage war against the Taliban in Afghanistan, leaders in maverick states who feared being toppled had new reasons to seek weapons of mass destruction (WMD), hoping to deter the arrival of American expeditionary forces. These deadly weapons were also useful to muscle weaker states or to counter similarly armed neighbors. The selection of WMD varied, depending on successes with indigenous production or foreign acquisition. The deterrent most vulnerable to pre-emptive attack—ocean-spanning ballistic missiles—was also the hardest to acquire. Thus, deterrence for leaders in states of proliferation concern is likely to rest on cruder instruments directed at closer targets, such as staging areas for American forces and nearby U.S. allies.

These varied recalibrations of deterrence had one connecting thread: Cold War calculations of MAD were widely displaced. MAD made perverse sense in a monumental struggle between mortal rivals during the Cold War, but no more. That bygone strategic competition produced many thousands of nuclear weapons and prospective targets for mushroom clouds. Both countries placed large numbers of these warheads on ballistic missiles that could traverse long distances in a matter of minutes. Improvements in guidance and warhead design meant that heavily fortified targets, such as missile silos and command and control centers, could quickly and euphemistically be placed "at risk." To avoid being disadvantaged in the event of a surprise attack, both countries maintained a significant portion of their strategic nuclear forces on "hair-trigger" alert.

Under these circumstances, the United States and the Soviet Union chose not to define MAD in minimal terms of, say, the demolition of a capital city, or ten important cities, or 50 percent of either nation's conventional military or military–industrial capacity. These targets could certainly be found in U.S. and Soviet nuclear war plans, but both nuclear rivals believed that the requirements of deterrence were far more exacting. War plans became inextricably linked to the superpower competition, in both its political and military dimensions. The requirements of nuclear deterrence became relative, not absolute. If one side seemed to be gaining a quantitative or qualitative advantage in nuclear forces, the other had to respond. What one side needed depended on what the other had, or was perhaps seeking. Nuclear forces, no less than superpower diplomacy, served the twin pursuits of seeking advantage and avoiding being placed at a disadvantage.

Nuclear deterrence therefore became synonymous with huge numbers of nuclear weapons, expansive target lists, and forces ready to fire. Under these circumstances, neither superpower could allow missile defense deployments to go unanswered. To do so would have accentuated perceptions of advantage or disadvantage. In 1972, Washington and Moscow reluctantly agreed to forgo national missile defenses that would be both ineffective and that would fuel even bigger nuclear arsenals.

MAD's precepts clearly need rethinking in an era of asymmetric warfare. Russia's national budget is now roughly the size of Belgium's, and the Kremlin is in no position to reconstitute a nuclear arms race. Instead, Moscow's nuclear forces face block obsolescence, and its command and control networks as well as military personnel will be stressed and underfunded over the next ten years or more. It no longer makes sense for the United States to cling to policies that keep dangerous, over-age Russian nuclear forces in the field and on alert.

Nor does it make sense to maintain expansive targeting lists and high alert rates against states with very small nuclear capabilities. After all, how many nuclear weapons does it take to deter far weaker states? If a small fraction of the U.S. nuclear arsenal fails to dissuade a national leader from taking precipitous risks, a much larger arsenal would be irrelevant for deterrence. And if a state of concern is so unhinged as to carry out a mass casualty attack against the United States that could quickly be traced back to its point of origin, does it really matter if the devastating response comes two days, two hours or fifteen minutes later? Nuclear overkill, high alert rates and defenselessness are particularly ill-suited for a new era of asymmetric warfare. A U.S. nuclear posture that continues to promote these attributes in other states is both counterproductive and dangerous.

New nuclear weapon states will certainly not emulate the size of Cold War arsenals, but their early moves have taken a familiar form. Even partial emulation creates special difficulties in Asia. China, India, and Pakistan have all declared that they will avoid the excesses of western nuclear theology, but they appear trapped in calculations where requirements are determined in relative, not absolute, terms. In just this fashion, domestic political, institutional, and geopolitical factors drove the competition upward between Washington and Moscow: Falling behind was not an option. Deterrence calculations will be of an entirely different (and wiser) scale in Asia, but MAD will also be harder to calibrate because the calculus of competition in southern Asia is triangular rather than bipolar. If nuclear capabilities grow on one leg of this triangle, pressures will also grow on the other two.

Thus, while all three states have declared their adherence to minimal, credible nuclear deterrence, no neighbor can take these official statements at face value. Pakistan can least afford MAD's competitive dynamic, yet it maintained two well-funded laboratories competing to produce nuclear weapons and ballistic missiles. The Indian government has officially adopted a "no-first-use" doctrine, while issuing an unofficial, draft nuclear posture that undercuts this core principle by embracing the western requirement of prompt nuclear retaliation. This is not at all helpful, since nuclear forces truly configured to retaliate quickly look indistinguishable from those postured to strike first. China has adopted the most pacific declaratory posture of any nuclear weapon state, but Beijing is also carrying out strategic modernization programs.

Declarations of good intentions are clearly insufficient in Asia. Meanwhile, calculations of deterrence acquire a momentum of their own. Thus, at the turn of the century, Pakistan was considering whether to place nuclear weapons on modified alert; India was contemplating whether to test thermonuclear weapons; and China was weighing how many ballistic missiles to deploy and how to solve the technical challenges associated with placing multiple warheads atop them to counter prospective U.S. missile defenses. In each case, it was difficult for Washington to argue for restraint, when emerging Asian nuclear powers were, in their own modest way, contemplating the emulation of U.S. practices. The Bush administration saw no particular reason to try; it cast aside the second strategic arms reduction accord that banned multiple warheads on land-based missiles, and it stopped the Clinton administration's hectoring of India and Pakistan on their nuclear modernization programs.

Cold War precepts against missile defenses also need to be rethought. The continued virtues of national vulnerability to missile attack are not self-evident in a new era of asymmetric warfare. There are many reasons to reconsider MAD's aversion to defenses. To begin with, accidents happen. Murphy's Law—if something can go wrong, it likely will go wrong—could also apply to a nuclear weapon atop a long-range ballistic missile. The U.S. intelligence community's conclusion that, "an unauthorized or accidental launch of a Russian or Chinese strategic missile is highly unlikely, as long as current security procedures and systems are in place"[2] does not inspire complete confidence, since Russia's security practices do not inspire complete confidence and since China's future course cannot be confidently predicted. In addition, countries in the Middle East and in Asia are acquiring ballistic missiles for leverage against neighbors, to keep U.S. expeditionary forces out, or for instruments of war-fighting. Covert supply networks—involving China, North Korea, and Russia—that help new states to extend the range of their ballistic missiles and to secure mass-casualty weapons are quite difficult to quash.

U.S. foreign and national security policies in troubled regions will henceforth be hampered without missile defenses. As with nuclear weapons, the political utility of missile defenses is likely to far exceed military utility, although the latter must be proven in order to secure the benefits of the former. In future years, the United States must be prepared to aid friends and allies in regions beset with ballistic missiles and WMD. During Cold War crises, Washington would signal resolve by increasing the readiness of U.S. nuclear forces or by moving ships or planes that could well be carrying nuclear weapons into harm's way. Now that the Cold War is over, signaling of this sort by the world's sole nuclear superpower is likely to be provocative and counterproductive to coalition warfare. Henceforth, the management of future crises and the signaling of alliance resolve will be served, in part, by moving theater missile defenses into harm's way.

These arguments do not constitute a blanket endorsement for national missile defenses, and they are insufficient reason to deploy hundreds of missile defense interceptors across the United States. They do, however, constitute grounds for a modest insurance policy of national territory against very low probability threats than could produce an extremely high number of casualties.

Many who reject this notion out of hand do not think twice about paying premiums for catastrophic damage on their home insurance policies. The size of this premium payment ought to be proportional, however, to the declared goal of limited national missile defenses.

Presidential candidate George W. Bush defined a limited defense as one necessary to meet two contingencies—"missile attacks by rogue nations or accidental launches."[3] These twin purposes do not require missile defenses sized to devalue or negate the nuclear deterrents of Russia and China. Thus, truly limited national missile defenses need not impair collaborative efforts with Moscow and Beijing against proliferation threats. If, however, the Bush administration proposes a "limited" national missile defense network of several hundred interceptor missiles, this is likely to be interpreted by Moscow and Beijing as a thinly veiled attempt to devalue or negate their nuclear deterrents. As a consequence, little help might be expected from either capital in future campaigns to counter proliferation. Moscow, in particular, is likely to view proliferation by oil-rich, friendly states as a means to counter overwhelming U.S. superiority while securing the resources needed for military acquisitions. While there are no guarantees that Moscow and Beijing would become partners against proliferation if Washington keeps national missile defenses limited, they are unlikely to provide much help if Washington is perceived as challenging the viability of their nuclear deterrents.

A second cardinal principle relating to missile defenses is the priority that must be attached to fielding systems aligned to the most likely and urgent threats. Those threats reside in troubled regions where the United States has long-standing alliance commitments, forward-deployed forces, and friends in need of protection. The threat posed by long-range ballistic missiles has decreased dramatically since 1987, while the threat posed by shorter-range missiles has grown significantly. Ocean-spanning ballistic missiles have not been used in warfare; theater ballistic missiles were used often by Nazi Germany and by Iraq and Iran in recent wars. States that have acquired ballistic missiles, and have worked hard to extend their range, are also working steadily to acquire weapons of mass destruction. Priority must therefore be given to theater, instead of national missile defenses. While national missile defenses can safely remain modest in pursuit of wider national security interests, theater missile defenses must provide robust coverage.

Debating Missile Defenses and U.S. National Purpose

A domestic U.S. consensus has yet to form over these conclusions at a time when American power is paramount, massive increases in defense spending appear to obviate the need for priorities, muscle flexing appears to be succeeding, and diplomacy is undervalued. One decade after the demise of the Soviet Union, political debate in Washington is marked by the absence of a compelling articulation for international cooperation or treaties, and by a highly motivated campaign against the latter. Arms control orthodoxy is in full retreat, symbolized by President George W. Bush's decision to withdraw from the ABM Treaty. Its basic tenets and themes no longer appear to fit the public mood or national circumstances. This slide was accelerated when supporters of arms control continued to defend Cold War-era treaties with unchanged arguments, when old concerns over arms race and crisis stability simply did not resonate any more.

The Cold War line-up of Hawks and Doves morphed into a debate between Dominators and Conciliators. The demise of the Soviet Union tilted domestic debates toward the preferences of Dominators. Political discourse trended toward coarseness and chest thumping. Cautionary tendencies concerning balance and equilibrium fell by the wayside. Why not take advance of the surprising gift of unchallenged U.S. superiority? And why continue to adhere to treaties that codified non-existent equality and constrained U.S. nuclear options?

While the end of the Cold War liberated Dominators to pursue unilateral impulses, it allowed arms controllers to revisit dreams of nuclear disarmament. The apparent successes of negotiating the Chemical Weapons Convention, the Comprehensive Test Ban Treaty (CTBT), and the indefinite extension of the Non-Proliferation Treaty in the 1990s were accompanied by a spate of studies analyzing new possibilities for the phased elimination of nuclear arsenals.[4] These visionary assessments—the first concerted effort of this kind since the Acheson–Lilienthal and Baruch plans—failed to resonate. Dominators soon checkmated the Clinton administration's incremental plans, and delivered a crippling blow by rejecting the CTBT. Deconstructionists on Capitol Hill who failed to abolish the Department of Education, the Internal Revenue Service, and the National Endowment for the Arts, finally succeeded in killing the U.S. Arms Control and Disarmament Agency. The rout was on. Dominators, clearly ascendant, began to search for more dragons to slay. Their overreaching will provide the basis for the subsequent rehabilitation of Conciliators.

Dominators were empowered by the successful opening campaign against terrorism in Afghanistan. This campaign quickly expanded into a broader effort against states of proliferation concern that aided and abetted terrorism. In his initial State of the Union address, President Bush took aim at an "axis of evil," consisting of Iraq, Iran, and North Korea.[5] These evil-doers were likely to be immune from the subtleties of diplomacy or treaty constraints. After this speech, it became easier to caricature the Bush administration's penchant for military options and disrespect for treaties. This cartoon image masked a harsh and uncontested truth: If Iraq, Iran, or North Korea were to succeed in their ambitions to become nuclear weapon-states, along with their continued acquisition of chemical and biological weapons, non-proliferation regimes would become hollow shells. Conciliators needed the help of Dominators to reaffirm these treaties and *vice versa*. Just as American diplomacy works best when backed up by muscle, the U.S. military needs well-functioning treaties to help prevent rampant proliferation and unilateralism. The weakness in this equation was not in U.S. power projection capability or force of arms, but in arms control.

Arms control accords need to be updated, reconceptualized, and strengthened for a new era of asymmetric threats. The bedrock international norm against the spread of nuclear weapons is enshrined in the Non-Proliferation Treaty, a contract between nuclear "haves" and "have nots." The "haves" promise to kick their nuclear weapon habit while the "have nots" promise continued abstinence. The question of nuclear testing fundamentally divides these two camps. The "haves" cannot credibly claim to be kicking their habit unless they agree to end permanently nuclear testing, which is why abstainers have long demanded the negotiation and entry into force of the CTBT. The CTBT provides essential backup for the Non-Proliferation Treaty.

Dominators blocked ratification of the CTBT on the grounds that nuclear weapons were central to U.S. national security, and that enduring nuclear deterrence required, in all likelihood, renewed testing. If the most powerful, richest, and most technologically advanced country in the world cannot forgo future testing, what messages are conveyed to smaller states looking for ways to neutralize more powerful adversaries? And if nuclear weapons are so central to post-Cold War conceptions of American power, what does this imply for the future of non-proliferation and disarmament treaties?

Dominators do not find these rhetorical questions very compelling because they place far more trust in nuclear weapons than in treaties. They argue that states have their own reasons for testing or acquiring nuclear weapons, and that treaties will not stop them. Sometimes, the loudest complaints against the nuclear club come from states wishing to join, as was the case with India prior to its nuclear tests in 1998. Other states, such as Iran, join this negative chorus because they are covertly looking for ways to neutralize U.S. military advantages, counter powerful neighbors, or project their own power and influence within their region.

There are, indeed, many reasons not to place too much faith either in non-proliferation treaties or the self-serving arguments made against them by those seeking the presumed rewards of WMD. Dominators do not wish to dismantle non-proliferation treaty regimes which, despite their weaknesses, establish international norms against acquiring and using these deadly weapons. Conciliators make the valid point that treaty regimes that are worth keeping are also worth strengthening. The rejoinder by Dominators is that strengthening measures are of little use against miscreants. Instead, they place far greater efficacy in corrective military action. These debates lead to *cul de sacs*, not consensus. Conciliators seek reassurance, while Dominators place their faith in compellance.

The net effect of this conjunction is the unraveling of non-proliferation regimes. Conciliators do not have the power to implement strengthening measures that require the Senate's confirmation, while the compellance posture preferred by Dominators is a surefire recipe for the militarization of U.S. non-proliferation policy. States fearing U.S. power projection capabilities will continue to seek deterrence through their own mass casualty weapons and varied means to deliver them. Rather than having a cautionary effect, successful instances of compellance could breed additional cases of proliferation. A successful, long-term strategy of containing and rolling back proliferation requires the leverage provided by Dominators and the tools favored by Conciliators.

During the Cold War, proliferation was contained because it was in the interest of both superpowers to do so. In a new era of asymmetric warfare, proliferation is generated by imbalances. It is abetted by powerful patrons that seek revenue, influence, and regional counterweights to U.S. power. Proliferation is about hedging one's bets in troubled regions, as well as hedging that the United States might swing from interventionism to insularity—America's peculiar bipolar disorder. Proliferation is also about emulation. New and aspiring members of the nuclear club are, after all, following well-worn paths to power and status. Nuclear powers cannot devalue for other states that which they continue to hold dear. The exercise of U.S. military might to stop other states from acquiring nuclear weapons while Washington prepares to resume nuclear testing constitutes another form of bipolarity, with the same dysfunctional result.

Some theorists of international relations believe that proliferation will have stabilizing effects, similar to those that kept the Cold War from becoming hot.[6] Even if one grants that offsetting nuclear capabilities stabilized superpower relations—a partially true, but nonetheless questionable assertion, given the close calls and crises that marked Cold War experience—there is scant evidence that proliferation is stabilizing in asymmetric contexts. To the contrary, in the one case of offsetting nuclear proliferation since the Cold War ended—that of South Asia—the evidence to date all points in the direction of instability. In this case, offsetting nuclear deterrence has made the Subcontinent "safe" for state-sponsored terrorism, intense crises, clashes between border forces, and limited warfare.[7]

The further march of proliferation, whether in Northeast Asia, the Persian Gulf, or elsewhere, will surely have negative repercussions. If the Visigoths outside the gates seek WMD, those inside the fortress will need them as well. New waves of proliferation not only serve to undermine established order, they undermine the re-establishment of order. Some regions of the globe will be blessedly free of these concerns; others will not. For those residing in troubled regions, proliferation will be the harbinger of dread and the handmaiden of disorder. Wherever proliferation becomes the norm, anarchy lurks in the shadows. Barriers against the use of WMD, painstakingly erected during decades of Cold War crises and reinforced by non-proliferation regimes, will be challenged. When these barriers are breached, anarchy claims additional ground. Every new instance of proliferation leaves citizens at the mercy of the ambitions of their leaders—or of neighboring leaders. If these leaders are responsible, they will embark on a decades-long effort to stabilize and reduce the dangers they have embraced, as was the case during the Cold War.[8] If regional ambitions override prudence, WMD could be used repeatedly in future warfare.

With good reason, then, Dominators gird for battle against proliferation. However, their preferred methods are so imbalanced as to guarantee longterm failure, even in the event of singular victories on the battlefield. Success in combating proliferation cannot be built on military action and compellance alone. The resort to force, when unaccompanied by parallel efforts to strengthen treaty regimes, can become a repetitive phenomenon. But even repetitive military "successes," when accompanied by scorn for arms control and non-proliferation treaties, would further weaken those regimes, setting the stage for more proliferation and more unilateral enforcement—unless the enforcer chooses isolationism instead. To be truly successful, the use of force to counter proliferation needs to be aligned with diplomatic efforts to strengthen the treaty norms one is ostensibly fighting to protect.

Dominators need the preferred instruments of Conciliators as much as treaty supporters need the muscle that Dominators would prefer to apply. When the United States seeks but fails to strengthen treaty norms because of the recalcitrance of other state parties, or when strengthening measures fail to alter the behavior of miscreants, then military action is not only justified, it could be essential to promote public safety and to maintain the integrity of treaty regimes. Indeed, the expressed readiness to act militarily might provide impetus to strengthening measures or improved behavior by states of proliferation concern. Conversely, when the United States rejects or refuses to ratify treaties, fails to pay its dues for treaty implementation, and rejects strengthening measures proposed by others without offering better alternatives, treaty regimes will be weakened—even if military action is successful.

The glaring weakness of the Bush administration's strategy to counter proliferation is the severe imbalance it reflects between defense and diplomacy. President Bush's "axis of evil" speech accentuated the tilt away from treaties and diplomacy, which are almost by definition an inappropriate and feckless instrument against evil. In the fiscal year 2003 budget, missile defense programs received slightly more funding than the Department of State. The administration altered the way it classified missile defenses, making it difficult to differentiate whether funding was going to national or theater defenses. All indications are, however, that funding for national ballistic missile defense, one of the lowest probability threats in an era of asymmetric warfare, exceeded that for defenses against short-range missiles, a far more likely threat.[9] Cooperative threat reduction (CTR) initiatives to safeguard dangerous weapons and materials in the former Soviet Union received approximately one-third of the funds allocated to maintain the U.S. stockpile of nuclear warheads and prepare for a resumption of nuclear tests. These grave imbalances reflect the preferences of Dominators skeptical of treaties and confident in the efficacy of muscling states of proliferation concern.

These imbalances were not unique to the Bush administration. Before the terrorist attacks on September 11, 2001, the United States was spending less than two-tenths of 1 percent of the Pentagon's budget on defending against chemical and biological weapons.[10] To help facilitate Senate consent to ratification of the CTBT, the Clinton administration pumped up funding for nuclear stockpile "stewardship" programs. Upon leaving office, the Test Ban Treaty remained unratified, but U.S. spending for the care of its nuclear stockpile exceeded funding for cooperative threat reduction by a margin of 2:1. Similarly, the Clinton administration allocated twice as much for missile defense as for CTR programs. Overall U.S. spending for nuclear deterrence was 100 times greater than funding for prevention or mitigation of a catastrophic event.[11] The Bush administration inherited these imbalances and further accentuated them.

A New Synthesis

Asymmetric threats are so diverse and difficult to defend against that every available instrument should be applied to this effort. It is profoundly unwise to reject summarily diplomatic and treaty-based tools to counter proliferation, in favor of pre-emptive military strikes or preventive warfare. Pre-emption might well be necessary in rare cases when compelling evidence exists of an impending attack by a state or terrorist group seeking WMD, but in most cases, the evidence of an impending strike will be ambiguous, and the quest for dangerous weapons will be lengthy. American soldiers deserve every opportunity to avoid facing the possibility of chemical, biological, or radiological attacks. Thus, worst-case analysis and the early resort to force could pose more risks than the determined and sustained pursuit of non-military means of redress. If these instruments are tried and found wanting, then the use of force can become a necessary and justifiable action. American military capabilities for this purpose are exceptionally strong, while U.S. interest in preventive diplomacy and strengthening measures for non-proliferation treaties has become quite weak. As long as these imbalances persist, and as long as preventive diplomacy and treaties are the object of scorn in Washington, proliferation will proceed apace, even if U.S. military action is successful.

A new synthesis is needed that combines the continued strengthening of U.S. power projection capabilities with a willingness to work with friends and allies against proliferation threats. In this synthesis, the conventional capabilities that Dominators seek make good sense, while contempt for treaties and multilateral organizations does not. The strengthening of non-proliferation regimes that Conciliators seek makes good sense, while the rejection of minimal national and robust theater missile defenses does not. Both camps agree with the need for deep reductions in deployed nuclear weapons while retaining nuclear deterrence and U.S. conventional superiority. They disagree on what broader purpose and strategic concepts should guide U.S. policy.

During the Cold War, Dominators were foiled by the twin constructs of MAD and the ABM Treaty. Having cast these aside with the demise of the Soviet Union, constraints against the unfettered pursuit of U.S. strategic superiority have been removed. This pursuit is doomed to fail, as it will corrode partnerships necessary to roll back proliferation. Conciliators know what they are up against—new, bunker-busting nuclear weapons, the resumption of nuclear testing, and the weaponization of space—but they have yet to articulate their own preferred strategic concept. A successful strategic synthesis must borrow from both camps. It must devalue deadly weapons alongside the deployment of missile defenses, and it must update the practice of arms control to address evolving threats.

If Dominators seek to fill the void created by nullifying the ABM Treaty and rejecting MAD with missile defenses and pre-emptive strikes, domestic divisions will surely grow and ties with allies will fray. A transition that is pursued without a domestic consensus will be halting, and could well result in the unraveling of domestic support both for treaties and nuclear programs. A bipartisan approach is essential to successfully present new U.S. thinking abroad. Moreover, a domestic consensus is needed to maintain strong U.S. alliances and to foil wedge-splitting strategies by Moscow and Beijing. Only a bipartisan approach can stand the test of time, alliance cohesion, and annual budget battles on Capitol Hill.

The Clinton administration never postulated, articulated, or defended a post-Cold War strategic concept governing nuclear forces, missile defenses, and arms control. The Pentagon's "bottom up" review of nuclear policy during President Bill Clinton's first term produced a reaffirmation of institutional interests, albeit with useful changes at the margin. There was no top down review during the second term. Instead, the Clinton administration continued to seek amendments to existing treaties, downsizing strategic arms reductions while at the same time modifying the ABM Treaty to permit limited defenses.

The absence of a new conceptual framework made each of the Clinton administration's decisions harder to implement and easier to oppose. President Clinton's separate efforts to down-size nuclear arsenals and deploy limited defenses never congealed at home or abroad. The Kremlin advocated even deeper cuts in lieu of missile defenses, but this initiative was opposed by the Pentagon as interfering with nuclear targeting plans. By expressing continued fealty to MAD's precepts while trying to engineer phased reductions, the Clinton team was caught in a domestic bind: Under the dictates of lingering Cold War concepts of nuclear deterrence, lower numbers and alert rates equaled less safety and security. Downsizing the U.S. nuclear arsenal remained constrained by requirements to place a great many targets at risk of prompt destruction.[12]

The phased introduction of limited national missile defenses added to these complications when pursued under the logic of MAD. Clinton administration officials argued that the Kremlin need not be concerned about limited defenses because Moscow maintained high alert rates and the ability to overwhelm defenses, but they failed to make a persuasive case. MAD continued to pit missile defenses against nuclear arms reductions and de-alerting, when the logic of post-Cold War circumstances called for all three. MAD's embellishments were understandable during the Cold War, but they prevented transition strategies and foundered on the politics of treaty ratification once the Soviet Union died. A successful transition from the known to the new required bipartisan support and a compelling, central organizing principle to replace MAD and reinforce arms control. Cooperative threat reduction constitutes the most compelling conceptual and programmatic replacement for MAD and reinforcement for arms control.

Transitioning from SALT to START to Cooperative Threat Reduction

The first phase of strategic arms control reached fruition during the Nixon administration. It occurred when the United States discarded the goal of American strategic superiority, adopting instead the guiding principles of "essential equivalence" and mutual deterrence. This shift permitted the launch of the strategic arms limitation talks and the negotiation of the ABM Treaty. A second, more ambitious, phase occurred in the Reagan administration, which ultimately leveraged the prospect of advanced missile defenses to achieve deep cuts in force levels. During this transition, the lexicon and purpose of negotiations changed from strategic arms limitation to strategic arms reduction. SALT was superseded by START.

The third crucial phase—and the challenge we now face—demands that we reach beyond the management and reduction of U.S. and Russian nuclear forces. The challenge ahead is even more ambitious—to combine strategic force reductions with a much larger enterprise of cooperative threat reduction. Cooperative threat reduction programs have been reduced in public discourse to a series of government programs to safeguard dangerous materials and weapons in the former Soviet Union. This is far too small a conception. Cooperative threat reduction deserves pride of place alongside military preparedness, preventive diplomacy, deterrence, and arms control as a core component of U.S. national security in an era of asymmetric warfare.

For those who doubt the elevation of CTR to this rank, consider how its absence would affect U.S. national, regional, and global security. By raising CTR up from its current bureaucratic confines, treaty regimes would be reinforced, friends reassured, partnerships against proliferation strengthened, and higher barriers constructed against the acquisition of WMD by maverick states. The time has come to start thinking about CTR as a strategic concept rather than as a government program. Strategic arms control and non-proliferation treaties rooted in Cold War experience need to be updated and strengthened by a broader conception of cooperative threat reduction.

Cooperative threat reduction would supplement written accords, not replace them. The codification of deep cuts provides for the reciprocity and access that are essential building blocks for a broader agenda of cooperative threat reduction. Strategic arms reduction remains important, but it no longer suffices to serve U.S. national security interests, nor those of other states threatened by proliferation. The United States and Russia would not be safer by jointly reducing their nuclear forces if, at the same time, lethal weapons and materials leaked out of the former Soviet Union. Likewise, if maverick states secure weapons of mass destruction by other means, U.S., regional, and international security would be significantly diminished. The parallel reduction of U.S. and Russian nuclear forces provides a means to secure a broader agenda of cooperative threat reduction keyed to proliferation threats.

CTR is an acronym associated with bilateral efforts between Washington and Moscow to safeguard dangerous materials and to take apart aging bombers, submarines, and missiles. This definition is far too confining. It must expand to include collaborative efforts in troubled regions beset by creeping proliferation. In the wake of the terrorist acts on September 11, 2001, Washington, Moscow and Beijing began to cooperate fruitfully against terrorists seeking weapons of mass destruction. The challenge ahead is to extend these patterns of cooperation against states that seek weapons that can produce mass casualties.

Strategic Cooperation or Competition against Proliferation

Proliferation tends to beget more proliferation. Cooperative threat reduction could provide the reinforcement needed to prevent the descent of non-proliferation treaty regimes into irrelevance. As former U.S. Ambassador to Russia Jack F. Matlock, Jr., has noted: "We need cooperation with Russia to secure our most fundamental security interests."[13] The same could be said about China. Moscow and Beijing need to assist Washington in stopping and reversing proliferation for this battle to be won. If any one of these capitals acts in ways that undermine non-proliferation treaty regimes, these accords will be weakened. At the turn of the century, all three capitals were acting contrary to the health and well being of non-proliferation treaty regimes.

Washington's actions have seriously weakened the Non-Proliferation Treaty. Republicans in the Senate rejected ratification of the CTBT and passed reservations to the Chemical Weapons Convention that handicapped the conduct of challenge inspections. The Bush administration has rejected a long-sought protocol to the Biological Weapons Convention without offering a better alternative to the difficult monitoring challenges associated with preventing the spread of these deadly microbes. The U.S. Congress is perennially late and short in paying its dues to treaty implementation bodies. These failings are reinforced by the actions of Moscow and Beijing, which have provided material and diplomatic support to the three countries constituting President Bush's "axis of evil." If the United States, Russia, and China do not change their harmful patterns of behavior, non-proliferation treaties will become dead letters.

Moscow and Beijing have an interest in seeking to stem proliferation— unless it is useful against American hegemony. The instinct to counter U.S.

power coincides with the interests of well-connected groups within Russia and China that stand to benefit from commercial transactions with states of proliferation concern. Stopping these transactions depends upon leadership calculations that weigh national interests and monetary gain against perceived U.S. ambitions. For example, as one close observer of Russian assistance to Iran in building nuclear power plants has observed, "the United States sees only risk and no benefit" in nuclear exports to Iran, whereas Russia "sees a manageable risk and significant [economic] benefit."[14]

Even if Washington seeks improved ties, Moscow and Beijing might continue to aid and abet proliferation by maverick states—if not actively, then by placing impediments before U.S. diplomatic initiatives to toughen export controls or inspection regimes. Washington's ability to change the calculus of decision in Moscow and Beijing depends upon finding the right mix of incentives, reassurance, and disincentives. If Washington is perceived as primarily interested in seeking to reinforce its strategic superiority at the expense of their nuclear deterrents, Moscow and Beijing will surely continue to pick and choose when to support (or undermine) non-proliferation regimes. After all, Washington also behaves in this manner, given its long-standing friendship with Israel and its improved ties with India and Pakistan.

If proliferation proceeds unabated, Washington could seek to alter this course by taking military action against regimes that have accumulated WMD. Military action poses a host of problems, however, including the risk of catastrophic losses to U.S. expeditionary forces and nearby friends and allies, as well as the increased likelihood of retaliatory terrorist acts on American soil. Pre-emptive strikes are not a part of the U.S. military or political culture; unless they succeed in short duration, they could engender bitter domestic controversies. Even if successful, they could distance Washington from its friends and allies, and raise difficult questions about why military action against proliferation is pursued in some cases, while proliferation is condoned elsewhere. Moreover, each pre-emptive strike would constitute a vote of non-confidence in treaty regimes, which could further weaken them.

The use of American military power to defeat proliferation could also prompt more proliferation, if other threatened states conclude that mass-casualty weapons constitute the best deterrent against an overwhelmingly powerful foe. Each exercise of U.S. military power against proliferation could result in Washington having more work to do, while receiving less help from others. Moscow and Beijing might conclude that the benefits of this scenario—preoccupying Gulliver in regional firefighting—is a more attractive alternative than helping Washington to curtail proliferation in Iraq, Iran, and North Korea.

Dominators reject this bleak prognosis, believing that the successful exercise of U.S. power projection could have a bandwagon effect against proliferation. In this view, the success of U.S. forces in Afghanistan—the charnel grounds for earlier great power expeditions—has already had profoundly positive demonstration effects. As a consequence, the Bush administration has signaled to other potential foes that adventurism would be met with strength. But what if containment, thus reinforced, were followed by a successful instance of rollback? What if, for example, Saddam Hussein were not merely contained, but removed from power, and his covert stockpiles of chemical and biological weapons eliminated? Would not this success, following closely on the heels of routing the Taliban and al-Qaeda network, lead to voluntary or involuntary rollback elsewhere? For this analysis to be correct, U.S. military forces would need another rout on the battlefield, followed by much-chastened behavior by Moscow and Beijing, as well as by states of proliferation concern that might be next in the line of U.S. fire.

Terrorism presented a common enemy to Washington, Moscow, and Beijing. Thus, Russia and China provided diplomatic support for the use of force by the United States in Afghanistan. In doing so, they received wider U.S. latitude to carry out "anti-terrorism" measures within their own countries. In contrast, Moscow and Beijing are unlikely to provide diplomatic support for U.S. military strikes against trading partners that pursue WMD. Diplomatic support for states of proliferation concern could also substitute for military assistance to those under attack by U.S. forces.

Would Russia and China change their habits of providing assistance to states of proliferation concern if the United States were to overthrow Saddam Hussein? The answer to this question depends heavily on the overall context of U.S. relations with both major powers. Will regime change in Iraq be pursued in the context of strategic partnership or cooperation, or in the context of extending U.S. hegemony? If the latter is the case, then leaders in Moscow and Beijing are likely to smile in photo-opportunities with U.S. officials while continuing to assist maverick states that could offer hard currency while preoccupying Gulliver. In other words, proliferation might be one element to help balance a hegemonic power. For every proliferation-bent regime that the United States seeks to isolate, Moscow and Beijing are unlikely to join Washington's posse—unless their national security interests are also threatened directly by the seeker of WMD. The possibility of catastrophic failure will attend every exercise of U.S. military power to counter proliferation, while "successful" military campaigns are likely to overextend American power and strain U.S. alliances. Over time, domestic divisions could immobilize U.S. national security policies.

This troubling scenario is not a forgone conclusion. An alternative scenario—one in which Moscow and Beijing line up alongside Washington in common cause against proliferation in states of concern—remains possible. This hopeful scenario, however, requires that Washington actively pursue cooperative partnerships with both Moscow and Beijing. President Bush and Russian president Vladimir Putin have both expressed the desire to forge a strategic partnership. Their success would depend on the sum total of Washington's initiatives—including those regarding Russia's ties with NATO, arms control accords, missile defense deployments, and military space programs—and whether, in Moscow's view, these add up to strategic cooperation or the pursuit of U.S. hegemony.

The Bush administration has not sought a strategic partnership with China. Instead, U.S.–China ties have been marked by a mixture of competitive and cooperative pursuits. Trade is an important area of cooperation, while the status of Taiwan could become the primary source of contention. Given the impressive demonstrations of U.S. power projection, Beijing is unlikely to seek a near-term resolution of the Taiwan issue by force of arms, as long as Taipei does not seek independence—a course of action that Washington could persuasively counsel against. In addition to the Taiwan issue, Beijing will measure Washington's strategic objectives by U.S. initiatives on nuclear weapons, missile defense deployments, and military space programs. If the sum total of U.S. plans are viewed by Beijing as not undercutting its vital national security interests, cooperation on proliferation could be forthcoming. This can be measured, as in the case of Russia, by the cessation of commercial transactions bearing on proliferation, as well as by Beijing's diplomatic stance on hard proliferation cases.

If this hopeful scenario of unilateral cooperation against proliferation in states of concern were to occur, results would be easy to measure. But how might Washington successfully promote such cooperation? The exercise of sanctions against China did not work in the Clinton administration. To succeed in changing Russian and Chinese practices that facilitate proliferation, carrots must exceed the benefits of commercial transactions with states of proliferation concern. These incentives must be reinforced by the likely imposition of disincentives that hurt more than sanctions.

It is evident from continued Russian and Chinese support for states of proliferation concern that neither tentative multilateralism nor triumphal unilateralism provides for an effective mix of incentives, reassurance, and penalties. The Clinton administration's awkward combination of incremental arms reduction, cooperative threat reduction, sanctions, and limited national missile defenses certainly did not generate good behavior by either Moscow or Beijing on hard proliferation cases. Nor is the Bush administration's nuclear posture review, withdrawal from the ABM Treaty, and evident enthusiasm for missile defenses likely to foster a better track record in both capitals, given the threat these initiatives pose to the Russian and Chinese nuclear deterrents. Indeed, the Bush administration's initial moves are likely to be interpreted by Moscow and Beijing as the pursuit of devaluation, if not nullification, of their deterrents.[15] In this context, the Bush administration's clever formulation that U.S. "missile defenses do not threaten any state that would not threaten us" is unlikely to provide comfort.[16]

Success in turning Moscow and Beijing against proliferation in states of concern will require a balanced approach that draws from the preferences of Conciliators and the instruments favored by the Dominators. This mix will include reassurance measures designed to demonstrate that U.S. military dominance would not be extended to the nullification of the Russian and Chinese nuclear deterrents; written accords with Moscow governing strategic arms reductions along with monitoring arrangements that provide confidence in faithful implementation and insurance against reversibility; strengthening measures for non-proliferation regimes; and wide-ranging programs of cooperative threat reduction with both major powers. At the same time, Washington must clarify that if Moscow and Beijing continue to undermine these regimes by providing support for states of proliferation concern, the United States would have to adjust upward its defense preparations against such threats. While these preparations would be primarily geared to counter maverick states, they would also have negative ramifications for the defense postures of Russia and China.

This mix of incentives, reassurance measures, and disincentives will be discussed below. It will no doubt make for awkward juxtapositions and inconsistencies in U.S. policy, but the complexities of proliferation as well as U.S. relations with both major powers leave no better choice. Harmonization of non-proliferation policy is an ideal that eludes practitioners. The prescriptions of Conciliators and Dominators each have their own separate coherence, but neither approach, by itself, leads to success. A melding of preferences in now required. The resulting inconsistencies are tolerable, as long as they result in success against proliferation.

Reassurance Amid Power Imbalances

During the Cold War, the two nuclear-armed superpowers attempted to reassure each other through treaties that affirmed national vulnerability and that obligated both countries to accept intrusive monitoring arrangements. Strict reciprocity, codified in treaties, was the key to successful monitoring. With the demise of the Soviet Union and the rise of asymmetric warfare, U.S. national security policy will no longer rely on making a virtue of national vulnerability. Nor can reassurance be codified in treaties, since the ABM Treaty is beyond rehabilitation and since accords governing strategic nuclear capabilities will not mask the distinctly unequal power of the signatories. How can mutual reassurance, which is essential if the United States, Russia and China are to collaborate against proliferation, be provided under conditions of significant and growing inequality?

The strategic concept of cooperative threat reduction could help fill the void created by the U.S. withdrawal from the ABM Treaty and by the rejection of MAD. If properly conceived and implemented, cooperative threat reduction could provide reassurance to Moscow and Beijing that the United States seeks partnership rather than subservience. Alternatively, if Washington seeks to fill the void created by its disaffection from treaties primarily with missile defenses, coercive diplomacy, and power projection, the United States is likely to have little help in rolling back proliferation. The central paradox in seeking to replace treaties with superior firepower is that apparent success makes the resort to force more likely and more problematic.

A balanced approach is needed to succeed in countering proliferation. Without positive complements, "counter-proliferation" policies that rely heavily on military means will become a lonely pursuit. Cooperative threat reduction could help provide that balance, if it is elevated alongside deterrence, defense, arms control, and diplomacy as a core component of U.S. national security policy. At the same time, missile defenses and power projection capabilities would have essential roles to play in an era of asymmetric warfare, since the threat of resorting to the use of force could empower other means of persuasion. Collaborative steps to promote cooperative threat reduction could take many necessary forms, including the adoption of strengthening measures for multilateral non-proliferation and disarmament accords; new bilateral understandings between the United States and Russia that promote reassurance alongside deep cuts; and creative diplomatic undertakings to reduce tensions within regions beset by proliferation.

If all of these instruments fail, and if the use of force becomes necessary against determined and dangerous proliferators, success must be swift and dramatic. Failure is not an option, since the failed exercise of military power would further weaken treaty regimes and the U.S. appetite to enforce them, resulting in far greater proliferation. Successful military action must still be accompanied by cooperative threat reduction initiatives and strengthening measures for non-proliferation treaties. Otherwise, the subsequent use of force becomes more likely—and more lonely.

The elevation of cooperative threat reduction to a strategic concept—rather than viewing such activity as a collection of bureaucratic programming initiatives —would be as momentous as the two earlier shifts in U.S. arms control policy. Each of these shifts resulted from dynamic underlying tensions that, when skillfully juxtaposed, generated a creative synthesis. In the first instance, the acceptance of vulnerability laid the groundwork for a process of strategic arms limitation. In the second major shift, the threat of ambitious defenses became the fulcrum leveraging extraordinary reductions in strategic arms. The dynamic underlying tension for the third shift is the pursuit of cooperative threat reduction under conditions of U.S. strategic superiority, when America's freedom of action is seemingly greatest.

Why should the United States pursue a strategic concept of cooperative threat reduction when its power is unchallenged? To begin with, U.S preeminence will be tested—but not in head-on collisions. Instead, U.S. military and economic strength will be challenged by unconventional means, and Russia's aging Cold War stocks of dangerous weapons and materials provide the most plentiful, but far from the only, sources to neutralize U.S. advantages. Cooperative threat reduction is not to be confused with charity. Instead, it is a common sense, practical means to protect national interests, including the safeguarding of friends and allies. Successful CTR programs extend U.S. advantages and guard against the most lethal challenges to America's military dominance and economic well-being. Cooperative threat reduction is a national interest-based strategic concept—but one that also serves the interests of regional and international security. To paraphrase Thomas C. Schelling and Morton H. Halperin, cooperative threat reduction "is a promising, but still only dimly perceived, enlargement of the scope of our military strategy."[17]

The paradoxical pursuit of cooperative threat reduction at a time of unparalleled U.S. strategic superiority calls for a surge in creative, conceptual thinking akin to that pursued by the founding fathers of strategic arms control in the late 1950s and early 1960s. The paradox we now face is every bit as profound as the acceptance of vulnerability to achieve strategic arms limitations in the 1970s and the parallel pursuit of deep cuts and ambitious missile defenses in the 1980s. The current shift from MAD to cooperative threat reduction is both required and vastly complicated by the disparity of power between the United States and Russia. It is further complicated by the need to find a mix of defense and deterrence that is compatible with threat reduction. A new strategic synthesis is waiting to be developed, one that employs cooperative threat reduction alongside deterrence, preventive diplomacy, arms control, and non-proliferation accords to reduce the dangers posed by Russia's decline and the rise of asymmetric threats.

The Rise and Stagnation of Cooperative Threat Reduction

During the Cold War, enormous intellectual and diplomatic efforts were devoted to creating treaty regimes governing the most deadly weapons known to humanity. It took extraordinary political capital to convince powerful government institutions, politicians, and concerned citizens that treaty constraints on nuclear forces and missile defenses were both wise and necessary. The creativity, time and effort involved in crafting these accords—selecting measuring units, devising treaty constraints to establish mutually agreed stabilization measures, and (hardest of all) agreeing upon intrusive verification arrangements to give these accords political standing and durability—helped keep the Cold War from becoming hot.

In the first decade of the post-Cold War period, very little creativity was directed toward treaty instruments. Instead, the Clinton administration applied itself to amending, downsizing, or adjusting existing accords to deal with new circumstances. At the same time, the enterprise of cooperative threat reduction expanded greatly. Initial successes were driven by the exigencies and opportunities created by the surprising demise of the Soviet Union. In 1991, presidents George H.W. Bush and Mikhail Gorbachev took parallel and reciprocal steps to remove from the field the least safe and secure nuclear weapons when the Soviet Union was coming apart.[18] One year later, the Open Skies Treaty was negotiated, permitting cooperative aerial inspections from Vancouver to Vladivostok. This much-undervalued accord provided the basis for monitoring and reassurance between states with significant disparities in both military and verification capabilities.[19] Also at the end of the administration of President George H.W. Bush, senators Sam Nunn and Richard Lugar rallied their colleagues on Capitol Hill to enact legislation authorizing the executive branch to dismantle and safeguard dangerous weapon systems and materials in the former Soviet Union. This began under the auspices of the Pentagon, and soon extended to the Department of Energy, which undertook extensive "lab to lab" contacts to safeguard poorly protected fissile material in the former Soviet Union.

In Washington parlance, these combined programs became known as "Nunn–Lugar" CTR initiatives. They began to be implemented in serious fashion during the Clinton administration. By February 2002, CTR programs in the former Soviet Union had secured the deactivation of 5,829 nuclear warheads; destroyed 445 inter-continental ballistic missiles and 429 missile silos; eliminated 92 strategic bombers and 368 launchers from ballistic missile-carrying submarines; destroyed 291 submarine-launched ballistic missiles, 21 ballistic missile-carrying submarines, and 483 long-range cruise missiles; and sealed 194 nuclear test tunnels.[20] Assistance has been provided for nuclear weapons storage security and transportation security. Construction was nearly completed on a large, secure fissile material storage facility, and the United States began working to improve the safety and security at Russian chemical weapons storage sites. Security upgrades were implemented for 750 metric tons of highly enriched uranium and plutonium. Radiation detection equipment was installed at Russian border crossings to help detect and interdict nuclear smuggling. Plutonium-laden fuel rods from nuclear power reactors have been secured.

During the Clinton administration, cooperative threat reduction was being practiced every day by the Department of Defense and the Department of Energy in scores of laboratories, military bases, and research institutes in the former Soviet Union. A new initiative under the aegis of the Department of State, called the International Science and Technology Center Program, sought to combat "brain drain" to states of proliferation concern. Fledgling initiatives to find gainful commercial employment for workers in Russia's "nuclear cities," as well as for skilled workers who previously produced chemical and biological weapons in the former Soviet Union, were undertaken. Operating under expanded guidelines, the Pentagon's On-Site Inspection Directorate carried out training courses and inspections in over fifty countries within and around the former Soviet Union.

The breadth of these activities stood in stark contrast to the congealed state of nuclear negotiations. During the Clinton years, treaties and cooperative threat reduction underwent a reversal of roles. Throughout the Cold War, treaties were central. They were supplemented from time to time by confidence-building measures and freestanding accords to reduce nuclear dangers. These spin-offs were, in essence, CTR arrangements, but this terminology did not come into vogue until the Nunn–Lugar initiatives. Then, during the Clinton administration, bilateral U.S.–Russian treaty talks stalled and multilateral negotiations in the Conference on Disarmament in Geneva, which produced the Comprehensive Test Ban and Chemical Weapons Convention, ground to a halt. While the entry into force of the START II accord and revisions to the ABM Treaty were blocked by legislative maneuvers in Washington and Moscow, the Nunn–Lugar programs grew and prospered, enjoying broad bipartisan support. Creative effort and initiative shifted from treaty making to CTR initiatives. The most visionary pragmatist in the Clinton administration, Secretary of Defense William J. Perry, began to articulate the replacement of MAD with Mutual Assured Safety.[21]

Whatever the terminology one favored for the overarching goal behind these efforts, CTR programs promised what treaty talks between presidents

Bill Clinton and Boris Yeltsin could not—concrete results that blended prag-matism with idealism. The fieldwork undertaken to secure dangerous weapons and materials in the former Soviet Union was visionary in concep-tion, and yet practical in its execution. Unlike MAD, the concept and prac-tice of cooperative threat reduction was affirmative. New bonds were forged in the United States and Russia between those who worked in partnership to reduce common threats. During the Cold War, bilateral treaties and non-proliferation accords were largely separate undertakings. The successful prac-tice of CTR fused these two enterprises, reinforcing the deep cuts mandated by bilateral treaties while strengthening non-proliferation regimes by safe-guarding dangerous materials. Moreover, CTR programs helped the United States forge new patterns of cooperation against the threat of proliferation in the newly independent states of the former Soviet Union and Warsaw Pact. Whereas treaty making divided Washington, CTR initiatives were consen-sual, reinforcing American diplomacy as well as U.S. national security.

In addition, cooperative threat reduction could be adapted to meet new circumstances and threats far more easily than treaties. Flexibility was a great virtue, if the executors of CTR programs were given leeway by their bureau-cratic overseers. CTR programs were ideally suited to address the new threat hierarchy presented by the demise of the Soviet Union and the rise of asym-metric warfare. "The most urgent national security threat to the United States today," concluded one blue-ribbon panel, "is the danger that weapons of mass destruction or weapons-usable material in Russia could be stolen or sold to terrorists or hostile nation states and used against American troops abroad or citizens at home."[22] This report concluded that a three- to four-fold funding increase for CTR programs was urgently needed.

In principle, the strategic concept of cooperative threat reduction could be adapted to increase not only national, but also regional and international secu-rity. Threat reduction could be pursued bilaterally or multilaterally, such as the collaborative effort by the United States, South Korea, and Japan during the Clinton administration to freeze and then disassemble North Korea's dangerous nuclear and missile programs. CTR initiatives could be embedded in bilateral or multilateral treaties, or they could be carried out as unilateral or reciprocal initiatives. CTR programs could involve military, political or economic incen-tives, or some combination thereof. The creative application of cooperative threat reduction was bounded only by political will, creative diplomacy, and resources. The Clinton administration's biggest success—and probably its most meaningful contribution—in the arms control field was translating the concept of cooperative threat reduction, as proposed by senators Nunn and Lugar, into far-ranging practices after the demise of the Soviet Union.

Despite the many virtues of cooperative threat reduction, these programs lost momentum in the latter part of the Clinton administration. CTR initiatives, like arms control, have no equilibrium point. Progress is hard won, but not self-sustaining. Further progress comes from the top down, not from the bottom up. If top-down pressures to move forward are absent, backsliding will almost certainly occur. In the case of arms control, backsliding was abetted by the advance of weapons' technology, domestic skeptics, powerful bureaucratic interests, and Soviet mischief making. In the case of cooperative threat reduction, applied technology was not the problem; gaining access to sites in the former Soviet Union was. In arms control accords, access was based on strict reciprocity, but in CTR, access was mostly a one-way street. The United States wanted more and more of it, while the Kremlin became increasingly unsure of U.S. intentions. Mischief making was extremely modest by Cold War standards, when proxy wars were fought under the umbrella of MAD and strategic modernization programs were pursued to tilt the scales of nuclear deterrence. In the case of CTR, Americans worried that Russia wasn't living up to its promises. The Kremlin's worries were more profound, suspecting that CTR programs were vehicles to make Russian disarmament irreversible and to simplify U.S. targeting.

The stagnation of cooperative threat reduction resulted from many factors, including distracted U.S. leadership, the disaggregation and lack of coordination of CTR programs, bureaucratic micromanagement, and a perceptible shift in the politics of U.S. national security away from cooperation with Russia. Top-down leadership was needed to counter bureaucratic overseers who, when working on potentially controversial initiatives, naturally tended to move slowly and cautiously. Contractual paperwork dictated pacing. The fear of negative reviews bred an excess of caution. Not everyone on Capitol Hill believed in cooperative threat reduction. For some, U.S. tax dollars were being used to pay for activities that Russia should have been financing by itself. In this view, by defraying the costs of dismantling missiles, bombers, and submarines, and by helping to pay for the safeguarding of dangerous materials, the United States might actually be helping Moscow to spend its scarce resources on new weapons.

These arguments had a simple rejoinder: If the United States did not subsidize CTR activities, they would either not be carried out or be given a very low priority by Moscow. Either way, U.S. national security would be endangered. Toward the end of the Clinton administration, those believing in "win-win" outcomes lost ground to zero-sum thinking. Lingering Cold War mindsets carried over from nuclear negotiations to cooperative threat reduction. Those working in the field who were enthusiastic about CTR initiatives often encountered skepticism by program managers in bureaucracies responsible for implementing them. A vocal minority remained skeptical about CTR programs on Capitol Hill, as well. No individual was in charge of coordinating efforts that ranged over many departments. President Clinton was preoccupied with higher-profile matters, foreign and domestic. Nearly every assessment of CTR programs cited their lack of coordination and executive branch leadership as critical handicaps.[23]

Ten years after getting underway, cooperative threat reduction began to stagnate. Exceptional work continued, despite bureaucratic obstacles in Washington and Moscow, especially in providing assistance for treaty-mandated reductions and in safeguarding dangerous materials. When measured against the complete absence of CTR programs when the Cold War ended, this track record, as one close observer has noted, was "nothing short of dramatic ... But if judged against the scale and urgency of the threat, or the opportunities available to address it, current efforts still fall woefully short."[24] The visionaries who helped launch CTR initiatives had moved elsewhere. Their absence was filled by program managers wearing green eyeshades, who announced that, if the scope of the program were to expand, the Kremlin would have to open padlocked doors. This assertion was entirely true, but also exceptionally narrow-minded. Revealing the secrets behind closed doors could make America safer, but this information could also make Russia more vulnerable. Cooperation and trust were essential ingredients in this enterprise, but they were lacking.

One of the visionary pragmatists who helped start CTR programming in Russia during his directorship of the Los Alamos National Laboratory, Siegfried S. Hecker, offered this ten-year retrospective of CTR programming: The good news, Hecker wrote, was that "nothing really terrible happened within the Russian nuclear complex in spite of the difficult times faced by the Russian people." The bad news was that "the problems in the Russian nuclear complex were much greater and more pervasive that either Russians or Americans realized ten years ago." Moreover, Hecker noted, U.S. initiatives to reduce threats at Russian nuclear facilities and bases lacked "a clear, coherent and sustained" strategy, resulting in "a patchwork quilt of nuclear programs—often lacking coordination not only within Russia, but also within the U.S. interagency community." Furthermore, some of the programs promoted by the United States did not adequately incorporate Russian strategic objectives, forcing the Russian government to choose between following its national interest and receiving much-needed financial assistance.[25]

In the absence of leadership insisting on a wider field of view, the gulf between program managers in Washington and CTR implementers in the field widened. In Washington, the "golden rule" of cooperative threat reduction became "we have the gold; therefore we make the rules." In the field, this translated into program planning and execution that, in Hecker's delicate phrasing, "did not meet the demands of sensitive cooperative programs."[26] Cooperative threat reduction became less cooperative. Its scope narrowed to those programs where U.S. financing suited Russian needs. "The bank account of trust and good will built up early in the decade," Hecker observed, "was drawn down steadily to near bankruptcy by the end of the decade":

> [T]he window of opportunity appears to be closing, both because Russia does not need our money as desperately and because the security services have begun to close up the [nuclear] complex. To make progress now, the spirit of trust and partnership must be renewed, and a common set of objectives must be developed to meet the national security interests of both nations."[27]

Cooperative threat reduction efforts followed the same pattern as other arms control ventures during the Clinton administration. Initially, these programs were infused with energy and produced dramatic successes. By the end of President Clinton's second term, however, the enterprise was foundering. While the program's scope grew, its vision shrunk. The incoming Bush administration made matters immediately worse by treading water for almost one year while reviewing CTR programs. It then concluded—not surprisingly in the wake of the September 11, 2001 terrorist attacks—that CTR was absolutely essential and deserving of a larger infusion of funds. At the same time, the Bush team endorsed a new U.S. nuclear posture designed to defeat adversaries, withdrew from the ABM Treaty, and pursued the prompt deployment of national missile defenses—steps that were hardly designed to build trust and mutual confidence. While the need for CTR was never greater and more resources would be applied to varied tasks, the conditions required to succeed were receding into the distance.

Reviving Cooperative Threat Reduction

Assessments of CTR efforts to date usually arrive at the same conclusions.[28] First, these studies conclude that CTR activities are absolutely essential to U.S. national security. Second, the scope and pace of CTR activities must be accelerated greatly into the sensitive areas of weapons safety and security; "consequence management" in the event of a nuclear accident or emergency;

and technical cooperation in stockpile stewardship. Third, these studies invariably call for a much-accelerated effort to secure nuclear materials that can cause widespread and lasting damage; extend transparency and cooperation beyond the dismemberment of missiles, submarines, and bombers to the disassembly of nuclear warheads; help Russia to downsize and provide gainful employment to skilled scientists that have worked previously on nuclear, chemical, and biological weapons programs; and properly train and equip those manning border checkpoints.

These expanded horizons for cooperative threat reduction in Russia would not occur in a vacuum. Achieving these goals, as the authors of these studies note, would require a political context of strategic cooperation between Moscow and Washington. If the Kremlin has reason to believe that greater transparency and U.S. intrusiveness would result in further weakness, CTR programs will remain confined to narrow areas in which bilateral interests coincide, such as providing American financial support for the disassembly of obsolescent weapon systems. Put another way, if the Kremlin believes that the risk of providing access to sensitive areas outweighs the benefits of increased security at these sites, Moscow will forgo the security upgrade.

During the Cold War, transparency and intrusive monitoring were reciprocal obligations that were codified in treaties. Reassurance was also provided by the ABM Treaty, which facilitated cooperation by mandating national vulnerability. With the Bush administration's withdrawal from the ABM Treaty and rejection of MAD, new reassurance measures with Russia will be required if the promise and vision of CTR programs are to be realized.

CTR initiatives with China have been extremely modest, reflecting a relationship between wary competitors rather than partners. During the Clinton administration, a modest "lab to lab" program was initiated between U.S. and Chinese nuclear scientists, but this program was suspended amid congressional concerns and inquiries over Chinese espionage. If resumed, bilateral CTR initiatives with China would remain quite modest. Beijing's nuclear deterrent is quite small, and transparency is anathema to Chinese strategic culture. The dark cloud of a potential clash over the Taiwan question is never too far off on the horizon.

For these and other reasons, if the promise of cooperative threat reduction between Washington and Beijing is to be realized, it will be forged through collaboration on regional security issues along China's periphery. Washington and Beijing have found common ground in seeking to defuse the Kashmir dispute and in encouraging Pakistan's military leaders to sever their ties to Islamic militant groups. The fluidity of events in South Asia opens space for collaborative diplomacy by Washington and Beijing. Both capitals could also work together to dampen another potential flashpoint in northeast Asia. Chinese leaders have heeded U.S. proliferation concerns to a greater extent with respect to North Korea, but this restraint could vanish if bilateral relations sour. The same is true with respect to Iran. The biggest impediment to realizing the promise of bilateral threat reduction is, of course, the Taiwan issue. If Taipei moves toward independence and if Beijing counters with coercive moves, bilateral relations would be on a collision course. This is hardly a forgone conclusion, however. Wise management of this issue could result in a prolonged period of quiet across the Taiwan Strait and the parallel pursuit of cooperative threat reduction around China's periphery. U.S. military primacy would help Beijing from engaging in coercive moves against Taiwan, while Washington's diplomacy would encourage Taipei not to create a *causus belli*. For this rosy scenario to occur, restraint by Beijing and Taipei would need to be matched by Washington's conscious choice to accept Beijing's nuclear deterrent.

CHAPTER 8

Fateful Choices

P roliferation is a "make or break" issue for cooperative threat reduction
(CTR). A successful transition from Mutual Assured Destruction
(MAD) to cooperative threat reduction requires that Moscow and
Beijing constrain their material or military support for states seeking
weapons of mass destruction. If leaders in Russia and China place a higher
priority on hard-currency transactions with states such as Iran and Iraq than
on improved ties with the United States, then the scope of CTR efforts
would remain limited to programs that provide narrowly defined mutual
benefits. Ongoing programs to dismantle and safeguard Russia's Cold War
arsenal clearly fall within this narrow framework. Cooperation on early
warning for missile launches might also proceed, given the clear dangers associated with Russia's blind spots resulting from the diminishment of its Cold
War constellation of radar stations and satellites. A larger conception for
cooperative threat reduction—the true partnership needed to properly safeguard dangerous materials at the source and to reorient Russia's nuclear,
chemical, and biological warfare centers—would, however, fall victim to the
Kremlin's continued material support to states of concern. U.S. cooperation
with China on sensitive regional security issues will also be colored by
Beijing's stance on proliferation.

A successful transition from MAD to cooperative threat reduction also
requires that Washington discard some bad habits. If the United States seeks
to impose one-sided rules for implementing threat reduction programs,
Russia and China are likely to balk. Similarly, if Moscow and Beijing perceive
that Washington seeks to devalue or negate their deterrents through missile
defenses and the weaponization of space, they will likely limit their support

for U.S. counter-proliferation initiatives to instances where threats are jointly perceived. Pipelines to "old friends" that can pay for assistance with hard currency are likely to remain open. Alternatively, if Washington is perceived as accepting a nuclear deterrent relationship with Russia and China, the pace of a collaborative transition could pick up along with the scope of CTR efforts.

Two Key Indicators of Reassurance

Consequently, one key indicator of American strategic objectives for both Moscow and Beijing will be the architecture chosen for U.S. missile defense deployments. The preferred U.S. architecture could facilitate or retard a successful transition from MAD to cooperative threat reduction. Similarly, some missile defense architectures could strengthen alliances, shore up non-proliferation regimes, and send useful signals to states brandishing missiles and weapons of mass destruction (WMD). Other missile defense architectures could vastly complicate these dangers. If Russian or Chinese leaders conclude that Washington seeks to negate their nuclear deterrents, the transition from MAD to cooperative threat reduction will be stillborn.

The second key indicator of U.S. strategic objectives for Moscow and Beijing will be whether Washington seeks to seize the "high ground" of space. Space has long been a medium in which military functions such as weather forecasting, communications, signals intelligence gathering and photo reconnaissance have occurred. However, the weaponization of space—deploying what the Soviets used to call "space strike" weapons in orbit or satellite killers on the ground—was sidestepped during the Cold War. One reason why an arms race in space did not occur was the ability of the Soviet Union to compete. Russia and China will be watching whether, in the absence of a superpower counterweight, Washington will now seek to extend and reinforce its terrestrial superiority by dominating space. If so, not only would their conventional military inferiority be accentuated, but their nuclear deterrents might be readily negated. The U.S. approach to the weaponization of space will therefore be critically important for a transition from MAD to cooperative threat reduction. The more the United States takes the lead in pursuing anti-satellite weapons or weapons in space, the less Russia and China can be expected to cooperate in reducing asymmetric threats.

Missile Defense Architecture

The transition from MAD to cooperative threat reduction will fail unless it is harmonized with a parallel transition from nuclear overkill to a mix of much-reduced nuclear offense and discriminating missile defense. The management of these dual transitions faces downside risks and unintended consequences at every turn. The alternative of continuing the Cold War practice of avoiding risk by not deploying missile defenses is, however, no longer an option. Conceptually, the net effect of missile defense deployments should reinforce reductions in nuclear forces, reassure allies, support non-proliferation partners, and reduce the salience of missiles and WMD. This is a heavy load to place on military technology, let alone technology that remains largely unproven.

The argument laid out in the preceding chapters suggests three layers of risk management. The first layer is to establish the priority of theater over national missile defenses. A higher priority for theater missile defenses is mandated because shorter-range missiles pose far greater threats than ocean-spanning missiles. The numbers of theater ballistic missiles is expanding, while deployments of missiles of intercontinental distances are greatly contracting. Theater ballistic missiles were first used on the battlefield during World War II, and they have now become staples of warfare in the Middle East. If war breaks out across the Taiwan Strait or on the Korean peninsula, theater ballistic missiles will almost certainly be used—missiles that could carry WMD. In the event of warfare, it is essential for the United States to destroy these missiles before they are launched or before they land. Theater missile defenses are therefore essential instruments of alliance solidarity and protection. Forward deployments of theater missile defenses could negate perceptions of a "Fortress America," while underscoring the U.S. commitment to aid friends and allies threatened with proliferation.

Attacks by ocean-spanning ballistic missiles that would provide unmistakable proof of origin are perhaps the least likely threats to America in an era of asymmetric warfare. Nonetheless, a modest insurance policy against this unlikely, but devastating, eventuality is warranted. "Nobody can predict," as Fred Charles Iklé wrote, "that the fatal accident or unauthorized act will never happen ... The hazard is too elusive."[1] Former Secretary of Defense William J. Perry came to the same conclusion:

> Both prevention and deterrence ... could fail in the face of terrorism, and there is always the possibility, however remote, of an accidental or unauthorized launch from another nuclear power. Any of these contingencies would create a catastrophe, so it is reasonable for the United States to seek "catastrophic insurance," much as individuals buy earthquake insurance to cover the possibility that their house might be destroyed by such an event.[2]

American politics offers up strange juxtapositions on the point. Those who are inclined to support national health insurance tend to oppose even limited catastrophic insurance in the form of national missile defenses, while those who staunchly oppose national health insurance plans are eager to spend enormous sums for missile defenses. A balanced approach would set premium payment for limited national missile defenses at a low level, consistent with the low probability of an unauthorized launch of a ballistic missile by a major power or a suicidal launch by an "undeterrable" leader of a rogue state.

The second layer of risk management associated with missile defense deployments is to avoid paying unnecessary premiums for national coverage—overpayments that would set in train inflated nuclear requirements elsewhere. During the Cold War, nuclear requirements were sized against worst cases. In other words, the United States (and the Soviet Union) needed to have sufficient retaliatory nuclear forces after a surprise attack to nullify any advantage to the attacker. As a consequence, nuclear forces on both sides reached astronomical heights. It is also possible to fall into this trap with missile defense insurance policies. The worst case of a "limited" long-range missile attack against the United States is posed by a rogue submarine commander of the Russian Navy. In this scenario, as many as 120–200 warheads accompanied by sophisticated countermeasures to foil missile defenses could be launched against U.S. targets. A "limited" national missile defense against this worst-of-all-limited cases, would require hundreds of interceptors across the continental United States, or space-based interceptors, or both. A "limited" missile defense of this kind would be indistinguishable from a missile defense designed to negate the Russian and Chinese nuclear deterrents. The United States could then expect Moscow and Beijing to do everything in their power to maintain their deterrents, while trying to tie down Gulliver with whatever means are possible—including continued material support to states of proliferation concern.

The second layer of risk management—guarding against oversized national missile defense deployments—appears achievable. There is unlikely to be a domestic consensus in Washington on seemingly oversized national missile defenses. And if past continues to be prologue, the ambitions of missile defense enthusiasts for their definition of "limited" deployments on national territory will be whittled down over time by budgetary priorities, technical difficulties, and political mood swings. During the 1970s, a twelve-site national missile defense system was reduced to two locations, and then to one, which was soon abandoned. As former Secretary of Defense Harold Brown noted, previous national missile defense plans "have had enough political cachet to be approved. None of them has had enough to be built."[3] This formula might be modified somewhat in light of contemporary circumstances, but not much.

If Washington avoids the Cold War trap of sizing national missile defenses against worst cases, how much would be enough? If the message the United States wishes to convey to Russia and China is the pursuit of cooperative threat reduction, then national missile defenses would be sized sufficiently to counter proliferation rather than the deterrents of major powers. A counter-proliferation architecture would rely heavily on theater missile defenses, and lightly on national missile defenses.

If a state of proliferation concern is able to deploy a handful of ocean-spanning missiles, a few dozen missile defense interceptors should be sufficient to counter this modest threat. While the launch of a few ocean-spanning missiles against the United States is unlikely to occur, one can never be sure. Moreover, if Washington is going to pay high premiums for theater missile defenses designed to protect deployed U.S. forces and citizens living abroad (as well as friends and allies), Washington should also be willing to pay for a modest insurance policy for citizens living at home. One virtue of sizing national missile defenses against a minimal, low-probability threat is that the money saved could be applied to higher priorities. A second virtue is that Washington would signal that it seeks to pursue a CTR agenda with Moscow and Beijing.

By reducing the premium paid for national missile defenses while pursuing theater missile defenses vigorously, Washington would signal its pursuit of a non-proliferation agenda rather than a compellance strategy directed against Russia and China. A non-proliferation strategy would seek protection where it is needed most, while encouraging Russia to expand the scope of CTR programs from deployed forces to stockpiled missiles and warheads. At the same time, it would seek to depress China's strategic modernization plans, thereby minimizing cascade effects in India and Pakistan.

What if Washington has the wisdom to signal properly and Moscow or Beijing do not get the message? If Russia and China continue to provide military or material support for states of proliferation concern, then U.S. defensive preparations would naturally increase, while prospects for cooperative threat reduction decrease. Among the accounts likely to grow are both theater and national missile defenses, since the domestic U.S. checks against upscaling these programs would be weakened by proliferation abroad. Put another way, if Russia and China aid and abet bad news abroad, they are likely to encourage the U.S. defense posture they most fear. The costs to Beijing and Moscow of maintaining their deterrents against the growth of U.S. missile defenses could exceed the income gained from hard-currency transactions with states of proliferation concern. These costs would also be greater than the penalties imposed by U.S. sanctions in previous cases of proliferation.

Granted, the utilization of missile defense deployments to convey reassurance and to penalize misbehavior is a very difficult balancing act. If the right balance is not struck, or if balance is lost, then carefully planned layers of risk management could fall by the wayside, while proliferation dangers multiply. Moreover, there is inevitably a lag time associated with balancing strategies, a dynamic that bedeviled U.S. and Soviet efforts at strategic arms control. Despite the many difficulties involved, there appears to be no better missile defense balancing mechanism than domestic U.S. politics—at least for the foreseeable future. Given domestic discord over national missile defenses, treaties, and nuclear testing in the United States, it is probably unrealistic to expect that the right balance could be maintained by consistency, consensus, or divine providence. Instead, whatever balance is struck will eventuate through the natural interaction of contending political forces. Partisan division has many unfortunate side effects, but it does have the virtue of whittling down excess.

This is obviously a very tricky business, but in a period of partisan divide over the utility of nuclear weapons and national missile defense, the search for equilibrium will be elusive. Instead, a rough and movable balance will evolve, the mixed result of political maneuvering at home and changing perceptions of the rise or diminishment of foreign threats. National missile defense enthusiasts in Washington will continue to push for expansion; domestic skeptics will continue to push for contraction. The more Dominators overreach in seeking to slay foreign dragons, testing nuclear weapons, seizing the high ground of space, or overbuilding national missile defenses, the more they will empower Conciliators who oppose these initiatives. Conversely, the more ineffectual Conciliators are in using force, and hesitant in taking steps to shore up national security in troubled times, the more they will cede ground to Dominators. There are inevitable lag times and dislocations associated with American domestic politics, but over time and in the long run, domestic divisions are likely to produce the missile defense architecture that serves national purposes and that Moscow and Beijing deserve.

This should not be construed as a terribly mechanistic and predetermined process. American politics does not lend itself very well to mathematical equations. Balance depends in large part on perceptions, and perceptions are, by their very nature, variable and discordant. Threat perceptions can be mutually reinforcing or utterly confused. These phenomena have certainly not ended with the Cold War, and they, too, could play havoc with our search for balance. Mutual misperceptions could reinforce each other. What if fears of prospective missile defenses prompt increases in nuclear requirements, generating a vicious cycle before the checks and balances of U.S. domestic balances take hold? In other words, might not a modified version of the action–reaction syndrome appear for asymmetric threats?

This concern is certainly valid and cannot be dismissed. As discussed earlier, however, caution is advised before jumping on another action–reaction bandwagon. During the Cold War, many factors contributed to the absurd size of superpower nuclear arsenals, even with little or no deployed national missile defenses. In a post–Cold War environment, Russian nuclear forces will continue to drop even with U.S. national missile defenses, and China will continue to seek the least expensive means of establishing a viable deterrent. Some Russian analysts predict that the Kremlin's operational strategic offensive forces would fall to perhaps 700 warheads over a ten-year period.[4] The Central Intelligence Agency predicts Chinese strategic modernization to perhaps 100 warheads in 2015. These estimates do not provide the basis for a strategic arms race. In conditions of asymmetric warfare, the action–reaction syndrome could take very different forms than during the Cold War, as discussed below.

The third layer of risk management against possible negative repercussions of deploying national missile defenses is to establish thresholds against deploying dedicated instruments of space warfare, such as satellite killers and space-based interceptors. By keeping national missile defenses limited and terrestrially bound, the United States would signal to Russia and China its strong preference for cooperative threat reduction, while dealing sufficiently with maverick states. This third layer is also the most important, because weapons in space pose the greatest threat to the Russian and Chinese deterrents. Thus, the field-, flight-, or space-testing of instruments designed to disable or kill objects in space would nullify whatever reassurance is provided by maintaining very limited, terrestrially based, national missile defenses. U.S. attempts to seize the high ground of space would be perceived globally as a dangerous exercise in hegemonic overstretch. This agenda is likely to open rifts with U.S. allies, prompt a closer strategic partnership between Russia and China, accelerate the unraveling of treaty regimes, and place at risk space-dependent global commerce. Forbearance in this realm, on the other hand, opens many doors to cooperative threat reduction.

A Space Sanctuary?

Most conveners of blue-ribbon panels are poorly positioned to implement their recommendations, but not Secretary of Defense Donald H. Rumsfeld.

Before becoming President George W. Bush's surprise choice to run the Pentagon, Rumsfeld chaired not one, but two panels that bore his strong imprint. The first Rumsfeld Commission report concluded that ballistic missile threats were "evolving more rapidly" than estimated by the U.S. intelligence community. Worse, "the U.S. might well have little or no warning before operational deployment" of missiles able to reach U.S. soil.[5] This report had powerful repercussions, reshaping intelligence assessments of foreign missile programs, empowering national missile defense advocates on Capitol Hill, and placing the Clinton administration on the defensive.

The second Rumsfeld Commission dealt with space. It called for the United States to develop "the technologies and operational capabilities that its objectives in space will require." These objectives included the development and deployment of "the means to deter and defend against hostile acts directed at U.S. space assets and against the uses of space hostile to U.S. national interests." Rumsfeld warned against a "Space Pearl Harbor," since the means to deny, disrupt or destroy space systems were now more easily acquired in the global marketplace. The report based its dire warnings on the assumption that space warfare was "a virtual certainty": "[W]e know from history that every medium—air, land, and sea—has seen conflict. Reality indicates that space will be no different." The Rumsfeld Commission therefore called for "superior space capabilities," including the ability to "negate the hostile use of space against U.S. interests." A robust deterrence strategy for space would require "power projection in, from and through space." Moreover, senior political and military leadership needed "to test these capabilities in exercises on a regular basis."[6]

The Rumsfeld Commission's analysis and recommendations were strikingly evocative of the worst periods of the Cold War, when fears of surprise attack and calls for seizing the high ground of space were often sounded. For example, after the launch of Sputnik, Lyndon Baines Johnson (an aspiring presidential candidate who chaired the Senate's stinging investigation of a space gap) concluded, "[O]ut in space, there is the ultimate position—from which total control of the earth may be exercised ... our national goal and the goal of all free men must be to win and hold that position."[7] The Reagan administration's Strategic Defense Initiative (SDI) was the purest expression of this goal, combining military necessity and the Soviet threat with boundless technological optimism. During this time, the U.S. Air Force adopted a space policy predicated on the assumption that "spacepower will be as decisive in future combat as airpower is today."[8]

The sanctity of space was breached with the launch of Sputnik in 1957. The placement of a satellite orbiting the earth meant that it was but a matter of time before critical information could be gleaned from space and passed along to enhance war fighters on the ground. Sputnik also posed the frightening question of whether weapons would be circling the earth, ready to be cast down like thunderbolts at a moment's notice. To the surprise of many, and the gratitude of still more, Sputnik did not lead to the weaponization of space during the Cold War. There is no public evidence that either the Soviet Union or the United States deployed objects in space that could blind, disable, or destroy satellites. Nor did the two superpowers, locked in the vice of geopolitical and ideological competition, move beyond the most rudimentary efforts to test these capabilities on the ground.

Space was not weaponized during the Cold War largely because the United States and the Soviet Union both concluded that they had more to lose than to gain from celestial clashes. With the end of the Cold War and the removal of the Soviet counterweight, space warriors have a new opening to extend U.S. military superiority and to pre-empt challengers. The logic of asymmetric warfare provides a second, reinforcing impetus to weaponize space. States that cannot compete militarily with the United States might find the covert development of space warfare capabilities less expensive, less technically challenging, and more rewarding. If lesser powers can find the means to create havoc in space, they just might be able to tie Gulliver down.

Consequently, the challenge of avoiding the weaponization of space is quite different and conceivably greater now than during the Cold War, when the cautious principles of mutual deterrence extended into space. Back then, maintaining space as a "weapons-free zone" meant preventing the use of the moon as a future base of military operations. One enthusiast in the U.S. Air Force argued, "It has been said that, 'He who controls the moon, controls the earth.' Our planners must carefully evaluate this statement. For if it is true (and I, for one, think it is), then the United States must control the moon."[9] The alternative was a treaty forbidding the "appropriation by claim of sovereignty, by means of use or occupation, or by any other means" outer space, including the moon "and other celestial bodies."[10] This was the path chosen by presidents Dwight D. Eisenhower, John F. Kennedy, and Lyndon Baines Johnson, ultimately resulting in the 1967 Outer Space Treaty. This treaty also barred states parties from placing in orbit around the Earth any objects carrying "nuclear weapons or any other kinds of weapons of mass destruction, install such weapons on celestial bodies, or station such weapons in outer space in any other manner."[11]

The old terms of debate favored a space "sanctuary," in part because the anti-weaponization option appealed to our higher selves: Those who had botched things pretty badly on earth might still be able to protect the heavens from damaging human intervention. While the deployment of satellites that assisted military missions proceeded apace, weaponization was curtailed. Soon after Sputnik, other satellites began orbiting the earth, providing essential tasks for military forces. Satellites in space also provided civilian, commercial, scientific, and arms control tasks, including the taking of pictures to monitor treaty obligations.

The vulnerability of U.S. satellites that provided essential military tasks sorely tempted Soviet strategists, and *vice versa*. Nevertheless, space never became a shooting gallery during the Cold War. Had this begun, it would have surely spread quickly to earth. Vulnerability in space was akin to the mutual assured destruction relationship on earth. The United States and the Soviet Union still retained the means to create utter havoc in space by virtue of their huge missile inventories. These missiles could be reprogrammed to detonate their nuclear warheads in space, creating disabling fields of debris and radiation through which satellites passed.[12] Thus, both superpowers retained "residual" capabilities to fight in space. It was, however, in both superpowers' nature to design, test, and deploy more specialized means of space warfare. Surprisingly, both exercised remarkable restraint in the pursuit of "dedicated" anti-satellite (ASAT) weapons.

The United States and the Soviet Union competed intensely to gain a qualitative edge in tank or submarine warfare, air combat, and strategic nuclear forces—but not over ASATs. Both countries worked on rudimentary ASAT capabilities, but these programs were half-hearted and episodic. The United States maintained two ASAT interceptors on Johnston Island in the South Pacific from 1964 to 1975. One of these tests, utilizing a 1.4 megaton warhead, inadvertently damaged three satellites and set off burglar alarms in Hawaii. The Soviets tested ASATs from 1968 to 1971 and again from 1976 to 1982. During this three-decade stretch, the Soviet Union tested twenty ASATs, while the United States tested a grand total of thirty-three. This might seem like a lot, until one recalls that each superpower regularly flight-tested dozens of missiles *annually* during this period. While missiles aimed at each other were kept at the ready, deployed U.S. and Soviet ASAT systems were mothballed.[13]

The most succinct rebuttal to the Rumsfeld Commission's contention that the weaponization of, or conflict in, space is inevitable is that neither occurred during the Cold War.[14] The twin impulses of seeking advantage and fearing disadvantage produced approximately 70,000 nuclear warheads in the United States, and another 55,000 in the Soviet Union.[15] In contrast, there is no available evidence during the Cold War that a single weapon had been deployed in space. Despite the presumed military advantages of seizing this high ground, both superpowers shied away from turning space into a home for ASATs.

Anarchy—at least the man-made kind—is not a natural condition in space. Nor is anarchy inevitable on the sea-bed floor or on Antarctica—other regions where nations have recognized and advanced "the common interest of all mankind" to promote "peaceful purposes" and to avoid conflict.[16]

These restraints were essentially voluntary. Formal constraints on space warfare have been minimal, beginning with the Outer Space Treaty's prohibitions on WMD and military bases on celestial bodies. Needless to say, this was the low hanging fruit of space arms control. The most useful space weapons were ones that did not cause large bands of radiation and debris through which one's own satellites would have to traverse. In 1972, Washington and Moscow added important treaty-based protections against space warfare. The ABM Treaty prohibited space-based interceptors as a component of missile defense systems, and added specific protections for satellites that each side depended upon to monitor the other's compliance. Under the terms of the now-defunct ABM Treaty, both sides agreed not to interfere with these "national technical means" of verification.

The Carter administration tried to expand the envelop of formal treaty constraints on space warfare by proposing a ban on ASAT weapons, but got tripped up over problems of scope and verification. A complete ban on ASAT capabilities was impractical, since it would capture all ocean-spanning ballistic missiles, high-performance missile defenses, and even the space shuttle— all of which were also capable of damaging, destroying, or disabling satellites. A narrower approach focusing on "dedicated" ASATs—kill vehicles expressly designed to demolish or disable satellites—was pursued, but ran foul of monitoring difficulties. Determining whether ASAT kill vehicles were being covertly produced and that existing ASATs had all been destroyed required vast transparency. The Carter administration's efforts were also subject to the criticism that, with so many residual means to kill satellites, a narrow-casted ban on "dedicated" ASATs had limited value.[17] The ASAT talks foundered when U.S.–Soviet ties frayed.

Rather than risk a destabilizing contest in space warfare, every U.S. administration save one during the Cold War decided to quietly hedge against a Soviet ASAT program, rather than to ratchet up an open competition. Research and development programs were maintained to keep this option open, while overt testing was minimized. For example, during the administration of President Gerald R. Ford, the Pentagon's top research and development chief broadcast U.S. preferences to the Kremlin:

The Soviets have developed and tested a potential war-fighting anti-satellite capability. They have thereby seized the initiative in an area which we hoped would be left untapped. They have opened the specter of space as a new dimension for warfare, with all that this implies. I would warn them that they have started down a dangerous road. Restraint on their part will be matched by our own restraint, but we should not permit them to develop an asymmetry in space.[18]

The Reagan administration sought to replace this hedging strategy with the SDI, which had the immediate benefit of stopping Soviet ASAT tests. Instead, the Kremlin reverted to pursuing less visible hedges, clearly worried about Washington's high-technology challenge. SDI eventually succumbed to technical, economic, and political constraints. Domestic and foreign antipathy to war-fighting in space was so great that SDI enthusiasts could not successfully defend the concept in its most simple and stark terms, i.e. as a way to achieve security and escape the mutual hostage relationship with the Soviet Union by dominating space. Instead, the Reagan team tried to argue, with complete implausibility, that SDI would facilitate a cooperative transition in U.S.–Soviet relations.

The Reagan administration refused to negotiate any constraints on ASATs, in part to protect its SDI program. Instead, the Reagan team pushed for ASAT tests and deployments, ostensibly to redress an imbalance favoring the Kremlin, to deter Soviet attacks, and to counter threats posed by Soviet space systems. Democratic majorities on Capitol Hill pushed back, passing amendments calling for ASAT negotiations while blocking flight tests.

These Cold War rationales for pursuing ASATs no longer apply. In the absence of a superpower competitor, the United States can be confident of "winning" a space arms race—if "winning" is defined as succeeding in applying advanced technologies and deploying superior war-fighting capabilities in space. But in an era of asymmetric warfare, weaker competitors might still field capabilities that could cause havoc with satellites upon which the exercise of U.S. military capabilities depends. Indeed, they might do so even if the United States refrained from weaponizing space.

As was the case during the SDI debate, the connections between ballistic missile defenses and ASATs are complex and difficult to sort out. To begin with, ASATs constitute a threat to missile defenses, because successful intercepts rely on satellites to detect missile launches and provide targeting information. The ability of missile defenses to function properly therefore depended on the continued functioning of space systems. These protections could be sought through arms control arrangements, informal or tacit constraints, or by dominating space and destroying opposing ASATs before they could cause harm.

To complicate matters further, advanced missile defenses could also function as ASATs. The powerful ground-based interceptors or interceptors based in space designed to shoot down an incoming warhead could be reprogrammed and retooled to shoot down satellites. (Thus, America's renewed interest in missile defenses is doubly unsettling to Moscow and Beijing.) A ban on all advanced missile defense interceptors because they might have ASAT potential would also foreclose defenses against missiles that threatened U.S. allies and forward-deployed forces. Because a complete ban on missile defenses is not sensible, ASAT arms control would have to be pursued through other means.

The architecture and scope of American missile defense programs is therefore crucial, because they could make space warfare more or less likely. If U.S. missile defense plans suggest ambitions to extend what the Joint Chiefs of Staff call "full spectrum dominance" into space,[19] and if U.S. missile defense plans are accompanied by ASAT tests, Moscow and Beijing would react vigorously and, perhaps, in concert. When pursued in tandem, extensive missile defenses and ASATs could not only threaten nullification of the Russian and Chinese nuclear deterrents, but also render both leaderships blind. Thus, if Washington wishes to have Moscow and Beijing become partners in combating proliferation and in pursuing cooperative threat reduction, taking the lead in flight-testing and deploying ASATs would be a rather poor idea.

Attempts to formalize these understandings in a multilateral treaty could affirm the international community's widespread interest against weaponizing space, but these negotiations are bound to be tendentious and time-consuming. Many states in the 66-nation Conference on Disarmament in Geneva, which has jurisdiction for negotiations regarding the peaceful uses of outer space and which operates by consensus, favor an international convention banning space warfare, but these negotiations are likely to be bedeviled by previous problems of defining the treaty's scope and being able to monitor satisfactorily some of the convention's core obligations. An inclusive ban on space warfare-related activities, absent verification arrangements, would be hortatory in nature and would invite replication of the false promise of the Biological Weapons Convention, where some countries signed, and then ignored with impunity, core treaty provisions. Even if a future U.S. administration were to support and complete negotiations on an expansive international convention prohibiting space warfare-related activities, it may have difficulty receiving the Senate's consent to ratification.

An international convention that does not include the United States and other major space-faring nations is unlikely to provide reassurance. The Conference on Disarmament might have more success in clarifying and reaffirming strong international opposition to space warfare by narrowing its focus to banning activities that are most verifiable, such as the flight testing of anti-satellite weapons or the testing of weapons designed for other purposes in an "ASAT mode." Corollary prohibitions might apply to testing that causes space debris.

Even these more narrowly drawn and verifiable prohibitions would be strenuously opposed by those who seek U.S. dominance in space. The immediate need is to establish customary practices favorable to space commerce and to clarify unhelpful ones. Because the testing of advanced missile defenses is already underway, and because these interceptors can also be used for the purpose of anti-satellite warfare, it would be wise not to wait for the Conference on Disarmament to complete its work and for national legislatures to consent to ratification. Instead, it makes sense for space-faring nations to negotiate and implement bilateral or multilateral accords to avoid dangerous practices in space. These "rules of the road" for space would support space commerce, while making it harder and more repellant for states to cross critical thresholds toward weaponization.

One model worth emulating is the Incidents at Sea Agreement between the U.S. and Soviet navies. Negotiated in 1972 after a series of provocative naval incidents, it has been widely replicated by other bilateral and multilateral agreements. The purposes of "IncSea" accords include the avoidance of collisions, dangerous maneuvers or simulated attacks, blinding, and other reckless acts.[20] These types of rules are as applicable in space as at sea. Another example of establishing rules of the road is the 1989 Prevention of Dangerous Military Activities Agreement between the United States and the Soviet Union. This accord was designed to minimize the risk of inadvertent escalation, restrict the use of lasers, regulate military maneuvers, and prohibit interference with communications and command and control networks in peacetime.[21]

The IncSea Agreement and the Dangerous Military Activities Agreement are not treaties; they are executive agreements that do not require congressional approval. Nonetheless, they help establish international legal obligations. The "proliferation" of agreements prohibiting dangerous military practices in space, as on the high seas, can reinforce customary practices that facilitate space commerce rather than space warfare. The negotiation of rules of the road to prevent dangerous military activities in space would go against the impulse to maintain U.S. freedom of action and to exploit American advantages. Virtually the same critique was lodged against the IncSea Agreement, which is now widely valued.

If Washington has the wisdom not to confuse "leadership" with seizing the high ground of space, it could propose that space-faring nations engage in mutual information exchanges, transparency- and confidence-building measures, as well as site visits to provide reassurance that field- and space-based testing against satellite targets, testing in an anti-satellite mode, or testing in space against objects on earth are not being carried out. Devising transparency and monitoring measures to support the information exchanges associated with these provisions will not be easy, but more difficult verification problems have been tackled successfully with creativity and ingenuity.

Agreed rules of the road regarding activities in space are necessary, but insufficient. Even if such reciprocal reassurance measures could be implemented, they would relate only to observable, but not covert capabilities. Complete restraint in forgoing space warfare capabilities by Washington might not be reciprocated by Moscow and Beijing. Indeed, Washington must presume that they are working on ASATs behind closed doors. (Moscow and Beijing would surely have the same presumption.) The best insurance policy against cheating—and the best way to prevent ASAT flight tests and deployments—is to hedge. These hedges would be problematic, since they could be rapidly deployed, but there is no way to monitor with confidence what is transpiring behind closed doors. In other words, in asymmetric warfare, as during the Cold War, potential adversaries would have the means—whether residual or covert—to damage each other's satellites. This does not make space warfare inevitable. To the contrary: Space warfare can be avoided in the future, as in the past, if restraint accompanies residual capabilities, if covert ASAT capabilities reinforce restraint, and if field or space testing is avoided.

Just as in the Cold War, America's choice is whether to hedge wisely in space warfare, or to seek to dominate the competition, as the Rumsfeld Commission recommends. Given the extraordinary lead the United States enjoys in space-related activities, the weaponization of space is inevitable in the near-term only if the Pentagon takes the lead in this effort. A hedging strategy is clearly preferable. While asymmetric warfare could well lead weaker powers to covertly develop space warfare capabilities, power differentials could also reinforce restraint so that closeted capabilities are not deployed or used. If Russia or China were to move beyond covert research and laboratory programs to flight-test or deploy ASATs, they would not have this field to themselves for very long. They must surely know that outright cheating or pressing on the margins of agreed measures would prompt a vigorous U.S. response, as was the case during the Cold War. Neither Russia nor China has an interest in a competition over deploying or testing space warfare capabilities. Thus, the dictates of asymmetric power call for Russia and China to keep their ASAT developments under wraps. The same is true for the United States, which does not require deployed space warfare capabilities to disrupt Russian or Chinese satellite operations: Washington has quite sufficient conventional military capabilities that could disable or destroy satellite ground links.

The conditions of asymmetric warfare suggest that the covert development of ASAT capabilities may well be inevitable—but not the flight-testing or deployment of those capabilities. In times of U.S. superiority, no less than during the Cold War, it remains very much in the U.S. national security interest not to lead a competition in space warfare. Crisis stability and ASATs do not go well together: in the event of ASAT use, the blind would be leading the blind— unless, as suggested by the Rumsfeld Commission report, the United States succeeds in dominating the high ground of space. Pre-emption in space is a far more attractive and feasible option for Washington than for Moscow or Beijing.

U.S. attempts to seize the high ground of space would generate intense blocking action on Capitol Hill, where bipartisan approaches are needed not only to ratify treaties, but also to deploy missile defenses and weapons in space. The pursuit of space warfare capabilities would further alienate U.S. allies, while increasing the likelihood of bilateral Russian–Chinese strategic cooperation. Without strong alliances and help from Moscow and Beijing, proliferation problems would grow more acute, coalition building against proliferation threats would become harder, and the demise of non-proliferation treaties would become more likely. What remains of bilateral U.S.–Russian arms control accords would unravel. Put simply, the quest to weaponize space inevitably would generate less security on the ground—and more proliferation.

There are, in addition, powerful new economic reasons to avoid the weaponization of space. By 2010, the U.S. Space Command estimates that there will be 2,000 operating satellites, compared to roughly 600 today. Much of this growth will be tied to civilian and commercial applications, especially communication-related sectors. Beginning in 1996, commercial space revenues have exceeded government space expenditures, and this gap continues to widen. The U.S. Space Command projects that by 2003, the Global Positioning System will generate $16 billion in revenues. Space policy expert James Oberg estimates that in 2000, space technology industries realized $125 billion in profits. By 2005, global telecommunications revenues could reach $1.2 trillion, and by 2010, the cumulative U.S. investment in space could well reach $500–$600 billion—equaling that of current U.S. investments in Europe.[22]

With the global economy so intimately tied to assets in space, the flight-testing and deployment of ASATs would create dangerous perturbations in satellite-dependent commerce. A glimpse of this future was provided by the failure of one Galaxy IV satellite in May 1998. When the satellite's spacecraft control processor failed, 80 percent of U.S. pagers—37 million users—were unplugged. Some radio and television stations were knocked off the air, while gas stations and retail outlets were unable to verify credit card transactions. The Rumsfeld Commission cites this as a harbinger of future vulnerability in space to malefactors, and further reason to implement its recommendations. It contends that space warfare capabilities are now needed because the United States is more vulnerable in, and more dependent on, space. The first assertion is debatable; the second is incontrovertible. On economic grounds, however, a far stronger case can be made to try to head off warfare in space, rather than leading this charge.

Nuclear Ambitions

The British war historian and strategist B. H. Liddell Hart defined strategy as "the art of distributing and applying military means to fulfill ends of policy."[23] Under this reasonable definition, nuclear strategy is an oxymoron. The means of nuclear strategy—the targeting of an adversary—could certainly be justified as serving the ends of deterrence. If, however, deterrence ever broke down, and if war plans were truly implemented, there would be no "art" to distributing and applying nuclear detonations. Means and ends would become indecipherable and horrific. Had nuclear exchanges taken place during the Cold War, the most crucial objective would have been escalation control, and not comparative advantage or other definitions of victory.

Escalation control was the province of political leaders; nuclear strategists sought escalation dominance and other doctrinal devices to maximize deterrence. The resulting war plans have had their own internal logic based on targeting lists and damage expectancies. These plans were, however, unlikely to pass two significant external tests. The first test was public support. The more the cold logic of nuclear deterrence was explained in public discourse, the more it was likely to appall the general public and their elected representatives. The problem of public scrutiny was avoided by pinning the highest classification of nuclear war-fighting plans. Indeed, the successful maintenance of these plans required that they not be the subject of detailed debate.

The second test, as noted above, was escalation control. Once the nuclear threshold was crossed, escalation control would be predicated on shared cost/benefit calculations with an adversary to whom one was meting out mortal damage. Mutual abilities to calibrate and control such calculations amid the radiological ruin of a nuclear war would also be needed. The fragility of these assumptions does not require explanation. As a consequence, the cold logic of nuclear war fighting has had every prospect of breaking down once multiple mushroom clouds begin to form. Escalation control, in other words, loses meaning the deeper one side or the other enters the domain of its nuclear war-fighting plans.

These conundrums were addressed by some of the finest minds during the Cold War. Nonetheless, nuclear strategy continued to be an oxymoron or, as Lawrence Freedman wrote, a "muddle" and "a contradiction in terms."[24] Political leaders who dutifully signed off on nuclear war plans understood this fully, which is why, in every deep crisis of the Cold War, they sought mightily to avoid crossing the nuclear threshold. The disconnect between nuclear strategists and political leaders has been most evident during these periods of heightened tension.[25] McGeorge Bundy, who stood beside President John F. Kennedy during the harrowing days of the Cuban missile crisis, described this divide as follows: "In the real world of political leaders, a decision that would bring even one hydrogen bomb on one city of one's own country would be recognized in advance as a catastrophic blunder ... Political leaders, whether here or in Russia, are cut from a very different mold than strategic planners. They see cities and people as part of what they are trying to help—not as targets."[26] When confronted with the very real prospect of a nuclear exchange, political leaders and their advisors have tried to make sure that command and control over nuclear forces remained intact. Then they asked the nuclear strategists, in effect, to leave the room.

Nonetheless, Armageddon strategists have been given wide latitude to ply their craft. For the last four decades, there has been little political benefit—and considerable political risk—in questioning the basic premises of nuclear war-fighting plans. The discourse of political leaders on this subject seldom moved beyond affirmations of nuclear deterrence, which resonated quite positively with the public. The protectors of nuclear doctrine could therefore fend off attempts at radical reform simply by declaring that deterrence would be endangered. The requirements of nuclear deterrence could be downsized, but not questioned. Besides, few were properly cleared to enter these domains. Presidents and cabinet officers quickly moved on to other projects. Inherited war plans were modified to fit evolving targets and capabilities, and then put in the safe, from which it was fervently hoped they would never be retrieved.

As nuclear capabilities evolved, so, too, did concepts of nuclear deterrence, from massive retaliation, flexible response, assured destruction, counterforce and countervailing strategies, and other permutations. None of these constructs persuasively answered Liddell Hart's fundamental requirements of strategy. No doctrine of nuclear weapon use could satisfactorily answer how the application and distribution of nuclear detonations could successfully achieve political ends. No one was able to square means with ends. Deterrence strategists dodged these dilemmas by arguing that their craft was about avoiding war. And sure enough, as long as a nuclear war did not start, nuclear strategists could claim success. The contradictions and trap doors embedded in targeting plans remained concealed, and the general public was satisfied that rationality would prevail. The single-most public indicator of nuclear doctrine—the number of deployed nuclear warheads—was, after all, dropping downward, and the two superpowers were (usually) negotiating responsibly to further reduce nuclear dangers.

The illogic of nuclear strategy remained intact throughout the Cold War because true believers held the keys to the kingdom. Every successive evolution in nuclear doctrine appeared to address one set of weaknesses while raising another.[27] The Eisenhower administration briefly flirted with "massive retaliation." Secretary of State John Foster Dulles warned publicly that, "The way to deter aggression is for the free community to be willing and able to respond vigorously at places and with means of its own choosing."[28] The evident difficulties in skipping significant rungs in the escalation ladder soon led to notions of "flexible response," which then became an invitation to pursue open-ended nuclear requirements.

Next came the construct of "assured destruction," which was conceived by the "whiz kids" in Robert McNamara's Pentagon. "Assured destruction" entered the lexicon in 1964 as "the ability to deter a deliberate nuclear attack upon the United States or its allies by maintaining at all times a clear and unmistakable ability to inflict an unacceptable degree of damage upon any aggressor, or combination of aggressors—even after absorbing a surprise first strike."[29] Assured destruction was determined to be achieved by the killing of 20–25 percent of an adversary's population and 50 percent of its industrial capacity. This, as Freedman noted, was "calculated as much by reference to the law of diminishing marginal returns when applied to nuclear destructiveness as by any sense of the Soviet threshold of tolerance."[30]

There was only one good reason to use assured destruction as a guideline for determining nuclear requirements: political leaders could say "no" to the incessant requests by military departments and nuclear strategists for more and better nuclear capabilities. This was not a good enough reason, however, to embrace the targeting of population centers. As Fred Charles Iklé unerringly concluded, "'assured destruction' fails to indicate what is to be destroyed; but 'assured genocide' would reveal the truth too starkly."[31] Assured destruction was followed by counterforce targeting. The increased accuracy and lethality of U.S. warheads, now multiplied atop missiles, enabled nuclear strategists to place hardened military targets and leadership bunkers "at risk." Burgeoning strategic arsenals in the 1970s and 1980s were thus given new purpose. Unfortunately, many of these targets also happened to be within, or in lethally radioactive proximity to, cities.

The consequence of genocide remained lurking in the background of these doctrinal refinements, but the word dared not be mentioned in serious company; to do so would result in the expulsion of the mentioner. To find the last recorded example of truth telling from within, one must go back to 1949, when a distinguished advisory committee deliberated in deep secrecy on whether the Truman administration should pursue the H-bomb, then called "the super." The members of the advisory committee concluded that the use of hydrogen bombs "would involve a decision to slaughter a vast number of civilians. We are alarmed as to the possible global effects of the radioactivity generated ... [T]here is no inherent limit in the destructive power that may be attained with them. Therefore a super bomb might become a weapon of genocide."[32] "Super" bombs expressly tailored for counterforce targeting subsequently became the backbone of nuclear deterrence for Washington and Moscow.

A central dilemma of nuclear deterrence was that proposed strengthening measures equated usability with utility. Nuclear weapon strategists argued that the more "usable" the weapon was, i.e. the more weapons' effects could be tailored to specific targets while reducing collateral damage, the more deterrence would be strengthened. Meanwhile, national leaders acted upon a much different calculus, since they were firmly uninterested in crossing the nuclear threshold. These parallel universes survived intact after the Cold War ended. The quest for usability continued unabated. Thus, the Bush administration has been urged to pursue a uniquely designed "earth-penetrating" warhead to burrow toward the hardened leadership bunker or the underground cache of lethal weapons held by a maverick leader. A new and improved capability in this regard might well require renewed nuclear testing.[33]

Nuclear weapons strategists have long argued that the dictates of deterrence require continued refinements. Skeptics of nuclear deterrence seek to sidestep this dark and deep pit by pointing to the "existential" aspects of nuclear deterrence.[34] In this view, the mere holding of the weapon suggests a possibility of use, and hence deterrence. Serious nuclear strategists are made of sterner stuff. In their view, weapons need to be specifically tailored, modernized, and tested repeatedly to demonstrate usability.

These dictates led the United States and the Soviet Union to test nuclear weapons in excess of 1,700 times, or an average of more than once every two weeks, during the Cold War. The quest for utility and its equation with usability lends itself to varied explanations. In a Cold War context, these refinements could be explained as a bloodless surrogate for competition on the battlefield, or as a natural consequence of domestic politics and pressure groups. Additionally, the ceaseless quest to refine nuclear war-fighting capabilities could be viewed as a product of having overlarge and competing nuclear weapon laboratories. Another explanation, less explored than the rest, is that nuclear war-fighting capabilities continue to be refined because nuclear strategists continue to seek the means to escape from deterrence.[35]

The ultimate escape from deterrence is to devise a nuclear war-winning capability. In this context, the search for "strengthening" deterrence becomes indecipherable from the quest for decisive advantage, which could be gained only by covering an adversary's target set, *in toto.* The language of negotiation and public diplomacy was that of sufficiency and equality, but the numbers inscribed in treaty texts were always consistent with the dictates of targeting. The success of strategic arms limitation talks was predicated on the mutual abandonment of strategic superiority and the acceptance of national vulnerability. (The Nixon administration explicitly abandoned strategic superiority in lieu of "sufficiency.") And yet, the ink was not even dry on the 1972 strategic arms limitation accords, when both superpowers immediately set their sights on deploying significant increases in warhead numbers and accuracies. While diplomats searched for strategic stability, nuclear strategists engaged in the ceaseless quest of winning—or at least not losing—nuclear exchanges.

In the jargon of nuclear deterrence, "damage limitation" was king. "Damage limitation" meant targeting opposing nuclear forces that could do incalculable harm to one's homeland. To succeed at damage limitation, one had to target and destroy opposing nuclear forces before they could be launched or could reach their intended targets. The ultimate weapons for damage limitation were "prompt hard-target-kill capabilities"—super-accurate, super-lethal warheads atop fast-flying missiles. The Soviet Union held an excess of these warheads on land-based missiles; the United States countered by distributing these warheads on land, on missile-carrying submarines, and on cruise missiles. U.S. and Soviet damage limitation strategies were both fundamentally escapist in nature: their purpose was to escape the logic of mutual deterrence.[36]

The most significant constraint in escaping from mutual deterrence during the Cold War was, of course, the ABM Treaty. Thanks especially to the deployment of multiple independently targetable re-entry vehicles (MIRVs) and improved guidance, U.S. and Soviet nuclear strategists succeeded in building up warhead numbers, tailoring weapons' effects and increasing damage expectancies against hardened targets. Nevertheless, their best efforts at damage limitation were foiled by the utter vulnerability of national territory to however many warheads might survive a pre-emptive attack. With the U.S. withdrawal from the ABM Treaty, these calculations could finally be revisited. A long-sought war-winning capability was now theoretically possible for the United States.

This prospect—along with the need to take countermeasures to re-establish deterrence—is surely being weighed in Moscow and Beijing. The scope of such countermeasures would depend on the financial and technical means applied to these tasks. It would also depend on their perceptions of the ambitions behind the Bush administration's withdrawal from the ABM Treaty. This, in turn, would depend in significant measure on the proposed scope and architecture of U.S. missile defenses, and on U.S. ambitions for weaponizing space. Much therefore depends on whether the United States decides, in vastly altered circumstances, to escape from deterrence. There are, however, alternative escape routes available.

Alternative Nuclear Postures

In several respects, the Bush administration's nuclear posture review (NPR), released in January 2002, moved in the right direction. First, it proposed to reduce U.S. strategic forces over a ten-year period to comparable levels agreed to by presidents Clinton and Yeltsin in 1997—a force structure of approximately 2,000 warheads, of which perhaps 1,700 would be ready for immediate use. These reductions constituted a welcome 85 percent reduction from Cold War apogees of deployed warheads on "strategic nuclear delivery vehicles"—intercontinental-range bombers, land-based missiles, and ballistic missile-carrying submarines. Second, the Bush NPR proposed to reduce the "hard" alert level of U.S. nuclear forces over a ten-year period from approximately 2,500 warheads to perhaps 750 warheads. (However, approximately 500 additional warheads could be placed on alert relatively quickly by repositioning submarines, and more still by readying strategic bombers.)[37] Third, the Bush NPR proposed to remove additional strategic bombers from nuclear war plans. All of these steps were advertised as evidence of the administration's break with Cold War nuclear practices and a reaffirmation of prior declarations that Russia was no longer an enemy.

On the other hand, the Bush administration's NPR certainly did not treat Russia as a friend. In addition to establishing the goal of reductions to between 1,700 to 2,200 operationally deployed warheads on strategic forces, the NPR also appeared to set requirements for another 3,000 warheads that could be deployed in days, weeks or months, and thousands more in an "inactive reserve" status.[38] Russia, in contrast, would likely retain, over a ten-year period, perhaps 700 operationally ready nuclear warheads on its strategic forces, with very modest capabilities to deploy additional missiles, submarines, or bombers to increase this number.[39] The 1,700 deployed U.S. warheads projected by the Bush administration would, in other words, provide ample coverage of a wide range of targets in Russia and China. And if target coverage were to become a problem over this ten-year period, the NPR expressly permitted adding warheads to meet new needs from the reserve stockpile that would be maintained rather than dismantled. Indeed, the administration's desire for flexibility was so great that the obligations assumed under this accord would be in effect for a single day—after which all obligations would cease. The accord's monitoring provisions would lapse prior to the 24-hour period of obligation.[40]

Moreover, the NPR added conventional strike capabilities to U.S. nuclear war plans, a long-standing worry for Moscow and Beijing, while calling for upgrades in communication and intelligence for real-time targeting. By rejecting ratification of the second strategic arms reduction accord, the Bush administration retained the capability to deploy multiple warhead missiles atop its land-based missiles—a capability that Russia would be hard-pressed to retain and China would find difficult to develop for its mobile missiles. The most lethal MIRVed missile in the U.S. arsenal, the Peacekeeper, would be retained in storage, as would its missile silos. On top of this, the United States would overlay "limited" but ill-defined and open-ended missile defenses.

With good reason, Moscow and Beijing might conclude from the Bush administration's NPR that the United States wished to escape from nuclear deterrence and to trade in MAD for a nuclear war-winning posture. This negation strategy was infeasible as long as the ABM Treaty prohibited national missile defenses, but might conceivably be within reach during a new era of U.S. dominance and unilateralism.

While the NPR was suggestive of this ambition, it was far from definitive. Russian and Chinese perceptions could be reaffirmed, disabused, or reshaped by subsequent decisions taken by Washington. For example, joint U.S. and Russian efforts to make reductions irreversible by agreeing to dismantle warheads in a verifiable manner, or to destroy missile silos capable of launching MIRVed missiles, could rub some of the hard edges from the Bush administration's plans. The subsequent sizing of U.S. missile defenses to counter proliferation threats, rather than to negate the Russian and Chinese nuclear deterrents, would have similar reassuring effects, as would restraint in avoiding the flight-testing and deployment of dedicated space warfare capabilities.

A clear and clean break from Cold War nuclear deterrence practices is long overdue. But what kind of a departure is called for? U.S. strategic superiority opens up two radically different paths. Both paths seek the same destination—a prolonged period of safety against the dangers posed by weapons of mass destruction. And both would seek to extend and prolong U.S. military superiority. One path would pursue these objectives by maintaining nuclear war-fighting and missile defense capabilities sufficient to take on all comers and to win decisively. This approach places a premium on advanced technology and numerical superiority. It assumes that dominance could be successfully applied to the art of war at its most apocalyptic level. The other path, equally radical in approach, assumes that a nation enjoying strategic superiority would willingly choose not to extend U.S. dominance to the art of war at its most consequential level. This approach would seek a partnership with Russia and China against proliferation, rather than seeking to negate their deterrents.

The Bush administration's NPR took many steps down the first path, that of seeking to escape the construct of mutual deterrence by negating the nuclear capabilities of major powers as well as maverick states. What would an alternative U.S. nuclear posture look like? It might have at least eight key elements.

First, because the United States would seek to extend its conventional military superiority, and because it has more to lose than to gain by the development, testing, and deployment of new nuclear weapon designs, an alternative nuclear posture would heartily endorse the Comprehensive Test Ban Treaty (CTBT). Since no country can maintain an advanced nuclear stockpile as well as the United States, the longer a global moratorium and ban on nuclear testing lasts, the more it favors U.S. national interests. It would then follow that Washington should ratify the CTBT and strongly support the international monitoring and challenge inspection system associated with this treaty.

Second, an alternative path would embrace the development of nuclear warhead designs that are utterly reliable and that would not need to be tested. The very first nuclear weapon design—the bomb that leveled Hiroshima—did not need to be tested prior to its use because the scientists of the Manhattan Project knew that its simple design, based on highly enriched uranium, was sure to work. A "back to the future" approach to nuclear deterrence would produce uranium bombs that would provide 100 percent assurance of detonations under conditions of the CTBT's indefinite duration. This warhead would not require a hugely expensive "stockpile stewardship" program—although other warheads in the U.S. stockpile would. In addition, as Stephen M. Younger has noted, "Such designs would require a significantly smaller industrial plant for their maintenance … Simpler weapons might be maintained with higher confidence for longer periods by a weapons staff that has little or no direct experience with nuclear testing."[41] Uranium bombs could be designed for a range of yields, but they would not be capable of destroying the entire panoply of targets in U.S. nuclear war plans.

A third element of an alternative, radical departure from Cold War-like concepts of nuclear deterrence would be to drop the numbers of deployed nuclear weapons below the number of targets in Russia. In other words, verifiable reductions would be low enough to disallow the successful, prompt execution of nuclear war-fighting plans.

Fourth, the destructive power of available warheads would be progressively reduced. Over time, warheads designed to kill hardened silos and underground command centers would be replaced by warheads that reflect an acceptance of mutual deterrence between responsible nations. The development and stockpiling of "back to the future" Uranium bombs that never need to be tested support this requirement, since they would have insufficient yield to destroy hardened military targets.

Fifth, the clear and clean break from nuclear war-fighting strategies of deterrence could also be demonstrated by the collaborative, verifiable dismantlement of stockpiled warheads designed for tactical nuclear warfare and for missiles specifically designed to destroy multiple targets.

Sixth, further collaborative reductions in alert rates would signal the same general intention.

Seventh, a clear and clean break from Cold War concepts of nuclear deterrence could be clarified by the issuance of declaratory statements by responsible nuclear powers against any targeting that would result in the destruction of cities. During the Cold War, the United States rejected the targeting of cities, *per se*, while maintaining many targets in war-fighting plans that happened to be co-located with cities, or down-wind of them, such as hardened leadership bunkers, command and control nodes, and war-supporting industry, as well as garrisons, air bases, and missile fields that were within or close to metropolitan areas. Soviet targeting plans were similar in many respects. In other words, the deeper either or both sides delved into their nuclear war-fighting plans, the more genocidal they became. The massive damage from prompt nuclear effects would be compounded by delayed biospheric destruction. These plans remain in place.

The public identification of targets within and downwind of major metropolitan areas is an instructive exercise.[42] It clarifies the genocidal nature of U.S. and Russian nuclear war plans, and the excessive number of warheads retained to execute these plans. Mutual commitments to avoid the genocidal targeting of cities could not be verified, unlike most of the other proposals listed above. And needless to say, in *extremis*, a nuclear power could revert to the targeting of cities as the ultimate deterrent against a stronger foe. In effect, the targeting of cities would remain the last refuge of nuclear deterrence. Indeed, extraordinarily deep and verifiable reductions—to tens of warheads—would increase the likelihood of city strikes in the event of a breakdown of deterrence. But we are far, far distant from reductions to this minimal number.

The current structure of nuclear war plans owes much to the building blocks erected during the Cold War. The size of these tall edifices continues to reflect the inclusion of counterforce targeting, "ground zeroes" within or nearby cities, and damage limitation strategies of deterrence. Russian nuclear war plans will necessarily have to move away from these constructs, as its nuclear forces contract. The United States, however, could easily continue to maintain elaborate targeting plans. If the load-bearing beams of this structure were removed—such as targets within cities—the entire construction could go wobbly. The internal coherence of these war-fighting plans depends on keeping them within the nuclear family of deterrence strategists. With good reason, then, the architects of these war plans fend off external reviews and in-depth public elaborations.

This imposing, secret edifice, however, cannot obscure an essential truth known intuitively by political leaders throughout the Cold War: Safety in the throes of a deep crisis required setting aside elaborate nuclear targeting plans and focusing instead on the imperative to avoid a momentous crossing of the nuclear threshold. There is nothing more apolitical than plans to fight a nuclear war—unless it is plans to fight and win such a war. If a terrible moment of choice to cross this threshold arrives, and cannot be avoided, responsible political leaders are likely to seek a "minimal" demonstration of the horrors that lie ahead. Elaborate targeting lists—even those considerably pared down after the collapse of the Soviet Union—reflect a de-oxygenated military culture that has never seen the field of battle.

The eighth element of an alternative nuclear posture is a thoroughly familiar one—written accords that codify mutual obligations and provide intrusive monitoring arrangements to assess implementation. There is much to be said for clarifying mutual obligations and securing legislative approval. Such arrangements provide greater reassurance against reversibility than informal understandings, and reassurance, as has been noted in earlier chapters, is an essential element of cooperative threat reduction. Moreover, the only treaty-based provisions for reciprocal U.S. and Russian monitoring and intrusive inspections that currently exists—the verification arrangements of the first Strategic Arms Reduction Treaty—expire in 2009, or one year before the Bush–Putin treaty obligations take effect. The extension and expansion of these arrangements would certainly facilitate a wider range of CTR activities, perhaps including verified warhead dismantlement.

Written agreements also have disadvantages. Legislative concerns in either the United States or Russia could continue to delay or prevent the entry into force of the accords reached by unpopular or untrusted political leaders. The scope of agreed reductions has heretofore been limited to deployed forces, but as reductions proceed, the dismantlement of warheads and non-deployed missiles grows in importance. Yet expanding the scope of written accords to cover new areas could be very complicated and difficult to negotiate.

Alternatively, future reductions in deployed or non-deployed nuclear forces could be carried out by means of unilateral or reciprocal measures. This approach also has both advantages and disadvantages. Unilateral or reciprocal measures would be easier to implement than written accords, but they would also be easier to reverse. Intrusive monitoring arrangements for written agreements are spelled out; they would be voluntary or non-existent for unilateral or reciprocal initiatives. Take, for example, the 1991 initiatives carried out by presidents George H. W. Bush and Mikhail Gorbachev, removing the least safe and secure nuclear weapons from operational status. Ten years later, press reports indicated that some of these tactical nuclear weapons were returned to the Baltic region, presumably to compensate for Russian conventional military weaknesses.[43] This episode has complicated CTR initiatives in Russia. Nonetheless, the 1991 Bush–Gorbachev initiatives continue to be widely appreciated, especially in light of subsequent concerns over the acquisition by terrorist groups of "loose nukes" in the former Soviet Union.

If unilateral steps are pursued entirely as a substitute for written accords, many new problems could result. Even ambitious reassurance initiatives could be undermined or nullified by negative initiatives, such as moves to deploy space-based or anti-satellite weapons. The rejection of written accords and bilateral treaties would not be reassuring at home or abroad, and could have spillover effects, undermining multilateral accords, such as the Non-Proliferation Treaty. The net effect of jettisoning treaties, if compounded by moves to negate Moscow's deterrent, could be profoundly unsettling, prompting the sharp curtailment of cooperative initiatives underway with Russia.

Heavy reliance on unilateral measures could have another negative dynamic: The intended recipients of reassurance measures could become the central arbiters of their utility. National leaders could stress an absence of reassurance in order to prompt further initiatives to alleviate their expressed concerns. Legislative prerogatives would also need to be taken into account in a strategy that seeks to replace written accords with reassurance measures. If initiatives are not reciprocated fully, legislators could become disenchanted with this process and take blocking action.

When unilateral measures and reassuring initiatives are utilized as a supplement rather than as a substitute for written accords, downside risks and unintended consequences are reduced. The combination of written accords plus reassurance measures is more powerful than either standing alone. Again, the 1991 Bush–Gorbachev initiatives are instructive, since they came quickly after the First Strategic Arms Reduction Treaty was negotiated. In the absence of structured cooperation covering strategic arms reduction, informal arrangements covering tactical nuclear weapons would have been harder to orchestrate then—or in the future. Written accords offer more reassurance than informal arrangements, while unilateral or reciprocal measures offer more flexibility as well as powerful symbolism. Some changes, such as revisions in nuclear targeting or reducing the alert status of nuclear forces, can be realized only by unilateral or parallel steps. The combination of written accords and reassurance measures provide a strong foundation to keep alliances healthy, strengthen non-proliferation regimes, and reassure essential partners.

What might such a combination of written accords and reassurance measures entail? The preferred mix of deterrence and reassurance suggested here would include long-term written agreements placing the United States and Russia on an extended trajectory of very deep reductions in operationally deployed warheads. The objective of this proposed transformation in U.S. and Russian nuclear deterrence would not be reductions *per se*. Instead, it would be reductions in the size and character of deployed strategic forces, as well as the warheads they carry, to the point where they could not execute, promptly and successfully, nuclear war plans. Reductions of this nature would require considerable transparency, not only regarding deployed forces, but also production lines and inventories of missiles and warheads. Parallel, verifiable dismantlement of stockpiled warheads would be required. The exact number that would be reached as a result of such reductions is less important than mutual reassurance along the way. The extent of such reductions, however, would surely be far lower than those proposed in the Bush administration's NPR. How much lower would depend on the evolution of cooperative U.S.–Russian relations.

Reductions in U.S. nuclear forces below the Russian target set would still provide ample coverage of targets in China. A different kind of reassurance would be required for Beijing, given the sparseness of China's nuclear capability. Reassurance in this case requires the sizing of U.S. national missile defenses against maverick states, without seeking to negate Beijing's deterrent. Such reassurance ought not to be freely given. Instead, it ought to be contingent upon China's assistance in countering proliferation. The depth of U.S. reductions *vis-à-vis* Russia would therefore depend, in part, upon the extent of China's strategic modernization program, and the degree to which Beijing would be willing to accept transparency in return for reassurance.

As discussed above, a long-term process of deep cuts would be supplemented by bilateral accords establishing rules of the road against dangerous military practices related to space. Such accords would also require cooperative monitoring practices and far greater transparency than space-faring nations are accustomed to. Additional reassurance measures would relate to the architecture and extent of national missile defenses. Since it is unlikely that the United States would undertake written accords constraining national missile defenses, activities in this realm would henceforth be observable through transparent budget deliberations and deployments in the United States. Voluntary, reciprocal transparency measures to assess production runs of ocean-spanning missiles and missile defense interceptors could provide mutual reassurance.

As noted earlier, U.S. national missile defense requirements would naturally result from an interactive process of perceived threats and responses. To the extent that Russia and China become partners in restraining proliferation, especially proliferation related to extended-range missiles, U.S. requirements for national missile defenses would be depressed. Likewise, to the extent to which Beijing moderates its strategic modernization programs, missile defense enthusiasts in the United States would lose standing for added deployments. Conversely, bad news abroad would generate increased worries for Russia and China about U.S. deployments. The checks and balances of domestic U.S. politics must now substitute for the ABM Treaty.

Strategic Superiority Revisited

The alternative nuclear posture described above is every bit as far-reaching as a strategy that seeks to negate the Russian and Chinese deterrents. It, too, could be critiqued as "apolitical," and no less a form of escapism as the ambitions of nuclear weapon strategists. After all, the hierarchy of might has always mattered in international relations. Imbalances in nuclear capabilities were presumed to be important during the Cold War, especially in areas of Soviet advantage. With the demise of the Soviet Union, overwhelming U.S. strategic superiority might well reinforce preferred U.S. outcomes in regional contingencies or in direct confrontations with Russia and China. Dominance is not given away, and one never knows when strategic superiority could come in handy. Besides, presidents leave matters of nuclear strategy to those who would recoil with horror from most of the heresies discussed above.

And yet, if this is not the time to consider a clear and clean break from Cold War nuclear practices, then when is? The objectives sought in this exercise are the maintenance of American conventional military primacy alongside the prevention of proliferation and terrorism. Which of these two clear and clean breaks from Cold War practices stands a better chance to achieve safety from weapons of mass destruction? A far stronger case can be made that U.S. safety and primacy are better served by cooperative threat reduction, partnership, and the disassembly of nuclear war-fighting plans than by seeking to affirm U.S. dominance through nuclear war-winning capabilities, space warfare, and robust national missile defenses.

To begin with, the path preferred here reflects an acceptance, rather than an escape, from a mutual deterrence relationship with Russia and China. This approach would not be unconditional, however, since the maintenance of limited national missile defenses would require help from Moscow and Beijing against states of proliferation concern. Cooperation begets reassurance, while proliferation begets U.S. military capabilities that are displeasing to Beijing and Moscow. The approach suggested here reflects, in essence, a political compact. It places technology at the service of national security objectives—but it does not place too much faith in that technology.

This approach is designed to reaffirm U.S. primacy by reducing the only threats that could cause grave harm—those posed by proliferation, terrorism, and weapons of mass destruction. Progress down this path requires cooperative threat reduction to complement U.S. preventive diplomacy and military might. This approach strikes a balance between triumphant unilateralism and hesitant multilateralism. It employs the leverage provided by Dominators to secure outcomes that Conciliators favor. It therefore calls for strengthened non-proliferation treaty regimes as well as improved U.S. power projection capabilities. Proliferation cannot be successfully combated by diminishing either one while championing the other; advances on both fronts are required. There is no safety in enforcement actions without strengthened non-proliferation treaty regimes and cooperative threat reduction. As William J. Perry has noted, a mixed strategy of deterrence, prevention, and defense is the right approach for an era of asymmetric warfare.[44] Proliferation requires a reaffirmation of international order as well as dominant U.S. power projection capabilities.

The choices about nuclear strategy, missile defenses, and space warfare advocated here are not surrogates for "giving away" U.S. dominance. The gift of U.S. primacy is not something to be given away. Moreover, no country, or combination of countries, could challenge American military primacy for the foreseeable future. The question of choice therefore relates to which national security policies are most likely to provide maximum safety against proliferation and terrorism during a period of U.S. military dominance. The right choices require coherence and balance.

An approach that is dismissive of treaties and multilateralism while relying on military and technical superiority is anything but coherent and balanced. Those who choose unfettered strategic superiority while rejecting strengthening measures for non-proliferation treaty regimes increase

U.S. muscularity at the expense of cooperative threat reduction—a false and damaging choice in a new era of asymmetric warfare. By positing treaties against the further extension of U.S. military primacy, Dominators would distance the United States from its allies. The United States would remain militarily supreme, while becoming an increasingly lonely sheriff, beset with an increasing case load of bad actors.[45] Likewise, the choice of seeking to escape from nuclear deterrence against major powers will have fateful consequences, since Russia and China would do whatever is necessary to secure their deterrents.

The time has again come to ask, as Henry A. Kissinger once did, "What in the name of God do we mean by strategic superiority? What is the significance of it, politically, militarily, operationally, at these levels of numbers? What do you do with it?"[46] Shortly before stepping down as Secretary of State in January 1977, Kissinger returned to this theme. "Military superiority has no practical significance," he said, "under circumstances in which both sides have the capacity to annihilate one another … Those who are still talking about superiority are not doing the American people a service."[47]

Does Kissinger's bottom line still hold true, now that the Cold War is over and a great and growing disparity in power has emerged between the United States and all others? Without question, America's conventional military superiority continues to matter greatly. But what about U.S. nuclear superiority? How important is U.S. dominance in nuclear forces, space operations, and missile defenses? How much added value, and at what cost, might Washington expect by pushing for even greater disparities in these capabilities? Given the current and growing differential in conventional military capabilities, why would the United States need to reinforce its superiority with war-winning nuclear forces, robust national missile defenses, and space warfare capabilities? What new political, military, and operational advantages might be expected from a completely unfettered and expansive notion of U.S. strategic superiority? In the realms of international relations and domestic politics, is this scenario achievable or sustainable?

The successful pursuit of unfettered U.S. strategic superiority and its extension into space would require a domestic political consensus, extraordinary advances in technology, and supine responses by Moscow and Beijing, among other conditions. Even then, would U.S. strategic superiority, backed up by extensive missile defenses and space warfare capabilities, be able to prevent, say, all but five detonations by Russian or Chinese nuclear forces over American cities? If so, would this be acceptable? How about all but one or two detonations? In a new era of asymmetric warfare, would the attempted negation of the Russian and Chinese nuclear deterrents decrease or increase the likelihood of mass casualties produced by other means?

A nuclear war-winning posture is an all-or-nothing proposition. But "winning" against a major nuclear power would not prevent horrific destruction, whether during the Cold War or in a new era of American primacy. Maverick states seeking to deter U.S. power projection capabilities pose a very different problem: It might, indeed, be technically and militarily possible to prevent one, two, or five detonations carried out by new seekers of nuclear status. This is a core requirement of countering proliferation in an era of asymmetric warfare; the United States can and should seek to escape from being deterred by maverick states. But why should Washington seek a comparable escape from deterrence with Russia and China?

Even if the far-reaching proposals outlined here were adopted, the United States would retain, for the foreseeable future, conventional and nuclear superiority over Russia and China. Washington would enjoy the benefits of these advantages in future military contingencies and crises, should they arise. It is therefore difficult to see what added benefits on the battlefield would accrue to the United States from seeking to negate the Russian and Chinese nuclear deterrents. And it is easy to foresee multiple disadvantages in attempting to do so. The attempted escape from a nuclear deterrent relationship with those whose help is essential to combat proliferation and terrorism makes as little sense during an era of U.S. primacy as during the Cold War.

Admiral Arleigh Burke once said, "You very seldom see a cowboy, even in the movies, wearing three guns. Two is enough."[48] Whatever advantages are conferred by U.S. nuclear superiority will not be multiplied by the unfettered pursuit of national missile defenses and space warfare capabilities. Shortly after the end of the Cold War, Robert Jervis wrote, "If the United States acts as though nuclear weapons are highly useful, it may convince others of this very point more than it would like."[49] While this is true, it is also true that, in an era of U.S. primacy, others might seek weapons of mass destruction even if Washington pursues consistent and coherent policies to devalue these weapons. There is, in other words, no substitute for U.S. power projection capabilities, preventive diplomacy, and strong alliances to counter proliferation. There is also no substitute for strengthened non-proliferation treaties and disarmament regimes for weapons of mass destruction. An approach that systematically weakens and devalues treaties while strengthening military instruments is counterproductive and dangerous.

The varied "successes" of those seeking to hollow out or withdraw from treaty regimes that are essential to contain and roll back proliferation have done considerable damage. Anti-treaty forces in the U.S. Senate passed conditions to the Chemical Weapons Convention barring the removal of samples beyond American jurisdiction taken during inspections. They have also empowered the president to reject challenge inspections, notwithstanding the treaty's clear obligations in this regard. When employed by suspect states, these provisions could foreclose the uncovering of "smoking guns." Not satisfied with killing the CTBT, opponents have also withheld U.S. dues for preparatory efforts to carry out inspections. The Bush administration stood alone in withdrawing support for a protocol to strengthen compliance with the Biological Weapons Convention. It is self-defeating to seek military successes against proliferation while at the same time weakening diplomatic and treaty-based instruments necessary for this extended campaign.

Triumphant U.S. moralism heightens incoherence on such matters. During the war against terrorism in Afghanistan, amid growing concerns that Osama bin Laden and his al-Qaeda network would attempt to obtain nuclear, biological, and chemical weapons, President George W. Bush warned, "This is an evil man that we're dealing with. And I wouldn't put it past him to develop evil weapons to try to harm civilization as we know it."[50] Weapons of mass destruction do not acquire labels of "good" and "evil" depending on who holds them. They might, however, be necessary evils, depending on national perspective and historical or geopolitical circumstance. The existence of weapons of mass destruction requires concerted efforts to prevent their use, reduce their stockpiles, and diminish their salience in international relations. In the absence of progress toward these objectives, proliferation will proceed apace.

Considerable harm has been done by the waging of guerrilla warfare against non-proliferation treaty regimes. The damage done is repairable— but this would require a U.S. approach to countering proliferation that fires on all cylinders. Diplomacy needs to accompany muscularity; treaty regimes need to be rehabilitated; concerted steps to diminish the salience of weapons of mass destruction need to accompany improvements in U.S. power projection capabilities; space needs to be protected from those who would seek to "seize" this high frontier; new and "improved" nuclear weapon designs need to remain untested; deep cuts in nuclear war-fighting capabilities need to proceed apace; reassurance needs to accompany deterrence in great power relations; and cooperative threat reduction needs to be elevated to a central component of U.S. national security strategy.

Cooperative Threat Reduction and Transition

We are entering a third major transition in strategic arms control. The first transition took place in the period from the late 1950s to the early 1970s, when unrealistic, rhetorical policies built around general and complete disarmament and the quest for nuclear superiority gave way to a new enterprise of strategic arms control. The concept of "essential equivalence" in the Nixon administration was essential to this transition; without it, negotiations predicated on mutual security could not begin. The second transition occurred in the Reagan administration, when strategic arms control evolved into strategic arms reductions. The leverage provided by President Ronald Reagan's SDI was central to this transition from the management of an arms race to its significant contraction. This phase lasted from the 1980s until shortly after the Soviet Union collapsed.

The third transition, now underway, is marked by concerns over proliferation, terrorism, and asymmetric warfare. The most problematic threats during this phase are not the strategic nuclear delivery vehicles that preoccupied arms controllers and strategists in the previous two transitions. They are instead "loose nukes," lax controls over deadly materials, and the crossing of proliferation thresholds. The core concept needed to manage this third transition and to secure a safer future is cooperative threat reduction. CTR safeguards dangerous materials and weapons at the source, and reassures states whose assistance is critical to successfully contain and combat proliferation. Cooperative threat reduction helps to fill the void created by partisan divisions in the United States over treaties, while strengthening non-proliferation regimes. Cooperative threat reduction is about partnership and collaboration, which are essential complements to U.S. power projection capabilities.

One key element of the third transition in strategic arms control is replacing MAD with a new mix of nuclear offense and missile defense. This transition offers great opportunity as well as multiple dangers. To succeed, this transition must demonstrably reduce proliferation dangers. If the mix of nuclear offense and missile defense is badly conceived, it could easily compound these dangers. This transition must be pursued in partnership with Russia and China, the two countries most likely to feel threatened by the displacement of MAD. A successful transition from MAD to a mix of nuclear offense and missile defense is not possible without parallel efforts at cooperative threat reduction.

The time has finally come, as J. Robert Oppenheimer foresaw in 1953, to envision "defense and [strategic arms] regulation" as "necessary complements." Oppenheimer added:

> A more effective defense could even be of great relevance should the time come for serious discussion of the regulation of armaments. There will have been by then a vast accumulation of materials for atomic weapons, and a troublesome margin of uncertainty with regard to its accounting—very

troublesome indeed if we still live with vestiges of the suspicion, hostility and secretiveness of the world of today.[51]

A "serious discussion" of such matters must now extend well beyond operationally deployed warheads on ocean-spanning missiles and bombers. The transparency measures needed for these tasks must be devised with due regard for keeping the most essential secrets, while unstitching layers of secrecy woven into the Cold War competition. We must now build upon the intrusive monitoring and inspection provisions painstakingly negotiated during the Cold War to enter the domains of stockpiled dangers, production lines, and warhead dismantlement. The "vast accumulation of materials" that Oppenheimer anticipated has indeed occurred, and now constitutes the basis for many nightmare scenarios. CTR measures are ideally suited for the daunting agenda before us.

The transition from MAD to a mix of nuclear offense and missile defense has begun without adequate conceptualization or discussion. We know intuitively that the old scales of nuclear deterrence, in which missile defenses carried virtually no weight, no longer make sense. We also know intuitively that, in the future, as the scale of nuclear offense is depressed through progressive reductions in nuclear force levels, targeting requirements, alert rates, and the dismantlement of excess capacity, the other scale of missile defenses will rise. But the particulars of a reassuring transition have not been carefully integrated. Instead, these matters have been left to nuclear strategists and missile defense enthusiasts whose inputs are essential, but whose scope is far too narrow.

It is necessary to be clear about the most meaningful subtractions from one scale and additions to the other. Reductions in nuclear offense would be helpful, but would not ensure the transition that is now imperative. Likewise, the wrong additions to missile defense capabilities would badly impair prospects for a cooperative transition. Widespread deployments of theater missile defenses are absolutely necessary, while limiting national missile defenses is equally necessary. The imperatives of securing alliance relations, improving prospects for collaborative initiatives with Russia and China, and correlating defenses with the threat spectrum all mandate a significant tilt toward defenses against missiles that cannot reach U.S. shores. Oppenheimer was prescient on this matter, as well. Defenses, he argued, must "mean, even to our allies, who are much more exposed and probably cannot be well defended, that the continued existence of a real and strong America will be a solid certainty which should discourage the outbreak of war."[52] If theater missile defense deployments are designed properly, the threshold against nuclear weapons' use would be raised, while proliferation threats are dampened.

Keeping national missile defenses limited and exercising restraint on the weaponization of space would not only provide reassurance to Russia during a decade of decline, but also give Moscow added reasons to expand the scope of CTR efforts. At the same time, the pursuit of robust theater missile defense programs would signal to Beijing and Moscow that Washington would respond purposefully to the coercive use of ballistic missiles. These mixed messages have become essential for regional and international security. The right mix of missile defenses can affirm that the United States seeks partnerships, not subservience, and that Washington does not seek to make new enemies, but is prepared for whatever contingencies adversaries might present.

Transition strategies are extremely hard to execute in an environment of strongly competitive U.S.–Russian or U.S.–Chinese relations. A cooperative transition is less daunting in a period of U.S. primacy, when major powers have good reason to avoid confrontations with Washington, and when Washington has ample latitude to complement military superiority with reassurance and CTR measures. If the United States chooses wisely, circumstances are quite compatible with a transition from MAD to a mix of nuclear offense and missile defense. To succeed, this transition would need to be partial and not complete; the addition of missile defenses needs to be discriminatory, weighted heavily against proliferation concerns. The evolving mix of nuclear offense and missile defense would signal resolve in regional contingencies, as well as intended cooperation with major powers. The *sine qua non* of a successful transition is Washington's acceptance of nuclear deterrence relationships with Moscow and Beijing.

The transition away from MAD would not seek to balance or reverse the scales of nuclear offense and missile defense. In dealings with major powers, the United States would not seek a Maginot Line of national missile defenses, either on the ground or in space. The draw down of bloated Cold War-legacy arsenals and targeting strategies would take a very long period of time. A complete reversal of these scales would require multiple transformations— in great power relations and in the perceived role of nuclear deterrence, for starters—that are well worth envisioning, but require even more ambition than the bare outlines of the transition strategy discussed here.[53]

Conceptualizing the Future

The transition from MAD to cooperative threat reduction requires as much effort and intellectual content as earlier transitions. Moving away from MAD to a mix of nuclear offense and missile defense is far from a simple exercise. This process faces many serious technical and political hurdles. If the transition is driven primarily by technological enthusiasm or political triumphalism, it is very likely to go badly awry. Those who seek a safer alternative future are obliged to expend as much intellectual capital conceptualizing the next transition as the founding fathers of arms control did in the late 1950s and early 1960s. These pages provide little more than a beginner's sketch suggesting a way forward. There is much work to do in producing an improved set of drawings.

The old foundations of strategic arms control, necessarily erected upon the acceptance of national vulnerability during the Cold War, have been washed away by the demise of the Soviet Union and the rise of asymmetric warfare. The cornerstone of this earlier construction, the ABM Treaty, lies in ruin. Those who believe in strategic arms control and reducing proliferation dangers are now obliged to re-think their craft. A new construction is required. It must be erected upon a broad domestic political base, and must appeal to allies and major powers. This construction requires muscle as well as tact; power projection as well as diplomacy. Our new construction will require strengthened non-proliferation treaty regimes, written compacts governing arms reductions, and rules of the road to avoid space warfare. Our previous fixation with numbers is now a secondary matter; the mix and content of these instruments are far more important. More important still, is the larger conceptualization to which these components would serve.

Conceptualization usually occurs in academia or think tanks, after which it is embraced by a government that invites conceptualizers in. Thus, the Kennedy and Nixon administrations enlisted the brainpower of those who charted the new territory of strategic arms control before making their way to Washington. The Reagan administration enlisted the harshest critics of strategic arms control, with deconstructionists eventually giving way to the architects of a new enterprise of deep cuts. Similarly, the administration of President George W. Bush borrowed heavily from those who spent the Clinton years thinking hard about how nuclear strategy might be altered to conform to a new era of U.S. strategic superiority. Dominators did their homework; their preferences for nuclear weapons, missile defense, and space policy were ready to be translated into policy once Bush took office.[54]

In contrast, Conciliators have been tardy in doing their conceptual homework. Little work was done in this regard within the Clinton administration, when operational and tactical concerns dominated the nuclear agenda. By the time President George W. Bush took office, there was only one strongly articulated agenda for the nuclear future. This agenda is seriously imbalanced and, unless significantly altered, will not lead to a safer future. An alternative agenda needs to be conceptualized and vigorously pursued, one that serves as the basis for a new strategic synthesis combining U.S. primacy with cooperative threat reduction. Primacy alone is insufficient to reduce the dangers associated with proliferation and terrorism. When primacy abets the unraveling of treaty regimes, valuable ground is lost. In a new era of asymmetric warfare, American leadership needs to be collaborative as well as singular. Success over the long haul requires finding the right balance between assertive unilateralism and tentative multilateralism.

Notes

Introduction

1. Herman Kahn, *Thinking About the Unthinkable* (New York: Horizon Press, 1962), p. 13.
2. For an account of domestic divisions during the Cold War, see Michael Krepon, *Strategic Stalemate, Nuclear Weapons and Arms Control in American Politics* (New York: St. Martin's Press, 1984).
3. For the full text of President Bush's speech, see "Remarks by the President to Students and Faculty at National Defense University," May 1, 2001, available online at http://www.whitehouse.gov/news/releases/2001/05/20010501-10.html (accessed February 21, 2002).
4. I am indebted to George Perkovich for this notion.
5. President Bush, "Remarks ... at National Defense University," May 1, 2001.
6. Donald G. Brennan, *Arms Treaties with Moscow: Unequal Terms Unevenly Applied,* Agenda Paper No. 3 (New York: National Strategy Information Center, 1975).
7. *The Henry L. Stimson Center Award Presentation to Secretary of Defense William J. Perry* (Washington, DC: The Henry L. Stimson Center, September 20, 1994), p. 16.
8. Thomas C. Schelling and Morton H. Halperin, *Strategy and Arms Control* (New York: The Twentieth Century Fund, 1961), p. 2.

Chapter 1   The Paradigm Shifts

1. Harry Bayard Price, *The Marshall Plan and its Meaning* (Ithaca: Cornell University Press, 1955), p. 52.
2. Bruce Springsteen, *The Human Touch,* Columbia Records (1992).
3. Garrick Utley, "The Shrinking of Foreign News," *Foreign Affairs* Vol. 76, No. 2 (March–April 1997), pp. 2–10.
4. Stephen Ansolabehere and Shanto Iyengar, *Going Negative* (New York: Free Press, 1995).
5. Sarah Binder and Steven Smith, *Politics or Principle?: Filibusters in the U.S. Senate* (Washington, DC: The Brookings Institution, 1997), p. 91.
6. Dan Caldwell, "The SALT II Treaty," in Michael Krepon and Dan Caldwell (eds.), *The Politics of Arms Control Treaty Ratification* (New York: St. Martin's Press, 1991), p. 313.

7. This account relies heavily on Terry L. Deibel, "Inside the Water's Edge: The Senate Votes on the Comprehensive Test Ban Treaty," National War College, unpublished manuscript.

8. See *Jump-START: Retaking the Initiative to Reduce Post-Cold War Nuclear Dangers* (Washington, DC: Committee on Nuclear Policy, February 1999).

9. Jonathan B. Tucker, "The Chemical Weapons Convention: Has It Enhanced U.S. Security?" *Arms Control Today* Vol. 31, No. 3 (April 2001), pp. 8–12; Amy E. Smithson, *Rudderless: The Chemical Weapons Convention at One and One-Half,* Report No. 25 (Washington, DC: The Henry L. Stimson Center, 1998); and Jonathan B. Tucker (ed.), *The Chemical Weapons Convention, Implementation Challenges and Solutions* (Washington, DC: Monterey Institute of International Studies, April 2001).

10. Among the predictors of "megaterrorism" were Richard Falkenrath, Robert D. Newman, and Bradley A. Thayer, *America's Achilles' Heel: Nuclear, Biological and Chemical Terrorism and Covert Attack* (Cambridge, MA: MIT Press, 1998); Jessica Stern, *The Ultimate Terrorists* (Cambridge, MA: Harvard University Press, 1999); Ashton Carter and William J. Perry, *Preventive Defense: A New Security Strategy for America* (Washington, DC: The Brookings Institution Press, 1999). For a minority view that future terrorism involving weapons of mass destruction is likely to remain on a small scale, see Amy Smithson and Leslie-Anne Levy, *Ataxia: The Chemical and Biological Terrorism Threat and the U.S. Response,* Report No. 35 (Washington, DC: The Henry L. Stimson Center, October 2000).

11. The term "revolution in military affairs" is of nebulous origin. In the 1970s and 1980s, Soviet military literature referred to "military–technical revolutions." In the early 1990s, Pentagon planners such as Andrew Marshall and his assistant Andrew Krepinevich argued that technology was necessary but not sufficient for revolutionary change, and focused on operational and organizational aspects of change. See Andrew Marshall, Director of Net Assessment, Department of Defense, Memorandum for the Record, Subject: Some Thoughts on Military Revolutions (July 27, 1993), pp. 1–4. For subsequent expositions on the subject see Eliot A. Cohen, "A Revolution in Warfare," *Foreign Affairs* Vol. 75, No. 2 (March–April 1996), pp. 37–54 and William Owens and Edward Offley, *Lifting the Fog of War* (New York: Farrar, Straus & Giroux, 2000).

12. See Chapter 3, "The 1993–94 Nuclear Posture Review," in Janne Nolan, *An Elusive Consensus: Nuclear Weapons and American Security after the Cold War* (Washington, DC: The Brookings Institution Press, 1999). An earlier account can be found in David B. Ottaway and Steve Coll, "Trying to Unplug the War Machine," *Washington Post* (April 12, 1995).

13. This phrase was used within the Department of Defense to describe the policy codified in the 1994 Nuclear Posture Review. The first public reference was made by Bill Gertz, "The New Nuclear Policy: Lead But Hedge," *Air Force Magazine* (January 1995), p. 36. The first official use of the phrase came in the form of

testimony to Congress: Prepared Statement of Deputy Assistant Secretary Susan J. Koch, Testimony before the Subcommittee on Strategic Forces, Senate Armed Services Committee, 104th Congress, 1st Session (March 29, 1995).

14. Steven Mufson and Dana Milbank, "U.S. Sets Missile Treaty Pullout," *Washington Post* (December 14, 2001).

15. "Beyond The ABM Treaty," *Washington Post* (December 14, 2001); "Out With A Whimper," *Wall Street Journal* (December 14, 2001).

16. Michael Wines, "Facing Pact's End, Putin Decides To Grimace And Bear It," *New York Times* (December 14, 2001).

17. Elisabeth Rosenthal, "China Voices Muted Distress At U.S. Blow To ABM Pact," *New York Times* (December 14, 2001).

18. Keith B. Payne, Study Director, *Rationale and Requirements for U.S. Nuclear Forces and Arms Control*, Volume I, Executive Report (Fairfax, VA: National Institute for Public Policy, January 2001), pp. vii–viii, 9.

19. Michael Howard, "Reassurance and Deterrence: Western Defense in the 1980s," *Foreign Affairs* Vol. 61, No. 2 (Winter 1982–3), p. 316.

20. Payne, *Rationale and Requirements for U.S. Nuclear Forces and Arms Control*, Volume I, p. viii.

21. *Ibid.*, pp. 5–7.

22. Colin S. Gray and Keith Payne, "Victory is Possible," *Foreign Policy* No. 39 (Summer 1980), p. 14.

Chapter 2 *Prioritizing Threats and Responses*

1. See, for example, Richard A. Falkenrath, Robert D. Newman, and Bradley A. Thayer, *America's Achilles' Heal, Nuclear, Biological and Chemical Terrorism and Covert Attack* (Cambridge, MA: MIT Press, 1998); and Jessica Stern, *The Ultimate Terrorists* (Cambridge, MA: Harvard University Press, 1999).

2. There are two essential databases of acts of terrorism. However, both use different definitions and neither is completely satisfactory. The Department of State defines an act of terror as "the premeditated, politically motivated violence perpetrated against noncombatant targets by sub-national groups or clandestine agents usually intended to influence an audience." During the decade of the 1990s, the State Department lists 2,925 fatalities and 20,547 injuries associated with acts of terror by conventional explosives. This definition fails to capture incidents that result from domestic terrorism or internal conflict. See "Patterns of Global Terrorism–2000," U.S. Department of State (April 2001), accessible at http://www.state.gov/s/ct/rls/pgtrpt/2000/index.cfm?docid=2420. The Monterey Institute for International Studies compiles an open-source database of global terrorism associated with weapons of mass destruction, but this database includes incidents involving tear gas, pesticides, salmonella, and acid attacks. For an account of the Tokyo Subway attack, see Amy E. Smithson and Leslie-Anne Levy, *Ataxia: The Chemical and Biological Terrorism Threat and the U.S. Response,*

Report No. 35 (Washington, DC: The Henry L. Stimson Center, October 2000), Chapter 3.

3. The Commission on America's National Interests, *America's National Interests* (July 2000), pp. 3–8.

4. Final Report of The United States Commission on National Security/21st Century, *Road Map for National Security: Imperative for Change* (March 15, 2001), p. xiii.

5. *Ibid.,* pp. 12–13.

6. *Seeking A National Strategy, A Concert for Preserving Security and Promoting Freedom,* The Phase II Report on a U.S. National Security Strategy for the 21st Century (April 15, 2000), pp. 7–8.

7. *A Report Card on the Department of Energy's Nonproliferation Programs with Russia,* The Secretary of Energy Advisory Board, United States Department of Energy (January 10, 2001), p. 1.

8. U.S. Department of Defense, Office of the Secretary of Defense, *Proliferation: Threat and Response* (January 2001), p. 1.

9. National Intelligence Council, *Global Trends 2015, A Dialogue About the Future With Nongovernmental Experts,* NIC 2000–02 (December 2000), p. 14.

10. See, for example, Colin Gray, "Is Deterrence Reliable?" in *Explorations in Strategy* (Westport: Praeger, 1966), pp. 31–52; and Keith B. Payne, *Deterrence in the Second Nuclear Age* (Lexington: University Press of Kentucky, 1996).

11. "Foreign Missile Developments and the Ballistic Missile Threat Through 2015" (January 2002), available online at http://www.cia.gov/nic/pubs/other_products/Unclassifiedballisticmissilefinal.htm.

12. Raymond Aron, "From American Imperialism to Soviet Hegemony," *The Atlantic Quarterly* (Winter 1979–1980), p. 499.

13. See John Pike, "Part C. Counterforce" in *The Last 15 Minutes,* Joseph Cirincione and Frank von Hippel (eds.) (Washington, DC: The Henry L. Stimson Center, 1996).

14. Richard L. Garwin, "Boost-Phase Intercept: A Better Alternative," *Arms Control Today* Vol. 30, No. 7 (September 2000), pp. 8–11; and Theodore Postol, "Hitting Them Where It Works," *Foreign Policy* No. 117 (Winter 1999/2000), pp. 132–3.

15. See Dennis M. Gormley, *Dealing with the Threat of Cruise Missiles,* Adelphi Paper 339 (Oxford: Oxford University Press, 2001); Dennis M. Gormley and Scott McMahon, "Proliferation of Land-Attack Cruise Missiles: Prospects and Policy Implications," in Henry Sokolski (ed.), *Fighting Proliferation: New Concerns for the Nineties* (Maxwell Air Force Base, AL: Air University Press, 1996); and David Tanks, "Assessing the Cruise Missile Puzzle: How Great a Defense Challenge?" (Cambridge, MA: The Institute for Foreign Policy Analysis, October 2000).

16. Frank Heilenday, *V-1 Cruise Missile Attacks Against England: Lessons Learned and Lingering Myths From World War II* (Santa Monica, CA.: The RAND Corporation, 1995), pp. 4–8; Gregory Kennedy, *Vengeance Weapon 2: The V-2 Guided Missile* (Washington, DC: The Smithsonian Institution Press, 1983),

pp. 40, 52; Richard K. Betts (ed.), *Cruise Missiles: Technology, Strategy, Politics* (Washington, DC: The Brookings Institution, 1981), p. 5; James Phinney Baxter III, *Scientists Against Time* (Boston: Little, Brown & Co., 1950), pp. 234–5; Vannevar Bush attributed a 95 percent success rate for V-1 intercepts, in *Modern Arms and Free Men, A Discussion of the Role of Science in Preserving Democracy* (New York: Simon & Schuster, 1949), pp. 86–87. This might be drawn from the last day of mass V-1 attacks, when 104 were detected by early warning radar but only four reached London.

17. United Nations Special Commission, Final Compendium of Reports to the Security Council, S/1999/94 (January 29, 1999), pp. 28–30.

18. James A. Baker with Thomas M. DeFrank, *The Politics of Diplomacy: Revolution, War and Peace 1989–1992* (New York: G. P. Putnam's Sons, 1995), p. 383; George Bush and Brent Scowcroft, *A World Transformed* (New York: Alfred A. Knopf, Inc., 1998), p. 452.

19. Anthony Cordesman, *Iraq and the War of Sanctions* (Westport: Praeger, 1999); Theodore A. Postol, "Lessons of the Gulf War Experience with Patriot," *International Security* Vol. 16, No. 3 (Winter 1991), p. 119; United States Department of Defense, "Information Paper: Iraq's Scud Ballistic Missiles," at http://www.iraqwatch.org/government/U.S./Pentagon/dodscud.htm.

20. Major General Thabit Sultan, quoted in Dilip Hiro, *The Longest War: The Iran–Iraq Military Conflict* (London: Grafton, 1989), p. 135.

21. Hiro, *The Longest War*; Anthony Cordesman, *Iran's Military Forces in Transition: Conventional Threats and Weapons of Mass Destruction* (Westport: Praeger, 1999); Anoushiravan Ehteshami, "Iran in the 'War of the Cities,'" in *Ballistic Missile Proliferation* (Alexandria, VA: Jane's Information Group, March 2000), pp. 147–54. Richard Speier, "Iranian Missiles and Payloads," in *Iran's Nuclear Weapons Options: Issues and Analysis* (Washington, DC: The Nixon Center, January 2001).

22. This estimate comes from former Minister of Defense of South Korea, Chun Yong-Taek in "Missile Proliferation on the Korean Peninsula and Consequences of the Theater Missile Defense (TMD) Program," in P. Cotta-Ramusino and M. Martellini (eds.), *Missile Threats and Ballistic Missile Defense: Technology, Strategic Stability and Impact on Global Security* (Como: Landau Network Centro Volta, 2001), p. 16.

23. Raj Chengappa, "Pakistan Threatened India with Nuclear Attack during Kargil War: Army Chief," *The Newspaper Today* (January 12, 2001); and Chengappa, *Weapons of Peace, The Secret Story of India's Quest To be a Nuclear Power* (New Delhi: Manas Publications, 2000), pp. 8–9, 437.

24. US Government Printing Office, *Soviet Military Power: Prospects for Change, 1989* (Washington, DC: GPO, 1989), p. 34; *Allocation of Resources in the Soviet Union and China*, Hearings Before the Subcommittee on International Trade, Finance, and Security Economics of the Joint Economic Committee, Congress of the United States, Ninety-Seventh Congress, Second Session, Part 8, p. 36.

25. Admiral Dennis Blair, address to Carnegie International Non-Proliferation Conference (March 16, 2000), at http://www.ceip.org/files/events/ BlairAddress2000.asp?p+8.

26. Brad Roberts, *et al.*, "China: The Forgotten Nuclear Power," *Foreign Affairs* Vol. 79, No. 4 (July–August 2000), p. 57.

27. See Philip C. Saunders and Jing-dong Yuan, "China's Strategic Force Modernization: Issues and Implications for the United States," in Michael Barletta (ed.), *Proliferation Challenges and Nonproliferation Opportunities for New Administrations*, CNS Occasional Paper #4 (Monterey, CA: Center for Nonproliferation Studies, September 2000). Also see David Shambaugh, "Facing Reality in China Policy," *Foreign Affairs* Vol. 80, No. 1 (January–February 2001), p. 52—he mentions hundreds of missiles; and Robert Manning, Ronald Montaperto, and Brad Roberts, *China, Nuclear Weapons, and Arms Control: A Preliminary Assessment* (Washington, DC: Council on Foreign Relations, May 2000).

28. "Foreign Missile Developments and the Ballistic Missile Threat Through 2015," p. 5.

29. Department of Defense, *Selected Military Capabilities of the People's Republic of China*, Report to Congress pursuant to Section 1305 of the FY97 National Defense Authorization Act (April 1997), p. 2.

30. For an elaboration of this argument, see Joseph Cirincione, "Ballistic Missile Threat Evolves," Carnegie Endowment for International Peace, Proliferation Brief, Vol. 2, No. 13 (September 10, 1999) and "The Exaggerated Ballistic Missile Threat," in P. Cotta-Ramusina and M. Martellini, *Missile Threats and Ballistic Missile Defense: Technology, Strategic Stability and Impact on Global Security* (Como: Landau Network Centro Volta, 2001), pp. 23–36.

31. The research and analysis by Mark A. Stokes concludes that a missile attack on Taiwan by the People's Liberation Army would target key airfields, command and control centers and naval facilities, perhaps involving hundreds of missiles in the opening stages of a conflict. Other missiles would be held in reserve. *China's Strategic Modernization: Implications for the United States* (Carlisle, PA: U.S. Army Strategic Studies Institute, September 1999). Also see Denny Roy, "Tension in the Taiwan Strait," *Survival* Vol. 42, No. 1 (Spring 2000), and U.S. Department of Defense, *The Security Situation in the Taiwan Strait*, Report to Congress Pursuant to the FY99 Appropriations Bill (February 26, 1999), at http://defenselink.mil/pubs/twstrait_02261999.html.

32. John Pike and Peter Voth, "Current Plans for Missile Defense," in "NMD: Jumping the Gun?" *Disarmament Forum*, UNIDIR/DF/2000/4. Also see Federation of American Scientists, "Arrow TMD," at http://www.fas.org/spp/ starwars/program/arrow.htm.

33. The section dealing with TMD deployments in East Asia draws extensively from a Henry L. Stimson Center working group report, *Theater Missile Defenses in the Asia-Pacific Region*, Report No. 34 (Washington, DC: The Henry L. Stimson

Center, June 29, 2000). The working group was convened by Kenneth W. Allen, and drew on the expertise of James R. East, David M. Finkelstein, Banning Garrett, Bonnie Glaser, Michael J. Green, Michael Krepon, Michael McDevitt, Eric A. McVadon, Mike M. Mochizuki, Ronald N. Montaperdo, James Mulvenon, Benjamin L. Self, and David Shambaugh. Kenneth W. Allen was the principle drafter of the report's sections dealing with South Korea and Taiwan.

34. Chun Yong-Taek, in P. Cotta-Ramusina and M. Martellini, *Missile Threats and Ballistic Missile Defense: Technology, Strategic Stability and Impact on Global Security* (Como: Landau Network Centro Volta, 2001), p. 16.

35. The section draws heavily from the work of Benjamin L. Self, whose analysis appears in the Henry L. Stimson Center working group report, *Theater Missile Defenses in the Asia-Pacific Region*, Report No. 34 (Washington, DC: The Henry L. Stimson Center, June 29, 2000).

36. U.S. Department of Defense, *Report to Congress on Theater Missile Defense Architecture Options in the Asia-Pacific Region* (April 14, 1999).

37. Shirley A. Kan, *China: Ballistic and Cruise Missiles*, Congressional Research Service Report for Congress (updated May 27, 1998).

38. Bear Lee, "Defense Minister says TMD to Cost Taiwan $9.23 Billion," *Taiwan Central News Agency* (Internet) (March 24, 1999), *FBIS-CHI-1999-0324* (March 25, 1999).

39. "New Defense Minister Says TMD System Would Be Deterrent," *Taiwan Central News Agency* (Internet) (February 1, 1999).

40. Taiwan Relations Act (Public Law 96-8).

41. See, for example, Sha Zukang, "U.S. Missile Defence Plans: China's View," *Disarmament Diplomacy* No. 43, pp. 3–6.

42. Erik Eckholm with Steven Lee Myers, "Taiwan Asks U.S. to Let it Obtain Top-Flight Arms," *New York Times* (March 1, 2000); also see Barbara Opall-Rome, "Support Mounts in Taiwan for Ballistic Missiles," *Defense News* (April 26, 1999).

43. David Albright and Corey Gay, "Taiwan: Nuclear Nightmare Averted," *Bulletin of Atomic Scientists* Vol. 54, No. 1 (January–February 1998), at http://www.bullatomsci.org/issues/1998/jf98/jf98albright.html.

44. "Security and Stability in the Asia-Pacific Region" (Part 1 of 2), PacNet 18 (May 5, 2000) available at http://www.csis.org/pacfor/pac0018.html.

45. The Rumsfeld Commission's report can be accessed at http://www.brook.edu/fp/projects/nmd/rumsfeld98.htm.

46. DCI National Intelligence Estimate, President's Summary, NIE 95-19, accessible at http://www.fas.org/spp/starwars/offdocs/nie9519.htm.

47. *Ibid.*

48. Testimony before the House National Security Committee (February 28, 1996), accessible at http://www.fas.org/spp/starwars/congress/1996_h/h960228f.htm.

49. National Intelligence Council, "Foreign Missile Developments and the Ballistic Missile Threat to the United States Through 2015" (September 1999), accessible at http://www.cia.gov/nic/pubs/other_products/foreign_missile_developments.htm.

50. *Ibid.*
51. *Ibid.*
52. Albert Wohlstetter, "Is There A Strategic Arms Race?" *Foreign Policy* No. 15 (Summer 1974).
53. See Anne H. Cahn, *Killing Detente: The Right Attacks the CIA* (State College, PA: Pennsylvania State University Press, 1998).
54. "U.S. Bars Increase in Missile Forces," *New York Times* (January 9, 1959), and "U.S. Raising Missile Goals As Critics Foresee a 'Gap,'" *New York Times* (January 12, 1959). For other accounts of the controversies over the Pentagon's intelligence estimates during this period, see Jerome H. Kahan, *Security in the Nuclear Age, Developing U.S. Strategic Arms Policy* (Washington, DC: The Brookings Institution, 1975), pp. 41–66; Fred Kaplan, *The Wizards of Armageddon* (New York: Simon & Schuster, 1983), pp. 155–65; Stuart Symington, "Where the Missile Gap Went," *The Reporter* Vol. 26 (February 15, 1962); Daniel O. Graham, "The Intelligence Mythology of Washington," *Strategic Review* (Summer 1976), pp. 59–66; and Joseph Alsop, "Is There a Strategic Arms Race? II," *Foreign Policy* No. 16 (Fall 1974), pp. 83–88.
55. Henry Kissinger, *The Necessity for Choice* (New York: Harper, 1961), p. 15.
56. "Johnson Warns of U.S. Lag Behind Soviet," *New York Herald Tribune* (January 8, 1958).
57. Albert Wohlstetter, "The Delicate Balance of Terror," *Foreign Affairs* Vol. 37, No. 2 (January 1959), p. 211.
58. John F. Kennedy, *The Strategy of Peace*, Allan Nevins (ed.), (New York: Harper, 1960), pp. 37–38.
59. This was former Secretary of Defense Robert A. Lovett's pungent characterization. Joseph Alsop, "Is There A Strategic Arms Race? II," *Foreign Policy* No. 16 (Fall 1974), p. 85.
60. See Morton H. Halperin, "The Gaither Committee and the Policy Process" and "The Gaither Committee Report (Text)," in *National Security Policy-Making* (Lexington: Lexington Books, 1975).
61. "Gates Sees U.S. Safe," *Christian Science Monitor* (January 19, 1960).
62. "Kennedy Defense Study Finds No Evidence of a 'Missile Gap,'" *New York Times* (February 7, 1961); "U.S. Missile Lead Claimed in Study," *New York Times* (November 19, 1961).
63. *Military Implications of the Proposed SALT II Treaty Relating to the National Defense,* Report of the Hearings on the Military Aspects and Implications of the Proposed SALT II Treaty, together with Additional Views, Committee on Armed Services, United States Senate (Washington, DC: GPO, 1980), p. 2.
64. The occasion was a Friends of Freedom awards dinner of the Coalition for a Democratic Majority.
65. Paul H. Nitze, "Strategy in the Decade of the 1980s," *Foreign Affairs* Vol. 59, No. 1 (Fall 1980), p. 92 cited in William G. Hyland, "Setting Global Priorities," *Foreign Policy* No. 73 (Winter 1988–1989), p. 27.

66. Richard Pipes, "Why the Soviet Union Thinks It Could Fight and Win a Nuclear War," *Commentary* Vol. 64, No. 1 (July 1977), p. 168.

67. See Noel E. First and James H. Noren, *Soviet Defense Spending: A History of CIA Estimates, 1950–1990* (College Station, TX: Texas A & M University Press, 1998); and Raymond L. Garthoff, *The Great Transition, American–Soviet Relations at the End of the Cold War* (Washington, DC: The Brookings Institution, 1994), pp. 505–506; and Frances FitzGerald, *Way Out There In The Blue, Reagan, Star Wars and the End of the Cold War* (New York: Simon & Schuster, 2000), pp. 329–32.

68. A special commission chaired by former national security adviser Brent Scowcroft effectively declared the window closed after several Reagan administration deployment proposals for a new, heavy missile were rejected on Capitol Hill. See FitzGerald, *Way Out There in the Blue*, pp. 192–203.

69. See Christopher Andrew and Oleg Gordievsky, *KGB: The Inside Story of its Foreign Operations from Lenin to Gorbachev* (London: Hodder & Stoughton, 1990); "NIE 11-3/8-83, Soviet Capabilities for Strategic Nuclear Conflict, 1983–93 (March 6, 1984)," in Donald P. Steury, compiler *(Declassified) Estimates on Soviet Military Power, 1954–1984, A Selection* (Washington, DC: Center for the Study of Intelligence, Central Intelligence Agency, 1994); and Peter Vincent Pry, *War Scare* (Atlanta: Turner Publishing, Inc., 1997).

70. Jeane Kirkpatrick, "Dukakis' Dangerous Ideas," *Washington Post* (June 20, 1988). Emphasis in the original.

71. Frank Gaffney Jr., "No, It's Building UP," *New York Times* (November 17, 1989).

72. "Foreign Missile Developments and the Ballistic Missile Threat Through 2015," p. 18.

73. One survey found that most Russian scientists emigrated to Israel, Germany, and the United States, and "did not discover a single instance of a departure for such problem countries as Iraq or Iran. On the other hand, the emigration potential in the nuclear-missile complex remains dangerously high." Valentin Tikhonov, *Russia's Nuclear and Missile Complex, The Human Factor in Proliferation* (Washington, DC: Carnegie Endowment for International Peace, 2001), p. 3.

74. "Foreign Missile Developments and the Ballistic Missile Threat Through 2015," p. 5.

75. "When Bush Meets Putin," *Washington Post* (June 12, 2001).

76. According to budget figures compiled by the Ballistic Missile Defense Organization, in Fiscal Year 1999, Pentagon programs designed for theater missile defense received $2.1 billion, compared to $2.0 billion for national missile defenses. In the Clinton administration's outgoing budget, $2.3 billion was earmarked to fund national missile defenses, compared to $2.1 billion for theater missile defense.

Chapter 3   Missile Defense from the Cold War to Asymmetric Warfare

1. The United States Strategic Bombing Survey, *The Effects of Atomic Bombs on Hiroshima and Nagasaki* (Washington, DC: US GPO, 1946), p. 33.
2. Bernard Brodie, *The Absolute Weapon* (New York: Harcourt, Brace, & Co., 1946), p. 28.
3. The *New York Times Magazine* interview was published on June 23, 1946. Reprinted in Julia E. Johnsen, *The Atomic Bomb* (New York, The H. W. Wilson Co., 1946), pp. 101–2.
4. Spencer Weart and Gertrud Weiss Szilard (eds.), *Leo Szilard: His Version of the Facts* (Cambridge, MA: MIT Press, 1978), pp. 205–7 cited in William Lanouette, *Genius in the Shadows: A Biography of Leo Szilard: The Man Behind the Bomb* (New York: Charles Scribner's Sons, 1992), p. 262.
5. The Acheson–Lilienthal Report concluded that, "Inherent in any plan of international control is a probable acceleration of the rate at which our present [nuclear] monopoly will disappear." From U.S. Department of State, *A Report on the International Control of Atomic Energy*, Publication No. 2498 (Washington, DC: US GPO, 1946).
6. "Atomic Weapons and American Policy," *Bulletin of the Atomic Scientists* (July 1953), p. 205. For more on Oppenheimer's thinking about transition strategies, see Chapter 6 of David Goldfisher, *The Best Defense: Policy Alternatives for U.S. Nuclear Security from the 1950s to the 1990s* (Ithaca: Cornell University Press, 1993), specifically pp. 175–98.
7. Text reprinted in Glenn T. Seaborg with Benjamin S. Loeb, *Stemming the Tide, Arms Control in the Johnson Years* (Lexington, MA: Lexington Books, 1987), p. 415.
8. Additional missile defense sites were slated for Alaska and Hawaii. For details of the Sentinel program, see "Scope, Magnitude, and Implications of the United States Antiballistic Missile Program," Hearings before the Subcommittee on Military Applications of the Joint Committee on Atomic Energy, 90th Congress, First Session, 1967.
9. Department of State Bulletin (October 9, 1967), p. 449.
10. Robert S. Norris, Andrew S. Burrows, and Richard W. Fieldhouse, *British, French, and Chinese Nuclear Weapons,* Nuclear Weapons Databook, Vol. V (Boulder, CO: Westview Press, 1994), p. 363.
11. See Morton H. Halperin, "The Decision to Deploy the ABM: Bureaucratic and Domestic Politics in the Johnson Administration," *World Politics* Vol. 25, No. 1 (October 1972), pp. 62–95.
12. Robert S. McNamara, *The Essence of Security, Reflections in Office* (New York: Harper & Row, 1968), p. 65.
13. Department of State Bulletin (October 9, 1967), p. 449.
14. *Detente and Confrontation, American–Soviet Relations from Nixon to Reagan* (Washington, DC: The Brookings Institution, 1985), p. 7.

15. Nixon's speech with contemporaneous commentary can be found in William R. Kintner (ed.), *Safeguard: Why the ABM Makes Sense* (New York: Hawthorne Books, 1969).

16. MIRVing was the placement of multiple independently targetable re-entry vehicles atop a missile, enabling each warhead to destroy with precision separate targets. See "Safeguard Antiballistic Missile System," Hearings Before Subcommittees of the Committee on Appropriations, House of Representatives, 91st Congress, 1st Session, 1969.

17. The Natural Resources Defense Council estimates that U.S. strategic nuclear force loadings at the end of 1969 were 5,882, compared to 2,036 for the Soviet Union. See http://www.nrdc.org/nuclear/nudb/datainx.asp.

18. Donald Brennen, "The Case for Population Defense," in Johan J. Holst and William Schneider, Jr. (eds.), *Why ABM? Policy Issues in the Missile Defense Controversy* (New York: Pergamon Press, 1969), p. 115.

19. Herman Kahn, "The Case for a Thin System," in Johan J. Holst and William Schneider, Jr. (eds.), *Why ABM? Policy Issues in the Missile Defense Controversy* (New York: Pergamon Press, 1969), pp. 66–80.

20. Brennan, "The Case for Population Defense," in Holst and Schneider, Jr. (eds.), *Why ABM? Policy Issues in the Missile Defense Controversy,* p. 117.

21. Brennan, "When the SALT Hit the Fan," *National Review* Vol. 24 (June 23, 1972), p. 689.

22. This extract from Weisner's testimony is reprinted in William R. Kintner (ed.), *Safeguard: Why the ABM Makes Sense* (New York: Hawthorne Books: 1969), p. 322.

23. "Nuclear Test Ban Treaty," Hearings Before the Committee on Foreign Relations, United States Senate, Eighty-eighth Congress, First Session, p. 758.

24. See William R. Kintner, "The Prudent Case for Safeguard," in William R. Kintner (ed.), *Safeguard: Why the ABM Makes Sense* (New York: Hawthorne Books, 1969), pp. 53–4; and "Safeguard Antiballistic Missile System," Hearings Before the Subcommittee on Appropriations, House of Representatives, Ninety-First Congress, First Session, p. 66. During the debate over President Reagan's Strategic Defense Initiative, these claims about being able to deal successfully with radar blackout were acknowledged to be false. As President Reagan's Defensive Technologies Study Team Report concluded, "1960s technology in computer hardware and software and signal processing was incapable of supporting battle management of a multitiered defense" (*Aviation Week and Space Technology* (December 5, 1983), p. 51).

25. Bernard Brodie, "How Much is Enough? Guns vs. Butter Revisited," California Seminar on Arms Control and Foreign Policy (August, 1975), p. 5.

26. "Strategic Arms Limitation Agreements," Hearings Before the Committee on Foreign Relations, United States Senate, 92nd Congress, 2nd Session, 1972, p. 186.

27. See Eugene J. McAllister (ed.), *Agenda for Progress: Examining Federal Spending* (Washington, DC: The Heritage Foundation, 1980), p. 16.

28. "The Effect of ABM on U.S.–Soviet Relations," in Abram Chayes and Jerome B. Weisner (eds.), *ABM: An Evaluation of the Decision to Deploy an Antiballistic Missile System* (New York: Harper & Row, 1969), p. 158.

29. Henry Kissinger, *White House Years* (Boston: Little Brown & Co., 1979), p. 540.

30. United States Arms Control and Disarmament Agency, *Documents on Disarmament, 1983,* Publication 125 (Washington, DC: US GPO, February 1986), pp. 199–201.

31. *Ibid.,* p. 200.

32. See, for example, Christopher Andrew and Oleg Gordievsky, *KGB: The Inside Story of Its Foreign Operations from Lenin to Gorbachev* (New York: HarperCollins, 1991); Andrew and Gordievsky (eds.), *Instructions from the Center: Top Secret Files on KGB Foreign Operations 1975–1985* (London: Hodder & Stoughton, 1991); Peter Vincent Pry, *War Scare, Nuclear Countdown After the Soviet Fall* (Atlanta: Turner Publishing, Inc., 1997); Benjamin B. Fisher, "A Cold War Conundrum: The 1983 Soviet War Scare" (Washington, DC: Central Intelligence Agency, Center for the Study of Intelligence, September 1997), available at http://www.cia.gov/csi/monograph/coldwar/source.htm.

33. *Pravda* (March 27, 1983).

34. ABC News transcript, "This Week with David Brinkley" (April 8, 1984).

35. "The President's Choice: Star Wars or Arms Control," *Foreign Affairs* Vol. 63, No. 2 (Winter 1984–1985), p. 276.

36. NBC News, "Meet the Press" (March 27, 1983).

37. James C. Fletcher, "The Technologies for Ballistic Missile Defense," *Issues in Science and Technology* (Fall 1984), pp. 24–5.

38. "Rhetoric and Realities in the Star Wars Debate," *International Security* Vol. 10, No. 1 (Summer 1985), p. 5.

39. "The Strategic Defense Initiative: Defensive Systems and the Strategic Debate," Lecture given to the California Seminar on International Security and Foreign Policy (November 1984).

40. *Strategy in the Missile Age* (Princeton: Princeton University Press, 1959), p. 200.

41. *Soviet Military Power,* 2nd ed. (Washington, DC: US GPO, March 1983), p. 101.

42. *Ibid.,* p. 106.

43. *Soviet Military Power,* 4th ed. (Washington, DC: US GPO, April 1985), p. 44.

44. "Soviet Capabilities for Strategic Nuclear Conflict, 1983–1993," NIE 11-3/8-83, Volume I—Key Judgments and Summary, in *Estimates on Soviet Military Power, 1954–1984, A Selection* (Washington, DC: Center for the Study of Intelligence, Central Intelligence Agency, December 1984), pp. 414, 433.

45. Nitze's speech is reprinted in Craig Snyder (ed.), *The Strategic Defense Debate: Can Star Wars Make Us Safe?* (Philadelphia: University of Pennsylvania Press, 1986), pp. 221–7.

46. Weinberger did take public exception to the cost-effectiveness criterion, asserting that, "if you can do it [protecting a continent and hundreds of millions of

people] it's cost effective" (Interview at the Godfrey Sperling Breakfast, January 6, 1987).

47. Strobe Talbott, *The Master of the Game: Paul Nitze and the Nuclear Peace* (New York: Alfred A. Knopf, 1988), p. 214.

48. Key first-person accounts have been provided by George P. Shultz, *Turmoil and Triumph, My Years as Secretary of State* (New York: Charles Scribner's Sons, 1993); Robert C. McFarlane and Zofia Smardz, *Special Trust* (New York: Cadell & Davies, 1994); Caspar Weinberger, *Fighting for Peace, Seven Critical Years in the Pentagon* (New York: Warner Books, 1990); and Kenneth L. Adelman, *The Great Universal Embrace, Arms Summitry—A Skeptic's Account* (New York: Simon & Schuster, 1989). For informed, but not necessarily consistent interpretations of what transpired, see Talbott, *The Master of the Game;* Don Oberdorfer, *The Turn* (New York: Poseidon, 1991); Peter Schweitzer, *Victory, The Reagan Administration's Secret Strategy that Hastened the Collapse of the Soviet Union* (New York: The Atlantic Monthly Press, 1994); Raymond L. Garthoff, *The Great Transition, American–Soviet Relations and the end of the Cold War* (Washington, DC: Brookings Institution, 1994); and Frances FitzGerald, *Way Out There in the Blue, Reagan Star Wars, and the End of the Cold War* (New York: Simon & Schuster, 2000).

49. Theodore A. Postol, "Lessons of the Gulf War Experience with Patriot (Use of Patriot Air Defense System During the Persian Gulf War)," *International Security* Vol. 16, No. 3 (Winter 1991), p. 119.

50. "From Brilliant Pebbles To Brilliant Eyes," *New York Times* (June 23, 1991).

51. "The New Administration and the Future of Arms Control," *Arms Control Today* Vol. 18, No. 10 (December 1988).

52. Senator Sam Nunn, "Arms Control in the Last Year of the Reagan Administration," *Arms Control Today* Vol. 18, No. 2 (March 1988).

53. Secretary of Defense William Perry, Department of Defense News Briefing, Subject: Ballistic Missile Defense Program (February 16, 1996).

54. Donald H. Rumsfeld, Dr. Barry M. Blechman, General Lee Butler, Dr. Richard L. Garwin, Dr. William R. Graham, Dr. William Schneider, Jr., General Larry D. Welch, Dr. Paul D. Wolfowitz, and R. James Woolsey, "Executive Summary of the Report of the Commission to Assess the Ballistic Missile Threat to the United States," Pursuant to Public Law 201, 104th Congress, July 15, 1998. The National Intelligence Estimate of "Emerging Missile Threats to North America During the Next Fifteen Years" (NIE 95-19) (November 1995), available at http://www.fas.org/spp/starwars/offdocs/nie9519.htm.

55. DCI, National Intelligence Estimate, "Emerging Missile Threats to North America During the Next 15 Years (NIE 95-19)" (November 1995); National Intelligence Council, "Foreign Missile Developments and the Ballistic Missile Threat to the United States through 2015" (September 1999).

56. Samuel Berger, "Is This Shield Necessary?" *Washington Post* (February 13, 2001); and Leon Fuerth, "Tampering With Strategic Stability," *Washington Post* (February 2, 2001).

57. Speech at the National Defense University (May 1, 2001), available online at http://www.whitehouse.gov/news/releases/2001/05/20010501-10.html.
58. Vernon Loeb and Thomas E. Ricks, "Bush Speeds Missile Defense Plans," *Washington Post* (July 12, 2001).
59. Steven Mufson and Mary Pat Flaherty, "Missile Defense Speedup Weighed," *Washington Post* (June 8, 2001); and James Dao, "Rumsfeld Outlines To NATO Fast Track on Missile Shield," *New York Times* (June 8, 2001).
60. Patrick E. Tyler, "Russia And U.S. See A Breakthrough On Divisive Issues," *New York Times* (October 19, 2001); David E. Sanger, "Bush and Putin Declare They Can Alter ABM Pact," *New York Times* (October 22, 2001); and Walter Pincus and Alan Sipress, "Missile Defense Deal Is Likely," *Washington Post* (November 1, 2001).
61. Press Conference by President Bush and Russian President Vladimir Putin, Portman RitzCarlton, Shanghai, People's Republic of China (October 21, 2001).
62. Steven Mufson and Sharon LaFraniere, "ABM Withdrawal A Turning Point In Arms Control," *Washington Post* (December 13, 2001); David E. Sanger and Patrick E. Tyler, "Officials Recount Road To Deadlock Over Missile Talks," *New York Times* (December 13, 2001).
63. Steven Mufson and Dana Milbank, "U.S. Sets Missile Treaty Pullout," *Washington Post* (December 14, 2001); Michael Wines, "Facing Pact's End, Putin Decides To Grimace And Bear It," *New York Times* (December 14, 2001).
64. I have borrowed this construct from George Perkovich.
65. Assistant Secretary of Defense J. D. Crouch, Special Briefing on the Nuclear Posture Review, Washington, DC (January 9, 2002), transcript available at http://www.defenselink.mil/news/Jan2002/t01092002_t0109npr.html; and Walter Pincus, "U.S. To Cut Arsenal To 3,800 Nuclear Warheads," *Washington Post* (January 10, 2002).
66. Speech at the National Defense University (May 1, 2001). See http://www.whitehouse.gov/news/releases/2001/05/20010501-10.html.

Chapter 4   Vulnerability, Risk, and Missile Defense

1. X [George Kennan], "The Sources of Soviet Conduct," *Foreign Affairs* Vol. 25, No. 4 (July 1947), pp. 566–82. Kennan offers the policy guidance that "In these circumstances it is clear that the main element of any United States policy toward the Soviet Union must be that of a long-term, patient but firm and vigilant containment of Russian expansive tendencies" (p. 575). In the end, "the United States has it in its power to increase enormously the strains under which Soviet policy must operate, to force upon the Kremlin a far greater degree of moderation and circumspection than it has had to observe in recent years, and in this way to promote tendencies which must eventually find their outlet in either the break-up or the gradual mellowing of Soviet power. For no mystical, Messianic movement—and particularly not that of the Kremlin—can face frustration indefinitely without eventually adjusting itself in one way or another to the logic of that state of affairs" (p. 582).

2. Charles Krauthammer, "The New Unilateralism," *Washington Post* (June 8, 2001).
3. State of the Union address (January 29, 2002).
4. Zbigniew Brzezinski, "Indefensible Decisions," *Washington Post* (May 5, 2000).
5. National Institute for Public Policy, *Rationale and Requirements for U.S. Nuclear Forces and Arms Control*, Volume I, Executive Report (Fairfax, VA: NIPP, January 2001), pp. 9–16.
6. Charles William Maynes has suggested a more nuanced topology consisting of "controllers," "shapers," and "abstainers." "Contending Schools," *The National Interest* No. 63 (Spring 2001), pp. 49–58.
7. The division within the community of Dominators has been characterized as between "pragmatic, non-ideological realists" and "hegemonists." Jonathan Clarke. "The Guns of 17th Street," *The National Interest* No. 63 (Spring 2001), p. 104.
8. "Proliferation Roundtable," Carnegie Endowment for International Peace (June 5, 2000).
9. William Kristol and Robert Kagan, "Reject the Global Buddy System," *New York Times* (October 25, 1999).
10. Charles Krauthammer, "The Bush Doctrine," *Washington Post* (May 4, 2001).
11. Commission to Assess United States National Security, Space Management and Organization (January 11, 2001), pp. 9, 16.
12. Alison Mitchell, "Senate Democrats Square Off With Bush Over Missile Plan," *New York Times* (May 3, 2001). For similar reactions, see "What Congressional Critics Are Saying about the President's Speech on Missile Defense," Council for a Liveable World, (accessed February 4, 2002).
13. Sidney D. Drell, "Arms Control: Is There Still Hope?" *Daedalus* Vol. 109, No. 4 (Fall 1980), p. 181.
14. Eugene J. Carroll, Jr., "Why Should We Care?" National Missile Defense, What Does It All Mean?" A CDI Issue Brief, Center for Defense Information (September 2000), p. 1.
15. Union of Concerned Scientists Executive Summary, *Countermeasures, A Technical Evaluation of the Operational Effectiveness of the Planned U.S. National Missile Defense System* (Washington, DC: UCS) (Spring 2000), p. xix.
16. Joseph Cirincione, *et al.,* Introduction, *White Paper on National Missile Defense* (Washington, DC: Lawyers Alliance for World Security, Summer 2000), pp. 3–4.
17. For a transcript of the Rumsfeld hearing, see FDCH Political Transcripts (January 11, 2001), eMediaMillWorks, Inc.
18. Charles Krauthammer, "Arms Control: The End of an Illusion," *The Weekly Standard* (May 7, 1999).
19. Executive Summary, *Report of the Commission to Assess the Ballistic Missile Threat to the United States* (July 15, 1998), pp. 5–6.
20. Daniel Gouré, *Defense of the U.S. Homeland Against Strategic Attack* (Washington, DC: The Center for Strategic and International Studies,

December 2000), pp. 11–12. Available online at http://www.csis.org/homeland/reports/defenseofushmld.pdf.

21. US Department of Defense, Secretary of Defense, *Proliferation: Threat and Response* (January 2001), p. 4.

22. Robert Walpole, Testimony Before the Senate Foreign Relations Committee (September 16, 1999).

23. Pew Charitable Trusts survey taken between January 3 and 7, 2001. The top five priorities of those surveyed were (1) keeping the economy strong; (2) improving the educational system; (3) reducing crime; (4) taking steps to make the Social Security system financially sound; and (5) adding prescription drug benefits to Medicare coverage. See The Pew Research Center for the People and the Press, "Clinton Nostalgia Sets in, Bush Reaction Mixed," released January 11, 2001, http://www.people-press.org/reports/display.php3?ReportID=18 (accessed February 4, 2002).

24. Unclassified chart prepared by the Joint Staff, "The Threat Spectrum," presented before congressional committees, 2000.

25. "60% in Poll Favor Bush, But Economy Is Major Concern," *New York Times* (March 14, 2001).

26. During the public announcement of the withdrawal notification, President George W. Bush stated, "We know that the terrorists, and some of those who support them, seek the ability to deliver death and destruction to our doorstep via missile. And we must have the freedom and the flexibility to develop effective defenses against those attacks ... I cannot and will not allow the United States to remain in a treaty that prevents us from developing effective defenses." For a complete transcript see http://www.whitehouse.gov/news/releases/2001/12/20011213-4.html (accessed February 4, 2002).

27. Robert S. McNamara, *The Essence of Security, Reflections in Office* (New York: Harper & Row, 1968), pp. 58–9.

28. Paul C. Warnke, "Apes on a Treadmill," *Foreign Policy* No. 18 (Spring 1975), p. 12. Warnke never characterized the two nuclear superpowers as "apes" in the article. This editorial embellishment caused Warnke added grief in subsequent dealings with Capitol Hill.

29. Carl Kaysen, "Keeping the Strategic Balance," *Foreign Affairs* Vol. 46, No. 4 (July 1968), p. 670. See also Harold Brown, "Security Through Limitations," *Foreign Affairs* Vol. 47, No. 3 (April 1969), p. 422 for this widely held premise.

30. Thomas C. Schelling and Morton H. Halperin, *Strategy and Arms Control* (New York: The Twentieth Century Fund, 1961), p. 9.

31. Glenn Snyder, "The Balance of Power and the Balance of Terror," in Paul Seabury (ed.), *The Balance of Power* (San Francisco: Chandler, 1965), p. 190.

32. A December 2001 assessment by the Central Intelligence Agency estimates that the People's Republic of China has the capability to deploy multiple, independently targetable re-entry vehicles on missiles housed in silos, but not road-mobiles. National Intelligence Council, *Foreign Missile Developments and the Ballistic Missile Threat Through 2015* (Langley, VA: Central Intelligence Agency,

December 2001), available online at http://www.cia.gov/nic/pubs/other_ products/Unclassifiedballisticmissilefinal.htm (accessed February 4, 2002).

33. Eliot A. Cohen, "Defending America in the Twenty-First Century," *Foreign Affairs* Vol. 79, No. 6 (November–December 2000), p. 45.

34. Kim R. Holmes, "Beyond Mutual Assured Destruction: The Role of Missile Defense in Ensuring Peace and Stability" (unpublished manuscript), p. 15.

35. For instance, from 1959 to 1964, the United States produced 90/ ICBMs. From 1963 to 1967, the Soviet Union produced 719 ICBMs. See "NRDC's Nuclear Data—Table of U.S. ICBM Forces from 1959–1996," available online at http://www.nrdc.org/nuclear/nudb/datab3.asp and "NRDC's Nuclear Data—Table of U.S.S.R/Russian ICBM Forces, 1960–1996," available online at http://www.nrdc.org/nuclear/nudb/datab4.asp.

36. National Intelligence Council, *Foreign Missile Developments and the Ballistic Missile Threat Through 2015* (December 2001).

37. Brad Roberts, Robert Manning, and Ronald Mantaperto, "China: The Forgotten Nuclear Power," *Foreign Affairs* Vol. 79, No. 4 (July–August 2000), pp. 59–60.

38. Bernard Brodie, *Strategy in the Missile Age* (Princeton: Princeton University Press, 1959), p. 303.

39. Cited in Michael Mandelbaum, *The Nuclear Question, The United States and Nuclear Weapons, 1946–1976* (New York: Cambridge University Press, 1979), p. 222.

40. McGeorge Bundy, "To Cap the Volcano," *Foreign Affairs* Vol. 48, No. 1 (October 1969), pp. 9–10, 12.

41. Kenneth Waltz, "Nuclear Myths and Political Realities," *American Political Science Review* Vol. 84, No. 3 (September 1990), p. 734.

42. *Ibid.*, p. 742.

43. Richard L. Garwin, "Superpower Postures in SALT: An American View," in Morton A. Kaplan (ed.), *SALT: Problems and Prospects* (Morristown, NJ: General Learning Press, 1973) p. 110.

44. George Rathjens and Jack Ruina, "BMD and Strategic Stability," *Daedalus,* Weapons in Space, Vol. II, Implications for Security, Vol. 114, No. 3 (Summer 1985), p. 242.

45. Snyder, "The Balance of Power and the Balance of Terror" in Seabury (ed.), *The Balance of Power* (San Francisco: Chandler, 1965), pp. 184–201.

46. Robert Jervis, *The Illogic of American Nuclear Strategy* (Ithaca: Cornell University Press, 1984), p. 31.

47. Bruce Blair, *The Logic of Accidental Nuclear War* (Washington, DC: The Brookings Institution, 1993), p. 9.

48. Scott Sagan, *The Limits of Safety: Organizations, Accidents, and Nuclear Weapons,* (Princeton: Princeton University Press, 1993), p. 264, emphasis in the original.

49. In February 2000, the People's Republic of China issued a white paper, which observed, *inter alia,* "if a grave turn of events occurs leading to the separation of Taiwan from China in any name, or if Taiwan is invaded and occupied by

foreign countries, or if the Taiwan authorities refuse, *sine die,* the peaceful settlement of cross-Straits reunification through negotiations, then the Chinese government will only be forced to adopt all drastic measures possible, including the use of force, to safeguard China's sovereignty and territorial integrity and fulfill the great cause of reunification." The Taiwan Affairs Office and The Information Office of the State Council, People's Republic of China, "White Paper—The One-China Principle and the Taiwan Issue" (February 21, 2000), available online at http://www.china-embassy.org/eng/7128.html.

50. "Did China Threaten to Bomb Los Angeles?" Carnegie Endowment for International Peace Issue Brief, Non-Proliferation Project, Vol. 4, No. 4 (March 22, 2001).

51. This figure does not include sea-launched ballistic missiles or warheads to be delivered by strategic bombers. See "NRDC Nuclear Notebook: Russian Nuclear Forces, 2001," *The Bulletin of the Atomic Scientists* Vol. 57, No. 1 (January–February 2001), pp. 78–9 and "NRDC Nuclear Notebook: U.S. Nuclear Forces, 2001," *The Bulletin of the Atomic Scientists* Vol. 57, No. 2 (March–April 2001), pp. 77–9.

52. D. G. Brennan, "The Case For Missile Defense," *Foreign Affairs* Vol. 47, No. 3 (April 1969), pp. 447–8.

Chapter 5   Missile Defense and the Asian Cascade

1. Glenn Snyder began to explore the instabilities associated with offsetting nuclear arsenals in *Deterrence and Defense* (Princeton: Princeton University Press, 1961). Robert Jervis gave content to this dilemma in *The Illogic of American Nuclear Strategy* (Ithaca: Cornell University Press, 1984). For its application to South Asia, see Michael Krepon and Chris Gagné (eds.), *The Stability–Instability Paradox: Nuclear Weapons and Brinksmanship in South Asia,* Report No. 38 (Washington, DC: The Henry L. Stimson Center, June 2001).

2. The Draft Report of the National Security Advisory Board on Indian Nuclear Doctrine (August 17, 1999), section 2.3.

3. David Shambaugh, "China's Military Views the World," *International Security* Vol. 24, No. 3 (Winter 1999–2000), p. 55.

4. The Badar-II was launched from the Russian Cosmodrome at Baikonur, Kazakhstan on December 10, 2001. See "Satellite Badar-II launched," *Dawn* (December 11, 2001) at http://www.dawn.com/2001/12/11/top5.htm (accessed December 11, 2001). For a description of Badar-II's projected capabilities see John Pike, "Pakistan and Earth Observation Systems" (November 28, 1999), at http://www.fas.org/spp/guide/pakistan/earth/ (accessed January 22, 2002).

5. See Roger Dingman, "Atomic Diplomacy During the Korean War," *International Security* Vol. 13, No. 3 (Winter 1988–1989); Jack Snyder, "*Atomic Diplomacy in the Korean War,*" Pew Case Studies in International Affairs, Case 359 (1993); and Gordon Chang, *Friends and Enemies: the United States, China, and the Soviet Union, 1948–1972* (Stanford: Stanford University Press, 1990), pp. 116–42.

6. "On the Ten Major Relationships," April 25, 1956, in *Selected Works of Mao Tsetung* (Beijing: Foreign Language Press, 1977), Vol. 5, p. 288.

7. Marshall Nie Rongzen, "How China Develops its Nuclear Weapons," *Beijing Review* (April 29, 1985), p. 17.

8. U.S. Department of Defense, Office of the Secretary of Defense, *Proliferation: Threat and Response* (January 2001), p. 14.

9. See Bates Gill and James Mulvenon, "The Chinese Strategic Rocket Forces: Transition to Credible Deterrence," *China and Weapons of Mass Destruction: Implications for the United States,* Conference Report (November 5, 1999), p. 13. This paper, prepared for the National Intelligence Council, can be accessed at www.cia.gov/nic/pubs/conference_reports/weapons_mass_destruction.html.

10. China reportedly increased its defense spending by 17 percent in both 2001 and 2002. "China Plans Major Boost In Spending for Military," *Washington Post* (March 6, 2001) and "China Raises Defense Budget Again," *Washington Post* (March 5, 2002).

11. Alastair Iain Johnston, "China's New 'Old Thinking': The Concept of Limited Deterrence," *International Security* Vol. 20, No. 3 (Winter 1995–1996), pp. 5–6.

12. Author's interviews at the Ministry of External Affairs and Ministry of Defence, New Delhi (November 2000).

13. U.S. Department of Defense, Office of the Secretary of Defense, *Proliferation: Threat and Response* (January 2001), p. 14.

14. *Ibid.*, p. 13. Also see *Global Trends 2015: A Dialogue About the Future With Nongovernmental Experts,* National Intelligence Council (December 2000), p. 55; and Stephen Lee Myers, "Intelligence Report Says U.S. Missile Defense May Stimulate China," *New York Times* (August 10, 2000).

15. National Intelligence Council, "Foreign Missile Developments and the Ballistic Missile Threat Through 2015," p. 10. This estimate can be accessed at www.cia.gov/nic/pubs/other_products/Unclassifiedballisticmissilefinal.htm.

16. See Philip C. Saunders and Jing-dong Yuan, "China's Strategic Force Modernization: Issues and Implications for the United States," in Michael Barletta (ed.), *Proliferation Challenges and Nonproliferation Opportunities for New Administrations,* CNS Occasional Paper #4, (Monterey, CA: Center for Nonproliferation Studies, September 2000); David Shambaugh. "Facing Reality in China Policy," *Foreign Affairs* Vol. 80, No. 1 (January–February 2001), p. 52; Robert Manning, Ronald Montaperto, and Brad Roberts, *China, Nuclear Weapons, and Arms Control: A Preliminary Assessment* (New York: Council on Foreign Relations, May 2000), pp. 49–50. Brad Roberts enumerates a continuum of possible responses to NMD deployment in "China," in James J. Wirtz and Jeffrey A. Larsen (eds.), *Rockets' Red Glare: Missile Defenses and the Future of World Politics* (Boulder, CO: Westview Press, 2001), pp. 183–211.

17. This term has been widely borrowed from Itty Abraham, "India's 'Strategic Enclave:' Civilian Scientists and Military Technologies," *Armed Forces and Society* Vol. 18, No. 2 (Winter 1992).

18. George Perkovich, *India's Nuclear Bomb, The Impact of Global Proliferation* (Berkeley: University of California Press, 1999), p. 421. For a well-sourced Indian perspective, see Raj Chengappa, *Weapons of Peace* (New Delhi: HarperCollins, 2000).

19. For an assessment of the factors behind India's tests, see Michael Krepon, "Introduction," in *The Balance of Power in South Asia* (Abu Dhabi: The Emirates Center for Strategic Studies and Research, 2000), pp. 1–10.

20. See, for example, Vajpayee's remarks before the Rajya Sabha on May 29, 1998 and his Independence Day Speech on August 15, 1998, which are accessible at www.indianembassy.org. Also see Foreign Minister Jaswant Singh's interview in *The Hindu* (November 29, 1999).

21. For the text of the report and an informed analysis of it, see Arvind Kumar (ed.), "Report on a Workshop on The Draft Indian Nuclear Doctrine," NIAS Report R1-2001 (Bangalore: National Institute of Advanced Studies, 2001).

22. Bharat Karnad, "A Thermonuclear Deterrent," in Amitabh Mattoo (ed.), *India's Nuclear Deterrent: Pokhran II and Beyond* (New Delhi: Har-Anand, 1999), pp. 109–49. An overview of non-official views can be found in Sumit Ganguly, "Potential Indian Nuclear Force Postures," *CMC Occasional Papers,* Occasional paper # 19 (Albuquerque, NM: Cooperative Monitoring Center, Sandia National Laboratories, January 2001), from which this analysis is drawn.

23. Vijai K. Nair, "The Structure of an Indian Nuclear Deterrent," in Mattoo (ed.), *India's Nuclear Deterrent: Pokhran II and Beyond,* p. 105.

24. K. Subramanyam, "Nuclear Force Design and Minimum Deterrence Strategy for India," in Bharat Karnad (ed.), *Future Imperilled: India's Security in the 1990s and Beyond* (New Delhi: Viking Penguin, 1994), pp. 177–95.

25. Jasjit Singh (ed.), *Nuclear India* (New Delhi: Knowledge World, 1998), p. 315.

26. Raja Menon, *A Nuclear Strategy for India* (New Delhi: Sage Publications, 2000), pp. 225–8.

27. Kapil Kak, "Command and Control of Small Nuclear Arsenals," in Singh (ed.), *Nuclear India,* p. 268.

28. Vijai K. Nair, "The Structure of an Indian Nuclear Deterrent" in Mattoo (ed.), *India's Nuclear Deterrent,* p. 88.

29. Menon, *A Nuclear Strategy for India,* p. 169.

30. Karnad, "A Thermonuclear Deterrent" in Mattoo (ed.), p. 142. Karnad suggests Chinese military targets as "secondary" targets.

31. The clearest exception to this standard was the Indian Navy's shelling of oil facilities in Karachi in December, 1971. However, acts of terror in urban areas presumably carried out with the support of intelligence agencies are not uncommon.

32. Ashley Tellis, "India's Emerging Nuclear Doctrine: Exemplifying the Lessons of the Nuclear Revolution," *NBR Analyses* Vol. 12, No. 2 (Seattle: The National Bureau of Asian Research, May 2000), p. 8. For an elaboration of Tellis' analysis, see *India's Emerging Nuclear Posture: Between Recessed Deterrence and Ready Arsenal* (Santa Monica: RAND, 2001).

33. *Ibid.*, p. 102.

34. Michael Quinlan, "How Robust is India–Pakistan Deterrence?" *Survival* Vol. 42, No. 4 (Winter 2000–2001), p. 152.

35. See, for example, the remarks of Indian Army Chief General S. Padmanabhan in "From One General to Another: We're Ready," *The Indian Express* (January 12, 2002).

36. Tanvir Ahmad Khan "Nuclear Risk Reduction," *Dawn* (April 7, 2001).

37. Quinlan, "India–Pakistan Deterrence?" *Survival,* Vol. 42, No. 4 (Winter 2000–2001), p. 150.

38. See, for example, http://www.fas.org/nuke/guide/pakistan/facility/khushab.htm.

39. See Bill Gertz, "Pakistan Builds Missile Sites," *Washington Times* (January 14, 2002). Also see Kanti Bajpai, P. R. Chari, Pervaiz Iqbal Cheema, Stephen Cohen, and Sumit Ganguly, *Brasstacks and Beyond: Perception and Management of Crisis in South Asia* (Urbana: University of Illinois, Urbana–Champaign, 1995); Stephen P. Cohen, P. R. Chari, and Pervaiz Iqbal Cheema, *The Compound Crisis of 1990: Perceptions, Politics, and Insecurity,* ACDIS Research Report (Urbana: University of Illinois, Urbana–Champaign, July 2000); and Raj Chengappa, *Weapons of Peace,* pp. 9, 327, 357. The extent to which Pakistan prepared to use its nuclear capability in the 1990 crisis has been wildly exaggerated by Seymour M. Hersh, "On the Nuclear Edge," *The New Yorker* (March 29, 1993), pp. 56–73. Hersh's account was repeated in William E. Burrows and Robert Windrem, *Critical Mass: The Dangerous Race for Superweapons in a Fragmenting World* (New York: Simon & Schuster, 1994). For a participants' account of the 1990 crisis, see Michael Krepon and Mishi Faruqee (eds.), *Conflict Prevention and Confidence-Building Measures in South Asia: The 1990 Crisis,* Occasional Paper No. 17 (Washington, DC: The Henry L. Stimson Center, April 1994).

40. Xue Litai, "Evolution of China's Nuclear Strategy," *Strategic Views from the Second Tier: The Nuclear Weapons Policies of France, Britain, and China,* John C. Hopkins and Weixing Hu (eds.) (New Brunswick: Transaction Publishers, 1995), pp. 167–89; You Ji, *The Armed Forces of China* (New York: I. B. Tauris, 1999), p. 88; and Menon, *A Nuclear Strategy for India,* p. 223. A drawing of Soviet submarine tunnel basing can be found in the fifth edition of *Soviet Military Power* (Washington DC: Department of Defense, March 1986), pp. 20–1.

41. This sad tale is best told in Ahmed Rashid, *Taliban: Militant Islam, Oil and Fundamentalism in Central Asia* (New Haven: Yale University Press, 2000).

42. See Musharraf's interview with Arnaud de Borchegrave, "Bin Laden 'Cult Figure' of Pakistani Muslims," *Washington Times* (March 21, 2001).

43. "Security Dilemmas of Nuclear-Armed Pakistan," *Third World Quarterly* No. 21 (October 2000), pp. 782, 790.

44. See P. K. Iyengar, *The Times of India* (February 10, 2000); "Corrupt Nuclear Yields," *Jane's Intelligence Review* (December 1, 1998), p. 20; and "Size of Indian Blasts Still Disputed," *Science* Vol. 281, No. 5385 (September 25, 1998), p. 1939.

45. See Alastair Iain Johnston, "China's New 'Old Thinking': The Concept of Limited Deterrence," *International Security* Vol. 20, No. 3 (Winter 1995–1996), pp. 5–42.
46. Robert S. Norris and William M. Arkin, "NRDC Nuclear Notebook: Chinese Nuclear Forces," *Bulletin of the Atomic Scientists* Vol. 56, No. 6 (November–December 2000), pp. 78–9.
47. Mark A. Stokes, *China's Strategic Modernization: Implications for the United States* (Carlisle, PA: Strategic Studies Institute, U.S. Army War College, September 1999), pp. 117–123 and Steven Lambakis, *On the Edge of Earth: The Future of American Space Power* (Lexington: University Press of Kentucky, 2001), pp. 147–50.
48. See chapters by Michael Quinlan and David S. Yost in *Strategic Views from the Second Tier: The Nuclear Weapons Policies of France, Britain, and China,* John C. Hopkins and Weixing Hu (eds.) (New Brunswick: Transaction Publishers, 1995).
49. Interview of Sha Zukang by Michael R. Gordon, "China Fearing a Bolder U.S., Takes Aim on Proposed National Missile Shield," *New York Times* (April 29, 2001), p. 6.
50. See Rajesh M. Basrur, "Nuclear Weapons and Indian Strategic Culture," *Journal of Peace Research* Vol. 38, No. 2 (March 2001), pp. 181–98.
51. Interview with C. Raja Mohan in *The Hindu* (November 29, 1999).
52. See R. Jeffrey Smith, "India Moves Missiles Near Pakistan Border," *Washington Post* (June 12, 1997); Perkovich, *India's Nuclear Bomb,* p. 396; Menon, *A Nuclear Strategy for India,* p. 202; and Pravin K. Sawney, "Pakistan Scores over India in Ballistic Missile Race," *Jane's Intelligence Review* (November 1, 2000).
53. "India's missiles in position: Fernandes," *The Times of India* (December 26, 2001) at http://www.timesofindia.com/articleshow.asp?catkey=843527949&art_id=1778730327&sType=1 (accessed January 22, 2002).
54. For a sense of the collateral damage that could be produced from various targeting options see the Natural Resources Defense Council, *The U.S. Nuclear War Plan: A Time for Change,* at www.nrdc.org.
55. See Herman Kahn's *Thinking About the Unthinkable* (New York: Horizon Press, 1962); also see Kahn, *On Escalation: Metaphors and Scenarios* (New York: Frederick A. Praeger, 1965).
56. Confidential interviews by the author (2001).
57. Confidential interviews by the author (2001).
58. The first passage of the Koran, Sura Anfal, also contains verses that dictate against unnecessary bloodshed and the protection of non-combatants. Sura Al-An'am states, "take not life which Allah has made sacred, except by way of justice and law." The second passage referenced is Sura 4, verse 97. (Email communications from Khalid Rahman, Institute of Policy Studies, Islamabad, August 8, 2001, and Sameer Ahmad, Stanford University, August 29, 2001.)
59. See Jessica Mathews, "Not Saddam But His Weapons," *International Herald Tribune* (March 5, 2002).

60. Bernard Brodie, "On the Objectives of Arms Control," *International Security* Vol. 1, No. 1 (Summer 1976), pp. 32–3.
61. For a comparative assessment of nuclear risks, see Michael Krepon, "Nuclear Risk Reduction: Is Cold War Experience Applicable to South Asia?", in Michael Krepon and Chris Gagné (eds.), *The Stability–Instability Paradox: Nuclear Weapons and Brinksmanship in South Asia*, Report No. 38 (Washington, DC: The Henry L. Stimson Center, June 2001).

Chapter 6 Reassessing Strategic Arms Control

1. This definition is borrowed from Joseph S. Nye, Jr., "Arms Control and International Politics," *Daedalus* Vol. 120, No. 1 (Winter 1991), p. 145.
2. Lawrence Freedman, "Arms Control: Thirty Years On," *Daedalus* Vol. 120, No. 1 (Winter 1991), p. 71.
3. Emanuel Adler, "Arms Control, Disarmament, and National Security: A Thirty Year Retrospective and a New Set of Anticipations," *Daedalus* Vol. 120, No. 1 (Winter 1991), p. 1
4. *Ibid.*, p. 3.
5. Thomas C. Schelling and Morton H. Halperin, *Strategy and Arms Control* (New York: Twentieth Century Fund, 1961), p. 1.
6. Adler, "*Arms Control*", p. 9.
7. Michael Howard, "Reassurance and Deterrence: Western Defense in the 1980s," *Foreign Affairs* Vol. 61 (Winter 1982–1983), p. 324.
8. Robert Jervis, *The Meaning of the Nuclear Revolution* (Ithaca: Cornell University Press, 1989), p. 225.
9. Thomas C. Schelling, "From the Airport Bench," *Bulletin of the Atomic Scientists* (May 1989), p. 30.
10. Schelling, "The Thirtieth Year," *Daedalus* Vol. 120, No. 1 (Winter 1991), p. 21.
11. Strobe Talbott, *The Master of the Game, Paul Nitze and the Nuclear Peace* (New York: Alfred A. Knopf, 1988), p. 15.
12. Schelling, "The Thirtieth Year," *Daedalus* (1991), p. 24.
13. Johan Jørgen Holst, "Arms Control in the Nineties: A European Perspective," *Daedalus* Vol. 120, No. 1 (Winter 1991), p. 84.
14. Thomas C. Schelling and Morton H. Halperin, *Strategy and Arms Control*, p. 1.
15. Thomas C. Schelling, "Reciprocal Measures for Arms Stabilization," in Donald G. Brennan (ed.), *Arms Control, Disarmament, and National Security* (New York: George Braziller, 1961), p. 169.
16. Hedley Bull, *The Control of the Arms Race* (New York: Frederick A. Praeger, 1961), p. 10.
17. Freedman, "Arms Control: Thirty Years On," *Daedalus* (1991), p. 74.
18. Holst, "Arms Control in the Nineties: A European Perspective," *Daedalus* (1991), p. 89.
19. Bull, *Control of the Arms Race*, p. 11.
20. Reprinted in B. H. Liddell Hart, *Deterrent or Defence* (London: Stevens and Sons, 1960), p. 23.

21. Glenn Snyder, *Deterrence and Defense* (Princeton: Princeton University Press, 1961), p. 226.

22. Robert Jervis, *The Illogic of American Nuclear Strategy* (Ithaca: Cornell University Press, 1984), p. 31.

23. Bernard Brodie placed the cost-saving objective topmost on his list of objectives for arms control. See "On the Objectives of Arms Control," *International Security* Vol. 1, No. 1 (Summer 1976), p. 19.

24. Speech before the United Press International editors and publishers (September 18, 1967).

25. Albert Wohlstetter, "Is There a Strategic Arms Race?" *Foreign Policy* No. 15 (Summer 1974), p. 10.

26. William Hyland, *Mortal Rivals: Superpower Relations from Nixon to Reagan* (New York: Random House, 1987), p. 43.

27. Henry Kissinger, *White House Years* (Boston: Little Brown & Co., 1979), p. 549.

28. *Consideration of Mr. Paul C. Warnke to be Director of the U.S. Arms Control and Disarmament Agency and Ambassador,* Committee on Armed Services, United States Senate, 95th Congress, 1st Session (Washington, DC: Government Publishing Office, 1977), p. 7.

29. Henry Kissinger, "Arms Control, Inspection and Surprise Attack," *Foreign Affairs* Vol. 38, No. 4 (July 1960), p. 73.

30. Josef Joffe, "How America Does It," *Foreign Affairs,* Vol. 76, No. 5 (September–October 1997), p. 27.

31. Kissinger, *White House Years,* p. 561.

32. Freedman, "Arms Control: Thirty Years On," *Daedalus* (1991), p. 75.

33. *Ibid.*

34. Joseph Nye, "Arms Control and International Politics," *Daedalus* Vol. 120, No. 1 (Winter 1991), p. 149.

35. Leslie Gelb, "The Future of Arms Control: A Glass Half Full?" *Foreign Policy* No. 36 (Fall 1979), p. 21.

36. Robert C. Toth, "Some Experts Doubt Value of Arms Pacts," *Los Angeles Times* (May 21, 1984).

37. Remarks by the President to Students and Faculty at National Defense University (May 1, 2001), and testimony by Secretary of Defense designate Donald H. Rumsfeld before the Senate Armed Services Committee (January 11, 2001).

38. "Detente," *Hearings before the Committee on Foreign Relations,* United States Senate, 93rd Congress, 2nd Session (Washington, DC: GPO, 1975), p. 164.

39. Michael Mandelbaum, *The Nuclear Question: The United States and Nuclear Weapons* (New York: Cambridge University Press, 1979).

40. Jervis, *The Meaning of the Nuclear Revolution,* p. 225.

41. Albert Carnesale and Richard N. Haass (eds.), *Superpower Arms Control, Setting the Record Straight* (Cambridge, MA: Ballinger Publishing Company, 1987), p. 355.

42. Freedman, "Arms Control: Thirty Years On," *Daedalus* (1991), p. 72.

43. Nye, "Arms Control and International Politics," *Daedalus* (1991), p. 160.

44. *Ibid.,* p. 154.

45. Holst, "Arms Control in the Nineties: A European Perspective," *Daedalus* (1991), p. 83.

46. Morton H. Halperin, "Arms Control: A Twenty-five Year Perspective," *F.A.S. Public Interest Report* Vol. 36, No. 6 (June 1983).

47. Thomas C. Schelling, "What Went Wrong With Arms Control?" *Foreign Affairs* Vol. 63, No. 2 (Winter 1984–1985), p. 220.

48. *Ibid.,* pp. 225–229, emphasis in the original.

49. Roy Gutman, "The Nay-Sayer of Arms Control," *Newsday* (February 18, 1983), cited in Raymond L. Garthoff, *The Great Transition: American–Soviet Relations and the End of the Cold War* (Washington, DC: The Brookings Institution, 1994), p. 504.

50. Colleen Barry, "Russia Warns U.S. on Missile Defense," Associated Press (February 4, 2001).

51. These talking points were published in the January 2000 issue of the *Bulletin of the Atomic Scientists,* accessible at www.thebulletin.org/issues/2000/mj00.

52. See *Jump-START, Retaking the Initiative to Reduce Post-Cold War Nuclear Dangers* (Washington, DC: Committee on Nuclear Policy, February 1999).

53. Federation of American Scientists, Natural Resources Defense Council, Union of Concerned Scientists, "Toward True Security, A U.S. Nuclear Posture for the Next Decade" (June 2001).

54. Testimony of R. James Woolsey before the Senate Select Committee on Intelligence (December 4, 1996).

55. For the particulars of this concern and proposed remedies, see Bruce G. Blair, Harold A. Feiveson, and Frank N. von Hippel, "Taking Nuclear Weapons off Hair-Trigger Alert," *Scientific American* (November 1997). Also see John Steinbruner, *The Significance of Joint Missile Surveillance,* CISS Occasional Papers (Cambridge, MA: American Academy of Arts and Sciences, July 2001).

56. Commencement speech at the United States Military Academy (May 27, 2000).

57. See Lisbeth Gronlund, George Lewis, Theodore Postol, and David Wright, "Highly Capable Theater Missile Defenses and the ABM Treaty," *Arms Control Today* Vol. 24, No. 83 (April 1994), pp. 3–8.

Chapter 7   *From MAD to Cooperative Threat Reduction*

1. This insight has been borrowed from George Perkovich.

2. Robert Walpole, Speech before the Nonproliferation Roundtable at the Carnegie Endowment of International Peace (September 17, 1998), transcript available online at http://www.cia.gov/cia/public_affairs/speeches/archives/1998/walpole_speech_091798.html; also see National Intelligence Council, "Foreign Missile Developments and the Ballistic Missile Threat to the United States

Through 2015" (Central Intelligence Agency, September 1999), available online at http://www.cia.gov/cia/publications/nie/nie99msl.html.

3. George W. Bush, "Missile Defense Now," *Washington Times* (May 25, 2000).

4. See, for example, *Report of the Canberra Commission on the Elimination of Nuclear Weapons* (Canberra: Australian Department of Foreign Affairs and Trade, 1996); "An Evolving U.S. Nuclear Posture," *The Second Report of the Steering Committee Project on Eliminating Weapons of Mass Destruction* (Washington, DC: The Henry L. Stimson Center, December 1995); Barry M. Blechman and Cathleen S. Fisher, "Phase Out the Bomb," *Foreign Policy* No. 97 (Winter 1994–1995), pp. 79–95.

5. George W. Bush, "State of the Union," (Washington, DC) (January 29, 2002), transcript available at http://www.whitehouse.gov/news/releases/2002/01/20020129-11.html (accessed March 15, 2002).

6. See Kenneth N. Waltz, *The Spread of Nuclear Weapons: More May Be Better,* Adelphi Paper 171 (London: International Institute of Strategic Studies, 1981). Also see Waltz, "More May Be Better," and "Waltz Replies to Sagan," in Scott D. Sagan and Kenneth N. Waltz, *The Spread of Nuclear Weapons: A Debate* (New York: W.W. Norton, 1995), pp. 1–47, 93–115. Specifically, on Europe, see John J. Mearsheimer, "Nuclear Weapons and Deterrence in Europe," *International Security* Vol. 9, No. 3 (Winter 1984–1985), pp. 19–46.

7. Michael Krepon and Chris Gagné (eds.), *The Stability–Instability Paradox: Nuclear Weapons and Brinkmanship in South Asia,* Report No. 38 (Washington, DC: The Henry L. Stimson Center, June 2001); also see Scott D. Sagan, "More Will be Worse" and "Sagan Replies to Waltz" in Sagan and Waltz, *The Spread of Nuclear Weapons,* pp. 47–93, 115–37.

8. Michael Krepon, "Nuclear Risk Reduction: Is Cold War Experience Applicable to South Asia?," in Krepon and Gagné (eds.), *The Stability–Instability Paradox,* pp. 1–14.

9. For a historic baseline and an attempt to sort through the Bush administration's classifications, see Congressional Research Service, *Appropriations and Authorization for FY2002: Defense* (Washington, DC: CRS, February 2002), pp. 59–62. The number used for the FY2003 budget request for ballistic missile defense (BMD) includes the $800 million cost of the Space-Based Infrared Sensors-High (SBIRS-High), crucial to the functioning of a potential missile defense and with limited utility for anything but missile defense, with the $7.8 billion figure for BMD to reach a total of $8.6 billion. This is significantly higher than the State Department request of $8.1 billion. See Department of Defense, "Details of Fiscal 2003 Department of Defense (DoD) Budget Request," Press Release (February 4, 2002), available online at http://www.defenselink.mil/news/Feb2002/b02042002_bt049-02.html and Secretary of State Colin Powell, Testimony before the Senate Foreign Relations Committee (February 5, 2002), available at http://www.state.gov/secretary/rm/2002/7797.htm.

10. John F. Sopko, "The Changing Proliferation Threat," *Foreign Policy* No. 106 (Spring 1997), p. 18.

11. Fred Charles Ilké, "The Second Coming of the Nuclear Age," *Foreign Affairs* Vol. 75, No. 1 (January–February 1996), p. 124.

12. For a discussion of the ramifications of the requirement of "prompt hard-target counterforce capabilities" on force sizing, see Jan Lodal, *The Price of Dominance* (New York: Council on Foreign Relations Press, 2001).

13. "Odom's Russia: A Forum," *The National Interest* No. 66 (Winter 2001–2002), p. 117.

14. Siegfried S. Hecker, "Thoughts about an Integrated Strategy for Nuclear Cooperation with Russia," *The Nonproliferation Review* Vol. 8, No. 2 (Summer 2001), p. 11.

15. Natural Resources Defense Council, "Faking Nuclear Restraint: The Bush Administration's Secret Plan for Strengthening U.S. Nuclear Forces" (February 13, 2002), available online at http://www.nrdc.org/media/pressreleases/020213a.asp.

16. "Interview with Ambassador Robert G. Joseph, U.S. National Security Council," conducted by Leonard S. Spector, *The Nonproliferation Review* Vol. 8, No. 3 (Fall–Winter 2001), p. 5.

17. Thomas C. Schelling and Morton H. Halperin, *Strategy and Arms Control* (New York: The Twentieth Century Fund, 1961), p. 1.

18. See Raymond L. Garthoff, *The Great Transition: American–Soviet Relations and the End of the Cold War* (Washington, DC: The Brookings Institution, 1994), pp. 490–491; James A. Baker III with Thomas M. DeFrank, *The Politics of Diplomacy: Revolution, War, and Peace, 1989–1992* (New York: G. P. Putnam's Sons, 1995), pp. 658–9; George Bush and Brent Scowcroft, *A World Transformed* (New York: Vintage, 1998), pp. 544–547.

19. See Michael Krepon and Amy E. Smithson, *Open Skies, Arms Control, and Cooperative* Security (New York: St. Martin's Press, 1992); Defense Threat Reduction Agency, Department of Defense, *The Treaty on Open Skies*, prepared by Kirk W. Clear and Steven E. Block (Dulles, VA: DTRA, April 1999); John C. Baker, Kevin M. O'Connell, and Ray A. Williamson (eds.), *Commercial Observation Satellites: At the Leading Edge of Global Transparency* (Santa Monica, CA: Rand and ASPRS, 2001); Yahya A. Dehqanzada and Ann M. Florini, *Secrets for Sale: How Commercial Satellite Imagery Will Change the World* (Washington, DC: Carnegie Endowment for International Peace, 2000).

20. Defense Threat Reduction Agency, "Cooperative Threat Reduction Scorecard," available online at http://www.dtra.mil/ctr/ctr_score.html (accessed March 14, 2002).

21. *The Henry L. Stimson Center Award Presentation to Secretary of Defense William J. Perry* (Washington, DC: The Henry L. Stimson Center, September 20, 1994), p. 16.

22. *A Report Card on the Department of Energy's Nonproliferation Programs with Russia*, Howard Baker and Lloyd Cutler, Co-Chairs (Washington, DC: The Secretary of Energy Advisory Board, United States Department of Energy, January 10, 2001), Executive Summary, p. iii.

23. Matthew Bunn, *The Next Wave: Urgently Needed New Steps to Control Warheads and Fissile Material*, (Cambridge, MA and Washington, DC: Harvard University Managing the Atom Project and the Nonproliferation Project of the Carnegie Endowment for International Peace, April 2000); *A Report Card on the Department of Energy's Nonproliferation Programs with Russia*, Howard Baker and Lloyd Cutler, Co-Chairs; Commission to Assess the Organization of the Federal Government to Combat the Proliferation of Weapons of Mass Destruction (Deutch–Spencer Commission), *Combating Proliferation of Weapons of Mass Destruction* (July 1999), available online at http://www.senate.gov/~specter/11910book.pdf; Kenneth N. Luongo, "The Uncertain Future of U.S.–Russian Cooperative Nuclear Security," *Arms Control Today* Vol. 31, No. 1 (January–February 2001), pp. 3–10; Oleg Bukharin, Matthew Bunn, and Kenneth Luongo, *Recommendations of Accelerated Action to Secure Nuclear Material in the Former Soviet Union* (Princeton: Russian American Nuclear Safety Advisory Council, 2000); and Siegfried S. Hecker, "Thoughts about an Integrated Strategy for Nuclear Cooperation with Russia," *The Nonproliferation Review* Vol. 8, No. 2 (Summer 2001), pp. 1–22.
24. Bunn, *The Next Wave*, p. vi.
25. Hecker, "Thoughts ... "*The Nonproliferation Review*, pp. 1–2.
26. *Ibid.*
27. *Ibid.*, p. 3.
28. See n. 22 above.

Chapter 8—Fateful Choices

1. Fred Charles Iklé, "Can Nuclear Deterrence Last Out the Century?" *Foreign Affairs* Vol. 51, No. 2 (January 1973), p. 272.
2. William J. Perry, "Preparing for the Next Attack," *Foreign Affairs* Vol. 80, No. 6 (November–December 2001), p. 36.
3. Hearings, Senate Foreign Relations Committee, *The START Treaty in a Changed World*, 100th Congress, 1st Session, 1992, p. 106.
4. See Alexander Pikayev, "Russia and the United States: Searching For A New Strategic Framework?", unpublished paper presented to the Workshop on the Perspectives of the Treaty on Non-Proliferation of Nuclear Weapons in the 21st Century: Towards the 2005 NPT Review Conference, Tokyo, Japan (February 27, 2002).
5. Executive Summary, *Report of the Commission to Assess the Ballistic Missile Threat to the United States* (July 15, 1998), pp. 5–6.
6. *Report of the Commission to Assess United States National Security, Space Management and Organization* (Washington, DC) (January 11, 2001), available online at http://www.defenselink.mil/pubs/space20010111.html (accessed March 14, 2002).
7. *New York Times* (January 8, 1958).

8. Statement by Major General Thomas Moorman, U.S. Air Force director for space and Strategic Defense Initiative programs, quoted in *Aviation Week & Space Technology* (January 30, 1989), p. 17.

9. Brigadier General Homer A. Boushey, Deputy Director, Research and Development, quoted in "Moon Bases Called Vital," *Christian Science Monitor* (January 30, 1958).

10. Article II of the Treaty on Principles Governing the Activities of States in the Exploration and Use of Outer Space, Including the Moon and Other Celestial Bodies. This treaty entered into force on October 10, 1967.

11. Article IV of the Treaty on Principles Governing the Activities of States in the Exploration and Use of Outer Space, Including the Moon and Other Celestial Bodies.

12. William J. Durch, *Twenty-First Century Threat Reduction: Nuclear Study Results from DTRA/ASCO*, Report prepared for the Advanced Technology Division, Advanced Systems and Concepts Office, Defense Threat Reduction Agency (DTRA) (November 30, 2001).

13. For two accounts of this history that arrive at very different policy prescriptions, see Paul Stares, *The Militarization of Space, U.S. Policy, 1945–1984* (Ithaca: Cornell University Press, 1985), and Steven Lambakis, *On The Edge of Earth, The Future of American Space Power* (Lexington: The University of Kentucky Press, 2001).

14. Also see John E. Hyten, *A Sea of Peace or a Theater of War: Dealing with the Inevitable Conflict in Space*, ACDIS Occasional Paper (Urbana: University of Illinois at Urbana–Champaign, April 2000).

15. William M. Arkin and Robert S. Norris, "Nuclear Notebook," *Bulletin of the Atomic Scientists* (December 1993), p. 57. For annual totals, see William M. Arkin and Robert S. Norris, "Global Nuclear Stockpiles, 1945–2000," *Bulletin of the Atomic Scientists* (March–April 2000), p. 79.

16. The preambular language of the Antarctic Treaty (1959), the Outer Space Treaty (1967), and the Seabed Arms Control Treaty (1971) all have similar phraseology. See *Arms Control and Disarmament Agreements, Texts and Histories of the Negotiations* (Washington, DC: United States Arms Control and Disarmament Agency, 1996 edition).

17. For a detailed discussion on merits (and demerits) of various arms control options for anti-satellite weapons, see Donald L. Hafner, "Approaches to the Control of Antisatellite Weapons," in William J. Durch (ed.), *National Interests and the Military Use of Space* (Cambridge, MA: Ballinger, 1984), pp. 239–70.

18. Malcolm R. Currie, Director of Defense Research and Engineering, Address before the Air Force Association, *Aviation Week and Space Technology* (November 8, 1976), p. 13.

19. See, in particular, Department of Defense, *Joint Vision 2020* (Washington, DC: Government Printing Office, May 30, 2000), available online at http://www.dtic.mil/jv2020/jvpub2.htm.

20. David Winkler, *Cold War at Sea: High-Seas Confrontation Between the United States and the Soviet Union* (Annapolis: Naval Institute Press, 2000).
21. Bob Woodward and R. Jeffrey Smith, "U.S.–Soviet Pact to Curb Incidents," *Washington Post* (June 7, 1989); Michael Dobbs, "New Pact Addresses Accidental Conflicts," *Washington Post* (June 13, 1989).
22. See testimony of General Richard B. Myers before the Subcommittee on Strategic Forces of the Senate Armed Services Committee (March 22, 1999), available online at http://www.senate.gov/~armed_services/statemnt/1999/990322rm.pdf and James Oberg, *Space Power Theory*, at http://www.jamesoberg.com/books/spt/spt.hml.
23. B. H. Liddell Hart, *Strategy: The Indirect Approach* (London: Faber & Faber, 1968), p. 334.
24. Lawrence Freedman, *The Evolution of Nuclear Strategy* (New York: St. Martin's Press, 1981), p. xviii.
25. The obvious exception to this rule was President Richard M. Nixon and his national security adviser, Henry A. Kissinger.
26. McGeorge Bundy, "To Cap the Volcano," *Foreign Affairs* Vol. 48, No. 1 (October 1969), p. 12.
27. I have borrowed here from the titles of two essential books on this subject, Robert Jervis, *The Illogic of Nuclear Strategy* (Ithaca: Cornell University Press, 1984) and Lawrence Freedman, *The Evolution of Nuclear Strategy* (New York: St. Martin's Press, 1981).
28. Secretary of State John Foster Dulles. "The Evolution of Foreign Policy," *Department of State Bulletin* 30, No. 761 (January 25, 1954), p. 108.
29. Alain C. Enthoven and K. Wayne Smith, *How Much Is Enough? Shaping the Defense Program 1961–1969* (New York: Harper Row, 1971), p. 174.
30. Lawrence Freedman, "The First two Generations of Nuclear Strategists," in Peter Paret (ed.), *The Makers of Modern Strategy: From Machiavelli to the Nuclear Age* (Princeton: Princeton University Press, 1986), p. 758.
31. Iklé, "Nuclear Deterrence" p. 281.
32. Herbert York, *The Advisors: Oppenheimer, Teller and the Superbomb* (San Francisco: W. H. Freeman & Co., 1976), p. 52.
33. Michael R. Gordon, "U.S. Nuclear Plan Sees New Weapons and New Targets," *New York Times* (March 10, 2002).
34. See McGeorge Bundy, "A Matter of Survival," *The New York Review of Books* (March 17, 1983).
35. I am indebted to George Perkovich for raising this point.
36. For an explanation of the origin and force structure consequences of damage limitation, see Jan Lodal, *The Price of Dominance: The New Weapons of Mass Destruction and Their Challenge to American Leadership* (New York: Council on Foreign Relations, 2001).
37. Interview with Robert S. Norris (March 6, 2002). Also see Natural Resources Defense Council, "Faking Nuclear Restraint: The Bush Administration's Secret

Plan for Strengthening U.S. Nuclear Forces," accessible at http://www.nrdc.org/media/pressreleases/020213a.asp.

38. *Ibid.*

39. Alexander Pikayev, "Russia and the United States: Searching For A New Strategic Framework?" (February 27, 2002).

40. For more on the treaty's provisions, see J. D. Crouch, "Special Briefing on the Nuclear Posture Review," The Pentagon (January 9, 2002), available online at http://www.defenselink.mil/news/Jan2002/t01092002_t0109npr.html.

41. Stephen M. Younger, "Nuclear Weapons in the Twenty-First Century, Los Alamos National Laboratory (June 27, 2000), p. 15, available online at http://www.fas.org/nuke/guide/usa/doctrine/doe/younger.htm.

42. Natural Resources Defense Council, *The U.S. Nuclear War Plan: A Time for Change* (Washington, DC: NRDC, June 2001), available online at http://www.nrdc.org/nuclear/warplan/index.asp.

43. Bill Gertz, "Russia transfers nuclear arms to Baltics," *Washington Times* (January 3, 2001).

44. Perry, "Preparing for the Next Attack," Foreign Affairs, Vol. 80, No. 6 (November–December 2001), p. 33.

45. I have borrowed this metaphor from Richard N. Haass, *Reluctant Sheriff: The United States After the Cold War* (New York: Council on Foreign Relations Press, 1997).

46. Kissinger was exasperated at the time by critiques of the Ford administration's efforts to negotiate a second strategic arms limitation accord. Press conference (July 3, 1974), reprinted in *Survival* Vol. 16, No. 5 (September–October 1974), pp. 239–46.

47. Kissinger reversed field during the ratification hearings on the SALT II Treaty, warning that Soviet strategic superiority would "exponentially" increase the Kremlin's willingness to run risks. See Frances FitzGerald, *Way Out There in the Blue: Reagan, Star Wars, and the End of the Cold War* (New York: Simon & Schuster, 2000), p. 97.

48. This observation was offered at Kissinger's Harvard University seminar on March 24, 1960. David Alan Rosenberg, "The Origins of Overkill, Nuclear Weapons and American Strategy, 1945–1960," *International Security* Vol. 7, No. 4 (Spring 1983), p. 71.

49. Robert Jervis, "Weapons Without Purpose? Nuclear Strategy in the Post-Cold War Era," *Foreign Affairs* Vol. 80, No. 4 (July–August 2001), p. 147.

50. "Bin Laden Seeks to Gain Nuclear Arms, Bush Says," *Los Angeles Times* (November 7, 2001).

51. "American Weapons and American Policy," *Foreign* Affairs Vol. 31, No. 4 (July 1953), pp. 534–5. For more on Oppenheimer's views, see David Goldfischer, *The Best Defense: Policy Alternatives for U.S. Nuclear Security from the 1950s to the 1990s* (Ithaca, NY: Cornell University Press, 1993), Chapter 4.

52. *Ibid.,* p. 534.

53. See, for example, David Goldfischer's concept of "mutual defense emphasis," in *The Best Defense: Policy Alternatives for U.S. Nuclear Security from the 1950s to the 1990s* (Ithaca, NY: Cornell University Press, 1993); William J. Durch's concept of minimum deterrence joined by minimum defense in "Rethinking Strategic Missile Defenses," in Ivo H. Daalder and Terry Terriff (eds.), *Rethinking the Unthinkable: New Directions for Nuclear Arms Control* (London: Frank Cass, 1993), p. 181; Freeman Dyson's concept of "Live and Let Live," *The New Yorker* (February 27, 1984), pp. 101–2; and "An Evolving U.S. Nuclear Posture," *The Second Report of the Steering Committee Project on Eliminating Weapons of Mass Destruction* (Washington D.C.: The Henry L. Stimson Center, December 1995).

54. The two most important studies in this regard were the *Report of the Commission to Assess United States National Security, Space Management and Organization* (January 11, 2001) and National Institute for Public Policy, *Rationale and Requirements for U.S. Nuclear Forces and Arms Control*, Volume I, Executive Report (Fairfax, VA: NIPP, January 2001).

Index

Patriot missile, 54, 65–70, 96, 158
Peacekeeper missile, 179, 239
Pentagon, 2–3, 8, 24, 34, 36, 38–41,
  45–6, 50–1, 53, 61–2, 67, 78–9,
  84, 90–1, 93, 97, 104, 107–8,
  113, 141, 181, 197–9, 209, 224,
  227, 235
People's Liberation Army, 123
  see also China
Perle, Richard, 179
Perry, William J., 14, 71, 97–8, 209
Persian Gulf
  proliferation in, 35, 54–8, 62–3,
    127, 196
  war, 17, 19, 27, 50, 55, 57–8,
    96, 113
  see also Iran; Iraq
Pipes, Richard, 78
Post-Cold War
  U.S. military superiority and, 6, 10,
    15, 19, 42
  MAD and, 6, 9–10, 14, 36–9
  Classical arms control and, 7, 14,
    116–25
Pre-emptive strikes, 59, 78, 88, 122,
  148–51, 156, 160, 162, 179, 183,
  188, 198, 202, 225, 237
Prevention of Dangerous Military
  Activities Agreement, 230
Prithvi missiles, 155
Putin, Vladimir, 33, 40, 100–1, 182,
  204, 242

Rabin, Yitzhak, 22
RAND, 89
Reagan, Ronald,
  missile defense and, 5, 91–6, 131
  strategic arms control and, 5, 26–7,
    167, 175–80, 200, 250, 253
  weaponization of space and, 224, 228
  Chemical Weapons Convention and,
    21, 33
Rice, Condoleeza, 48

Rogue states
  missile defense and, 52–5, 72–5,
    81–4, 98–9, 105
  see also Asymmetric warfare; "Axis of
    evil"; Iraq; Iran; North Korea
Roosevelt, Franklin D., 85
Rudman, Warren, 48–9
Rumsfeld, Donald H., 100, 106,
  112, 129
  Commission to Assess the Ballistic
    Missile Threat to the United
    States and, 72–6, 79, 97–8,
    112, 224
  Commission to Assess National
    Security Space Management and
    Organization and, 110, 224,
    226, 231, 233
Russia
  CTR programs and, 7–8, 13, 28–9,
    35, 96
  proliferation and, 103, 127, 183,
    191, 201–2, 207, 243
  missile defense and, 9–10, 53–6,
    106, 116–17
  weaponization of space and, 10,
    12, 152, 161, 204, 217–18,
    231–2

Safeguard system, 88–90, 92
Schelling, Thomas C., 2, 15, 116,
  178–9, 207
Schlesinger, James, 49, 93
Schneider, William, 90
Scowcroft, Brent, 48
SCUD missile, 54–9, 73–4, 96
Second Strategic Arms Reduction Treaty
  (START II), 3, 27, 32–3, 39, 180,
  184, 187, 191, 209, 239
Sellers, Peter, 3
Senate Armed Services Committee, 78
Sentinel system, 86–8, 92
September 11, 2001, 2–3, 6, 24, 45–7,
  49–52, 135, 147, 197, 201, 214